COSMOS, CHAOS AND THE WORLD TO COME

Cosmos, Chaos and the World to Come

The Ancient Roots of Apocalyptic Faith

Norman Cohn

Yale University Press · New Haven and London 1993

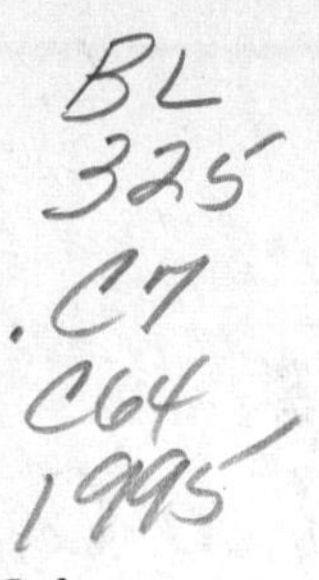

First published in paperback 1995

Set in Baskerville by Best-set Typesetter Ltd., Hong Kong
Printed and bound in Great Britain by The Bath Press, Avon

Library of Congress Cataloging-in-Publication Data

Cohn, Norman Rufus Colin.
Cosmos, chaos and the world to come: the ancient roots of apocalyptic faith / Norman Cohn.
p. cm.
Includes bibliographical references and index.
ISBN 0-300-05598-6 (hbk.)
0-300-06551-5 (pbk.)
1. Creation—Comparative studies. 2. Cosmogony—Comparative studies. 3. Eschatology—Comparative studies. I. title.
BL325.C7C64 1993
291.2'4—dc20 93-1294
CIP

A catalogue record for this book is available from the British Library.

Acknowledgement is made of kind permission to quote from the following: G. Vermes, *The Dead Sea Scrolls: Qumran in Perspective* (Collins, London, 1978) and G. Vermes, *The Dead Sea Scrolls in English*, 2nd edition (Penguin, Harmondsworth, 1975). Quotations from the Old Testament (or Hebrew Bible) are generally taken from the Revised Standard Version. However, quotations from the Book of Daniel are taken from the New English Bible, and so are a number of other passages, duly indicated in the Notes. In keeping with critical orthodoxy the divine name has been rendered throughout not by 'Lord' but by Yahweh. Quotations from the New Testament are taken from the NEB, except for a couple of quotations from the RSV, also indicated.

Frontispiece: God fighting Zu. Assyrian relief 865–860 BC from Nimrud, Temple of Ninurta. *British Museum*

Is there any thing which can either be thoroughly understood, or soundly judged of, till the very first cause and principles from which originally it springeth be made manifest?

Richard Hooker, *Of the Lawes of Ecclesiastical Politie* (1593)

Contents

Foreword

This book investigates the deepest roots and first emergence of an expectation which is still flourishing today. That there will shortly be a marvellous consummation, when good will be finally victorious over evil and for ever reduce it to nullity; that the human agents of evil will be either physically annihilated or otherwise disposed of; that the elect will thereafter live as a collectivity, unanimous and without conflict, on a transformed and purified earth — this expectation has had a long history in our civilisation. In overtly Christian guise it has exercised a powerful fascination down the centuries, and continues to do so; and in secularised guise it has been easily recognisable in certain politico-social ideologies. On the other hand there have been great civilisations, some of them lasting thousands of years, that knew nothing of any such expectation. So where and how did the expectation originate? And what kind of world-view preceded it?

Those questions have been preoccupying me, on and off, for almost half a century — in fact ever since I wrote my first study of collective beliefs, *The Pursuit of the Millennium*, in the years immediately after the Second World War. They had, of course, preoccupied others before me; but the standard answers left me unsatisfied. I doubted whether 'primitive' or 'archaic' peoples everywhere and at all times really imagined time as revolving in long, repetitive cycles, punctuated by periodic destructions and re-creations of the world and/or of mankind. And was it really so certain that the first to expect a single, final consummation were Jews and Christians? The whole matter seemed to call for re-examination.

Some twenty years ago I set out to re-examine it. This book summarises the conclusions which bit by bit, over that long span, have forced themselves upon me.

Wood End,
Hertfordshire, England

Acknowledgements

For several years after I began work on this book I was Astor-Wolfson Professor in the University of Sussex, a personal appointment that left me far more time for research than is normally enjoyed by British academics. I am correspondingly grateful to David Astor and to the Wolfson Foundation. I also recall with keen appreciation the year that I spent as a Fellow of that admirable academy, the Netherlands Institute for Advanced Study at Wassenaar.

During my long haul I was greatly fortified, stimulated and enlightened by talks with, and letters from, Mary Boyce and Robert Carroll. Finally they crowned their benefactions by reading and commenting on the completed manuscript. I am truly beholden to them both. My thanks go also to Geza Vermes for encouraging me to undertake and persevere with this enterprise, and to him and to Henry Saggs for their thoughtful — and fruitful — bibliographical suggestions. To Robert Baldock and his colleagues at the Yale University Press, London, I am indebted for the scrupulous care with which they prepared the book for publication.

What I owe to my wife and to my son Nik is beyond all reckoning. But for their encouragement the book would never have been completed, and but for their criticism it would have had even more shortcomings than it has.

For such errors, oversights and other blemishes as remain, I am of course solely responsible.

PART ONE

The Ancient Near East and Beyond

CHAPTER I

Egyptians

Cosmos, in the sense of all-embracing, all-pervading order, was taken for granted in the Ancient Near East: everything in heaven and earth, in nature and in society, had been established and set in order by the gods and was still watched over by the gods.

Not that cosmos was undisturbed. There were chaotic forces, restless and threatening. And here too gods were at work. If some gods were benign, others were not — and some gods could be now benign, now destructive. Every Near Eastern world-view showed an awareness not only of order in the world but of the instability of that order.

Nevertheless the ordered world was imagined as essentially unchanging. Changes were of course seen to occur, technological advances were made — but none of this gave rise to expectations of a future that would be radically different from anything known in the present or in the past: as things had been, so they would remain. At the heart of every Near Eastern world-view was a sense of immutability.

Elaborated by priests and theologians, these world-views were adopted happily enough by those belonging to the upper strata of society: for monarchs and administrators and scribes they served to justify a social order that brought such manifest benefits to the privileged. But that does not mean that they were repudiated by the common people. After all, the concern with order and chaos reflected a very general experience of the way things were. Ordinary folk knew very well how easily all their plans could be upset and all their work undone: each garden and field might be endangered by flood or drought, each herd and flock might be seized by some predatory band from outside the society and by common thieves within it. For succour people relied on the state — which was almost always a monarchy. Oppressive as it was, the state nevertheless stood for order. Vigilance in upholding the law and in frustrating and punishing crime, vigilance also in warding off foreign enemies and when appropriate defeating them in battle — all this not only enabled the state to survive but affirmed and strengthened the ordered world. The regular and effective functioning of that great defender, the state, and of its supreme embodiment, the king, belonged to the same all-embracing order as the movements of the sun and the moon and the stars, the rotation of the seasons.

Because they were rooted in everyday reality the interpretations offered by priests and theologians were generally accepted even by those who had only a vague understanding of them. And because they were not abstract philosophical systems but religious world-views, they were able to condition not only the behaviour of individuals but the political, social and economic life of society.

And of course these world-views were all totally ethnocentric: always the society concerned was placed firmly at the centre of the ordered world.

2

Awareness of cosmos and of what threatened it was nowhere more highly developed than in Egypt.[1]

The very life of Egypt has always depended on the Nile. Most of the country is desert and rainfall is inadequate to support crops or livestock. Agriculture is possible only in a narrow strip of land on either side of the great river, and never could have been practised but for the annual inundation that flows northwards for some 600 miles between late June and late September. Ancient Egyptians were deeply impressed by the contrast between the 'Black Land', as it was called after the deep black mud deposited by the inundations, and the 'Red Land', the desert, fearful and deadly. And then there was the erratic behaviour of the Nile itself. Until modern technology enabled dams to be built, the river might overflow one year, fall too low the next — and either meant famine. All this helped to generate a sense of a world perpetually endangered. And so did the contrast, always so dramatic in Egypt, between day and night: bright day, when the sun, splendid, omnipotent, creator and sustainer of life, sailed high over the land, and the night that so abruptly swallowed up the sun — a time full of menace, when life was suspended.

By the Early Dynastic or Archaic Period danger had taken on a further meaning. Like many other parts of the globe, Egypt had been populated for tens of thousands of years by tiny, isolated groups of hunters. During the fourth millennium small, scattered settlements of farmers spread along the Nile valley, and in the second half of that millennium chiefdoms or small states began to form. By *c.*3050 BC warfare between these proto-kingdoms had resulted, by a process whose course is still being debated, in the creation of a unified kingdom embracing the whole of Egypt. But political security was gone for ever. From then on existence was perceived largely in terms of conflict, actual or potential.

The course of Egyptian history was less tranquil than is often supposed. It is true that Egypt — protected by desert to the west, by the Mediterranean to the north, and to the east by the Red Sea — was less exposed to invasion than most Near Eastern states. Nevertheless Egypt too went through periods of political turmoil. If the Archaic Period and the Old Kingdom (*c.*3050–2160 BC)[2] witnessed a great flowering of civilisation, they were followed by the two centuries of weak rule, civil war and economic collapse known as the First Intermediate Period (2160–1991). If the Middle Kingdom (1991–1786) saw a restoration of peace and prosperity, that was followed by the Second Intermediate Period (*c.*1786–1540), when Egypt, split into two kingdoms, was culturally and politically dominated by foreigners. Under a strong line of native kings the New Kingdom (1540–1070) became the centre of an empire extending from Nubia to Asia Minor — but only at the cost of ever-recurring wars. And after the New Kingdom came a slow and this time irremediable decline, during which Egypt was conquered first by the Persians, then by Alexander the Great, before being absorbed into the Roman empire in 30 BC. Naturally the Egyptian world-view was affected by these convulsions. It was all too clear that, however strong the Egyptian state might seem, it was never absolutely secure. The ordered world, identified with that state, was always at risk.

3

Egyptians did not believe that the world had been created out of nothing: material of some kind had been there always. They imagined the original creation as a shaping of that formless material into an ordered world.

There were many versions of how that happened — the most influential, from the third millennium onwards, being associated with the great religious centres at Heliopolis (originally called On), Memphis and Hermopolis. There was agreement on essentials. The world had not been shaped by a god who had existed for ever and ever — what had existed for ever and ever was chaos. Often that chaos is described in negative terms: it cannot be explained, it is not like anything, it is the negation of the present, existing world. It is what existed 'before the sky existed, before earth existed, before men existed, before the gods were born, before death existed'.[3] Yet chaos was not imagined as immaterial: it was a boundless ocean, called Nun. Darkness was on the face of the deep, for there was as yet no sun. But within that dark, watery abyss lay, in a latent state, the primal substance out of which the world was to be formed. Also submerged somewhere within it was the demiurge who was to do the forming. But the demiurge too existed only as potentiality, not yet aware of himself or of the task that lay ahead.

About the first step in the making of the world there was also widespread agreement. At a certain moment — it was known as 'the first time' or 'the first occasion' — a tiny island rose out of the water: the primordial hillock. This notion surely reflects the experience, repeated each year, of the inundation and reflux of the Nile — the spectacle of a land almost submerged and then emerging from the waters renewed, covered with fresh soil, and soon green, full of living creatures, fertile, ready for cultivation: an annual genesis. Perhaps — as some scholars have suggested — there were even vague recollections, handed down from generation to generation of peasants, of a time when most of Egypt was swamp, flooded by a Nile that had not yet carved out its bed, with only scattered islands emerging. However that may be, there were not many places of any importance that did not claim to be built upon or around it. Memphis, Heliopolis, Hermopolis, Thebes, Esna, Edfu, Dendera, Crocodilopolis were only a few of the centres where the ordered world was supposed to have begun.

The Nun was there before any god, was even sometimes called 'father of the gods', but it was not an active force. The organising, ordering of the world had to be carried out by the demiurge. But what did this involve? It did not, for Egyptians, involve conflict: the demiurge does not appear, in the hymns addressed to him, as fighting against chaos or chaos monsters. His significance is quite other. The original chaos was an undifferentiated, unitary state, and the demiurge embodied the process of differentiation and definition. Whereas the original chaos was boundless, there were bounds to the ordered world that began to emerge with the demiurge. Again, the demiurge brought light where there had been primordial darkness — and in the light things could exist separately. Through the demiurge oneness was transformed into multiplicity.[4] If the original state is described as the time 'when two things had not yet come into existence', the demiurge is called 'the One, who makes himself into millions'.[5]

The theologians of Heliopolis and Hermopolis held that the demiurge was the sun-god Ra, those of Memphis that he was the earth-god Ptah.[6] All agreed that he came into full existence at a moment when the primordial hillock emerged. While in the Nun he had been in a state of 'somnolence' or 'inertia', but as he became aware of himself he transformed himself. Not begotten of any father, not conceived by any mother, of his own volition he gave himself a body and entered upon active existence.

The demiurge in Memphite doctrine, Ptah, was also called Tatenen, 'the earth rising up' — which linked him both with the primordial hillock and with the soil emerging from the annual inundation. Ptah made the world, he created the gods, their temples and their images. He was the master of matter. He founded the provinces and cities of Egypt. Food and drink, the material sustenance of life, were his gift. He was the founder of all arts and crafts, patron of building, sculpture, metallurgy. It was he who set the heavens in their proper place and kept them there, and the sun was his creation and subordinate to him.

But the most influential theology was the Heliopolitan. By the middle of the third millennium the sun-god Ra (or Re) had become the great god of the city of Heliopolis, and he soon became identified with the ancient tribal god of the Heliopolitans, Atum (meaning 'the Completed One'), with the scarab-god Khepri ('he who comes into existence'), with the falcon-god Horus, with the god of horizons Akhti. Indeed, in the course of Egyptian history Ra became identified with most of the deities who were worshipped as supreme gods in the various cities — who thereupon shed their original attributes and acquired the dignity of sun-god and self-creating demiurge. So the obscure Amun, god of Thebes, became the mighty Amon-Ra when, with the beginning of the New Kingdom, Thebes became the capital of the ruling dynasty.

None of this diminished the supremacy of Ra, or his all-importance as demiurge. Nor was his stature diminished in the theologies, such as those of Hermopolis or Esna, which maintained that Ra came not directly from the Nun but was created by demiurges who had come out of the Nun. Indeed, as priests struggled to reconcile the various theologies the sun-god became a truly universal presence. His only serious rival was the god Osiris — of whom more later. And it was only very late — in the Graeco-Roman period — that the cult of Osiris finally ousted that of Ra.

How the demiurge first became manifest was a subject for imaginative elaboration. According to texts in the temple at Edfu, he came flying out of the primordial darkness in the form of a falcon and settled on a reed at the water's edge. The Hermopolitan priests were still more imaginative. According to them, immediately after 'the first occasion' eight primitive deities, some frog-like, some serpent-like — and all of them, therefore, closely related to the watery chaos

— created a lotus-flower in the temple lake at Hermopolis; from this Ra emerged as a child. The Hermopolitans also told of a cosmic egg that hatched on the hillock. But iconography favoured yet another version, of Heliopolitan origin. Weary of floating in the Nun, the demiurge climbed on to the hillock in human form, already equipped with eyes, mouth, tongue, hands, heart, arms, legs, penis.

The first creations of the demiurge were the god of the air Shu and a goddess, probably of moisture, called Tefnut; he created them, in one version, by masturbation, in another, by spitting. These were Heliopolitan versions. Memphite theology was subtler: Ptah conceived in his heart the gods he intended to create, then gave his ideas concrete existence by means of his tongue, i.e. by speech. It was generally agreed that, once created, Shu and Tefnut produced the earth — imagined as a flat platter with a corrugated rim — and the sky, imagined as an inverted pan, resting on supports to hold it safely away from the earth. Earth and sky mated and produced two divine couples. With the appearance of these deities a gradual process began which in the end populated the world with gods, human beings and animals. Here the potter-god Khnum played a major part, moulding each embryo on his wheel and then placing it in the mother's womb.

Egyptian gods had much in common with human beings. It is true that in prehistoric times Egyptians, like many primitive peoples, gave animal forms to most of their deities; but already in the Archaic Period and the Old Kingdom more and more gods were given human or partly human forms. More importantly, the gods had some of the limitations of human beings. Except for the demiurge they were neither omniscient nor omnipotent: events could take them by surprise, and they were not always able to influence them. Nor did the gods even enjoy eternal life. Not only had they all, except the demiurge, been created by earlier gods — they could grow old and die. There are myths that describe the sun-god himself as ageing, withdrawing from active rule and installing another god as his representative. At Thebes, Edfu and Hermopolis there were even tombs of gods who were supposed to have lived and died in the remote past. All this emphasised the kinship between gods and human beings.

That is not to say that there was no gulf between them. The gods lived beyond the limits of the earth — in the heavens or in the netherworld — and human beings had no direct contact with them. Yet they operated on earth, and very powerfully. A field of force surrounded each deity, magical power radiated from each, to affect whatever claimed his or her attention. Moreover, diverse though they were, gods and goddesses formed a community, almost a family:

their parental, filial, marital and other relationships, together with their various personalities and functions, constituted the hidden dynamics of the universe. It was an awe-inspiring notion, and Egyptians were in fact awed by the might and majesty of their deities — how deeply may be sensed even now in the colonnaded chamber at Karnak, with its 134 giant columns ranged in sixteen rows.

But awe was combined with love; as one hymn puts it, 'I prostrate myself in fear of thee, I look up to thee in love.'[7] As Egyptians saw it, men and women were not created to serve the gods as their slaves but for their own sake, like the gods themselves. Indeed they were convinced that when the demiurge organised the world he delighted in adjusting it, with its sunlight and its plants and animals — and its gods — to suit human needs. His example set the tone for the other gods: almost all of them were benign. To be dependent on such beings was no hardship.

Besides, Egyptians knew that, like themselves, gods were both bound and sustained by the all-embracing principle of order, called *ma'at*.

4

The concept of *ma'at* was developed in response to the needs of the Egyptian state.[8] As soon as that state was formed it became clear that such a complex polity, embracing peoples of diverse origins and often with conflicting interests, required a body of rules. Only a body of rules, systematically thought out and authoritatively imposed and enforced, could avert chaos. The word *ma'at* meant 'base' — like the base of a throne. And *ma'at* was in fact the base on which the legal system of Egypt rested. An early king would call himself 'lord of *ma'at*', and claim to have conceived of *ma'at* in his heart and decreed it with his mouth.

Soon *ma'at* acquired a far wider significance: the word was used to indicate a principle of order so all-embracing that it governed every aspect of existence. The equilibrium of the universe and the cohesion of its elements, the rotation of the seasons, the movements of the heavenly bodies, the diurnal course of the sun — and amongst human beings, proper observance of religious obligations and rituals by the priests, fair dealing and honesty and truthfulness in personal relations — all this was included in *ma'at*. In Egyptian thought, nature and society were imagined as two sides of one and the same reality: whatever was harmonious and regular in either was an expression of *ma'at*.

It was not for nothing that the hieroglyph for *ma'at* recalled the primordial hillock, for *ma'at* came to be imagined as the base on which the ordered world itself rested. *Ma'at*, it was believed, had been there from the very moment when the ordered world began to emerge from primordial chaos, in fact it symbolised the pristine state of the world: the demiurge established it when he climbed to the top of the primordial hillock.

In Memphite theology the earth-god Ptah is called 'lord of *ma'at*', and the pedestal with which he is commonly represented is likewise shaped like the hieroglyph of *ma'at*.[9] In the Heliopolitan theology it was of course the sun-god Ra who was 'lord of *ma'at*'. Here the establishment of *ma'at* coincided with the first sunrise. Moreover, each dawn was felt to call that original event out of the depths of the past. In the Egyptian climate each sunrise was (and is) wonderfully brilliant; to ancient Egyptians it seemed a daily miracle, a repetition of 'the first occasion'. And what followed was scarcely less wonderful. The sun-god was imagined as each day traversing the sky in a boat and passing through the netherworld each night in another boat. The successful voyage through the perilous netherworld, accomplished with the aid of lesser gods, the triumphant reappearance at dawn — all this was an ever-renewed proof that the sun-god had the power to sustain and renew the ordered world.

The sun-god and *ma'at* were so closely associated as to be inseparable. *Ma'at* sustained Ra's life: a hymn to the sun-god proclaims that 'thy nourishment consists of *ma'at*, thy beverage is *ma'at*, thy bread is *ma'at*, the garment of thy body is *ma'at*'.[10] Eventually there was also a goddess called Ma'at. She too was intimately related to the sun-god — sometimes she is even called his daughter. The goddess Ma'at accompanied Ra as he sailed across the sky in his boat; often she is portrayed standing at the prow, as pilot. So guided, Ra pursued a course whose straightness was itself an affirmation of perfect and indestructible order.

From the heights of heaven Ra observed the activities of human beings and judged them.[11] Those who felt themselves wronged could lay their complaints before him in the knowledge that he would see justice done, for he was a just and incorruptible judge. An official who had been unjustly dismissed could appeal to the sun-god to reinstate him and to punish his powerful persecutor. Especially the least privileged and most defenceless could rely on his support: he protected orphans, the downtrodden, the poor, against arbitrary tyranny. All this is expressed at length in hymns dating from the New Kingdom, but it is clearly implied already in the famous 'Instruction' for King Merikare, which dates from *c.*2050 BC.[12]

In his judicial capacity Ra had the support of the crew of the sun-boat. The goddess Ma'at of course helped him, and so did four baboons who sat at the boat's prow. Living with *ma'at*, detesting everything that ran counter to it, they ensured that the strong did not oppress the weak — and in so doing, we are told, they offered up *ma'at* to Ra and made the gods content.[13] But most of all Ra relied on his secretary and deputy, the moon-god Thoth, who was sometimes called his son.[14] What this implied is shown by a phrase in a hymn to Ra: 'Daily Thoth writes *ma'at* for thee.'[15] Thoth too is shown at the prow of the sun-boat. It was his task to crush the opposition that Ra encountered during the voyage — and that too was an affirmation of *ma'at*.

Thoth was endowed with the wisdom and insight that he needed in order to impose and maintain *ma'at* amongst gods and human beings. As 'legislator in heaven and on earth' he saw to it that the various gods kept to their proper spheres of activity, that in human society the various professional bodies fulfilled their proper functions, that nations respected each other's frontiers and that fields were kept to their proper boundaries.[16] As 'lord of laws' he taught the gods about *ma'at*: when conflicts arose between gods, he settled the dispute and re-established peace and harmony. He also stood by the supreme authority on earth, Pharaoh, in his adminstration of government. Thanks to his vigilance, a human being who transgressed against *ma'at* could expect to be punished, whether in this life or in an afterlife. An enemy of every form of disorder, Thoth was ceaselessly on the watch to ensure that *ma'at* was respected throughout the universe.

5

The political and social embodiment of *ma'at* was the Egyptian state, and the essence of the Egyptian state was the monarchy, which was regarded as a divine institution.[17] The lengthy historical process by which a number of clans and tribes and proto-kingdoms had been fused into a single state under a single king was identified, in imagination, with the moment when the primordial hillock emerged from the waters and the sun-god ascended to take up the government of the universe.

According to official history, Egypt had originally been ruled by gods. The first ruler of all was the sun-god himself. He was succeeded by his sons and daughters, then by his grandchildren, always as royal couples, and they in their turn were succeeded by a line of demi-gods and demi-goddesses, or 'spirits'. The human kings of Egypt were descended from these and were their rightful heirs.

In reality the history of the Egyptian monarchy was turbulent enough: the succession was often decided by civil war, and the founder of a new dynasty was often simply an ambitious and ruthless usurper. Nevertheless, the monarchy was always presented as the guarantor of rightness in the world, and the triumph of the existing dynasty was always presented as an affirmation of the divinely appointed order.

The myth of Seth and Osiris is illuminating. Seth was the anomalous god. Whereas other gods could be symbolised by a real animal, such as a cat or a falcon, Seth alone had a purely fabulous creature as his symbol. His very birth was violent and abnormal — by his own effort he burst out of the side of his mother, the sky-goddess Nut — and it brought disturbance and conflict into the ordered world. He was an embodiment of crude physical strength, of sexual potency and unbridled, bisexual promiscuity, of unruliness. Destructive storms, the terrifying desert, everything that was exotic and therefore disconcerting could be linked to him. Also, he murdered his brother, the great god Osiris, dismembered his corpse and threw the pieces into the Nile.

This was an attack on legitimate monarchy, for Osiris was a king among the gods, second only to Ra. By slaying him before he had had time to beget an heir, Seth opened up the possibility of usurping the kingship. But Isis, wife and sister of Osiris, gathered the scattered members together, including the phallus. So she was able to present her husband with a posthumous heir, Horus — a living proof that parentage and the legitimate transmission of monarchy can triumph over even the most extreme violence. And in single combat Horus — partly thanks to his mother's command of magic, partly thanks to his own cunning — was able to overcome his father's murderer.

The final outcome was decided by the divine magistrates, sitting as a court at Heliopolis: Horus became king on earth, and so a god with whom the living pharaoh could always be identified; while Osiris was awarded dominion over the netherworld into which he had already descended. But Seth was not wholly rejected, either: if in one version of the myth he is awarded dominion over the realms outside the ordered world — the barren deserts, the foreign countries — in another version he is received back into the ordered world, as attendant of the sun-god.[18] And with the consolidation of legitimate monarchy, cosmos was reaffirmed.

Pharaoh was not only of divine descent, he was semi-divine himself. From the Old Kingdom onwards it was believed that on his death each king took his place amongst the gods. More importantly, while still on earth the king was perceived not only as the son of the gods and goddesses as a collectivity but, specifically, as 'the son of Ra.' In the New Kingdom the implication of the latter epithet was made explicit: the fiction was maintained that the sun-god, in the form of the ruling king, always mated with the king's chief wife, to produce a unique being standing halfway between the gods and mankind. The mating is portrayed on the walls of various temples, and the inscription that accompanies the picture in the temple of Amenhotep III (*c.*1391–1353) at Luxor shows how physical the mating was supposed to be:

> Words spoken by Amun-Ra, Lord of Karnak, pre-eminent in his harem, when he assumed the form of this her husband, King Menkheperura [Tuthmosis IV], given life. He found her as she slept within the innermost part of her palace. She awoke on account of the divine fragrance and turned towards His Majesty. He went straightway to her, he was aroused by her. He allowed her to see him in his divine form, after he had come before her, so that she rejoiced at seeing his perfection. His love, it entered her body. The palace was flooded with divine fragrance and all his odours were those of the land of Punt.[19]

The half-god Pharaoh and the true gods assisted each other, they exchanged services. Pharaoh approached the gods as the representative of the Egyptian people, making offerings on their behalf and soliciting favours for them in return. It was through Pharaoh that the people were able to fortify the gods and so enable them to sustain the world order. Conversely, it was through Pharaoh that the benign power of the gods was bestowed on the people. Gods and human beings alike depended on Pharaoh for their well-being.

If Pharaoh represented the people before the gods, he also represented the gods before the people. In particular he was Ra's representative. As one king put it, '[The god] created me as one who should do what he had done, and to carry out that which he commanded should be done. He appointed me herdsman of this land, for he knew who would keep it in order for him.'[20] The king's role was symbolised already in the ceremony of accession. The new king ascended his throne at dawn on the day immediately following the death of his predecessor — and this was perceived as commemorating and as it were renewing Ra's ascent of the primordial hillock. As the dawning of each day was perceived as a re-establishment of cosmos, so was the assumption of rule by a new king.

Like Ra himself, the king was 'lord of *ma'at*'; and in commemorative texts various kings are referred to as 'he who does *ma'at*', 'protector of *ma'at*', 'he who lives from *ma'at*'. In fact the king was thought of as literally united with *ma'at*, and ideally the whole people was supposed to be united with *ma'at* through him: '*Ma'at* has come after it has united itself [with King Horemheb]' — 'Thou [King Sethos] have fixed *ma'at* in Egypt; it has become united with everyone.'[21] By maintaining *ma'at* the king kept the state firmly integrated in the cosmic order and so ensured the well-being of society. Thus King Amenophis III (1417–1379) felt himself called 'to make Egypt flourish, as in primeval times, by means of the plans of *ma'at*', and Rameses IV (1166–1160) could declare, 'I have brought *ma'at* into this land.'[22]

The king expected that, if he preserved *ma'at* in the land, the gods would in return make the land prosper. Thus Rameses IV could appeal to Osiris, as god of the soil and of vegetation:

> 'And thou shalt give me high and plenteous Niles, in order to supply thy divine offerings, and to supply the divine offerings to all the gods and goddesses of South and North; in order to preserve alive the people of all thy lands, their cattle and their groves, which thy hand has made . . . And thou shalt be pleased with the land of Egypt, thy land, in my time.'[23]

The gods responded. The birth of Rameses II, whose long reign was to last from 1304 to 1237, was greeted by his divine father Amun-Ra with the declaration, 'I have put justice (*ma'at*) into its place' — with the result, we are told, that the earth was made firm, and heaven was satisfied, and the gods were content.[24] Likewise because Rameses III (1198–1166) did *ma'at* every day, Amun-Ra saw to it that the Nile floods brought abundance to the land and the people enjoyed all good things.[25]

A fertile Egypt was itself a sign of the presence of *ma'at*: the course of human affairs and the course of nature were not to be separated. A song written to celebrate the accession of King Merneptah, in the New Kingdom, conveys the relationship beautifully:

> Rejoice, thou entire land, the goodly time has come. A lord is appointed to all countries, . . . O all ye righteous, come and behold! Truth hath repressed falsehood, the sinners are fallen on their faces, all that are covetous are turned back. The water standeth and faileth not, and the Nile carrieth a high [flood]. The days are long, the nights have hours, and the months come aright. The gods are content and happy of heart, and life is spent in laughter and wonder.[26]

Ma'at found one of its main expressions in justice — in fact the very words for justice, for judging justly, for being found innocent, for being found right, all contain the root of the word *ma'at*. In his care for justice the king was supposed to model himself not only on Ra, but also, and even more closely, on Ra's assistant Thoth. Pharaoh was praised for 'laying down laws like Thoth'. He was called 'the good god, the heir to Thoth, who destroys what is evil and does what is true', 'who speaks justice like Thoth'. But justice meant much more than the impartial administration of the law. Pharaoh was expected to show infinite solicitude for his people: it was not for nothing that he compared himself with a shepherd, and carried a shepherd's crook as part of his regalia. The 'Instruction for King Merikare' details the qualities by which a newly and insecurely established pharaoh hoped to legitimise his rule: 'Do justice whilst thou endurest on earth. Quiet the weeper; do not oppress the widow; supplant no man in the property of his father; and impair no officials in their posts. Be on thy guard against punishing wrongly . . .'

The same 'Instruction' shows how royal solicitude was one expression amongst many of the all-embracing solicitude of the demiurge himself:

> 'Well directed are men, the cattle of the god. He made heaven and earth according to their desire . . . He made the breath of life [for] their nostrils. . . . He arises in heaven according to their desire. He made for them plants, animals, fowl and fish to feed them . . . He made the light of day according to their desire, and he sails by in order to see them . . . and when they weep he hears. He made for them rulers . . . , a supporter to support the back of the disabled. . . .'[27]

Through his god-like solicitude for the unfortunate the king confirmed that his rule was indeed divinely sanctioned.

In practice the administration of justice was delegated by Pharaoh to a vizier, and by him to a number of magistrates. All these were expected to collaborate in maintaining and strengthening *ma'at*. The vizier was actually called 'priest of *ma'at*'; while the autobiographical notices found in magistrates' graves bear witness to the same preoccupation. These men commonly aver that when they judged a case between two parties, both went away satisfied. And they would end by claiming to have shown themselves 'men of *ma'at*'. Needless to say, that was not always how it appeared to the parties themselves. But if complaints about biased and venial judges are frequent, that in itself shows how seriously people took the ideal of justice.

Nobody was more concerned with *ma'at* than the senior scribes, i.e. senior bureaucrats.[28] In a society where most people were illiterate these 'writing men' belonged to a highly esteemed élite. They wielded great power, for the whole administration of the state depended on them. They considered themselves to be 'men of the king' — but also believed that the supreme god had charged them with the task of promoting *ma'at* within the Egyptian community. They had a special responsibility for training future officials — and these in turn were expected to discharge their duties in accord with the dictates of *ma'at*. The heart of the good official was supposed to be so penetrated with *ma'at* that he could not possibly contravene the divinely appointed order. Most of all a counsellor at court was expected to act as *maʿat* required: 'Do *maʿat* for the king, [for] *maʿat* is that which the king loves! Speak *maʿat* to the king, [for] that which the king loves is *maʿat*.'[29]

The most detailed administrative arrangements could be perceived as affirmations of *maʿat*. A great feudal lord, for instance, would praise the king for having marked out the boundaries of his lands, and of the towns within his lands, and for having allotted him his share of the Nile and its flood-waters — and he would add that the king had done all this 'because of the great love he has for *maʿat*'.[30] Similarly King Amenemhat I (*c.*1991–*c.*1962) declared that he had fixed the boundaries of the shires to be as unalterable 'as the heavens' — and he had done so 'because he set such store by *maʿat*'.[31]

6

For an ethnocentric society there was no stronger affirmation of order in the world than victory in war. This was equally true whether the war was a colonial war in Nubia, or a civil war within Egypt itself, or, during the New Kingdom, war against a rival imperial power: always the enemy forces were perceived as forces of chaos. And in combating those forces too Egypt and its gods were allies. As one of the royal prayers puts it, 'Mayest thou let it be known in all the low country and all the hilly country that thou art the power of the pharaoh, thy son, against all the low country and all the hilly country. Thou grantest victory to Egypt, thine only land'.[32]

In countless Egyptian temples there is a picture, sculpted or painted, but always prominently displayed, showing one of the greatest gods presenting the king with the club of victory. The accompanying texts interpret the symbolism: 'Take to thyself the sword, O mighty king,' says the god Horus to King Seti I (1318–1304), . . . in order to smite the rebellious countries, that violate thy boundaries . . . they fall in their blood by the might of thy father Amon, who hath decreed thee might and victory.'[33] The god could also celebrate the victory that he and the king had won together — as Amun-Ra did for the benefit of King Thutmosis III (1504–1450):

> I have felled thine enemies beneath thy sandals,
> Thou hast smitten the hordes of rebels according as I
>   commanded you.
> The earth in its length and breadth, Westerners and Easterners,
>   are subject to thee,

Thou tramplest all countries, thy heart glad;
. . .
I have deprived their nostrils of the breath of life,
I have set the terror of thy majesty in their hearts,
I have caused thy victories to circulate among all
  lands,
My serpent-diadem gives light to thy dominion.
There is no rebel of thine as far as the circuit of heaven;
They come, bearing tribute upon their backs,
Bowing down to thy majesty according to my command.
I have made powerless the invaders who come before thee;
Their hearts burned, their limbs trembling.[34]

From the very beginning of Egyptian history monuments and official annals are at one in showing the king as invariably victorious. But how far does this reflect what really happened? Certainly not at all closely. To take one example: In 1285 BC, at Kadesh on the Orontes, Rameses II, with one of his four legions, was ambushed by the Hittites and their allies. The ensuing battle as described in Egyptian accounts has the air of a ritual drama, with everyone playing the part allotted by tradition. The enemy are rebels against Pharaoh's rule, and they are so numerous that they cover mountains and valleys like a horde of locusts. The king goes out of his tent in full ceremonial robes, with the uraeus-snake 'spitting fire' on his brow, mounts his chariot and alone, unsupported by any troops, supported only by the god Amun, tramples the enemy down and throws them into panic-stricken flight. Pharaoh and Amun together are more effective 'than millions of foot-soldiers and hundreds of thousands of chariots'.[35]

What was expected of the king did not and could not change, and it determined what was claimed for him. Rameses III (1198–1166) did not hesitate to claim for himself the astounding victory that Rameses II was supposed to have had over the Hittites — even though by his time the Hittites no longer existed as a political power. King Sahure (*c.*2455–2443) defeated the Libyans in battle — so his successor Pepi II appropriated the accounts of the victory for himself in every detail, although he probably never fought the Libyans at all. Tutankhamun (1361–1352), who died at the age of eighteen, was portrayed as victorious over peoples to the south and east of Egypt, although he is known never to have campaigned against them. To call such accounts falsifications of history is to miss the point. Their factual accuracy or inaccuracy was irrelevant: their intention was to show that the pharaoh in question had indeed fulfilled his allotted role, he had indeed affirmed and strengthened cosmos.

That same intention accounts for the wall paintings, to be found in many temples, showing long lines of prisoners of war, each representing a conquered city or country, waiting to be ritually massacred, often by Pharaoh himself. Modern historians believe that no such ceremonial massacres took place.[36] But since a hostile, or supposedly hostile, foreign power necessarily belonged with the forces of chaos, Pharaoh could not but annihilate it.

One of the cultic ceremonies performed in Egyptian temples was a ritual 'annihilation of enemies'. This normally took the form of a bloody sacrifice not of human beings but of wild animals—animals that for one reason or another were traditionally labelled as enemies of the gods. These victims were explicitly identified with 'rebellious' peoples. That explains why in many temples portrayals of Pharaoh's triumphs in battle are interwoven with portrayals of Pharaoh's hunting and slaying of wild animals. At Edfu, for example, we are shown an enormous net in which not only birds but animals and men are trapped — the men being prisoners of war, kneeling, their arms tightly bound. The king and two or three gods are pulling the net shut. Accompanying texts make it clear that such pictures were reinforced by ceremonies and spells designed to reduce and destroy the king's enemies.[37]

So central was this perception of Pharaoh and his role that not even conquest by a foreign power could shatter it. On the contrary, any foreign monarch who came to rule over Egypt was perceived as truly Pharaoh if he was willing to accept the pharaonic titulary and to serve the gods of Egypt. Both the Persian conqueror Cambyses and Alexander the Great had the good sense to comply. Those foreign rulers who failed to meet these expectations were themselves labelled as agents of chaos: their reigns meant a temporary absence of Pharaoh and of *ma'at*, a temporary victory of chaos.[38]

7

What we have called a religious world-view could just as well be called a political ideology, and the theologians who created and elaborated it could just as well be called political propagandists. They were to be found amongst the priests of the great temples, all of which owed their prosperity, indeed their very existence, to royal patronage. The values and attitudes of these men were the values and attitudes of the court. They felt it their sacred duty to ensure that the monarchy, and the state constructed around the monarchy, would endure. The same could be said of all the other literate men who wielded authority derived from the king, from high-ranking and wealthy officials and administrators down to the lower ranks of the bureaucracy and the priesthood. All these people were conservative in the original sense of the word: their overriding concern was to conserve.

By and large they succeeded: Egyptian society was extraordinarily stable. The country was sometimes invaded and conquered, the ambitions of great nobles sometimes precipitated civil war — but the only movement that might perhaps be called revolutionary was launched by a pharaoh. Between 1364 and 1347 King Akhenaten (Amenhotep IV) suppressed the cult of the old gods, including Amun-Ra, declared the Aten, i.e. the disc of the sun, to be the one true god, and identified himself with that. There is no reason to think that this innovation was made in response to popular demand, or that its prompt reversal by Akhenaten's son-in-law Tutankhamun ran counter to popular wishes.

There remain certain writings — the *Prophecies of Neferti* and the *Admonitions of Ipuwer* are the most important — which present the poor as comparable with foreign invaders: agents of chaos whose chance would come if ever royal authority were weakened.[39] They too have to be considered.

The *Prophecies of Neferti* tell of an Egypt open to foreigners and despoiled by them, and where moreover the traditional social hierarchy and traditional social and familial bonds have disintegrated:

> Lo, the great no longer rule the land
> . . .
> All happiness has vanished,
> The land is bowed down in distress
> . . .
> I show you the land in turmoil:
> The weak is strong-armed,
> One salutes him who saluted.
> I show you the undermost uppermost.
> . . .
> The beggar will gain riches,
> the great (will rob) to live.
> The poor will eat bread,
> The slaves will be exalted.

The disorder in society is reflected in a disordered nature. The Nile and the sun are both out of joint:

> Dry is the river of Egypt,
> One crosses the water on foot;
> One seeks water for ships to sail on,

Its course having turned to shoreland.
Shoreland will turn into water,
Watercourse back into shoreland.
. . .
Re will withdraw from mankind:
Though he will rise at his hour,
One will not know when noon has come;
No one will discern his shadow.[40]

The *Prophecy of Neferti* ends by hailing King Amenemhet I as the ruler who will reinstitute *ma'at* and expel chaos from the land.

The *Admonitions of Ipuwer* are concerned to show what happens when an (unspecified) king fails to exercise the authority that is rightly his.[41] In a land deprived of kingship a few men, ignoring traditional restraints, stir up strife unopposed. The result is revolution: 'Every town says, "Let us expel our rulers!" '. The traditional social hierarchy is totally destroyed: 'See now, all the ranks, they are not in their place.' — 'See now, the transformation of the people.' It is the turn of the great ones to 'hunger and suffer'.

The author shows what this means in practice. Judges are driven from the land, nobles are expelled from the royal palaces. Wearers of fine linen are beaten with sticks and set to work at the grindstones. Noblewomen roam the land, they are forced to carry heavy burdens and to sleep on bare boards — in fact they are treated as female slaves were normally treated. As for infants of noble birth, they are exposed on the hills to die, or else dashed against walls. Scribes are murdered, and their books of law are thrown into the street, to be trampled underfoot by beggars.

So far the *Prophecies of Neferti* and the *Admonitions of Ipuwer* — but did these things really happen? Egyptologists are fairly generally agreed that, though social disturbances did occur from time to time, there never was any such drastic upheaval. It seems that both the *Prophecies of Neferti* and the *Admonitions of Ipuwer* belong to a specific literary tradition, the description of states of chaos.[42] More than real events, these 'complaints' reflect the anxieties of the privileged, their sense of living on a tiny island of order and civilisation amidst a sea of disorder and barbarism. And they reflect, too, the need that the privileged felt for a strong king to hold social chaos at bay.

8

Hostile nations, rebels, troublemakers of every kind were not simply transgressors against *ma'at*; they were accomplices and instruments of superhuman powers of chaos. A principle that was the exact opposite of *maʿat* was also at work in the world. Egyptians called it *isfet* — which is often translated as 'falsehood' or 'injustice' but which meant more than that. *Isfet* denoted whatever ran counter to the rightness of the world, and it was a force to be reckoned with. For the ordered world always remained, like the primordial hillock, an island of order in an ocean of chaos that was threatening to overwhelm and obliterate it.

When the ordered world was shaped out of primordial chaos, that dark and watery mass did not cease to exist. The Nun still permeated the universe; it both surrounded the earth and filled the netherworld. Admittedly, it had its beneficent aspect. It was the source both of rain and — far more importantly — of the annual inundation. Again, each night the sun-god went down into the Nun, 'old' and 'weary' after the long day's journey, to rise next day refreshed and rejuvenated.[43] It is still true that the chaos surrounding the ordered world was a fearful and haunting presence.

As Egyptians saw it, *maʿat* was perpetually threatened by monstrous beings dwelling in the abyss of the netherworld — and the leader of these embodiments of *isfet* was the gigantic, dragon-like serpent Apophis, or Apep.[44] Apophis was a god, but an evil god — 'he of evil appearance', 'he of evil character' are among his epithets. His first beginnings are lost in the mists of time, but it was during the turbulent First Intermediate Period, when the stability that had characterised the Old Kingdom seemed lost for ever, that he first loomed up as a force of immense destructive power. And once there he remained, right down to the New Kingdom and beyond.

Apophis was an embodiment of primordial chaos. He had no sense-organs, he could neither hear nor see, he could only scream. And he operated always in darkness. As the sun-god's boat sailed through the underworld he tried again and again to block its passage by drinking up the imagined river on which it sailed. In every access of darkness — in an eclipse, in the waning of the moon, in a cloudy sky, but above all in those critical moments, the onset and the end of night — Apophis was at work.

As, at the day's end, the sun-boat went down over the horizon, Ra and the lesser gods manning the boat had to fight the serpent, and they had to do so anew each dawn. This battle on the borders of chaos and the ordered world was fought ferociously: Apophis was cut to pieces with knives, he was pierced with spears, he was burned with fire from the wrathful eye of the sun-god. And here Seth played a vital part: standing at the prow of the sun-boat, he pierced the serpent with his spear, so that the cosmic waters burst forth and the sun-god was able to continue on his way. No longer anomalous, no longer destructive, Seth appears here as a heroic, monster-slaying, world-preserving god. We shall be meeting many other such gods, some Semitic, some Indo-European.

It was a most necessary and urgent battle — for if Apophis had his way even once, the sun would come to a halt and the ordered world would come to an end. Egyptians were very aware of this, and they did what they could to assist the gods. Each day priests in many temples across the land — including the great temple of Amun-Ra at Karnak — recited liturgies celebrating the victory of the sun-god over the serpent. These liturgies seem to have been intended as a form of magic, aimed at destroying Apophis once and for all: 'He is fallen to the flame, Apophis with a knife on his head. He cannot see, and his name is no more in this land. I have commanded that a curse be cast upon him; I have consumed his bones; I have annihilated his soul in the course of every day; I have cut his vertebrae at his neck, severed with a knife which hacked up his flesh and pierced into his hide . . . I have made him non-existent . . . He is fallen and overthrown.'[45]

The vast liturgy of which these phrases form a tiny part is contained in a work known as *The Book of Overthrowing Apophis* — described in the text as a secret book, kept in the hall of the temple, and a treasury of words of magical power.[46] The book also contains instructions for the fabrication of a wax figure of Apophis. This is to be placed on the ground, and the priest is to stamp on it with his left foot until it is reduced to a shapeless mass. Then it is to be cut up with a flint knife, finally it is to be thrown on to a specially prepared fire. All this is to be done every morning, noon and night; and at times when the sun is obscured by clouds or rain, several such figures are to be burned.

Despite all this, Apophis never was destroyed, he was immortal. Moreover, he had always been there. The world and the gods had a beginning but chaos had no beginning, and nor had chaos-monsters. This was true not only of Apophis but of the whole army of strange, menacing beings — hybrid creatures, monstrous beasts, headless men — who are shown, on the walls of the tombs in the Valley of Kings, lining the banks of the underground river, threatening the sun-boat as it passes by. All these existed outside the ordered world, they were not part of creation, they were there from all eternity.[47] The most that could be achieved was to hold them at bay.

9

To repulse the dangers threatening the land of Egypt, to defend and perpetuate the realm of *ma'at* was a gigantic and unending task, requiring the unremitting efforts of gods and human beings, acting in collaboration. Temples and temple cult were there to ensure that collaboration was sustained, that cosmos was ceaselessly defended against the forces of chaos.

A Near Eastern temple was in no way comparable with a Greek temple or a Christian church. It was not a place where believers congregated to worship, indeed the interior was not even accessible to ordinary folk. It was a place of mystery, where priests performed complicated rituals in the presence of the god alone. Moreover, an Egyptian temple was itself an embodiment of cosmos. As each god in his sanctuary was experienced as the supreme force in the ordered world, so the building surrounding his statue represented the ordered world. In many cases the very structure of the building symbolised the emergence of the ordered world at 'the first occasion'. Such a temple was perceived as a re-creation of the primordial hillock where the demiurge had come to rest.[48]

A text in the temple at Edfu describes the relationship between myth and edifice. After the demiurge had arrived on the hillock, the area became a holy place requiring protection; this was provided by a reed wall. As the waters receded, the reed shelter was developed further until it became a complete reed temple, with the shelter containing the god — originally at the top of the hillock — still at a somewhat higher level than the rest. All this was faithfully copied in the stone temple: changing floor and ceiling levels reproduced the shape of the primordial hillock. Moreover, the waters of the Nun that had surrounded the original 'island of creation' were reproduced in the ornamentation of the brick wall surrounding the temple precinct: wavy lines, alternately concave and convex. The columns of the temple, with the capitals shaped to recall palms or lotus-flowers or reeds, represented the abundant vegetation of the island landscape. Some temple walls also have reliefs at their base showing plants, which seem to be growing from the very soil. So a new temple was regarded as representing the original reed shrine — and as possessing the same vast magical power as that.

Just as the primordial hillock had been an island of order surrounded by an ocean of chaos, so in the world beyond the temple precincts chaotic forces were still active. It was the function of the temple to reduce those forces to impotence.[49] To ensure the immunity of the temple itself the sacred precinct was surrounded with strong walls. Portrayals of Pharaoh brandishing his mace over the heads of prisoners of war, or slaying wild animals, served the same purpose at the level of symbolism: it was a way of holding the forces of disorder at bay. Again, in the cult the magical powers of the temple were permanently deployed to protect the god against the encircling chaos, and so to protect the ordered world itself. For though order had been established by the gods, and they were deeply concerned to ensure its survival, they could not ensure it without the constant assistance of human beings. The rites carried out in the temples provided that assistance.[50]

The rites centred on the statue or image of the god or goddess. The image was made in a temple workshop, but ceased to be lifeless matter and became a receptacle for the divine presence through an elaborate and secret rite of consecration, involving magic acts and utterances. In the course of this ceremony the image's eyes and mouth were 'opened', so that it could see and eat, and it was endowed with 'life'. But it could remain alive only with the help of further rites, correctly and regularly performed.

These rites are portrayed in scenes painted on the temple walls, with accompanying inscriptions. Each morning the officiating priests would take the statue of the god or goddess from the shrine where it had rested overnight, remove the previous day's clothing and make-up, cleanse and dress the statue afresh. But what, above all, gave the deity the strength to sustain the ordered world were the offerings supplied by the public: each day he or she was more than adequately fed. That the food was finally removed, untouched, from the temple building and divided amongst the priests in payment for their services made no difference, the deity was strengthened just the same.

The temple cult was inconceivable without Pharaoh. He had temples built and saw to it that dilapidated temples were restored. He ensured that regular and ample offerings were made in the temples. He endowed the temples with lands — and so generously that in the New Kingdom they owned about a third of the cultivatable land, with almost a fifth of the country's inhabitants.

Above all, Pharaoh was high priest in every temple. If one were to accept the wall paintings as historically accurate, one would have to conclude that he performed every rite in every temple in Egypt, unaided by priests. In reality he was probably present at the foundation ceremony of each temple, and he may or may not have performed the daily rite of the chief god of the state in the capital city. All other rites will have been performed by priests. Yet though the wall paintings cannot be literally true, they are so at a symbolic level: the king was felt to be present in the priest. It was his presence in the cult that guaranteed the continuity of the divinely appointed order. In one particular rite, which is always portrayed at the very back of the holy of holies, Pharaoh actually presents *ma'at*, either in the form of food or else in the form of a statuette of the goddess Ma'at, to the resident deity.[51] One cannot imagine a more telling symbolisation of what order meant to Egyptians.

10

Ordinary folk took it for granted that, just as the priests strove to sustain and strengthen *ma'at* through ritual, so they themselves should do so through their social behaviour — and that in itself implied conformity. Moreover, although their preoccupations did not coincide with the concerns of those who watched over the well-being of the state, they harmonised with them. For ordinary folk the supernatural world was always present. Little gods and beneficent spirits surrounded one, watching over one's everyday occupations and preoccupations, while harmful spirits, or demons, hovered nearby, awaiting their chance to inflict injury or sickness or death.[52]

Separate minor gods and goddesses supervised the marshlands bordering the Nile and the hunting and fishing that took place there; weaving and the making of clothes; the production of wine, oil and scented unguents; grain and harvest — indeed every aspect of economic life. Divine solicitude also influenced the individual fates of human beings. From the moment of conception the potter-god Khnum fashioned the child's body and the vital spirit within. Other deities watched over each birth and operated as midwives — chief among them the goddess of childbirth Ta-Uret (better known under her Greek name Thoeris). Thoeris was commonly represented in the form of a female, pregnant hippopotamus. People prayed to her in little chapels or in their own homes — as they did to the god Shed, who offered protection against accidents such as scorpion-stings, and to the grotesque dwarf god Bes, who was a jester and the god of fun and merriment.

Less ubiquitous, it would seem, than Mesopotamian demons, Egyptian demons were still dangerous enough. The great gods sent them to travel the earth, as their messengers, bearing sickness and death. Normally they moved — as did Mesopotamian demons — in groups of seven, or of multiples of seven, or in seven groups. Armed with knives, they cut out the hearts of those whom the gods had selected for destruction.

Demons could operate at any moment, but certain periods of transition were particularly favourable to them: the end of a day, the end of a month, the end of a year, the end of a decade. At such times, when order was disturbed, demons had free rein. People took what precautions they could. During the last five days of the year long prayers of supplication were addressed to the deities, especially to the lion-headed goddess Sekhmet, who was herself demonic. People also wore amulets representing Sekhmet, as vehicles of protective magic. Above all they invoked the aid of the beneficent little gods and spirits, for these were expert at combating demons. Thus, as demons armed with knives gathered about a newborn infant and its mother, good spirits similarly equipped gathered to fight them off.

So the gigantic unceasing struggle at the cosmic level between Ra and Apophis, order and disorder, had its counterpart in the vicissitudes of individual lives.

II

Egyptians did not welcome novelty, indeed they did not willingly admit its possibility. Each temple was supposed to be a continuation and re-creation of the first structure where the demiurge had rested on 'the first occasion'. Each king was the tireless defender of cosmos, ever victorious against the agents of chaos. Each battle, whatever its 'real' outcome, was perceived — like each temple ritual — as a reaffirmation of *ma'at*, a re-establishing of the ordered world as it emerged on 'the first occasion'.[53] The Egyptian ideal was not so much endless, unchanging duration as periodic regeneration and rejuvenation, repeated endlessly.

The god most closely associated with regeneration and rejuvenation was Osiris — the great god whom Seth had murdered and dismembered, but who had then been miraculously resurrected.[54] Sometimes Osiris was identified with the grain that is reborn after a period of burial underground, sometimes with the moon that shines again after a period of invisibility, sometimes with the Nile that produces a new inundation after a period of drought. There were rites to help Osiris make the required recommencements. In a sacred drama known as *The Mysteries of Osiris* a cake shaped like a mummy was planted with corn-seeds and watered: as it sprouted green shoots it symbolised and also encouraged the annual rebirth of nature. The same rite was performed at each new moon, so that the lunar cycle too could continue undisturbed.

The course of the sun was perceived as a model both of stability and of cyclical recurrence.[55] Various texts tell how in the last hour of the night the sun-god and all his attendant gods in the sun-boat enter into a giant snake as old people, weak with age, to emerge from it as still the same gods but now in the guise of young children; how the four baboons in the sun-boat open the eastern gates of heaven and let light stream into the world as it has always done; how the sun-god rises to repeat his original wonderful deed as he has always done.[56]

Different as they were, Ra and Osiris were nevertheless closely connected — a well-known relief even shows a ram-headed mummy inscribed, 'This is Ra when he comes to rest in Osiris daily' and 'This is Osiris when he comes to rest in Ra daily'.[57] Together the two great gods provided Egyptians with a pattern of death and rebirth, ending and beginning anew. This is evident, for instance, in the way reigns were reckoned. When a king died his successor ascended the throne at dawn on the following day — and this was perceived as a repetition of the first sunrise on the primordial hillock. The first year of the new reign was reckoned to run from that moment to the beginning of the inundation; with that event the second year began. So Pharaoh was linked both to Ra and to Osiris, so a reign was integrated into the cyclical rhythm of the world.[58]

Egyptians imagined time as stretching endlessly ahead — endlessly and changelessly too, save for the cyclical recurrences which were also endless. Perhaps — there are a couple of texts that suggest it — after millions of millions of years the time allotted to the world would run out, the sun would no longer follow its course, the heavens would fall, cosmos would revert to watery chaos.[59] But that was too remote a prospect to concern anyone very much. What mattered was that the ordered world should remain essentially unchanged — that nothing should happen that had no parallel in the present or in the past. Even when, in periods of political and social disaster, prophecies of a better future were produced, all that these looked forward to was a restoration of past order.[60] No pharaoh could hope to do more than re-establish conditions 'as they were in the time of Ra, in the beginning'.

12

The Egyptian yearning for regeneration and rejuvenation, for a reality beyond the attrition of time, found its supreme expression in beliefs about the afterlife.

In the long course of Egyptian history those beliefs fluctuated.[61] In the Old Kingdom the afterlife of the king became overwhelmingly important: the dead pharaoh was believed to ascend to the sky and to join the circumpolar stars — because they never disappear; or else — a much longer-lasting belief — to join Ra in the sun-boat, there to continue his royal duties, as defender of *ma'at*, and of Egypt as the realm of *ma'at*, for all eternity. The very architecture of the royal tombs, from the pyramids onwards, gave symbolic expression to these expectations. The king also granted funeral endowments to members of the royal family and to some favoured nobles, so that they could have tombs surrounding his own: clearly he hoped to enjoy their company in the afterlife. Peasants, on the other hand, seem to have expected no more than an indefinite extension of the laborious life they had lived on earth.

The First Intermediate Period witnessed what is often called 'the democratisation of immortality', but which seems, rather, to have been the democratisation of a beatific afterlife. First the nobility in general, eventually people at all levels of society looked forward to an afterlife that would be not only everlasting but also an improvement on this present life. These expectations were associated with the spread of the cult of Osiris. Already in the Old Kingdom the king, in addition to being the son of Ra, claimed to become Osiris on his death. Osiris also became associated with the rites performed at the king's accession and coronation; in the Middle Kingdom the new rulers even took him as their patron, in preference to Ra, who was so closely linked with earlier dynasties. But Osiris had more popular appeal than Ra had ever had. His strange fate — his murder and dismemberment by Seth, his subsequent resurrection and exaltation — was interpreted as an example of the suffering and vindication of the innocent. The less privileged members of society could see a meaning in that. Eventually Osiris came to be thought of as lord of the netherworld and of the blessed dead — and one who could grant resurrection to his followers. This was enough to ensure a widespread cult. Whereas other great gods remained remote in their temples, as a benign funerary god Osiris could be worshipped anywhere and by anybody, alongside the local and domestic gods who dealt with everyday affairs.

The blessed dead, it seems, were not thought to be wholly confined beneath the earth. The soul (*ba*) of a dead person continued to exist in the heavens, but the person could come alive only when the soul rejoined the body in the netherworld. This was possible because the souls of the blessed dead, in their millions, accompanied the sun-bark on its nocturnal journey. Revivification and rejuvenation were therefore transient — but they were experienced with such intensity that each night seemed equivalent to a lifetime on earth. Moreover, these reawakenings to a fuller, heightened life were destined to be repeated indefinitely: the blessed dead could look forward to an existence that would last millions of years.

For the rest, the beatific afterlife was imagined in very concrete terms.[62] The abode of the resurrected dead in the netherworld was called the 'Field of Reeds', and it was thought of as an unendingly fertile paradise, enjoying eternal springtime and producing regular and abundant harvests. Rich and poor alike were granted plots of land, which they were expected to cultivate. Such a prospect prompted the wealthy to equip their tombs with hundreds of figurines of labourers to do the cultivating for them, while even the poorest peasants often managed to provide themselves with one or two little clay slaves.

This afterlife was a vastly improved version of life as it was lived in Egypt — just as the netherworld was a mirror image of the Nile valley. The scenes that a noble would order to be painted, in advance, on the walls of his tomb show that he looked forward to all the pleasures he had enjoyed in his previous life — hunting, fowling, fishing, banqueting, and of course servants. Scenes of harvesting, slaughtering, baking, brewing, are often accompanied by a picture of the man himself seated at a heavy-laden dinner-table. For peasants and artisans the prospect cannot have been quite so blissful — but even they could look forward to an existence free from danger, ageing and sickness. And beer and bread, cool water, fresh breezes, good clothing were readily available to all.

By the Middle Kingdom every Egyptian, male and female alike, was eligible for these blessings. Though those who could afford it might still construct elaborate tombs, this was not necessary. Magical spells were more important. Spells that originally had been painted on the inside walls of pyramids, for the protection of the king, were now painted on the wooden coffins of ordinary folk; later, they were to become still more widespread, being written upon papyrus in the so-called *Book of the Dead* — which the Egyptians called the *Chapters of Coming Forth by Day*. Their object was always the same: to enable the deceased to emerge from the tomb and to evade the various traps and pitfalls that punctuated the route to the next world.

But magic was not everything. In order to qualify one must have worshipped Osiris, and one must have lived one's life in accord with *ma'at*. It was believed that at death a person had to face a trial, with judges (commonly Osiris himself, with some forty-two assistant judges), counsel for the prosecution and the defence, witnesses, even a clerk of the court (commonly the god Thoth). In a room which was often called the chamber of the double *ma'at*, i.e. the *ma'at* of life and death, the heart of the deceased was weighed against a feather, representing *ma'at*, to establish how far his conduct had been in accord with the divinely appointed order.

What this involved can be gauged from the so-called 'negative confessions' — self-exculpatory notices that people arranged to have deposited in their own graves. These commonly insist not only that the deceased has been punctilious in his offerings to the gods, particularly Osiris, but that he has not exploited or harmed his fellow-mortals. He has never killed or stolen. Not once has he caused shortages by deflecting the water-supply or by destroying growing crops. He has deprived nobody of his or her inheritance. In a word, he has been a man of *ma'at*.

It is significant that the deceased does not tell of the good he has done, only of the evil he has eschewed. A blissful afterlife was above all a reward for not adding to the evil in the world.[63] Those who had lived by *isfet* instead of by *ma'at* were excluded. Individual transgressors were denoted by the same word as political enemies, and both alike were liable to be linked with that ageless chaos monster, the serpent Apophis. A series of works about the netherworld, dating from *c.*1500 BC, tells what awaited them.[64] It was in every respect the opposite of what awaited the righteous. Naked, starving, deaf and blind, cut off from any contact with the sun-god or with Osiris, they were plunged into the chaos that surrounded the ordered world. For all human beings death meant going out of the ordered world into the chaos that had been there always — but whereas the righteous dead experienced only the rejuvenating power of the primordial ocean and re-entered the ordered world renewed and immortal, transgressors against *ma'at* underwent a 'second death'. Imagined sometimes as a terrifying darkness, sometimes as a sea of fire, sometimes as a demonic devouring crocodile, chaos swallowed them up. And if in some versions this meant annihilation, in others it meant eternal torment: a foretaste of the hell that was to haunt so many Christian minds in later ages.

Whatever the means, the aim was always the same: the elimination from the ordered world of everything that could impair it. The afterlife of the blessed dead, by contrast, belonged to the ordered world. Indeed, it was only in the afterlife that the divinely appointed order was fully realised. Living human beings and the blessed dead all inhabited the same world — but whereas the realm of the living was always liable to disturbance, full of conflict, that was not the case with the realm of the blessed dead. The point is beautifully made in another inscription from the New Kingdom:

> the region of the dead . . . the land of eternity, the just and fair, which has no terrors . . . Wrangling is its abhorrence, and no man there girds himself against his fellow. It is a land against which none can rebel; all our kinsfolk rest within it since the earliest day of time. The offspring of millions of millions are come thither, every one. . . . The span of earthly things is as a dream, but a fair welcome is given him who has reached the West.[65]

For individuals, an immense reassurance — but it implied no change in the world order: the tranquil realm of the blessed dead existed, and always would exist, alongside the troubled world of the living. That time was moving towards a universal consummation, when all things would be well for evermore and chaos would no longer threaten — that notion had no place at all in Egyptian thinking.

CHAPTER 2

Mesopotamians

The Sumerian-speaking peoples, who predominated in the extreme south of Mesopotamia, had their own notion of world order already at the beginning of historical times, around 3000 BC. And that notion was adopted and adapted by Akkadian-speaking peoples who lived partly alongside the Sumerian-speakers but mostly further north: Babylonians and Assyrians still adhered to it when they ruled over Mesopotamia in the second and first millennia.[1]

Like developed Egyptian civilisation, developed Mesopotamian civilisation lasted for almost three thousand years and remained remarkably uniform throughout that enormous span. Whether predominantly Sumerian or predominantly Semitic, whether radiating from Ur or Uruk or Nippur, or else from Agade or Babylon or Assur or Nineveh, it was always recognisably the same civilisation. Yet it was never a tranquil civilisation. Geography and history combined to make life in Mesopotamia even less secure than it was in Egypt.

Left to itself, Mesopotamia would have remained a hot, barren desert. Thanks to the irrigation that collected and channelled the silt-laden overflow of the Tigris and Euphrates it was a fertile land, with an agricultural system that could support a large population. But the work of irrigation was extremely strenuous. The floods, occurring between April and June, came too late for winter crops and too early for summer crops. Irrigation had to be perennial — which necessitated a network of canals and dikes, which in turn necessitated unremitting toil by a vast labour force.

Even then there was no guarantee. The Tigris and Euphrates were far less dependable than the Nile. A few years of lower water could turn the land into a desert, a single excessive flood could turn it into a gigantic swamp. Whatever man achieved in the way of irrigation and agriculture was always liable to be undone, the future was never predictable and always fraught with peril. At times torrential rains and scorching, dust-laden winds made life almost intolerable. And even at the best of times Mesopotamia was a difficult land to exploit.

It was by no means rich in natural resources: metal, stone, timber had to be imported. Life was one long struggle against a recalcitrant nature.

By the third millennium war was a further source of insecurity. To the west of the Euphrates lay the vast Syro-Arabian desert, with its scattered population of nomads. Mesopotamian peasants living on the alluvial plain were constantly harassed by these wild tribes, who raided their towns and villages. There was also perpetual tension, often exploding into violent conflict, between the inhabitants of the plains and the inhabitants of the foothills to the north. Endless guerilla war undermined one Mesopotamian kingdom after another. Again and again the land was invaded and conquered by foreign peoples from the highlands: Gutians, Elamites, Kassites, Persians.

Above all Mesopotamians fought one another. During the first half of the third millennium the Sumerian rulers fought one another for supremacy over Sumer with its dozen city-states. From the middle of the third millennium to the fall of Babylon in 539 BC countless monarchs in south and north, Sumerian and Semitic, fought one another in an effort to establish a realm embracing the whole of Mesopotamia. All these wars were accompanied by wholesale slaughter and destruction.

To Mesopotamians cosmos was very real — but so were the forces that threatened it.

2

Once upon a time, in the earliest Mesopotamian world-view, there was nothing but salt ocean, primordial, boundless. Later the ocean begat earth and sky, joined fast together. A god forced them apart and so created the present world or universe — which now rested, immersed, in the midst of the primordial ocean. The world consisted of the earth, imagined as a flat platter with a corrugated rim of mountains; above the earth, the vault of the sky, resting on the mountains and supported by the atmosphere, and with astral bodies rotating along it; beneath the earth, a mass of fresh water, called *abzu* or *apsu* (whence the English word 'abyss'); and further down still, beneath the *abzu*, another hemisphere, the netherworld, where lived the spirits of the dead.

By the third millennium the world in its entirety was perceived as a state. On the earth's surface that state did not extend beyond Mesopotamia and the countries that had dealings with Mesopotamia. Mesopotamia, and particularly its capital city — Babylon for Babylonians, for Sumerians probably Nippur — was the world's hub. The world was governed by Mesopotamian gods and goddesses.

Many of these gods and goddesses originally represented aspects of nature. In addition they functioned as individual patrons of the various city-states that developed in Sumer in the late fourth and early third millennia. Later a change of emphasis occurred: all deities came to be organised in a single, hierarchically structured pantheon — which, further expanded, was in due course taken over by the Babylonians and Assyrians. The pantheon was concerned with order in all its aspects — the order of society as well as the order of nature — in the whole world.

Originally the highest ranking god was the patron god of the city of Uruk, called An in Sumerian, Anu or Anum in the language of the Semites, Akkadian. His name was the Sumerian word for 'sky', and he was in fact a sky-god: rainfall belonged to him, as did the changing constellations and, through them, the times of the year with their different works and festivals. He was the father of all things: he engendered plants and trees, the gods were his children, and so too were the demons. An controlled everything, in nature and in society. His command directed all things in the way they should go. It was his will that lifted existence out of chaos and established the world order. Majestic, remote, he represented absolute authority — and all authority, divine or human, derived from him. The gods themselves knew it well:

> O An! thy great command takes precedence,
>   who could gainsay it?
> O father of the gods, thy command,
>   the very foundations of heaven and earth,
>   what god could spurn [it]?[2]

Scarcely less powerful than An was the god Enlil. He was a most complex figure. Patron god of the city of Nippur and god of the wind, he was the power that originally separated the sky from the earth and so created the world. He was also the power that sustained the rhythms of nature and fostered abundance and prosperity in the land. It was thanks to him that crops grew, that animals and fish and birds reproduced, that the canals were kept full of water. The life of society was sustained by him: without Enlil's warrant no city could be founded or populated, no cattle-pen or sheep-fold could be set up, no king or lord or priest or general could be appointed. Yet Enlil was not a purely benevolent deity. If, as lord of the moist wind of spring, he was the farmer's friend, as lord of the storm-wind he was a figure of dread, the ruthless executor of whatever destruction might be decreed by the gods.

In the end Enlil's role became almost as all-embracing as that of An. If An was lord of the sky, Enlil was lord of the earth and national god of Sumer. Like An he was called 'father of the gods'; and the first month of the year, in which the destinies of the year were decided, was consecrated to An and Enlil alike. Cosmic planner of infinite subtlety, cosmic administrator of infinite skill, Enlil was the embodiment of divine providence:

> Enlil, whose command is far-reaching, whose word is holy,
> The lord whose pronouncement is unchangeable, who forever
> decrees destinies,
> Whose lifted eye scans the lands,
> Whose lifted light searches the heart of all lands,
> Enlil who sits broadly on the white dais, on the lofty dais,
> Who perfects the decrees of power, lordship and princeship,
> The earth-gods bow down in fear before him,
> The heaven-gods humble themselves before him . . .[3]

Ruling, governing gods stood at the centre of the Mesopotamian world-view so long as Mesopotamian civilisation existed. When, in the course of the second millennium, the old world of Sumerian city-states was replaced by Semitic empires, An and Enlil tended to be overshadowed by the chief gods of those empires: Marduk in Babylonia, Asshur in Assyria. The underlying belief remained the same: Marduk and Ashur each became king of the gods and ruler of the world.

Immediately below An and Enlil were the god Enki (Akkadian Ea) — the patron god of Eridu — and the goddess Ninhursaga. Enki's responsibility was to implement the decisions of An and Enlil, to organise the world like a city-state and to keep it in good working order. Closely associated with sweet water, he instituted the regime of the Tigris and Euphrates, appointed a god to look after the canals and another to ensure that the marshes were kept stocked with fish and reeds. He also organised the rains and put yet another god in charge of them. God of intelligence and wisdom, he sponsored and protected arts and crafts, science, literature and beneficent magic. As for Ninhursaga — known as 'the lady of the womb' and 'the lady of form-giving' — she was the mother of all living things, 'the mother of all children'. In charge of the increase of flocks and the perpetuation of mankind, she took her place alongside An, Enlil and Enki as one of the greatest deities.

In their roles as world-rulers An and Enlil had a most efficient agent in the sun-god, whom the Sumerians called Utu and the Semites Shamash, and who was the patron god of Larsa and of Sippar. His special task was to maintain a principle to which both Sumerians and Semites attached great importance and which they indicated by words meaning 'straightness', 'rightness', 'truth' and also 'justice'.[4] In Akkadian the words were *kettu* and *mesharu*, and the sun-god was often called 'lord of *kettu* and *mesharu*': he could even be imagined and portrayed as having a goddess Kettu and a god Mesharu standing beside him. One is reminded of the Egyptian sun-god Ra, with his attendants the goddess Maʿat and the god Thoth. In Mesopotamia as in Egypt the sun's path was perceived as a perfect example of straightness, rightness. And here as there it was felt that the sun, as it followed that path, was perfectly situated to observe where right and justice were being respected and where infringed: he was 'the one from whom no secrets are hid'. There exist prayers that combine exultation over the sun's rising with praise of Shamash for dispensing social justice. Shamash was commonly represented carrying a rod, denoting straightness, and a ring, denoting completeness — symbols of order that could be borne also by the supreme, all-governing gods.

But if An, Enlil, Enki/Ea, Ninhursaga and Utu/Shamash carried the main responsibility for sustaining the ordered world, there were scores of lesser gods and goddesses whose task it was to look after either a particular city or else, at Enki's behest, a particular aspect of the world. Each ruled his or her domain by means of one or more of the entities that in Sumerian were called *mes*.[5] Although the term *me* cannot be adequately translated by any single word in any modern language, we have at least a rough idea of what it meant to Mesopotamians. A *me* operated as a rule, or law, or decree, regulating a particular element in society or civilisation. At the creation of the world An assembled all the *mes* and handed them over to the care of the other gods, his children. Thenceforth Enki guided or 'rode' the 'tens of thousands' of *mes*; while other gods were involved in the supervision and safekeeping of particular *mes*. The rule of the gods; the occupations of king, priest, shepherd; the crafts of the carpenter, the worker in metal, the worker in leather, the basket-maker, the scribe; uprightness, justice, truth; rejoicing, lamentation; trouble, strife; a rebellious land; destruction of cities; consuming fire; the hearth fire; art, music; every temple — all of these and many, many more had their own *mes*. Acting in concert the *mes* implemented the intention that the gods had for human beings — meaning, of course, for Mesopotamians.

On occasion all the gods came together in a grand assembly, held in the forecourt of Enlil's temple, the Ekur, at Nippur. Under the presidency of An the gods would take decisions concerning the government of the world. Wrongdoers, human or divine, were judged and sentenced. The assembly could depose kings and decree the transference of power from one kingdom to another, and even a major god might be temporarily banished. The gods could also — as we shall see — take emergency measures to save themselves from destruction.

3

Though invisible to human eye the gods were imagined — as their statues indicate — as human in form and as having human needs. Long before there were any human beings, they inhabited the world they had shaped. It was not human beings but gods who invented irrigation and agriculture, and they invented them to meet their own requirements. Moreover, in the beginning all the gods except the four highest worked at constructing and maintaining the canals and at sowing and harvesting. It was only because they grew tired of these exacting labours and downed tools that An created mankind at all. Everyone recognised that the one essential function of human beings was to relieve the gods of their chores. This dictated the attitude of Mesopotamians to the gods: they were their servants.

By the third millennium Sumer — a land rather smaller than Belgium — contained a good dozen city-states. Each city-state had its patron god, to whom it had been assigned when mankind was first created and to whom it had belonged ever since. This god had his temple in the city; and there he 'lived' — in an image made of precious wood and covered with gold-plated garments — very much as a human ruler lived in his palace. And there priests served him very much as courtiers served a human ruler — in an elaborate ritual, with each motion carried out strictly in accordance with traditional prescriptions.

Like Egyptian deities, Mesopotamian deities had to be fed. So had their consorts and offspring, who usually had temples of their own, and so had the priests and craftsmen attached to the temple. Already in the third millennium the offerings of food and drink were very ample. In later times the quantities that were supplied, day after day, to the temples in each city, became enormous: bulls and boars, scores of sheep and fowl, many hundredweights of bread, dozens of containers of wine and beer. Although all this must have constituted a burden on the population, there is no reason to think that it was resented — for how else could the gods have the strength to defend the city-state, or later the nation-state, at the centre of the ordered world?

As in Egypt, the order of the world was perceived as essentially unchanging — but whereas in Egypt that order was understood to have been determined by 'the first occasion', in Mesopotamia it was determined by heavenly prototypes. Thus a Mesopotamian temple was a replica not of a primordial hillock but of a heavenly temple — an earthly counterpart to the god's dwelling on high. As such it was a link between heaven and earth, an affirmation of the enduring relationship between earthly affairs and the realm of the gods.

No greater glory could come to a king than to be commissioned by a god to rebuild his ruined temple, for by so doing he would be reaffirming the divinely appointed order.[6] But the temple had to be built on exactly the same site, after exactly the same plan, in exactly the same materials, and with exactly the same ornamentation, as the former temple. When the last Mesopotamian king of all, Nabu-na'id of Babylon (555–539), was rebuilding a temple for the sun-god, the god himself showed him a foundation platform that had been laid down by one of the earliest Sumerian kings, and which nobody had seen since. That early temple, in turn, had been an exact copy of a still earlier temple which had been built by the gods themselves at the creation of the world, before human beings existed at all. The prototype of that primordial temple was preserved in heaven; so the king, in his rebuilding, was conforming to a super-terrestrial model which had existed, unchanging, since the beginning of all things.

That was how every king saw his work — from the great ruler of the first Babylonian empire, Hammurabi (1792–1750), to the Assyrian Sennacherib (7044–681), who claimed that in rebuilding a temple he had uncovered 'foundations whose structure had been sketched there from all eternity in the writing of heaven'. That was not all: throughout the rebuilding the gods not only prescribed the measurements for the temple but dictated the king's very gestures, so that these would repeat the gestures that they themselves had made when, in the beginning, they had constructed the first copy of the heavenly prototype.

4

War and the threat of war, which caused open villages to be replaced by fortified cities, also fostered the development of monarchy. And if originally a king was elected to meet a particular emergency, and surrendered his authority when the emergency was over, that ceased to be the case when war became normal. From the second millennium onwards permanent monarchy was the dominant form of government amongst Mesopotamian states, whether small or large, Sumerian or Akkadian. At the same time the king became a majestic figure, evoking awe and reverence in his subjects. A supernatural aura, which had always been attributed to deities, was said to surround him also.

Although Mesopotamian kings were seldom deified, they were at least divinely appointed.[7] The kingship, which existed independently of any king, had originally resided in heaven. The royal insignia had lain before An, and it was An who sent kingship and insignia down to earth. That happened soon after the creation of mankind, and for the best of reasons: human beings proved so stupid that rulers were needed to ensure that they would serve the gods as they were meant to do.

As heavenly king, An summoned each new king, presented him with the kingdom and the insignia, established him in his palace, gave him An's 'word'. And when An was largely replaced by Enlil, and then by Marduk and Ashur, the relationship between god and king was unchanged. A king of Assyria, ruling over millions, did so as the representative and instrument of the god Asshur, just as the king of an early Sumerian city-state had ruled over a few acres of land on behalf of the city's patron god.

A Mesopotamian state was the supreme expression on earth of the divinely appointed order, and the task of a Mesopotamian king was to ensure that within his realm that order was sustained. This too was equally true of the king of a Sumerian city-state and of the king of a Babylonian or Assyrian empire. When Gudea, king of Lagash, was instructed by an oracle to rebuild the city's temple, the instruction came from the patron god of Lagash, who in turn had received it from Enlil himself. Similarly an Assyrian monarch would consult either the national god Ashur or else the sun-god Shamash before embarking on a military campaign, or even before appointing a senior official. Assyrian historical inscriptions which tell what temples a king built, what irrigation works he carried out, what victories he won, were all intended not for human eyes but for the eyes of a god. That is why they were either placed before the god's statue or buried inside his temple. The purpose of each inscription was to show the god just how much the king had done to strengthen the ordered world.

The king also represented the people before the gods. So far from being an absolute, despotic monarch, he was constrained by innumerable religious duties — and in carrying these out he was supervised by an inflexible priesthood. To keep the gods well-disposed the king had to pray and fast and undergo ritual purifications and observe a host of magico-religious prescriptions. He had to prescribe the amount of the daily offerings to be made in each temple and to see to it that each temple had enough, in land and income, to make them. He had also to build new temples and to repair temples that had fallen into decay. In return for his conscientious discharge of all these obligations the gods could be expected to grant the land fertility. But here the king was further involved. The gods could send abundant rain — but it was the king's responsibility to ensure that irrigation was efficiently done and the canal system kept in working order.

In every way the well-being of the kingdom depended on the king. The king was referred to as 'he who maintains the life of the country'. The presence of a devout king on the throne was felt to guarantee that the cycle of the seasons would proceed smoothly, that the crops would ripen on time and would be abundant, that the generations would succeed one another without interruption. But always it was the gods who prescribed the king's duties and granted him his powers. Thus Lipit-Eshtar (1934–24) had been chosen by the gods An, Enlil and Ninlil to ensure that there would be plenty of cereals, thus Enlil had appointed Iddin-Dagan (1974–1954) to ensure that the people would have all the food and sweet water they needed.[8] An epithet which many a king — Sumerian, Babylonian, Assyrian — applied to himself was 'ploughman'. It was a way of claiming that the kingdom owed its fertility to the magic power with which the gods rewarded his devotion. The more zealous a king in serving the gods, the greater his efficacy as 'ploughman'.

As in Egypt, the king also called himself 'shepherd': he cared for the people on behalf of the gods, who were their real owners. And the first duty of the royal shepherd was to make justice prevail in the land. To say that Mesopotamians deeply respected the law would be a gross understatement — in their eyes the law was a divine creation, something revealed to the king by the gods, so that he could promulgate it in their name. Here the role of Utu/Shamash, god of the sun and of justice, was pre-eminent. Lipit-Eshtar's predecessor, Ishme-Dagan (1953–1935) made the point nicely:

> Utu has put what is right, the well-established word, in my mouth,
> to pronounce judgement, to reach a decision, to lead the people aright,
> to put justice before everything,
> to give right guidance to good people, to destroy the wicked . . .
> . . .
> so that the powerful man cannot do as he will . . .
> to destroy what is wicked, to let what is right increase . . .[9]

The association of the reigning monarch with the sun-god could be carried very far. In royal hymns Ur-Nammu (2113–2096) was described as predestined by the god Enlil to rule the land like Utu himself, Lipit-Eshtar as advancing in his splendour like the sun-god.[10] In the prologue to his famous code of laws Hammurabi compares himself with the sun precisely because of his concern for justice:

> Anum and Enlil named me
> ...
> to cause justice to prevail in the land,
> to destroy the wicked and the evil,
> that the strong might not oppress the weak
> to rise like the sun over the black-headed [people]
> and to light up the land.[11]

And on the celebrated Hammurabi stela the king is shown standing in front of the enthroned Shamash and receiving the laws from him.

Clearly, what *kettu* and *mesharu* meant, and what Utu/Shamash watched over, included much that nowadays would be called 'social justice'. Flood, drought, blight constantly forced peasants to borrow at high interest; and from the mid-third millennium onwards most of them were heavily in debt, and many were forced to sell themselves into bondage. Several kings, in their concern to forestall social unrest and political instability, declared a remission of such debts — and this too was presented as expressing the intention of Shamash. But indeed a ruler's concern for justice was supposed to involve the well-being of the people in all its aspects. The epilogue that Hammurabi gave to his code formulates that ideal:

> I rooted out the enemy above and below;
> I made an end of war;
> I promoted the welfare of the land;
> I made the people rest in friendly habitations;
> I did not let them have anyone to terrorise them.
> The great gods called me,
> So I became the beneficent shepherd whose sceptre is righteous;
> My benign shadow is spread over the city.
> In my bosom I carried the people of the land of Sumer and Akkad;
> They prospered under my protection;
> I have governed them in peace;
> I have sheltered them in my strength.[12]

5

Like Egyptians, indeed like all peoples in the Ancient Near East, Mesopotamians were convinced that the world order existed solely for the benefit of their gods and themselves. And at least from the third millennium onwards it was taken for granted that war was one of the most effective ways of strengthening that order. It was not for nothing that those vehicles of divine intention and activity, the *mes*, included a rebellious land, strife, consuming fire, destruction of cities. By defending his realm and by conquering new territories a king was not only fulfilling the original, most basic function of kingship — he was also obeying the will of the gods. It followed that he could fairly expect their assistance: when he embarked on a campaign it was always 'with the strength and power of the great gods'. A traditional formula of homage to the ruler of the Sumerian city of Uruk makes the connection quite explicit:

> The cracker of heads, the prince beloved of An,
> O! how he inspired fear after he had come!
> Their troops melted away, scattering from the rear,
> their men were unable to face him.[13]

The promise which, some two thousand years later, the goddess of war gave to the Assyrian king Esharhaddon expresses the same conviction: 'I am Ishtar of Arbela. I will flay your enemies and present them to you.'[14]

Akkadian Ishtar was the same goddess as Sumerian Inanna. She was the sister of Utu/Shamash — naturally enough, since justice in the land and victory over foreign foes were equally important manifestations of world order. She controlled thunderstorms and rain — and could on occasion withhold rain in order to compel a city to submit to another that she favoured. She was also capable of coming down on the land as a tempest, with thunder shaking the earth and lightning burning the farms. It was normal for a storm-god to be imagined as a warrior riding into battle on the clouds: this was the case with the male storm-god Ninurta, and it was also the case with Ishtar. Battle was called 'the dance of Ishtar', and the goddess herself boasted:

> When I stand in the midst of the battle,
>   I am the heart of the battle,
>   the arm of the warriors
> . . .
> My father [An] gave me the heavens,
>   gave me the earth,
> I am Inanna!
> Kingship he gave me,
> queenship he gave me,
> waging of battle he gave me,
>   the attack he gave me,
> the floodstorm he gave me,
>   the hurricane he gave me![15]

Throughout Mesopotamian history kings expected and experienced divine support in war, and in the most immediate, concrete way: not only Inanna/Ishtar but also patron gods were imagined as taking part in the battle. A stela made to commemorate the victory of a king of the Sumerian city of Lagash over the neighbouring city of Umma shows the patron god of Lagash, Ningirsu, casting his net over the foes of the city and cracking their skulls with his mace. That battle took place shortly after 2500 BC. A bas-relief made nearly two thousand years later shows the national gods of Assyria, Ashur, floating in mid-air over the king as he goes into battle, and holding his bow in exactly the same position as the king. And after the victory the king would attribute his success not to his own generalship but to his gods:

> Fear of the great gods, my lords, overwhelmed them, they saw my powerful storm troops and became crazed [with fright]. Ishtar, queen of attack and hand-to-hand fighting, who loves my priesthood, stepped to my side, broke their bows, and dissolved their battle formation, so that they all said 'This is our king!' At her exalted command they came over, one after another, to my side and took up position behind me, gambolled like lambs, and invoked me as lord.[16]

So in each victory gods and king together reaffirmed and strengthened the world order.

6

However tenaciously Mesopotamians clung to their belief in a divinely appointed and essentially unchanging order, they could not but recognise that in practice life within that order was desperately insecure. They knew well enough that chaotic forces were at work in the world, always had been, always would be. This awareness permeates much of Mesopotamian mythology of every period.

There is a type of myth, conventionally known as 'the combat myth', that tells how a god has defended the ordered world against the onslaughts of chaos.[17] In Mesopotamia the oldest of these myths are of Sumerian origin: they seem to belong to a tradition that was well established already in the third millennium.

The hero of the Sumerian myths is usually Ninurta, god of the thunderstorm and the spring flood. He was the favourite son of Enlil. He was also the protector of all Sumer, the guarantor of its prosperity and social harmony. Above all he was a mighty warrior — so mighty that when he arrived, fully armed, on his chariot festooned with battle trophies, he threw the assembled gods into panic. He was also able to induce his father Enlil to grant him a cult in Enlil's own temple, the Ekur at Nippur.

One myth, known mainly through an Akkadian version, tells of a combat between Ninurta and Anzu.[18] This monster was a bird, probably imagined as a huge eagle or vulture. It possessed supernatural powers and belonged to the realm of the gods. It seems to have been originally a benign creature, living on good terms with the gods. However, around 2000 BC it took on a sinister quality, as rebel against the gods, thoroughly malign, in fact a demon. Anzu had always been associated with Ninurta, as his heraldic beast and familiar. Now he became his adversary in a power struggle that would decide the fate of the world.

In Mesopotamia the royal power was imagined as an autonomous force, attached to the king but also residing in certain objects without which the king was powerless: not only crown and sceptre and royal robe but also the royal 'register of decisions' or 'register of destinies'. A Mesopotamian king had the right to decide the 'destinies' of his subjects — meaning what their careers and activities should be — and these decisions were transmitted, as written decrees, throughout the kingdom. It was believed that a summary of these decrees was also embodied in a register — although in reality no such register existed.

So replete with power were the royal insignia, including the fictional register of destinies, that a king deprived of them would, it was thought, become an ordinary person, without political significance or coercive power. The officials to whom the king delegated his authority in turn depended on the presence of the king at the head of affairs: if he disappeared all authority was nullified and the machinery of the kingdom ceased to function.

Now all this was equally true of the heavenly and cosmic realm. Enlil too had delegated his power to subordinates, the lesser gods. These attended to the good functioning of the various aspects of the world — but they could do so only as long as Enlil remained in possession of his insignia, including the register of destinies. But there was one period when Enlil necessarily put his insignia aside: while he took his morning bath. Unfortunately Enlil's trusted agent, his intimate and confidant, proved treacherous — as was known to happen also at human courts. This agent was the bird Anzu. Constantly watching Enlil as he presided majestically over the world, Anzu was overcome by envy and ambition: why should not he himself become sovereign over the gods? One morning, while Enlil was stripped of his regalia, Anzu seized the register of destinies and flew off with it to his hideout in the mountains. Immediately everything came to a standstill, the world sank into deathlike silence and inertia.

The gods, unable to fulfil their normal functions, came together in a council; this too was a transposition of what happened, in comparable emergencies, on earth. The chairman was not the incapacitated Enlil but the ancestor of all the gods, Anu. It was decided to seek out a champion, a god who would overcome Anzu, secure the register of destinies, and so set the world going again. After three gods had refused, on the grounds that the mission was an impossible one, the wise and wily Ea (Enki) persuaded the great goddess, mother of all the gods, to persuade her favourite, Ninurta, to undertake it. First Ninurta tried to overcome Anzu by enveloping him in 'the seven winds' as in a net; but Anzu, thanks to his possession of the register of destinies, was able to frustrate him at every turn. Again Ea intervened. Acting on his advice, Ninurta succeeded in cutting Anzu's feathers and piercing him with arrows; after which he cut his throat. The end of the poem is lacking, but we may assume that the source of power was restored to Enlil and that the lesser gods returned to their proper activities. As for Ninurta, his fame spread throughout the world.

Other myths tell how the ordered world was threatened by monsters rising from the *abzu* beneath the earth, and themselves endowed with all the destructive power of those chaotic waters. Labbu was a gigantic sea dragon, three hundred miles long and thirty miles high. From time to time it came ashore to devastate the land, killing people and animals and terrifying even the gods. Here too the first god chosen to deal with the monster refused combat. In the end the storm-god, riding on the clouds, succeeded in killing the dragon; and it seems that he was rewarded with kingship over the gods.

Then there was the demon Asakku, who came down to earth in a cloud or on the north wind: a spirit of nullity, who caused sickness, killed newborn animals and raised sandstorms.[19] In his fight with Asakku Ninurta was at first defeated but then, on the advice of his father Enlil, hurled the flood against the demon and, while it was overwhelmed, stabbed and killed it. Next the flood itself brought destruction on the earth. The gods responsible for irrigation and agriculture were reduced to despair. Again Ninurta plunged into action: he set a great pile of rocks in front of Sumer, to act as a dam. As for the flood that already covered the land, Ninurta canalised it into the Tigris, with admirable results:

> Behold now everything on earth
> Rejoiced afar at Ninurta, the king of the land;
> The fields provided much grain,
> The harvest of palm-grove and vineyard was fruitful,
> It was heaped up in granaries and hills.[20]

These Sumerian myths of a combat between god and chaos-monster are early examples — they were known already before 2000 BC — of a tradition that was to endure for millennia. It was also a very widespread tradition: as we shall see in later chapters, it was known to Vedic Indians, and almost certainly to Iranians too. In Mesopotamia it was to receive its most celebrated expression in Babylon, when it was already a thousand and more years old.

7

The famous Babylonian myth, or epic, *Enuma elish* (so called from its opening words, meaning 'When on high') tells of the exploits of the god Marduk.[21] Ninurta's exploits were certainly known to its author or authors, but the tale they tell is on a far grander scale.

Marduk had always been the patron god of Babylon, and already in the first period of Babylonian supremacy Hammurabi had promoted him to the dignity of supreme god. *Enuma elish* repeated that promotion, with the same political intention, in the second period of Babylonian supremacy, in late second millennium. And when, early in the first millennium, Assyria replaced Babylon as the dominant power, a new version of the story was produced, with Asshur as its hero.

Enuma elish presents a creation myth — and a far more elaborate one than the traditional cosmogony. The work opens with an account of how things were in the beginning. Neither earth nor sky existed — nothing but a watery chaos in which the fresh waters underground, Apsu (imagined as male), mingled with the salt waters of the sea, Tiamat (imagined as female). At first there were no gods — but then Apsu engendered two gods, who were born of Tiamat. Generations of gods followed, all inhabiting a formless void. The shaping of the world still lay in the future.

Yet as soon as they came into being the gods introduced a new principle into the world — movement. Apsu and Tiamat represented rest, inertia; unimaginably old, they wanted only to be left in peace. The gods, on the contrary, were active, restless. When they came together to dance, it was too much for Apsu. He complained to Tiamat that such behaviour was depriving him of rest by day, sleep by night — and announced his intention of smashing all the gods to bits.

Tiamat, as a mother, could not assent in the destruction of her offspring. But Apsu continued to plot their destruction, until the gods came to hear of it. Their reaction was panic — until Ea found a solution: by means of a magical spell he put Apsu to sleep. Then he stripped him of his crown and royal robe, killed him and established his own abode above him. So the waters underground were mastered — as Ninurta too had mastered them — while Ea set up his temple at Eridu, on the waters of a lagoon.

Marduk was born at Eridu as Ea's son. A magnificent creature from birth onwards, supernaturally wise and strong, he is the real hero of the myth. His adventures began when his grandfather Anu created storm-winds for him to play with. Now some of the gods were kept awake. These gods, kindred spirits to Apsu, succeeded where Apsu had failed: they persuaded Tiamat to take action herself against the main body of the gods, associates of Anu and Ea and Marduk — who after all were collectively responsible for depriving her of her consort Apsu.

Tiamat prepared for war and spawned troops to fight that war: monstrous serpents with sharp fangs, their bodies filled with poison. She even endowed these gruesome beings with a fearful, quasi-divine aura, so that anyone who looked on them would die of terror. And she added reinforcements: vipers, dragons, huge lions, mad dogs, mighty storm-demons, bisons, flying creatures, scorpion-men — all of them lethally equipped and thirsting for battle. To lead this host Tiamat appointed her second husband, the god Kingu — and to ensure his success she entrusted him with that supreme vehicle of power, the register of destinies.

When the news reached the gods, they were once more aghast. First Ea, that embodiment of wisdom, then Anu, that embodiment of authority, shrank back in terror at the sight of Tiamat. Finally the gods appealed to young Marduk. He agreed to tackle Tiamat, but on one condition: that the authority of all the gods should be given to him alone — in short, that he should be made king over the gods. This was granted. Marduk was given all the rights that went with kingship: power to promote and demote gods as he saw fit, authority to wage war, power to kill or spare prisoners of war.

Equipped with the royal insignia and armed with bow and arrows, a mace and a net, Marduk filled himself with blazing fire and mounted his storm-chariot. Like a thunderstorm, preceded by lightnings, followed by storm-winds, he faced Tiamat and her allies. Kingu and his army were at once overcome with terror; only Tiamat held her ground. Marduk tackled her in single combat. As she opened her mouth to swallow him he drove his 'evil wind' into her, jamming her mouth wide open and distending her belly. An arrow shot into her gullet cut through her insides and tore her heart asunder.

Tiamat dead, her followers were captured, disarmed and made prisoner, and Kingu was deprived of the register of destinies. Now the young god was free to deploy his power constructively. Standing on Tiamat's carcase he split her into two parts 'like a shell-fish'. Out of one half he made the sky and secured it: to prevent Tiamat's water from escaping he set bars in place and posted guards. In the newly created sky, at a spot immediately opposite the dwelling that his father had built over Apsu, he built an exact replica, his own heavenly dwelling. Next he made constellations and organised the calendar. The moon and the sun were instructed on how to conduct themselves. Finally Marduk made the earth, using the fluids in Tiamat's body to supply the rivers of Mesopotamia.

But if the myth of Marduk as it is told in *Enuma elish* is a cosmogonic myth, that need not have been true of the myth in its original form: the Marduk priests may well have promoted their god to the status of creator god, simply to show that he was worthy to be the patron god of a newly dominant Babylon. However that may be, it is certain that the combat myth did not always have cosmogonic implications. The unknown god who defeated the Labbu dragon, or Ninurta when he killed the Anzu bird, were clearly operating in a world that already existed — and so, as we shall see, was the Canaanite storm-god Baal, in all his exploits. In fact the combat myth as such was less concerned to explain how the cosmos came into being than to show how, in the face of ever-recurring threats, it has been preserved. This is true also of *Enuma elish.*

To preserve the world Marduk was named king in perpetuity 'king of the gods of heaven and earth'. And the young god was endowed with a new function: with Tiamat removed and the universe in being, he was charged with the task of administering it for the benefit of the gods, in return for their obedience. Marduk's first demand was that the gods build him a palace as a royal administrative headquarters — which could also serve, when necessary, as a residence for all the gods. This 'palace' was of course Marduk's temple at Babylon, Esagila — a massive symbol of order and permanence, known to Babylonians as 'the palace of heaven and earth', the seat of kingship.

The gods who had sided with Tiamat were granted their lives and set to work on building Esagila — but soon, moved by their display of gratitude and loyalty, Marduk decided to create new beings to do the work. Kingu, who had played such a large part in the uprising, was indicted and duly executed; and out of his blood Ea, at Marduk's prompting, fashioned mankind (and *Enuma elish* is not the only Mesopotamian work to claim that mankind bears the substance of a rebellious god . . .). Now all the gods could be given lighter tasks: one group was set to help in the administration of heaven, the other to superintend things on earth.

With his headquarters built Marduk invited all the gods to a feast. After the banquet the great gods completed arrangements for the good functioning of the world. The decrees or 'destinies' decided by the assembly were given their final form. Marduk was seated on the royal throne and received pledges of loyalty from all the gods. The oldest god of all, Anshar, Anu's father, defined the role of the new king:

> Surpassing be his lordship,
> may he have no rival,
> may he perform the shepherdship
> over the dark-headed people,
> and may they speak of his ways
> to the end of time.
> Let him establish large food portions
> for his fathers,
> let him see to their upkeep,
> take care of their sanctuaries . . .[22]

So Marduk's royal authority would ensure the well-being of the Mesopotamians and their gods. And the story ends with the gods reciting Marduk's fifty names, each name glorifying his power.

Enuma elish is a complex work, designed to serve many purposes. It not only exalts Babylon and Babylon's patron god, it explains how primordial chaos was mastered, how the ordered world was created, how kingly rule was established to maintain cosmos. And all these achievements are portrayed as achievements of youthful energy and enterprise. It is the vital young storm-god who sets everything in motion and ensures that movement — steady, controlled movement — will go on and on. This would have been impossible without killing not indeed 'the parents' — Marduk is unfailingly respectful towards his father, grandfather and great-grandfather — but that remote ancestor who preceded the gods, Tiamat. Like Apsu before her, Tiamat has to be killed because she stands for inertia, the dead weight of the past: if these two had their way the gods would remain for ever inactive, nothing would ever change, there would be no differentiation, indeed nothing would ever happen at all.

Marduk embodies not only dynamism but creative intelligence. By pardoning the gods who had sided with Tiamat, by providing all the gods with leisure and assigning them well-defined administrative tasks, he created conditions for a harmonious and enduring world order. So ordered, the world was like a well-run monarchical state, prosperous and at peace.

Yet the world was never totally secure. Although Tiamat had been killed long, long ago, and her waters were supposed to be contained behind bars in the heavens — somehow she still existed, as a constant threat to the world order. As sea she was there, spread over much of what was known of the earth's surface. More importantly, she was there as the supreme embodiment of chaos. As such she had to be periodically warded off and destroyed anew. The conclusion of *Enuma elish* contains a prayer that her floods may be held at bay for another year.

That was also one of the functions of the New Year festival known as the *akitu*. This was an ancient festival in which, over the centuries, a number of elements from different rites and cults had been combined. In the first millennium the *akitu* was celebrated in various cities in various months — in Babylon and in Ashur it was celebrated at the spring equinox — but always it represented the time when the gods decreed the destinies for the coming year.

On the ninth day of the twelve-day festival statues of the gods were borne in procession to a special temple, called the *akitu*-house, some way outside the city. In Assyria, where the *akitu* was also celebrated, King Sennacherib had the scene depicted on the copper doors of the temple, and provided the interpretation: 'a figure of Ashur, going to battle against Tiamat, carrying the bow, on his chariot . . . [besides] the gods who march in front and the gods who march behind him . . . [and] Tiamat and the creatures [that were] in her'.[23] It seems that in the *akitu*-house Tiamat was represented by a dais; when the statue of Marduk was taken there it was set on the dais to symbolise victory over Tiamat, while the statues of the other gods offered congratulations and gifts.[24] In the course of the festival the destruction of Tiamat was further symbolised by acts such as the smashing of a pot or the bisecting of a pigeon. The meaning of all this was made explicit when, in the seclusion of the *akitu*-house, a priest recited *Enuma elish* before a statue of the hero god: under the auspices of Marduk, order was reaffirmed in the universe.

In the New Year festival the Mesopotamian yearning for security found poignant expression. Faced with a climate that was liable at any moment to plunge the whole land into famine, Mesopotamians knew that the seasons could continue to succeed one another, moon and sun and stars could continue to revolve, life could go on, only if the gods could be persuaded to grant, again and again, a favourable decision. Faced with ever-recurring threats of invasion and conquest, they knew that they could go on only with Marduk's goodwill and assistance. Through the *akitu* the hopes and fears of every Mesopotamian were answered; nature was renewed, society was consolidated, anxiety was quieted, chaos was warded off for another year.[25]

8

From the human point of view the gods themselves could be a source of insecurity. As servants of the gods Mesopotamians knew better than to trust in the goodwill of their masters. That gods could act ruthlessly, could even be wantonly destructive and cruel — that was obvious already in the days of the Sumerian city-states, and it remained obvious so long as Mesopotamian civilisation existed.

These people knew well enough that the great gods were not only all-powerful but also inscrutable:

> A storm cloud lying on the horizon
> its heart inscrutable,
> His word, a storm cloud lying on the horizon,
> its heart inscrutable;
> the word of great An, a storm cloud lying on the horizon,
> the word of Enlil, a storm cloud lying on the horizon,
> its heart inscrutable . . .[26]

And again:

> Who knows the will of the gods in heaven?
> Who understands the plan of the underworld gods?
> Where have mortals learnt the way of a god?
> He who was alive yesterday is dead today.
> . . .
> I am appalled at these things; I do not understand
> their significance.[27]

Mere tiresomeness on the part of human beings could bring down merciless punishment. A myth embodied in an Akkadian poem from the mid-second millennium shows the gods behaving towards mankind in the same way as Apsu had behaved towards the gods.[28] After human beings were created to relieve the gods of their chores, they multiplied so rapidly that within 1200 years their clamour had become intolerable, 'the land was bellowing like a bull'. Enlil, unable to sleep, persuaded the gods to send plague — which effectively reduced the population and so the noise. However, after a further 1200 years the population and the noise were back where they had been. This time rain was withheld, to some effect. But still the problem recurred and Enlil was kept sleepless. Outraged, the gods combined to withhold both rain and the yearly flood for six successive years, with horrifying results: neighbours fell upon one another, parents killed and devoured their own children. Only the intervention of the benevolent Ea saved mankind: ostensibly by accident he let quantities of fish through to feed the starving.

Enlil, furious, decided on the total annihilation of mankind and bound all the gods by oath to co-operate in drowning all human beings in a flood. But again Ea intervened: without formally breaking his oath he contrived to warn a human servant of his, a sage called Atrahasis. This Mesopotamian Noah built a huge boat and loaded it with his family and with all kinds of animals. So this small group survived the seven days and nights of the flood. Meanwhile the gods, deprived of their customary offerings, became desperately hungry. When, at the end of the flood, Atrahasis prepared a sacrifice, they gathered round it like flies.

In the end Enlil assented in the survival of mankind — but only on condition that the numbers were kept down. So the gods invented the types of the barren woman and the virgin priestess, and created a demon who specialised in killing children.

The myth of Atrahasis is not intended as a criticism of the gods, let alone of Enlil. On the contrary, the poem ends by praising the 'great feat' that he had performed in making the flood. Ruthless the gods might be, but it was not for mere humans to complain. They must accept the world as it was — and at all costs avoid annoying the gods. Even so, fear of flood was an enduring feature of Mesopotamian life.

Defeat in war, and the horrors that flowed from defeat, were also greatly dreaded. It was not possible for Mesopotamians — as it was for Egyptians — to pretend that defeat never occurred: their historical experience was too grim for that. Sumerians already knew how easily the great gods could withdraw their favour from a city-state, and how impossible it was to oppose their decree. There exists a moving poem in which Ningal, patron goddess of Ur, grieves over the decision of the divine assembly, headed by An and Enlil, to destroy her city, and over her own inability to dissuade them. In the eyes of the modern historian Ur was captured, sacked and burned by wild hordes from the mountains. But in the eyes of the Sumerians the destruction was the work of Enlil himself, as god of the raging storm:

> When I was grieving for that day of storm,
> that day of storm, destined for me
>   laid upon me, heavy with tears
> . . .
> I could not flee before that day's fatality.
> Dread of the storm's floodlike destruction
>   weighed on me,
> . . .
> Truly I shed my tears in front of An.

Truly I myself mourned in front of Enlil:
'May my city not be destroyed!'
  I said indeed to them.
'May Ur not be destroyed!' I said indeed to them.
'And may its people not be killed!'
...
[Behold,] they gave instruction
  that the city be destroyed,
[behold,] they gave instruction
  that Ur be destroyed,
and as its destiny decreed
  that its inhabitants be killed.[29]

Defeat in war could also be perceived as a victory for chaos. The Neo-Babylonian *Poem* (or Epic) *of Erra* (or Era, or Irra) tells of the exploits of a god whose epithets include 'eminent son of Enlil', 'great lord' and 'champion of the gods'.[30] Nevertheless Erra was a god of war in its negative aspect — war as an orgy of destruction and slaughter. For many centuries 'Erra' had in fact been a name of the god Nergal, who ruled over the netherworld and the dead who inhabited it. As such, he was always a great killer. His one concern was that the population of his kingdom should grow and grow — and this he achieved not simply by arranging premature death for individuals but through epidemics and war. And he had troops — a host of demons known collectively as 'the Seven'. Originally created by Anu to terrify and kill human beings the moment they became noisy, the Seven operated in fire, in the storm-wind, in the lion's ferocity and the dragon's poison — and in war.

The story is told not directly but through a series of exhortations and protestations from the various personages involved. Urged on by the Seven, Erra tries to persuade Marduk to leave his palace. Marduk refuses: he remembers how when he vacated Esagila on a previous occasion, the ordered world went under in flood and chaos — and what a hard time he had reconstituting it. If he leaves now, the waters will again cover the land, daylight will turn to darkness, evil winds will blow, the Seven will come up from the netherworld and destroy every living being. Yet in the end the world-ruler shows himself gullible: when Erra promises to keep order in his place, he goes off to supervise the restoration of his dilapidated statues.

This gives Erra his chance. In a speech to his lieutenant Ishum he boasts that he will destroy the sunlight, turn day into night, make the land into rubble and towns into wilderness, lay waste the mountains and cut down the creatures living in them, stir up the seas and annihilate their riches, deprive cattle of their drink, strike down every human being.

Ishum agrees that Erra is capable of all this, and more. Ignoring Marduk's legitimate authority, he has 'undone the knot that holds the world together'. In Babylon he has provoked civil strife and indiscriminate massacre. Now disorder in society is causing disorder in nature: the river has run dry, while at sea great storms destroy the fishing fleet. And Erra is planning further destruction — and not only of people but of trees, buildings, boats, canals, even the netherworld. The heavens will quake, stars and planets will stray from their courses, the king of the gods will abdicate, the universe will no longer be governed at all. It is a tribute to Erra as, in effect, a chaos-monster of irresistible power.

Not that war as such was condemned. On the contrary, like all peoples in the Ancient Near East, Mesopotamians took it for granted that victorious war, fought under the auspices of the goddess of victory Innanna/Ishtar, was an affirmation of cosmos. Erra's warfare was warfare as suffered by the defeated. Scholars differ about the date at which the *Poem of Erra* was composed, but clearly it must have been inspired by some military disaster that befell Babylon. The author's aim, it would seem, was to explain how such a thing could happen to the city that Marduk had founded to be his residence and the capital of the universe. He sought an answer in the religious doctrine he knew: happenings on earth reflected happenings amongst the gods, so Babylon's misfortunes must reflect the replacement of Marduk by Erra.

The consequences of such a replacement were incalculable. The poem says as much. So long as Erra is exerting his destructive power, Marduk cannot return to that centre of the ordered world, his temple Esagil — but as soon as Erra is persuaded to redirect his rage and turn it against the nomads who were attacking caravans and raiding towns, everything changes. Marduk and the other gods take up their proper stations again, and order and fertility are restored. Nevertheless, the very fact that Erra could be imagined as ousting Marduk, even temporarily, shows how precarious, at times, cosmos must have seemed.

9

There were other embodiments of danger and disorder — demons, hosts of them, and all wholly devoted to destruction.[31] 'Born in the western mountain, brought up in the eastern mountain', those fearsome beings disported themselves in the desert, in waste ground and empty spaces: they were at home on the frontiers of the ordered world. Yet demons could go anywhere. On occasion they would force their way into the vault of heaven, cluster angrily around the moon-god and drive him from his throne. The resulting eclipse enabled them to attack the king and through him the whole country, sweeping over the land like a hurricane. Then it took all the power of Enlil, Ea and Marduk to save the world from disintegration.

More commonly demons attacked individuals in particular situations — in lonely places, or when asleep, or at meals, or in childbirth. Generally imagined as airy spirits, like breath or the wind, they were able to enter a house by passing through cracks or holes, or under the door. Asexual themselves, without mate or children, they destroyed familial bonds: they would make a man impotent, alienate a wife from her husband. Vampire-like, they drank people's blood and devoured their flesh. Wherever they passed they left poison behind them: human feet that walked that way would be covered in livid spots. Poison deadly as the venom of snake or scorpion spouted from their mouths or dripped from their claws. Demons were dirty, impure things, and gave out a bad smell.

The library of the last Assyrian king, Ashurbanipal, originally at Nineveh and now in the British Museum, includes a list of demons and kinds of demons, with their distinctive attributes.[32] Most of them are of Sumerian origin. There is Namtaru: son of Enlil and the queen of the netherworld Ereshkigal, he is the messenger of the king of the netherworld Nergal. As such he is the demon of plague and messenger of death: whomever he seizes must die at once and go to populate Nergal's realm. The female demon Lamashtu is a sterile and frustrated virgin who attacks pregnant women and women in labour, and kills their babies. She is commonly represented as a naked woman with the head of a lioness and feet like the claws of a bird of prey. Born in heaven as the daughter of Anu himself, she proved so wicked that she was cast down to earth. The hot wind that brings sandstorms from the desert is the work of the demon Pazuzu — imagined as a winged monster with four claws and a deformed head. Lilitu, a succubus who visits men at night, is impregnated by these contacts and bears more demons, known collectively as the *alu* and *gallu*. These in turn bring death to human beings: operating surreptitiously at night they strike people down like a falling wall. The pre-eminent demon of sickness is Asaku (Sumerian Asag). He is described as dwelling in a man's body, covering him like a garment when he walks about, in the end paralysing him. But there is also a special headache demon, responsible for incapacitating headaches such as accompany sunstroke.

Demons would be less successful if only people did not sin. If one sinned, the protective spirit or spirits who habitually watched over one departed, leaving the field open to demons. One or other of these would usurp the vacant place, and the sinner would be struck down with illness. Sooner or later this was bound to happen to everyone.[33] Mesopotamians made no distinction between antisocial behaviour and the infringement, even unwitting, of a taboo. If a person set members of a family against one another, or showed disrespect to his parents, or cheated as a tradesman, or moved a boundary stone, or seduced his neighbour's wife, or murdered his neighbour, he laid himself open to demonic attack — but so he did if he inadvertently ate garlic on the wrong day, or crossed a river or ascended a staircase or did gardening on the wrong day. It was impossible altogether to avoid sinning, so it was impossible to avoid demons and the afflictions they brought. Order existed in the world, but it did not exist for the convenience of human beings.

10

The gods had reserved immortality for themselves. By their decree death was the universal fate of human beings.[34] As that marvellous work the *Epic of Gilgamesh* puts it:

> Who, my friend, was ever so high
> [that he could]
> rise up to heaven
> and lastingly dwell with Shamash?
> Mere man, his days are numbered,
> whatever he may do, he is but wind.
> You are — already now — afraid of death.[35]

That fear too belonged to the human condition:

> The one who followed me,
> the rapacious one,
> sits in my bedroom, Death!
> And wherever I may turn my face,
> there he is, Death![36]

At the appointed time each human being must, as a disembodied soul, make his or her way down to the lowest level of the world, below the *apsu*. In that shadowy realm the light enjoyed by the living was replaced by darkness, sound and movement gave way to silence and immobility. No good awaited one who went

> To the land of no return . . .
> To the house from which he who enters never goes forth;
> To the road whose path does not lead back;
> To the house in which he who enters is bereft of light;
> Where dust is their food [and] clay their sustenance.[37]

Not that the dead ceased to exist: total annihilation was as unthinkable to Mesopotamians as it was to Egyptians. Like Egyptians, Mesopotamians were commonly buried with talismans, cooking and working utensils; they were also, at regular intervals, supplied with food and drink by their children.[38] In return for these attentions they would assist members of their family who were still alive, for instance in cases of sickness. But if they were neglected they would behave like those other denizens of the netherworld, the demons. A dead Mesopotamian who was not properly buried, or who was too soon forgotten, could bring physical or mental sickness upon his kin. Such anxieties were of course familiar also to Egyptians,[39] as they have been to many other peoples — but in Mesopotamia they possessed a singular urgency. There the same rituals of exorcism as were employed against demons were employed also against ghosts of the vengeful dead.

Even to the most fortunate of the dead the afterlife offered no consolation at all for the hardships endured on earth. True, there were gods in the netherworld — not only Nergal and his consort Ereshkigal but a whole host of lesser gods. But they were a severe and morose company, dwelling in their own well-defended palace, and they showed no favour to any of the dead. The prospect of a blissful afterlife, so real for Egyptians, did not exist for Mesopotamians.

Nor were Mesopotamians any more capable than Egyptians of imagining that the world could ever be made perfect, and immutable in its perfection. Fantasies of cosmos without chaos were not for them.[40]

CHAPTER 3

Vedic Indians

It was not only the technologically developed civilisations of the Fertile Crescent that produced world-views centred on a divinely appointed order that was basically timeless and unchanging, yet was never wholly tranquil. The proto-Indo-Iranian tribes who in the second half of the third millennium were living on the vast open steppes of southern Russia did the same.[1]

By 2000 BC, if not earlier, these tribes had split into two peoples, the Indo-Aryans and the Iranians. In the course of the second millennium the greater part of both peoples left the steppes. For whatever reason — maybe loss of pasturage through drought or prolonged frost, maybe pressure of population — whole tribes migrated, driving their herds with them. The main body of Indo-Aryans moved through Central Asia and Afghanistan, across the perilous passes of the Hindu Kush, and down into the Indus valley — where they arrived in successive waves, probably over a period of several centuries from around 1500 BC onwards.

The Indus valley was at that time rather similar to the valleys of the Nile, the Tigris and the Euphrates, in that it was easy to clear and was fertilised by an abundance of flood-borne silt. And like them it was a cradle of civilisation: excavations have revealed that the famous cities of Harappa and Mohenjo-daro controlled an empire that lasted from at least 2300 to 1750 BC. Shortly after 1750 some disaster befell this efficient and wealthy civilisation. It used to be thought that the disaster was an earlier Indo-Aryan invasion, but it is now thought to have been an earthquake — and one that caused the Indus to change its course and flood the agricultural land.

When the first Indo-Aryan tribes arrived, a couple of centuries later, they did not have to storm the massive brick ramparts of the major cities. But they had long-bows and arrows and bronze axes, and — most importantly — chariots with spoked wheels, drawn by two horses yoked abreast, and carrying two warriors. So equipped, they were well able to take such minor strongholds as remained, and to establish themselves as conquerors in the land. Not that they constituted a nation: happy to unite in subjugating the non-Aryan, dark-skinned people they called *dasas*, the tribes were no less happy to make war on one another.[2]

Each tribe was ruled by a *raja* or 'king', assisted by an entourage of noble warriors and a council of elders. In the early period the king was primarily a leader in war. In no sense divine, he was nevertheless closely connected with those heavenly kings, the gods. Victory in war and the subjugation of enemies, dominion, prosperity, wealth, the possession of heirs — these things were gifts of the gods, and they showed that a king was in harmony with the gods and with the cosmic order.[3] Yet in this warlike society the priests, or brahmins, always a powerful class, gradually came to appropriate a status higher than that of the warriors, including the *raja* himself. A king who infringed the rights of the brahmins was regarded as an offender against the divinely appointed order, and doomed himself and his kingdom to destruction.

Compared with the peoples of Harappa and Mohenjo-daro the Aryans were technologically backward. They built not in brick but in wattle and daub, so nothing remains of their buildings; and they left no statues or even figurines. On the steppes they had lived from stockbreeding of cattle and horses, and they still knew nothing of city life but lived in tribal villages, with their herds of cattle, horses, sheep and goats in nearby pastures. It is true that the economy soon changed from predominantly pastoral to mixed pastoral and agricultural: barley or wheat was reaped. But cattle retained their central role: farmers prayed for increase of cattle, the warrior's booty consisted mostly of cattle, the sacrificial priest received cattle in payment for his services. Cattle were in fact a sort of currency, and values were reckoned in heads of cattle.

Such was the society which, over the period 1500–1000 BC, gradually established itself in the 'Land of the Seven Rivers'.

2

Almost our only source of information about the invading tribes is the *Rig Veda*.[4] What it has to say about their social structure and economic organisation and wars is valuable but incidental. Being itself a religious work, it throws most light on the Indo-Aryan — or, as it is usually and appropriately called, the Vedic — world-view.

'Veda' means 'knowledge', and here it means knowledge of the superhuman powers that are active in the world, and of the way to influence them. That knowledge was believed to have been there for ever — until, once upon a time, long, long ago, it was 'seen' by certain sages in a state of visionary ecstasy. Ostensibly revealed by numinous experiences and sudden insights into the hidden origins and inter-connections of things, it offered magical techniques and rules for establishing contact and entering into collaboration with higher powers. And it was correspondingly valuable: as the one repository of eternal truth, the source of all understanding, the sole infallible guide to living, it was more potent than the gods themselves.

The real history of the *Rig Veda* is known. Although this collection of more than a thousand hymns in Sanskrit was written down around 600 BC, and the earliest extant text dates only from around 1200 AD, the hymns themselves were composed at a time when the Aryans were comparative newcomers in the sub-continent — mostly, it seems, around 1200 BC. Early in the first millennium the hymns were collected and arranged. By that time they were regarded as sacred, so not a word was permitted to be altered, and the priestly schools devised checks to ensure that no word was. Even when the art of writing was widely known, the hymns were rarely written down. Instead, they were transmitted orally from generation to generation of priests and singers in the priestly schools. The mnemonic capacity developed by these professionals ensured the survival of the hymns, essentially intact, down to the present day.

Most of them were composed and cherished by various priestly families, for use in the sacrificial cult. Though their content was largely based on widespread popular beliefs, it was cast in poetry of great sophistication. And though the collection served the interests of the Indo-Aryan or Vedic community as a whole, in that it catered for the desires of ordinary people for health, security, prosperity and offspring, it is permeated by the concerns of an intellectual élite.

The hymns of the *Rig Veda* include prayers and litanies and, above all, songs of praise, exalting particular gods and their mighty works, and intended, when recited or chanted, to strengthen them in their present activities. From the episodes they recount and from the hints and references they cast to and fro, one can reconstruct a coherent and all-embracing world-view.[5]

3

The *Rig Veda* knows nothing of the notions that were to flourish so vigorously in India in later times — of vast cycles of time slowly revolving, of a declension of ages to be followed by a new beginning and a new declension, over and over again, of individual souls passing meanwhile through thousands upon thousands of incarnations. Vedic Indians saw things quite differently. They took it for granted that the ordered world cosmos would not change: always imperfect, constantly threatened by destructive forces, it would nevertheless survive indefinitely as it now was.

On the other hand the cosmos had not always existed, but had been established at a certain moment in the past. The *Rig Veda* contains several accounts of how this come about.[6] In some of the most famous it is the god Indra who masters primordial chaos and brings the ordered world into being.[7]

Indra is the most important god in the *Rig Veda*: no less than a quarter of the hymns are dedicated to him — some 250, whereas no other god receives more than ten. The etymology of his name is unknown, but some of the epithets attached to him suggest that originally he personified the brute power of nature, and especially of the atmosphere: he is a storm-god, wielder of the thunderbolt, sender of rain. But he is also a divine warrior. As such he is described in anthropomorphic terms, as a giant with mighty arms and hands, voracious mouth and throat, a prodigious appetite. Eternally young and strong, stormy, violent, but also cunning, he is a formidable fighter. He travels on a golden chariot drawn by two sprightly dun-coloured steeds. When he throws his thunderbolt with a thousand jagged teeth it never misses its aim.

This divine warrior was a god of warriors. Not that his cult was practised exclusively, or even chiefly, by professional warriors: an entire tribe would worship him as its guardian — but a guardian whose care was needed above all in time of war. For — perhaps already on the steppe, certainly by the time they arrived in the Indus valley — the Indo-Aryan tribes had developed a warrior ethos. Although a warrior class existed, every able-bodied male was expected to bear arms. All alike would turn to Indra for support — and none more devoutly than the king, who was above all a warlord. Indeed, it has been plausibly argued that the exaltation of Indra was a way of legitimising the replacement of traditional tribal chieftains by such warlords.[8]

It seems that in early days the Bharatas were the most formidable of the tribes. The *Rig Veda* describes the Bharatas as 'cattle-hunters moving in hordes', and adds that the source of their strength is Indra. The Bharatas earned the enmity of the other tribes, who formed an alliance against them — which of course also invoked Indra's support. And everyone alike called on Indra for help in subjugating the *dasas*. They did not call in vain: as the untiring champion of the Indo-Aryans Indra captured hostile towns and annihilated their inhabitants, seized herds of horses and cattle from the enemy and bestowed them on his own people.

The bond between Indra and the Indo-Aryan tribes is shown as a very close one. The tribes with their horses and chariots move at the god's command, and he is portrayed as the author of their every victory. The fighting troops are summoned to model themselves on him, to be 'heroes in the style of Indra' and, by vanquishing the *dasas*, to carry out his work. This call is directed as much to the common people as to the professional warriors.

Indra is felt to be physically present in the midst of the battle: together with his fair-skinned companions he slays the dark men with his spear, he wields his sovereign might through the tribal kings. There is in the *Rig Veda* a battle-hymn that says it all:

> Indra — to be known through strength, hero pre-eminent, powerful, triumphant, exercising might, above every hero, above every fighter, born in might — mount the winning cars, finding cows! Him, cleaving cow-pens open, finding cattle with bolt in arm, winning the race and rushing forth with vigour —be heroes like him, O kinsmen of the clan! Hold fast to him, O comrades! Plunging with prowess into cowpens, Indra the uncompromising hero, of wrath hundredfold, subduer of troops, hard to be fought with — may he in battles be our aid![9]

Yet Indra is much more than warrior-god and storm-god. Known as 'he with a thousand testicles', he is possessed of boundless creative energy and triumphant vitality — and he has always exercised them for the benefit of human beings. He is lord of nature, he bestows fertility on the fields and on women, indeed every positive and helpful process is a manifestation of his beneficent power. The first and most overwhelming manifestation of that power was the cosmogony.[10] On the outermost edge of the world, or maybe in heaven, there was a cave belonging to a demon called Vala, meaning 'confinement'. There herds of cows were kept imprisoned. Their owners were demons too — though their name, Panis, was used also for the miserly rich who failed to make adequate offerings to the gods and their priests.

In this myth Indra appears as a priest-king. Guided by his divine bitch, and supported by a body of heavenly priests headed by the god Brhaspati, 'Lord of cultic song', he arrives at the cave and breaks it open. He does so not by force of arms but by offering a sacrifice and by singing sacred songs around the sacrificial fire. These songs are endowed with the magical power of *rita*, the divinely appointed order of the world, and Indra's deed is itself an affirmation of that order. The singing sets the cows free.

These cows symbolise the dawns — whence their reddish colour — and their liberation starts the succession of sunrises. Now the sun, hitherto confined in darkness, rides high over the world. Light pours forth, darkness is banished. And with the cows freed, nourishment becomes available not simply to priests but to mankind.

4

There is another and far more celebrated cosmogonic myth attached to Indra.[11] No hymn in the *Rig Veda* actually tells the story, but many hymns refer to it; and with the help of later Indian commentaries and reworkings, it is possible to reconstruct the myth from those scattered hints. It is clear that the ordered world came into being as a result of Indra's intervention in the war of the Adityas and the *rakshas* or *rakshashas*, meaning 'demons'. In the *Rig Veda* both *rakshashas* and Adityas are endowed with superhuman, magic power. The Adityas are variously identified in the *Rig Veda*, but they never number more than eight. The number of the demons is also indeterminate, but is often given as seven. Their leader is, or was before he encountered Indra, the arch-demon Vritra.

Adityas and demons were opposed in every way. The Adityas, who were generally imagined as human in appearance, were benevolent beings. They were the sons of the goddess Aditi, whose name probably meant 'freedom' and who represented above all the notion of wide-open nature, free from all restriction and obstruction. This was true of the whole family: in their various ways all the Adityas fostered ongoing, outgoing life. The demons did the opposite — indeed, in post-Rigvedic times they were called Danavas, a term denoting 'bondage', 'restraint'. Imagined as serpents or dragons or, sometimes, as boars, they devoted themselves to restraining, binding, obstructing.

In the beginning there were the cosmic waters, and these were held in or covered by Vritra. The arch-demon — whose very name meant 'restrainer', 'opposition', 'blockage' — was generally imagined as a gigantic snake (*ahi*) either lying on the primordial mountain or else with the mountain contained inside it, and the waters contained inside the mountain. He could also be imagined as a boar, lying on the waters. Treacherous and malignant, he dwelt on the borders of darkness.

The Adityas wanted the waters set free — not least because at that time the sun was contained in the waters as an embryo. Until the waters flowed and the sun was placed in the heavens the world could not function. Vritra and his associate demons would have none of this: the ordered world must not come into existence at all, so the waters must remain for ever imprisoned.

War broke out between Adityas and demons and, though the *Rig*

Veda does not relate its early stages but only hints at them, it is plain that the Adityas were worsted. Their remedy was somehow to call Indra into existence, as their champion. Born, it seems, of the sky as his father and the earth as his mother, he was the youngest of the gods. From the moment of his birth he was ready to do battle on behalf of his elders — but he imposed a condition: if victorious, he would be the king over the gods.

Indra's first step was to drink three great draughts of the stimulant soma. The draught transformed him, as no doubt he intended it should. In a moment he grew to such a size that he filled sky and earth. Terrified, his parents flew apart — and once separated, sky and earth would never be re-united; it was the first stage in the ordering of the world. The gods were still terrified of Vritra: they gave way before his power, at the sound of his hissing they shrank back like feeble old men, they deserted their champion. But Indra, undeterred, prepared for battle. He created a storm, personified in the god Rudra and his attendants the Maruts. Then, armed with the wonder-working thunderbolt, the *vajra*, that the craftsman-god had made for him, he hurled himself upon Vritra. It was a ferocious combat. First Vritra broke Indra's jaw but then, while the heavens shuddered at the monster's screams, Indra broke Vritra's jaw, smashed his face in, split his skull, killed him and left him lying on the ground. Finally Indra fought and slew the female arch-demon Danu, whose name also makes her a personification of restraint. Though she is described as Vritra's mother she must surely have been, originally, his mate — and so something of a counterpart to Babylonian Tiamat. Indra left her corpse lying upon the corpse of Vritra.

Now Indra was indeed supreme lord: the gods were glad to endow him with their powers and submit to his rule. And he set about constructing the ordered world. The primordial mountain, which had been loose and quaking, was fixed to the bottom of the cosmic waters, and the earth spread out around it. Then Indra divided the *Sat* from the *Asat*, the existent from the non-existent.

The *Asat* had always been there, it was primordial chaos. Now it was confined beneath the earth and separated from it by a great chasm. As the netherworld it became the habitation of Vritra and the other demons. The *Sat*, now organised in three parts, sky, atmosphere, earth, became the realm in which gods and human beings moved and had their being. In the under-surface of the stone sky a pathway was carved for the sun to travel along. Planted at last where it rightfully belonged, the sun shone out over the earth — and its revolutions were set going. As for the cosmic waters, they flowed out of the cave where Vritra had kept them enclosed — or else, in some accounts, out of the burst belly of Vritra himself — formed rivers and ran to the sea like birds to their nest or chariots in a chariot-race. These waters were also goddesses — and as such, called by the usual complimentary term, cows. Now Indra became their husband. Thanks to him the udders of these divine cows were full: the waters, changed into the most motherly of beings, became the heavenly ocean that provides the rain needful for life.

It was time for a great feast, at which all the gods sang Indra's praise. It was also time for the gods to take up their proper functions. The cosmic law, *rita*, was established; and in accordance with that law, and with their own natures, the gods set to work at their respective tasks.

That was not the end of Indra's heroic feats. There were other demons to be dealt with, and Indra slew them too. Moreover, whatever their names, those demons were all Vritra, and Indra's combats all had the same meaning: over and over again the waters had to be released, over and over again the sun had to be made available and safe, if cosmos was not to sink back into chaos.

5

The Indra myth is a pre-eminent example of a combat myth, and it has much in common with other such myths. Vritra is very much like the Egyptian Apep or Apophis. Like him, he represents primordial chaos: dwelling in everlasting darkness, he contains the cosmic waters. By attacking, piercing and slaying him the warrior-god — Indra or Seth — sets those waters free. At the same time the god frees the sun and enables it to move on its proper course. And if one considers the doublets of the Indra myth, the resemblance goes even further. The god Trita Aptya is Indra's close companion and duplicates some of Indra's feats — in fact, he may well be an earlier version of Indra himself. Now, the dragon that Trita Aptya slays is described as a screaming dragon — and the scream of Apep, rending the darkness, is an unforgettable feature of the Egyptian myth.

The parallelism with the Mesopotamian myths of Ninurta and Marduk is no less striking. The basic pattern is the same. Here as there the gods are helpless in face of a monstrous power. But then a warrior and storm-god appears — a heroic figure, younger, more enterprising and more courageous than the other gods. He tackles the monster, defeats and slays it. In recognition of his prodigious achievement, the storm-god is exalted over all, or nearly all, the other gods. He may even set the gods to work in the world, each in his proper station. A great feast of the gods is held to inaugurate the new age, and the praises of the young god are sung.

Between Indra and Marduk there is a further point of resemblance: both, by killing their monsters, become creator-gods. And the monsters likewise have much in common. Tiamat and Vritra are both powers making for sterility and inertia, hostile to life and activity. Of both it could be said that so long as that power remains dominant, nothing can ever happen. But that is not all: Tiamat and Vritra are both primordial ancestors, standing in an ambivalent, even tormented relationship with younger gods. Tiamat is so much aware of being the ancestor of the gods that, until provoked beyond endurance, she tries to defend them from her enraged husband. As for Vritra, one Rigvedic hymn describes some of the greatest gods — Varuna, Agni, Soma — as being contained inside him: the serpent is their 'father'.[12] And very reluctant they are to come out, even at Indra's behest. 'Unkindly I desert him who was kind to me, as I go from my own friends to a foreign tribe,' laments Agni. 'I have spent many hours within him. Now I choose Indra and desert the father. Agni, Soma, Varuna — they fall away', sighs Soma. Strange phrases these, applied to a father: one can only wonder whether Vritra himself was not sometimes imagined as the primordial mother, like Tiamat. However that may be, in both cases the ancestor has to be killed, so that younger gods can take their proper place in the world — the newly ordered world.

So one returns to Apep. He too is an ancestor, for he was there before the ordered world existed, indeed he was there before any of the gods. And if now he is a purely hostile, destructive figure, is that not because the benign, nurturing aspects of primordial chaos have been split off and attached to another cosmic snake — that world-encircling serpent into which all the gods and all the blessed dead go each night, to emerge rejuvenated, reborn, each morning?

One could continue. As we shall see in a later chapter, a version of the combat myth that was closely akin to the Vedic version flourished amongst the Scandinavians — and recently attention has been drawn to a Russian folktale that is also clearly derived from the Indra myth. So we are confronted with three separate traditions, Egyptian, Mesopotamian, Indo-European, all of them very ancient. To look for a common place of origin seems pointless — if the traditions have much in common it is because they express the same fears and hopes. In one form or another the myth flourished over vast areas of the ancient world. And what it says in all its forms is the same: that cosmos has always been threatened by chaos and always will be, yet has always survived and always will.

6

Cosmos existed, and endured, thanks to the immutable principle called *rita.*[13] As with Egyptian *ma'at*, *rita* cannot be translated by any single word in any modern language, but we know what it means. Etymologically *rita* means 'set in motion', and it was used to indicate the normal and right way for things to happen in the world. If in the *Rig Veda* it sometimes figures as an expression of the will of the gods, it can also figure as a mighty power independent of the gods, indeed as a power whose law the gods were bound to obey and whose demands they were bound to carry into effect.

The order of nature, which regulates the alternation of day and night and the cycle of the seasons, and the order of human life, by which each individual goes from birth to death, were both included in *rita*; and so was the ritual order, which prescribed just how sacrifices were to be made to the gods. The moral order, by which human beings were supposed to regulate their conduct and their relations with one another, was also part of *rita*: he who behaved in accord with the requirements of that principle would be just, upright, honest — and he would prosper, the winds would blow sweetly for him. Speech that was in accord with *rita* was truthful speech; conversely, where *rita* prevailed there was no place for lying — or for liars. But indeed the realm of *rita* was universal: the movements of the sun, the moon, the stars were its visible expression. It was also the force that set in motion whatever conserved and increased life: thanks to *rita* the day broke, rivers flowed, nourishing plants grew tall, cows gave their milk.

Certain gods were particularly concerned with the maintenance of *rita.*[14] Varuna was long thought by scholars to be a sky-god — indeed his name was thought to be identical with the Greek Uranos. That view is now discredited and he is recognised as essentially an all-controlling king. Much that was attributed to Indra was also attributed to Varuna: it was said that in the beginning he measured out the earth, fixed the sky in its place, set the course of the sun. Only, Varuna was no warrior god, the battles of the tribes were no concern of his. Remote and imperturbable, from his dwelling above the sky he watched over the cosmos and over *rita* as guardian and protector.

The physical world and human society alike were dependent on Varuna for the maintenance. It was thanks to his all-embracing power that earth and the heavens stood firm and immovable, nature continued on its normal regular course. Equally his will, as expressed in his ordinances, was the source of all law and all morality. Gods and human beings were bound to act in conformity with it — and

Varuna saw to it that they did so. It was thanks to his vigilance that human beings conducted themselves in accordance with *rita*. He had spies to keep him informed of their doings, and any offence against *rita* was punished. Any remissness in adoring the gods, including any error, even involuntary, in the ritual of sacrifice, was punished with sickness — which was itself a sign of disorder, *anrita*. Acutely aware of their insufficiency, people prayed to Varuna to forgive them their transgressions and to grant them happiness.

There were other offences against *rita*. Murder, cursing, deceit, drunkenness, anger, gambling, cheating at dice were all forbidden by Varuna. Moreover, each person had a particular function in society, appropriate to his or her place in the class structure. One was expected to devote oneself assiduously to fulfilling that function: it was a way of affirming that the world was in order. If one failed to do so, the operation of the cosmos would be impaired. Any such dereliction roused Varuna's wrath.

Worse still was to swear falsely. Swearing an oath was a religious act, performed with religious rites; and the words pronounced were endowed with supernatural force, which would turn back on anyone who swore falsely. To do such a thing was to ally oneself with the very principle opposed to *rita*.

So it is not surprising that Varuna was also god of the oath. It was in fact doubly appropriate because, amongst all the natural elements that he controlled, Varuna was most closely involved with water — and water was linked with oath-taking.[15] A person accused of wrong-doing, and who swore his innocence, could be required to submerge himself in water while an arrow was shot and retrieved. If he was still alive when the arrow was brought back his truthfulness, and thereby his innocence, were held to be established.

Varuna controlled rainfall, the regular flow of streams and rivers was his particular concern. But his connections with the waters went much further than that. According to the *Rig Veda* Varuna dwelt in the great ocean that surrounded the whole cosmos and from which, originally, the cosmos had emerged. Varuna's home was in those waters. There are indeed good grounds for thinking that the divine name Apam Napat, 'son of the waters', which was known both to the Vedic Indians and to the Iranians, and which must therefore be of Indo-Iranian origin, began as an epithet of Varuna.[16]

Presumably it was because of his association with the formless waters outside the ordered world that Varuna was also called god of the night. Guardian of the cosmic law, dwelling in the cosmic ocean, lord especially of the night sky, Varuna enveloped all things.

Mitra was Varuna's close associate, but kindlier, less awe-inspiring — and associated not with the night but with the day and sun, and not with water but with fire. He seconded Varuna in his care for human society, encouraging friendliness, agreement, the peaceful settlement of disputes. While Varuna, representing kingship in its static aspects, was the guardian of the great principle of *rita*, Mitra supervised the practical operation of *rita* in the world. To him who lived according to *rita* he was an ever helpful friend and ally.[17]

The noun *mithra* meant 'contract', but the word was used in a very wide sense. 'Contract' was understood as the basis of a relationship that was entered into voluntarily, and that united people in friendship and peace. Underlying it was the notion of a divinely sponsored integration, as opposed to chaotic and conflict-ridden separateness. Indeed, it seems that the prototype of all human contracts was felt to be a great cosmic contract that reconciled all opposites: light and darkness, night and dawn, life and death. Human affairs and the processes of nature were subject to the same order, *rita*, so the notion of contract was applicable to all alike.[18] So it was wholly appropriate that the god most intimately concerned with the operation of *rita* in the world should also be a personification of the contract.

Then there was Indra. Although it has sometimes been argued that Indra had little or no connection with *rita*, that is not what the *Rig Veda* says. There are in fact many passages where Indra, the only god to rival Varuna in kingly majesty, is portrayed as being, like him, the maker and protector of *rita*.[19] Or else he is shown as assisting Varuna in supervising the operation of *rita* in the world — just like Mitra. Indeed, the *dvandva* or 'pair' compound names Mitravaruna and Indravaruna are practically interchangeable: the collaboration they indicate is of the same kind in both cases.

It is said of Indra that he establishes order in the working of the universe and upholds the eternal law, that the regularity of nature is a manifestation of his power, that by *rita* he lights up the host of mornings, that he moves with steeds yoked by eternal order, even that he himself is *rita*. In one hymn he is actually identified with *rita*. As *rita* he opens the ears of the morally deaf and he inspires thoughts that prevent transgressions. In fact heaven and earth are his, the very cows offer their milk to him.

The evidence is abundant that this divine warrior and god of warriors, champion of the invading tribes in their wars with the native peoples, was also perceived as the power working in and guiding the whole ordered world. But how could it be otherwise, since in Vedic India as elsewhere victory in war was itself a supreme affirmation of the divinely appointed order?

And he remains a warrior: again and again he slays the demons that come up from the netherworld, threatening and damaging the world of *rita*. The god's war with the forces of chaos has not ended, in fact it can never end.

7

Gods and human beings alike depended on soma to strengthen and revitalise them.[20] Soma was a plant that grew, full of sap, in mountainous country. What plant it was has been extensively debated, and the debate is still in progress. Zoroastrian priests still use a plant called *hom* — which is a species of ephedra. However, it is far from certain that the *hom* of today is the same as the haoma/soma of three millennia ago. One of the more plausible suggestions is that the ancient plant was *pergamum harmala*, wild rue.[21]

An intoxicating drink was made from soma. Specially trained priests repeatedly bathed the plant stems in water and pressed them between stones, and strained and watered down the juice that emerged. The process was a solemn religious ritual. The poets who describe it in the *Rig Veda* note how their songs speed the work along, and how in return the soma reveals heavenly secrets to them and inspires their singing.

Soma was a powerful stimulant. It was felt to quicken thought, bestow poetic inspiration, heighten intellectual and physical energy. To the warrior it gave fresh courage, to the priest the mood he needed to offer up a fitting sacrifice. Sickness was cured by it, and sexual potency increased. Above all soma offered long life, it was an *elixir vitae*. Not only human beings but the gods themselves needed soma — in fact it was to soma that they owed their extraordinary strength and splendour. When, at the sacrifice, priests and gods drank soma together the bonds between the community and its gods were strengthened.

So boundless were the benefactions of soma that it could not be simply a plant, it must be a god. Soma is in fact described as the friend and protector of the other gods: they could rely on him to ward off their enemies and guarantee their well-being. He was praised in terms as glowing as those applied to the greatest gods. He was King Soma — king, of course, of plants and herbs, but also sometimes called king over gods and human beings, lord over all peoples, king of the world. He is even called creator and lord of the heavens, preserver of everything that exists. The soma sacrifice itself took on a cosmic import: the noise of the pressing was thunder, the woollen strainer represented clouds, the dripping juice was rain, which in turn fostered the growth of plants. As moisture Soma was in all plants, and in all creatures, human and animal, that fed on plants. Soma was also in all semen. In fact Soma was the power that ensured the continuation of the cyclical process on which all life depends. Ongoing life was his realm as it was Varuna's — only in his case it was life perceived as an unending process of reproduction.

Like Soma, Agni was both a phenomenon and a god, or rather, a phenomenon perceived as a god.[22] Agni was fire — the word is related to the Latin *ignis*. Like soma, fire was worshipped by the Iranians as devoutly as by the Vedic Indians, so it must have been a god already for the proto-Indo-Iranians. It could hardly have been otherwise. The peoples of the steppes will have depended on fire for their very survival. Originally they will no doubt have perceived it as the power that provided them with warmth in the bitter winters and enabled them to cook the meat that made up the greater part of their diet. But the Agni of the *Rig Veda* is much more than that.

The *Rig Veda* refers again and again to the waters as Agni's home. When, for instance, a priest consecrated a king by pouring water over him, he would invoke all the Agnis dwelling in the water. This association of fire and water, so paradoxical at first sight, ceases to be so when one recalls that water could signify the cosmic waters. Agni is called the child of the waters, and also the bull of the waters, meaning that he made them pregnant. It is as though fire were the primordial male power that went into the primordial female power in order to be reborn from it.[23]

A primordial, cosmic power, Agni could nevertheless be observed at work in the world. His flames were like hair, his eyes sparkled, his tongue licked at the trees, his sharp teeth ate them up. He could be terrifying as he burned up forest and steppe: then he was a manifestation of violent, all-conquering strength. But he was present everywhere on earth, and that gave him insight: he knew everything that happened, he was not to be deceived, he was a wise and cunning god. And he was present also in the sun, spreading his radiance in the sky and over the earth, bringing consolation, releasing energy.

Agni could be very helpful to human beings. He could also be a person's intimate friend, more intimate than any other god. At home in the domestic hearth and never absent from it, he was the benevolent patron and protector of the family, taking good care too of the cattle and the horses, driving away enemies, human and superhuman, warding off hardship and sickness. He was hostile to the demons that haunted the world, his sharp eyes detected them, his sharp teeth grasped them.

In the ritual of sacrifice Agni's role was central. Vedic Indians — and Iranians too for that matter — made their offerings over fire. Set alight, encouraged with melted butter, fire ate into the offerings — which meant that gods were partaking of them. It was Agni who invited the gods to the meal, who led them to the place, who saw to it that the offerings would be tasty. Often he was called the priest of the sacrifice. Like Soma he was a patron of such priests, protecting and fortifying them, and inspiring them to compose fine hymns and to recite them well. In return — again like Soma — he himself was praised in many hymns.

The Vedic pantheon included many other gods. Much esteem was already given to Vishnu, who was later to become a very great god indeed. He was Indra's close friend and assisted him in his fight with Vritra. And like Indra, he was an agent of liberation: by striding through the universe he made space for human beings to live and act freely and for the gods to exercise their powers. Benevolent and generous, he fostered fertility of every kind, watching over conception and birth, bestowing abundance of rain, food and all good things. The goddess of dawns, Usas, also figures prominently in the *Rig Veda*. Beautiful, eternally young, she rode a chariot drawn by reddish horses or cows. She destroyed not only darkness but also enmity, her light brought pleasure, well-being, success. Hymns in her praise rejoice in the regular return of daylight: if each night was experienced as an outbreak of chaos, each daybreak was experienced as a re-establishment of *rita*. Akin to Usas were the two male twins known as Nasatya, or else as the Asvin, 'owners of horses'. 'Grandsons of heaven', they represented the spreading light of daybreak. Each day they rode across the sky in their golden chariot. They too were destroyers of darkness, and of the demons that throve in darkness. They protected warriors in battle, and as doctors they helped women in childbirth.

Then there were cows.[24] The cow had much more than economic value, she symbolised everything that was most precious. In Vedic literature the goddess Usas is called a cow, and the rays of light at dawn are called a herd of cows. This stressed the sanctity of cows, for the first rays inaugurated the sacrificial ritual, on which the well-being of gods and human beings and the very survival of the ordered world depended. And a cow 'able to calve and to give milk' was the finest fee for the brahmin who performed the sacrifice.

The waters, perceived as a source of physical and moral healing, and themselves sanctified, were likewise called cows. The great goddess Aditi, mother of the Adityas, and the supreme symbol of freedom and development, was called a milch cow, and in Vedic ritual she was symbolised by a cow. Originally used as a figure of speech, a simile or a metaphor, in the end the word for 'cow' or 'cows' came to designate the holiest of beings. And as goddesses were considered to be cows, so the cow herself became holy. In one Rigvedic hymn a cow describes herself as one 'who knows the ritual spell, who raises up the sacrificial voice inherent in all pious devotions, a goddess arrived from the gods'.[25]

That did not mean that cows could not be killed. On the contrary, a cow was the finest offering that could be made to the gods.

9

By themselves the gods would not have had the strength to carry out their unending task of sustaining the ordered world and of strengthening *rita*. They depended on the sacrifices offered by human beings.

The role of sacrifice in Vedic society was different from its role in Egyptian or Mesopotamian society.[26] Naturally when the Indo-Aryans were living as semi-nomadic tribes on the Russian steppes, and afterwards during their long and laborious migration to India, they had no temples. This was still the case with the Vedic Indians. More importantly, the Vedic Indians seem to have known nothing of public or tribal or national rituals. When sacrifices were made to the gods they were made on behalf of an individual or a small family, and at home. In fact they were a form of private hospitality: the desired deities were invited to a meal in their honour. And that implied much more than a mere gift of food. A god was welcomed like a guest, offered refreshment after his journey, provided with a comfortable seat of soft grass, entertained with poetry and music. In return, the family concerned had the happy experience of sitting down together with a god or with several gods. It would also expect the god — like any human guest — to return the host's hospitality through a gift, a favour.

All but the simplest rituals required the participation of priests, who had to be paid — which meant that the main driving force behind the cult was the desire of prosperous individuals to further their own well-being. Nevertheless, it was as true of Vedic as of other ancient societies that to keep the ordered world in being required constantly repeated ritual sacrifices. How this process was understood is shown not only by the *Rig Veda* but also by the liturgical collection known as the *Yajur Veda* and above all by the *Brahmanas*, in which the songs and rites are described and interpreted for the benefit of officiating priests.

In Vedic sacrifice the offering was often a domestic animal (wild animals were excluded), but it could also be a plant. Whatever it was, it was perceived as being part of the sacrificer, i.e. of the person who provided the offering and on whose behalf the sacrifice was being made — and as representing the whole of that person. This was true whether or not a priest officiated: it was always the sacrificer who was offering himself up.[27]

Parts of the sacrificial animal or plant were consumed in the fire, and the gods were nourished by the savour that mounted to the skies. The rest was eaten by the sacrificer and the priest or priests — and that too was perceived as a consuming, a total destruction, of the offering. Finally the sacrificer rewarded the priests, lavishly: at each stage he had to be felt to be giving up something that was his own.

The gods depended on sacrifices for their well-being and indeed for their immortality. Without sacrifices they would become weak and would no longer be able to ensure the prosperity of the land and its inhabitants. Strengthened by sacrifices, they could be relied on to send rain — in India, the supreme manifestation of cosmic order. Rain at the right time made the plants grow, which provided nourishment for animals and human beings and so, by making sacrifices possible, for the gods themselves.

Heaven and earth, the domain of the gods and the domain of human beings, were totally dependent on one another, they could subsist only as two parts of a single whole. What enabled that whole to subsist was *rita* and what enabled that great principle to subsist was sacrifice: sacrifice was both the most powerful and the most indispensable support of cosmos.

Every sacrifice strengthened *rita*, including every sacrifice offered by the head of a household in the privacy of his own home; but the sacrifice offered by a king was particularly effective. A Vedic king was only a warlord ruling over quite a small principality, but he was nevertheless the richest member of the community. This enabled him to institute particularly costly sacrifices, for the benefit of his kingdom as well as of his reign. It was his duty to nourish not only the gods but also the brahmins: every royal sacrifice was accompanied by a lavish distribution of gifts to the brahmins. These gifts typically included cows and land to graze them on — for milk, clarified butter and milk curds were the favourite foods of the gods and formed part of every sacrifice. The brahmin for his part was wholly dedicated to strengthening *rita* — and he did it by officiating at sacrifices. Some brahmins also acted as counsellors to kings, and that too was perceived as an affirmation of *rita*, for the exercise of government was one aspect of cosmic order.

10

One god stood apart from the others: Rudra.[28] He was the god of the uncultivated land, the wilderness, and so of the dangerous and frightening aspects of nature. He was imagined as residing in the great mountain ranges in the north — whereas the other gods resided in the east — and as frequenting lonely, uncanny places. More prominent in folk belief than in the *Rig Veda*, he was at home with wild animals and serpents. He could figure as patron of hunters, but also as patron of thieves and robbers. He brought sickness and death to human beings and to cattle. If a few hymns were nevertheless addressed to him in the *Rig Veda*, and offerings made to him, it was in the hope of mollifying his hostility — for he could be moved to compassion and could even, on occasion, turn himself into a helpful doctor for man and beast.

Rudra stood on the margins of the ordered world, not wholly belonging to it yet not wholly alien either. It was a different matter with the demons. They were for ever striving to overthrow the gods and to take their place. In order to achieve their aim they had to weaken *rita* — and they had their ways of doing that.[29] Wherever a king interfered with the brahmins or with the normal practice of sacrifice, demons were at work. The same was true of any interference with the class structure — for the classes were defined not simply by their social roles but by their relationship to sacrifice. Such interference undermined the ordered world; if it was not checked, if the demons were not frustrated, cosmos would disintegrate into chaos. In practice, any prolonged drought was interpreted as a manifestation of chaos, and a sure sign that sacrifices had not been offered as they should have been.

Just as the demons had once tried to prevent the making of the ordered world, so now they strove to inflict damage on that world and on the human beings and animals living in it. There was no limit to their nefarious activities.[30] They threatened one's property, good fortune, health, life. In pairs or in whole bands, demons prowled the land. Sometimes they were imagined as more or less human in appearance, especially as woman-like, but distorted — yellow-eyed, three-headed. Sometimes they were imagined as reptiles or animals — mostly as snakes, but also as dogs, owls, vultures. There were demons that changed themselves into animals at night, and in that form flew through the air, congregated at cross-roads, pranced around houses. People prayed to the fire-god Agni to hold such creatures at bay. But demons did much worse: they brought sickness and disease. Some demons specialised in entering into their victims and eating them up from inside. At critical moments — after the death of a relative, or after a childbirth — a person was particularly liable to fall victim to the evil designs of demons.

Human beings could ally themselves with demons. An enemy could employ a demon to ruin a sacrifice, and so deprive the offerer of the benefits he expected. Sorcerers could employ demons — and so become themselves a sort of demon. It could also happen that a whole category of human beings came to be regarded as demonic. This was the case with the so-called *dasas*, the dark-skinned people who were in occupation of north India when the Indo-Aryans arrived. In legend particularly the leaders of the *dasas* are often demonised.

The permanent abode and power-base of the demons was the netherworld. The *Rig Veda* gives no systemtic account of the netherworld, but it offers many hints; one hymn is particularly illuminating.[31] We learn that beneath the earth there is an abyss, a bottomless pit shrouded in total and everlasting darkness. Human beings who have set themselves against *rita* go there: not only sorcerers but individuals who have shown too little regard for the gods or for the priests, or who had neglected their proper duties. For making the opposite of *rita, anrita*, their god, they are slain by those guardians of *rita*, Soma and Agni, and cast out of the ordered world.

For the ordered world, consisting of the earth and the sky and what is above the sky, operates according to *rita*. It is the realm of sun and of light and of the beneficent waters, it is the lap of the goddess Aditi, mother of the Adityas, which is the safe home of gods and of human beings. The netherworld, on the contrary, is the lap of Nirrti, 'destruction'. There the sun never reaches, there is no light or warmth, no fertilising water. In the netherworld *rita* does not obtain, it is *anrita*. It lies outside the ordered world, it is the realm of chaos.[32]

II

Apparently those who had transgressed against *rita* were not the only ones to go down, after death, into a gloomy, hopeless existence in the eternal darkness of the netherworld. It seems that originally, in proto-Indo-Iranian times, this was the universal fate, and that in Vedic times it was still the fate of the common people.

The *Rig Veda* has nothing to say about the common people — naturally enough, since it was composed by and for members of the privileged strata of society. To the privileged it offers a most agreeable prospect. Provided only that they had honoured the gods and made the proper ritual offerings, had been generous to the priests and fulfilled their proper functions in the world, such people had no cause to worry about the netherworld. On the contrary, they could look forward to an afterlife as happy as that which awaited the most fortunate members of Egyptian society.

Vedic Indians believed that each such individual had a spirit —

an impalpable substance, like a breath. But though the spirit was distinct from the body, it did not desert it for ever at the moment of death. At death the spirit made its way to heaven, easily and pleasantly — and once arrived there it met its body again. Not even cremation could prevent that: so long as the corpse had not been injured by bird or beast, and the bones had been collected afterwards and correctly arranged, the whole body was reconstituted in the next world, ready for the spirit to re-enter. Then life was resumed.[33]

The dead continued their lives in heaven, where they dwelt with the Fathers — the dead who had gone before them — and with Yama, the first man and therefore the first to die. Now he reigned, rather than ruled, in heaven. That blissful realm is repeatedly described in the *Rig Veda*: it is full of radiant light, and of harmony and joy.[34] Its denizens are nourished on milk and honey and of course soma. They make love — all the more deliciously because they have been freed from every bodily defect. The sound of sweet singing and of the flute is readily available. There are even wish-cows, which supply whatever is wished for. In short, the afterlife of the fortunate minority would be a much improved version of the life they had lived on earth — a life, too, that would be free, at last and for ever, from harassment by the restless agents of chaos.

But none of this had any bearing on the future of the world itself.

CHAPTER 4

Zoroastrians

At a time when the Vedic Indians were still imagining the world as held in timeless equilibrium, a totally new perception of time and of the prospects for mankind was emerging amongst the Iranians. The Iranian prophet Zarathustra — more generally known under a later, Greek form of his name, Zoroaster — came to see all existence as the gradual realisation of a divine plan.[1] He also foretold the ultimate fulfilment of that plan, a glorious consummation when all things would be made perfect once and for all.

When was all this achieved? There are two opinions, which cannot be reconciled. According to a Zoroastrian tradition the prophet lived 258 years before Alexander, which would place him in the middle of the sixth century BC; and this has been accepted by some eminent scholars. However, the tradition in question has been shown to derive from a late calculation based on a Greek fiction.[2] For more than a hundred years linguistic and archaeological evidence has been accumulating in favour of the alternative view — which is, that Zoroaster lived in a far earlier period, some time between 1500 and 1200 BC, when the Iranians were still settled pastoralists rather than farmers.[3] Zoroaster's own liturgical hymns, the *Gathas*, abound in references to the institutions, customs, technology and ways of thought of the traditional pastoral society — whereas not a single simile is drawn from agriculture. In one place the prophet even prays to the supreme god for the gift of a camel, a stallion and ten mares. For that matter the name Zarathustra probably meant either 'he who can manage camels' or 'he who has active camels'.[4]

As for the location of Zoroaster's activity, scholars disagree; some hold that his homeland was not far from the original homeland of the Iranians, somewhere south of the Urals, in what is now northern Kazakstan, others that it lay somewhere on the route of their migrations southwards — either in the extreme east of present-day Iran or in western Afghanistan. But all are agreed that the people from whom Zoroaster came eventually settled in eastern Iran. The efforts of the Zoroastrian priesthood of later times to situate the origins of the religion in western Iran have no justification in historical fact. The religion must have been already very old, must indeed have acquired the inviolability of antiquity, before it spread so far; for its scriptures contain not a single reference to any western Iranian king, people, place or tradition.

Alone amongst the founders of major religions, Zoroaster started as a priest of an older religion, the traditional religion of the Iranians — which means that from the age of seven or so he must have undergone the usual rigorous professional training. But if his mind always remained that of a priest steeped in age-old doctrines, it was also a passionate, original, adventurous mind. There is a tradition that from the age of twenty he led a wandering life for some years, frequenting visionaries and seers. Such people had existed for countless generations, and they had their own well-established spiritual disciplines. But Zoroaster's experience and achievement were to be unique. At some point he had illuminations, or hallucinations, in which he saw and heard the great god Ahura Mazda — Lord Wisdom — surrounded by six other radiant figures. From that time onwards he felt himself to be the divinely preordained prophet of a religious faith that differed greatly from the traditional faith.

Though Zoroaster never aimed at abolishing the religion of his ancestors, he did seek to reform it — and that was enough to attract the enmity of the traditionalist priesthood. As often happens — one thinks of Jesus, of Mohammed — Zoroaster failed to establish himself as a prophet in the district where he had been brought up; and after some years he moved elsewhere. At the court of a prince called Vishtaspa he found a home for life, where he was venerated and whence his doctrines were disseminated. He himself seems to have preached to all who would listen — to women as well as to men, to the poor and ignorant as well as to the rich and learned — and to have offered a blissful immortality to all who accepted his message. If, as seems likely, such a future had come to be regarded as reserved for princes, warriors and priests, these people must surely have been enraged at this attack on their monopoly. Fresh enmities sprang up: neighbouring princes took up arms to destroy the new faith. But the prophet's supporters were victorious in battle, and the faith survived.

Much in the early history of Zoroastrianism remains obscure, but there are good grounds for thinking that during the first thousand years of its existence the faith established itself over large areas of north-eastern and eastern Iran. Moreover, despite formidable geographical barriers, it penetrated into western Iran, which had been invaded and settled by the Medes (in the north) and the Persians (in the south); and did this so effectively that by the seventh century BC the hereditary priests of western Iran, the magi, were converted. The royal dynasty of the Achaemenians included many Zoroastrians by the early sixth century. The Persian monarch Cyrus the Great, who founded the first Iranian empire in 549 BC, was probably a Zoroastrian; if so, this must have facilitated both his conquest of Media, where many of the nobles were Zoroastrians, and his conquest of eastern Iran, where the oldest Zoroastrian communities were to be found. Certainly Zoroastrianism soon became both the religion of the royal house and the official religion of all Iran; and so it remained during the two centuries of the mighty Achaemenian empire. Even when that empire was conquered by Alexander the Great, in 334–331 BC, and the Achaemenian dynasty was replaced by the Macedonian dynasty of the Seleucids, Zoroastrianism continued to flourish. And during the eight hundred years of the second and third Iranian empires — the Parthian (or Arsacid) and the Sasanian — from the second century BC to the seventh century AD, it functioned again as a state religion.

In the mid-seventh century the Muslim armies that swept out of Arabia finally succeeded in overthrowing the Sasanian empire; and the great days of Zoroastrianism began to draw to a close. Although the ethical qualities instilled by Zoroaster's teachings have enabled the religion to survive countless vicissitudes, including much persecution and hardship, it gradually ceased to be, numerically, one of the world's major religions: in the 1970s there were only some 130,000 Zoroastrians. The majority — over 90,000 — live in the Indian sub-continent, whither their ancestors fled, many centuries ago, to escape from Muslim oppression; these are the Parsis (meaning 'Persians'). In Iran there are fewer than 20,000 Zoroastrians.

The impact of Zoroastrianism is a very different matter: though not generally recognised, it has been, and still is, immense. For some centuries before Christ Zoroaster's basic teachings were widely disseminated. In a later chapter it will be argued that they had much influence amongst Jews, and even more amongst the early Christians — and so, in the long run, upon the world-view of what was to become European civilisation.

2

Zoroastrianism possesses sacred scriptures, known collectively as the *Avesta* — which probably meant something like 'Authoritative Utterance'.[5] The extant *Avesta* is only a quarter of the original, and even that quarter was probably given written form only in the fifth or sixth century AD. Up to that time its preservation depended almost wholly on oral transmission, generation after generation, in priestly schools. However, though the time-gap between Zoroaster's proclamation and the sixth century AD is something like 2000 years, the transmission of his words seems to have achieved the same astonishing accuracy as the transmission of the *Rig Veda*.

Truncated as it is, the *Avesta* is still voluminous. It includes seventeen hymns composed by Zoroaster himself, the *Gathas*; these are couched in an east Iranian language so archaic that it is close to that of the *Rig Veda*. The remainder of the *Avesta*, also in an east Iranian dialect, is linguistically of later date — which is why it is commonly called the 'younger' or 'later' *Avesta*. It does not follow that its contents are also younger. On the contrary, present-day scholarship inclines to the view that, whatever accretions and modifications may have occurred in later centuries, the 'younger' *Avesta* contains much material that embodies the original teachings of Zoroaster, and even some material that was preserved by him and his followers from what was already in their time a distant past. Then, apart from the *Avesta*, there are the Pahlavi or Middle Persian books. These works underwent their final redaction only in the ninth and tenth centuries AD. However, they include both a summary of the whole of the original *Avesta* (the *Dinkard*) and long passages of translation of lost parts of the *Avesta*. Particularly instructive is the Pahlavi book known as the *Bundahishn* ('Creation'), which deals both with the making of the ordered world and with its final state.

Despite some obstacles, these various works have enabled scholars to reconstruct, with a reasonable degree of assurance, not only the teachings of Zoroaster himself and of the theologians who interpreted and elaborated upon those teachings, but also the world-view of the Iranian society into which he was born. As one would expect, this turns out to be closely akin to the Vedic world-view. In both, the notion of all-embracing order is central. Amongst the people that produced Zoroaster — scholars call them Avestans, from the *Avesta* — the Indo-Iranian word *rita* changed into *asha*; but what it meant did not change.[6] The pantheon that in various ways sustained *asha* was also broadly similar. The *Avesta* contains a number of *yashts*, or hymns of praise, dedicated to ancient, pre-Zoroastrian deities[7] — and some of these are exact counterparts of Vedic deities. The god of fire, Atar, has the same nature and functions as Agni, Haoma is the same god as Soma, the river-goddess Sarasvati figures in both pantheons.

Many lesser gods also contributed to sustaining *asha*: gods personifying such concepts as the hospitality owed to a guest, the prosperity to be expected from a marriage contract, the prayers that could ensure victory in battle. Such divinities might be 'abstract' but they were by no means remote: on the contrary, to their worshippers they were ever-present and highly individual powers. The same was true of the god who represented the souls of all useful animals, the god who represented healing and inspiration, and the gods personifying the sky, the earth, the sun, the moon — and many, many others. Most of these lesser gods also had Vedic counterparts.

The *Avesta* does however diverge from the *Rig Veda* in its treatment of the great gods who brought the ordered world into being and were still responsible for supervising it. Indra is mentioned only briefly, and then as a demon. Varuna is present — if he is present at all — only as the obscure 'Son of the Waters'. Iranian Mithra, on the other hand, stands out as a far more impressive figure than Vedic Mitra. The god who dominates the Avestan world-view is Ahura Mazda, 'Lord Wisdom'; and it is not clear that the Vedic priests had any knowledge of him.[8]

There is no agreement amongst scholars as to what these discrepancies mean. In the next chapter it will be argued that they have much greater implications than meet the eye. Meanwhile one fact is universally recognised, and can be taken as certain: that Zoroaster gave Ahura Mazda a position more exalted than any deity in the ancient world had ever occupied.

3

It was an ancient Indo-Iranian doctrine that in the beginning there had been only one of everything — one plant, one animal, one man. Perhaps it was through reflecting on this primordial singularity that Zoroaster arrived at the conviction that in the beginning there had been only one god. Certainly he proclaimed that once upon a time Ahura Mazda, the wholly wise, just and good, had been the one and only god. Himself uncreated, Ahura Mazda was the first cause of everything in the universe that is good, whether divine or human, animate or inanimate, abstract or concrete — in short, of *asha* and everything that is in accord with *asha*.

Ahura Mazda's unique dignity as maker and guardian of the ordered world is the theme of one of the finest *Gathas*:

> This I ask Thee, tell me truly, Lord. Who in the beginning, at creation, was the Father of Asha? Who established the course of sun and stars? Through whom does the moon wax, then wane? This and yet more, O Mazda, I seek to know.
>
> This I ask Thee, tell me truly, Lord. Who has upheld the earth from below, and the heavens from falling? Who [sustains] the waters and plants? Who harnessed swift steeds to winds and clouds?

> This I ask Thee, tell me truly, Lord. What craftsman created light and darkness? What craftsman created both sleep and activity? Through whom exist dawn, noon and eve, which remind the worshipper of his duty? . . .
>
> . . . Who made the son respectful in heed to the father?[9]

It followed that Ahura Mazda was supremely deserving of worship — and in the Zoroastrian creed the religion is in fact called 'the worship of Mazda'.

But if in the beginning Ahura Mazda was the only divine being, he was not the only being. Iranians had always recognised the existence of a principle that was the very negation of *asha* — a principle of falsehood or distortion, a force of disorder, incessantly at work in the world. They called it *druj*, meaning 'falseness', 'the Lie'; and the concept seems to have meant more to them than the corresponding term, *druh*, meant to the Vedic Indians. Zoroaster developed the concept further still: Ahura Mazda had a mighty antagonist in Angra Mainyu, who was the spirit of destruction, of active evil.

In the *Gathas* the prophet has left a summary of this, his central revelation: 'Truly there are two primal spirits, twins renowned to be in conflict. In thought and word, in act they are two: the better and the bad . . .'[10] The words with which, also in the *Gathas*, Ahura Mazda repudiates his great opponent drive the point home: 'Neither our thoughts nor teachings nor wills, neither our choices nor words nor acts, nor our inner selves nor our souls agree.'[11]

In Zoroaster's thought the twin spirits embodied the forces that maintained cosmos and the forces that strove to undermine it. Originally, superhuman and supernatural though they were, they had to make a choice between the two principles. Ahura Mazda, in accordance with his profoundly moral nature, chose to support *asha*, and Angra Mainyu, impelled by his moral perversity, chose to support *druj*. So a struggle began whose vicissitudes constitute the past, present and future of the world.

This reinterpretation of traditional notions had vast implications. For earlier generations the divinely appointed order, though constantly disturbed, had nevertheless been essentially static. This was still true of the Vedic Indians: of the world portrayed in the *Rig Veda* it could still be said that as things have been, they remain. For Zoroaster and his followers, on the contrary, nothing was static. Angra Mainyu's assault on *asha*, Ahura Mazda's defence of *asha*, went on and on, yet they would not go on for ever. The world was a battlefield, the battle was still in progress, but it would have an end.

Time itself was in motion, it was moving forward. In Zoroastrian theological writings a distinction is made between unlimited time, or eternity, on the one hand, and 'limited' or 'bounded' time on the other. The struggle between Ahura Mazda and Angra Mainyu is contained within 'limited time'; its conclusion will mark the end of limited time and the beginning of an eternity of bliss. For in the end Angra Mainyu will be destroyed, *druj* will cease to operate, *asha* will prevail totally and everywhere, cosmos will be rid for ever of the forces of chaos. Thus Ahura Mazda's intention will be accomplished, the divine plan will reach fulfilment. All this simply systematises what is implicit in the thought of the prophet himself.

4

From the very beginning, then, the two spirits stood face to face. But if the two were to wage a cosmic war, they needed allies — and since no possible allies were in existence, that meant that they had to create them. Their antagonism began to express itself actively, in creation and counter-creation.

Ahura Mazda carried out his work as creator through a being who probably derived from the Indo-Iranian artisan-god — the god who appears in the *Rig Veda* under the name of Tvastr and who is known, marginally, to the *Avesta* also. This being was Spenta Mainyu, meaning 'Holy Spirit' — Ahura Mazda's agent, who nevertheless was one with him.

Lord Wisdom started by creating six powerful divine beings to stand at his side — the radiant figures of the prophet's earliest revelation. One of these is *asha*, the names of the others can be translated as Good Thought, Dominion (rightfully exerted), Devotion, Wholeness, Immortality; no doubt they correspond to key concepts in the traditional intellectual culture. Known collectively as *Amesha Spentas* ('Holy Immortals' or 'Bounteous Immortals'), they are all subordinate to Ahura Mazda and act only in accordance with his will.

Zoroastrians have also continued to worship the gods of the traditional Indo-Iranian pantheon, especially such as have a *yasht* dedicated to them in the *Avesta*; though whether Zoroaster himself also numbered these amongst the beings created by Ahura Mazda, or whether they were reintroduced into the religion at a later state, is a matter on which scholars disagree. But there is no dispute about Ahura Mazda's greatest creative act: with the help of the six Holy Immortals, he brought the ordered world into being.

Zoroaster's cosmogony, as embodied in the *Gathas*, was later elaborated and made explicit by generations of Zoroastrian theologians. The result is most fully described in the Pahlavi *Bundahishn* — which, though it reached its final form only in the ninth or tenth century AD, abounds in direct quotations from earlier sources, some of them containing very archaic material indeed.[12]

The original source seems to have been a cosmogonic myth that was established already before Zoroaster, and which must itself have been formed by centuries of reflection in the priestly schools. Its outline can be divined from the *Bundahishn*. It told how the gods created — or rather arranged, organised — the cosmos in seven stages or 'creations'. The first and second 'creations' were of the sky — a huge round shell, made of stone — and of water, which half-filled the shell. Next the earth was brought into being, as a great flat dish floating on the water; and then, in the middle of the earth, a single plant, a single animal (a bull) and a single man. Fire came last, and it took two forms — as visible fire, and as an unseen vital force pervading all the animate 'creations'.

At first the fiery sun stood still overhead: the world was motionless, changeless, held at noontide. The beginning of the moving, changing world we know was determined by the fate of the first bull, the first man and the first plant.

In the beginning the three existed quietly at the centre of the world. The bull — 'the Uniquely-created Bull' — was gigantic, white, bright as the sun; it lived on a river-bank. On the opposite bank stood the man, whose name Gayo-maretan (Pahlavi Gayomard) meant 'Mortal Life'; as broad as he was tall, and as bright as the moon. Change began when both bull and man were sacrificed by the gods; and from their seed came the multiplicity of animals and human beings.[13] As for the plant — imagined as 'moist and milky, without twigs or bark' — the gods pounded it, and from its sap came all plants.

So the cycle of life was set in motion, with death following life and one generation succeeding another. The sun began its regular journeying across the sky, the seasons began to follow their regular course. The ordered world had come into being and — so long as human beings did their part — it would never fail.

The thinkers who elaborated this cosmogony were no doubt more interested in the origins and physical nature of things than in moral and spiritual problems. Zoroaster, on the other hand, was less concerned with the process of creation than with its purpose. When he took over the ancient doctrine he reinterpreted it drastically, to fit his own, profoundly ethical world-view. Again according to the *Bundahishn* — and here its evidence is borne out by Zoroastrian ritual, as it has been preserved down the ages — the prophet placed each of the seven 'creations' under the care of one of the great Holy Immortals: the sky under Dominion, water under Wholeness, the earth under Devotion, plants under Immortality, animals under Good Thought, while man was placed under the care of Ahura Mazda himself, or of his Holy Spirit, and fire was placed under the care of *asha*.

Long before Zoroaster's time, the Indo-Iranians had seen a divinity in fire. For Vedic Indians as for Iranians fire was a major cult-object, to which offerings were made in the daily act of worship. By associating fire with the all-embracing principle of order itself the prophet gave it a still profounder meaning, as the life-force within all the 'creations'. He laid it down that his followers should pray in the presence of fire, fixing their eyes upon it and thinking the while of *asha*, of justice and truth. His words were never forgotten. When, in Achaemenian times, Zoroastrians built their first temples, the place in the sanctuary that in many religions would have been occupied by an image was given over to a sacred, ever-burning fire. And to this day Zoroastrians pray in the presence of fire — whether it be a family praying before a hearth fire, or priests praying before a ritual fire, or any individual before the great natural fires of the sun and moon.

So each of the seven 'creations' was cared for by a Holy Immortal. But 'care' is too vague a term. Each of the great Holy Immortals was virtually identified with his particular 'creation', immanent in it as well as protecting it. For instance, Devotion and the lowly earth were the spiritual and material aspects of one and the same thing; the Holy Spirit, proceeding from the supreme god, was imagined as entering into and inhabiting every righteous person; and the principle of order, justice and truth was present in all fire. The great Holy Immortals had in fact a double significance: they were both personifications of the highest spiritual values and guardians of the physical world, they dwelt on high with Ahura Mazda yet permeated existence on this earth. By conceiving them Zoroaster wove the spiritual and the material together, so that the physical world itself — or rather, whatever was good and wholesome in the physical world — was seen as impregnated with moral purpose and directed by spiritual striving.

Zoroastrian theologians have always taught that Ahura Mazda first made the world in a spiritual, disembodied state, but then transformed it into the material, visible, tangible world we know. This transmutation of the incorporeal into the corporeal was in no sense a fall, a degeneration — it was a completion, a fulfilment: for Zoroastrians to be material is an added good.

The very making of the ordered world had a moral purpose, which was the defeat of Angra Mainyu. It was intended to attract the hostility and destructive fury of that terrible power. By creating it

Ahura Mazda created a setting in which his allies could wage concerted warfare against the forces of chaos, confounding them and in the end reducing them to nothingness; a trap into which Angra Mainyu would fall and where he would wear himself out.[14]

The portion of 'limited time' during which the world is attacked by Angra Mainyu is known as 'the time of mixture'. It is an appropriate term, for the attack was designed from the start to ruin the purity of each of the seven 'creations'. Though the sky was made of 'the hardest stones', the evil spirit pierced it. Then he contaminated the water, so that much of it became salty; and invaded the soil, turning much of it into desert. Even fire, the purest of all created things, he polluted, by mingling smoke with it. Above all he destroyed those 'creations' which were alive — the orginal plant, the orginal animal, the original man.

So the killing that in the traditional teaching had been carried out by the gods as a sacrifice was now carried out by Angra Mainyu, out of sheer malice. But the result was the same: the making of the changing, ongoing world we know. For Ahura Mazda and the Holy Immortals met Angra Mainyu's murderous attack with a massive counter-attack: to replace the single beings he had killed they created a multiplicity of plants and animals and human beings. In other words, the multiplication of living beings, which in the traditional world-view sprang simply from the beneficence of the gods, is now revealed as part of Ahura Mazda's strategy for reducing Angra Mainyu to impotence. And what at first looked like Angra Mainyu's greatest victory is shown to have ended in irreversible defeat.

5

Just as Zoroaster transformed traditional notions about how the world was ordered, so he or his followers transformed traditional notions about what human beings owed to the gods.

Iranian gods — 'the Immortals', 'the Shining Ones', as they were called — were mostly well-disposed towards their worshippers, but they also needed their support. Sacrifice had the same rich significance for Iranians as it had for Vedic Indians. It was a form of hospitality for which a return was expected, but it was not only that. Individuals might worship a god to obtain his favour but — as in Vedic India and in other ancient societies — worship had another, wider purpose: to enable and encourage the gods to act for the common good. Gods and goddesses who were properly worshipped, with eloquent praises and generous sacrifices, were both more inclined and better equipped to maintain *asha*. Fertility and prosperity, morality and fair dealing, victory in war — all these various manifestations of *asha* depended on the exertions of gods who had been propitiated and fortified by the prayers and offerings of human beings.

Sacrifices were regularly offered by each household. The offerings consisted essentially in ingredients representing the vegetable and animal kingdoms — commonly milk, butter, pieces of meat, the sap of plants. There were also daily priestly sacrifices with a highly developed ritual, based on Iranian cosmogony, which — as we have seen — was different from the Vedic. Each day priests re-enacted, symbolically, the original sacrifice by which the gods had established the ordered world. At these services all the 'creations' — stone, water, earth, plants, animals, fire — were represented by objects consecrated by the priest, who himself represented the 'creation' of man. Through these consecrations every aspect of the cosmos was purified and blessed.[15]

As with the Vedic Indians, the place where the sacrifice was made was no temple but a small piece of level ground under the open sky, consecrated by prayers and marked off by a furrow, to exclude the forces of chaos. Each sacrifice was made to a particular deity, who was invoked by name, with proper ritual words and with the abundant praise appropriate to an honoured guest. After the service the meat from the sacrificed animal — which on special occasions might be a horse or bull or cow — was shared between priest and worshippers. The god himself was fortified by the odour of the cooked meat. He was also offered a refreshing drink of milk, pomegranate and *haoma* — for the wonderful plant-cum-priest-cum-god was as central to the Iranian as to the Vedic cult. As a passage in the *Avesta* puts it: 'Even the slightest pressing of *haoma*, even the slightest enjoyment of *haoma*, is enough to destroy a thousand demons.'[16]

Thanks to the steady stream of sacrifices, priestly and individual, the processes that the gods had inaugurated in the beginning would continue endlessly: the sun would always rise, rain would fall, plants would grow, the world would remain habitable for human beings. But for such sacrifices, darkness, drought and wilderness would cover all the earth.

All these traditional obligations were accepted by Zoroaster and gladly taken on by his followers; indeed, they underlie Zoroastrian ritual to this day. But the prophet recognised other, weightier obligations, and these too have continued to be recognised down the ages. Every Zoroastrian knows that amongst all the creatures that Ahura Mazda created to populate the world, human beings carry a uniquely heavy responsibility and have the possibility of rendering a uniquely valuable service.

Just as, in the beginning, the two spirits chose to be respectively good and evil, so each individual must choose between the constructive and destructive values represented by the two spirits. At the very centre of Zoroastrianism is the notion of free choice. Those who choose aright become, after the Holy Immortals and the gods, the most precious of Ahura Mazda's allies in his struggle with Angra Mainyu. The intention of the supreme god is, precisely, that human beings shall be his chief protagonists amongst mortal creatures, upholding *asha*, fighting *druj*. In the cosmic drama they have been allotted the part of a collective saviour: step by step, in collaboration with the divine powers, they are meant to prepare the world for its salvation.[17]

The means by which this is to be done are at once spiritual and material — for, as always in Zoroastrianism, the two are so interwoven as to be indistinguishable. A human being is expected to do everything in his or her power to foster the well-being and prosperity of the world, but also his or her own well-being and prosperity. To do so is itself an affirmation of the highest values, a fulfilment of the supreme religious duty. A passage in the Pahlavi treatise known as *Selected Precepts of the Ancient Sages*, or alternatively as *The Book of the Counsel of Zartusht*, and which is in effect a Zoroastrian catechism, summarising what every boy and girl of fifteen must know before confirmation, illustrates the point nicely: 'Man's first [duty] on earth is to profess the religion and to practise and worship according to it. Second, he should take a wife and beget earthly progeny. He should be diligent in this and not neglectful of it. Third, he should turn the soil into plough-ground and cultivate it. Fourth, he should treat domestic animals properly. Fifth, a third of his days and nights he should attend the priests' school and inquire after the wisdom of just men; a third of his days and nights he should work and create prosperity; and a third of his days and nights he should eat and take pleasure and rest.' Alongside this one may set a passage from the liturgical text known as the *Vendidad*, or *Against the Evil Beings*: 'Who sows grain sows *asha*, and promotes and nurtures the . . . religion with a hundred new dwelling places . . . When the grain is prepared the demons begin to sweat; when milling [or winnowing] is done, the demons howl; when the dough is ready, the demons break wind.'[19]

The first of these passages dates from the Islamic period, the second probably from the late Parthian period, and both are obviously intended not for pastoralists but for settled farmers. Nevertheless, they accord well with the teaching of the prophet himself: already in the *Gathas* the righteous man is he who cherishes and conserves the 'good' creation. In the *Gathas* the righteous man is typically the good herdsman: patient, disciplined, brave, he is ever on the alert to defend the 'good' creation against the predators, animal and human, that menace its well-being.[20] Cattle-herding is in fact treated as a model for ethical behaviour in general, and the good herdsman occupies a place very similar to that of the good shepherd in the Bible.

There is another way in which a Zoroastrian is expected to assist Ahura Mazda: by the strict observance of a number of laws of purity. These involve much attention to personal cleanliness, and they also include a number of ritual requirements. Their common purpose is to strengthen the ordered world — Ahura Mazda's 'good' creation — and to weaken the forces of chaos, embodied in Angra Mainyu's counter-creation. This can be achieved only by keeping the two rigorously apart. A corpse, for instance, represents a victory for Angra Mainyu, and if it is permitted to come into contact with any part of the 'good' creation will tend to undermine the whole. Anyone who allows a dead body to touch earth or water thereby encourages drought in summer and deep snow in winter — disasters that in turn kill the 'good' cattle. The same is believed of dirt, rust, mould, blight and also of anything that issues from the human body — not only excrement but dead skin, cut nails, shorn hair, above all blood. In the Pahlavi books animal species that are harmful to human beings — insects such as ants, beetles, locusts, reptiles such as scorpions, lizards and snakes, beasts of prey such as wolves — are likewise labelled as instruments of Angra Mainyu, brought into being to serve as his allies in his struggle to impair the ordered world.[21] It is the duty of a Zoroastrian to destroy such creatures.

These elaborations on the prophet's dualistic doctrine may well have been formulated quite early in the history of the religion. Thanks to them Zoroastrians stood, from the beginning, in a very different relationship to cosmos from other peoples in the ancient world, save only for the Jews. In other societies people might strive, by their offerings and by their general behaviour, to assist the priests in sustaining the order of the world; but a Zoroastrian was more constantly and directly involved. His or her obligations permeated the whole of life. On the one hand this represented a democratisation: all members of the community took part, through the ordinary tasks of everyday life, in sustaining and strengthening the ordered world — indeed, they were all engaged in preparing the way for that final consummation when the world would be made perfect. On the other hand the rules regarding daily living, which proliferated down the centuries, set a barrier between Zoroastrians and other people: again like the Jews, Zoroastrians were a people apart.

6

Ahura Mazda had other important allies among the mortal creatures that he brought into existence. Though not as explicitly sanctified as in Vedic India, cattle were valued as an integral part of the community, along with human beings. In Zoroaster's eyes the maternal, mild-natured, nutritive cow was the supreme representative of the 'good' animals on which human life depends. And that was not all: the cow and ox — just like the sheep or lamb in the Bible — could easily be made into symbols of persecuted goodness. While the devout and regular sacrifice of a bull or cow was approved by the prophet, as it had been by proto-Indo-Iranians and still was by Vedic Indians, he was outraged by the way bands of cattle-raiders would seize whole herds and drive them from their green pastures, to be either used as draught animals or else slaughtered and eaten. He saw himself as the champion of these cattle-victims. A whole *Gatha* is devoted to the plight of the cow, defenceless in a world given over to violence. When the 'soul of the cow' appeals to Ahura Mazda for succour the reply is that the only effective help must come from Zoroaster.[22]

Dogs too are valuable allies. In the long ages before the horse was domesticated the pastoralists relied on dogs for herding — and the deep respect they acquired for these loyal and affectionate animals passed into Zoroastrian teaching. There was much oral literature about dogs; a surviving fragment — a chapter of the *Vendidad* — describes how the herdsman's dog, being a creature of the Holy Spirit, spends every night killing the creatures of the Evil Spirit and warning against those plagues of the pastoral life, wolves.[23] Still today Zoroastrians not only regard the dog as a righteous creature, they hold a dog's gaze to be purifying, a power that drives away demons. At a Zoroastrian funeral, for instance, a dog has to be present, to purify the corpse with its gaze and so strengthen the 'good' creation. But indeed all animals that are helpful to man are perceived as helpful also to Ahura Mazda in his struggle with Angra Mainyu. In return, all such creatures are deserving of considerate treatment.

Then there were the *fravashis* — who may have been the spirits of dead Zoroastrian heroes but may also have been simply the spirits of the ancestors; in any case they acted as guardians of the living. They were imagined as winged warriors, female like the Valkyries, living and very potent. We hear how tens of thousands of *fravashis* would advance, 'seeking each to obtain water for her own family, for her own village, for her own tribe, for her own country'. They were invoked in time of war, and not in vain: 'Then when a powerful ruler of the land is threatened by hostile foes, he calls on them, the powerful *fravashis* of the just. They shall come to help . . . ; they are made to fly down to him like well-winged birds. They serve him as weapon and arms . . .' And they exerted themselves to ensure the continuance of the people: 'It is by their splendour and glory that females conceive children . . . give birth easily, have a wealth of children.'[24]

Fravashis are numbered amongst the divine beings who sustain and strengthen *asha*. There exists a hymn in which Ahura Mazda himself pays tribute to them, as indispensable allies. But for the intervention of the mighty souls of the just, he says, all power would have passed to *druj*; Angra Mainyu would have conquered everything on earth — and once established, he would never have yielded up his rule.[25]

For Angra Mainyu too had mighty allies. Iranians had always felt themselves to be surrounded by demons, and in the *Avesta* the demonic host is interpreted as constituting the host of the Evil Spirit.[26] The *Gathas* tell how in the beginning the demons chose to ally themselves with Angra Mainyu, with the result that they 'rushed into Fury, with which they have afflicted the world and mankind'.[27] Above all, demons seduced people into worshipping them, and they were still doing so. Zoroaster certainly knew of a cult devoted to certain demons, and he was appalled. A cult designed to placate and propitiate the maleficent powers at work in the world would have appealed to very many people who were plagued by the hazards and miseries of life — but in the eyes of Zoroaster and his followers it could only be a negation of all that Ahura Mazda intended for his good world.

The number of demons was vast, and all were intent on assisting Angra Mainyu in his efforts to ruin the 'good' world of Ahura Mazda's making. Whatever harmed cattle or blighted crops was personified as a demon. The natural environment was full of demons. The wilderness beyond the limits of the settlement and the grazing ground was a place of dread, not to be entered on pain of death. In the darkness of the night, too, demons flourished. It was only the rising of the sun that prevented them from destroying everything in the world, so that not even the gods would find a place to stay.

Demonic too were all those tendencies in human beings — such as wrath, envy, sloth — that lured them to offend against the principle of order. So was everything that assaulted a person in his or her body: old age, sickness, hunger and thirst were all imagined as demons striving relentlessly to impede the operation of *asha*. Above all, death was a triumph for the demons. A frightful she-demon called Nasu settled on a corpse at the moment of death, and other demons with names meaning 'he who binds the body', 'he who drags the body away', clustered around. It would be a mistake to interpret these demonic operations in terms of modern notions of health or hygiene — they were incidents in Angra Mainyu's assault on the 'good' creation. That is why only the corpse of a righteous Zoroastrian suffered in this way — the corpse of a servant of *druj* was immune, for such a person had no place in Ahura Mazda's realm.[28]

The laws of purity were regarded as safeguards against the demonic hosts. The *Vendidad* details the precautions one must take after cutting one's nails. One must bury the scraps while uttering a magic spell, and trace a furrow nine times around the spot. Then one must dedicate the scraps to the owl, as the bird beloved of *asha*, so that it can use them as darts and arrows against the demons. Otherwise they will fall into the grasp of the demons themselves, to become their darts and arrows.

At least the more important of the demons were known as *daevas*. Traditionally the term had been applied to all divine beings indiscriminately, but for Zoroaster, and for Zoroastrians ever since, *daevas* were negative counterparts of the Holy Immortals. Just as these were dedicated to the maintenance of *asha*, so the *daevas* were dedicated to its ruination. *Yasht* 13 describes how formerly the *daevas* were even able to block the movement of the heavely bodies: 'the stars, the moon, the sun and the lights formerly stood motionless at the same place, because of the hostility of the *daevas*, because of the attacks of the *daevas*'.[29] That machination was thwarted by the *fravashis* — but at other times it is Mithra who, borne on his chariot, and armed with bows and arrows and his great mace, puts the *daevas* to flight.

The *Gathas* do not name any *daevas*, but the *Vendidad*, which names a host of demons, singles out five as particularly powerful and sinister: Indra, Saurva, Nanghaithya, Taurvi and Zairi.[30] Scholars disagree as to what these demons represented. The fact that two of them have names that correspond with names of Vedic deities has led some scholars to postulate a conflict between Iranians and Indo-Aryans for the land of Iran, in the course of which the Iranians came to see the gods of the enemy as demons.[31] Other scholars have argued that the demonised gods were not of Indo-Aryan but of proto-Indo-Iranian origin — that they were in fact the gods particularly revered by cattle-stealing warriors amongst the Iranians themselves.[32] However, the passage in the *Vendidad* in which these demons figure, combined with the comments that the *Bundahishn* and the *Dinkard* make on those same demons, suggests a different interpretation.

In the *Vendidad* the five arch-demons appear in an exorcism designed to accompany the ritual cleansing of a person who has been contaminated, for instance by contact with a corpse. The intention is to drive all five away 'from this house, from this borough, from this town, from the very body of the man defiled by the dead, from the very body of the woman defiled by the dead; from the master of the house, from the lord of the borough, from the lord of the town, from the lord of the land; from the whole body of the holy world'.

The *Bundahishn* has more to tell. There Saurva is presented as the demon who encourages anarchy and drunkenness, and seduces Zoroastrians into rejecting the sacred shirt and girdle that are an inseparable part of their attire. Taurvi and Zairi are demons who introduce poison into plants and animals, and so cause drought and famine; they also seduce Zoroastrians into walking barefoot or inadequately shod. Except etymologically, Nanghaithya seems to have had nothing in common with Vedic Nasatya, which was another name for the Asvins, those twin gods of daybreak and daylight who so frustrated the demons who prowl at night. Nanghaithya, on the contrary, seems to have been a demon of death. As for the chief of the band, there is no reason to doubt he is the same Indra as we meet in the *Rig Veda*, changed from a mighty god into an equally mighty demon. In the *Dinkard* he is described as the spirit of disobedience and apostasy, who leads Zoroastrians away from the path of right conduct. He is in fact a personification of *druj* — which makes it wholly appropriate that the Holy Immortal who is to destroy him at the great consummation should be Asha Vashishta, who is the personification of *asha*.[33] How the helpful, beneficent Indra came to be perceived in such a negative way will be considered in the next chapter.

To sum up: the references in the *Vendidad*, the *Bundahishn* and the *Dinkard* show that the great *daevas* were supreme embodiments of the forces of chaos, second in destructiveness and deadliness only to their creator and commander, Angra Mainyu (or, as he came to be called, Ahriman) himself.

7

Zoroastrian tradition holds that the thinking, and the revelations, that led the prophet to his novel interpretation of existence belong to the earlier part of his life, before he established himself at Vishtaspa's court. There is no reason to doubt the soundness of the tradition: Zoroaster's world-view clearly was coloured by his own experience at a time when he was himself in a defenceless position and was kept constantly aware of what was happening to other defenceless people.

Zoroaster was a fully qualified priest of the traditional religion, but he must have started life as a poor man — and one who suffered greatly under his poverty and the powerlessness that went with poverty. In the *Gathas* he appeals to Ahura Mazda for material succour: 'I know why I am powerless, Mazda; I possess few cattle and few men. I lament to thee.' — 'Who is found as protector for my cattle, who for myself . . . ?'[34] The cow joins in lamenting the powerlessness of her protector — 'a man without strength, whereas I wished for one ruling with power.' 'When shall one ever appear who will give him effective help?'[35] asks the cow, while Zoroaster himself makes a precise request: 'This I ask thee, tell me truly, Lord, how shall I gain that reward, namely ten mares and a camel . . . ?'[36] That, however, is not the heart of the matter. Underlying the interpretation that Zoroaster gives to the age-old concepts of *asha* and *druj* is an acute sense of a relatively peaceful social order threatened by aggression from outside. He evidently knew two kinds of tribes. There were tribes which lived mainly from their cattle and sought nothing but good pastures. And there were tribes which were true war-bands, ruthless, delighting in violence, eager to despoil and kill peaceable herdsmen. The prophet identified with the former, abominated the latter.[37]

There are in fact good grounds for thinking that the *Gathas* were composed while a society which had existed almost unchangingly for centuries, and which had never possessed very destructive weaponry, was coming into conflict with, and was being replaced by, a society of a new kind — more warlike and better equipped for war. Early in the second millennium groups of young Indo-Aryans went down through the passes of the Caucasus to the rich kingdoms in the south, to become mercenaries in the armies of warring princes. There they became acquainted with the chariot warfare that was to transform the art of combat throughout the eastern Mediterranean. Some of these Indo-Aryans stayed permanently in distant lands — but others returned to the steppes as professional warriors, bringing with them their chariots and their new fighting skills. For these adventurous and ruthless men the old tribal way of life, with its customs and its customary law, no longer had much meaning. Alongside traditional tribes headed by tribal councils there appeared warrior-bands headed by warrior-chieftains, and devoted less to cattle-rearing than to cattle-raiding.[38]

From the evidence of the *Gathas* (including linguistic evidence) it has been convincingly argued that originally proto-Indo-Iranian society, and the Indo-Aryan and Iranian societies that succeeded it, had no class of professional warriors: all adult males except priests were herdsmen.[39] Of course the tribes sometimes fought one another over disputed grazing grounds, but their campaigns can hardly have been more than skirmishes. It was a different matter when professional warriors appeared. Chariots enabled chieftains and their bands of retainers to raid tribal settlements over wide areas, carry off whole herds of cattle, kill human beings on a scale previously inconceivable. And if this way of life was first introduced to the steppes by returning Indo-Aryans, it did not long remain their monopoly. If only to defend themselves, Iranian tribes in their turn had to master chariotry and a new kind of tactics. Life on the steppes changed utterly as it passed into a typical 'heroic age', turbulent, restless, with military prowess as its highest value and the seizing of booty as its highest aim.[40]

The *Gathas* certainly seem to reflect the tensions and miseries of a time when this new way of life was establishing itself. In these hymns, just as the conscientious herdsman is presented as the righteous man *par excellence*, so the wicked man *par excellence* is the man who acquires fame and fortune by stealing cattle: 'Those wicked ones who appear in grandeur as lords and ladies, they too have ruined life, stealing the property of the [rightful] inheritor . . . Mazda declared ill things for them who with [their] habit of pleasure have ruined the life of the cow . . .'[41] These people are strengtheners of *druj*, upholders of what is false, agents of chaos. They are 'those who with ill purpose increase with their tongues fury and cruelty, they the non-pastors among pastors, for whom evil deeds prevailed, they having no good deeds, they serve the *Daevas*, which is the religion of the wicked man'.[42] There is no reason to doubt that the chief of those *daevas* was the warrior-god Indra. Zoroaster permitted no mercy to these 'followers of the Lie': they must be defeated and killed.[43]

The message does not seem to have evoked much response, or gained the prophet much of a following, in his homeland. He moved elsewhere — and the people amongst whom he settled must have included professional warriors, since they were able to wage and win wars in defence of the new faith. Nor did he remain a poor, defenceless man. In his new home he converted first the ruler's wife and then the ruler; was accorded every honour; and married into a powerful family. All this is to be found in Zoroastrian tradition, and it has been accepted by most modern scholars.

Zoroaster's historical significance is not affected by the prosperity that eventually came his way. He is the earliest known example of a particular kind of prophet — the kind commonly called 'millenarian' — and the experiences that determined the content of his teaching seem also to have been typical. Prophets who promise a total transformation of existence, a total perfecting of the world, often draw their original inspiration from the spectacle not simply of suffering but of one particular kind of suffering: that engendered by the destruction of an ancient way of life, with its familiar certainties and safeguards.[44] Zoroaster would seem to have been just such a prophet.

8

Zoroastrian teachings both about the state of individuals after death and about the state of the world after the end of 'limited time' were revolutionary in their day. Hints of those teachings are contained in the *Gathas* themselves, but for a full account one must turn, again, to the *Bundahishn*. When one reflects that the relevant passages are translations of lost Avestan material dating from the middle of the first millennium BC, if not earlier, they are startling indeed.[45]

Before Zoroaster's time beliefs about the afterlife had developed amongst the Iranians in much the same way as amongst the Vedic Indians. At first it was believed that all the dead led a bleak and shadowy existence beneath the earth. Later it came to be believed that a few select individuals — princes and warriors and priests who had observed all the requirements of *asha* and been generous in their offerings to the gods — would dwell after death in a paradise in the sky, enjoying sun and light and every pleasure of the senses. The fate of each individual was decided at a bridge over an abyss: only the souls of a privileged few would be able to cross it, the rest would plunge straight down into the joyless and comfortless netherworld.[46]

The prophet took over the notion of the bridge but gave it a new moral content. In his teaching all human beings — women as well as men, the lowly as well as the privileged — may hope to attain heaven; the one indispensable qualification is ethical achievement — naturally, in Zoroastrian terms. At the bridge each individual's thoughts and words and deeds, from the age of fifteen onwards, are weighed against one another. If those which accord with Zoroastrian notions of goodness weigh heavier, he or she goes to 'the luminous mansions of the sky', to dwell in the presence of Ahura Mazda and the Holy Immortals. If, on the contrary, evil thoughts and words and deeds weigh heavier, he or she goes to the netherworld. And already in the *Gathas* the netherworld has acquired a new meaning: it is the abode of the Lie, the proper realm of Angra Mainyu. It is also a place of punishment where, in darkness, amidst cries of woe, with the foulest food for nourishment, the souls of the damned are tormented. In a word, the netherworld has turned into hell: that notion too seems to have been an innovation of Zoroaster's.

Zoroaster seems to have modified traditional notions in another respect. Before him it had been believed that the few privileged souls who went to heaven were reunited, after the lapse of a year, with their bodies, changed into immortal flesh. The *Gathas* suggest that the prophet would have none of this. For him, apparently, heaven was populated by disembodied souls. At the end of 'limited time', on the other hand, there was to be a universal bodily resurrection.

The men who composed the Avestan material knew well enough that universal bodily resurrection would seem incredible to many, and they supplied a splendidly poetic response. 'From where', they make Zoroaster ask, 'shall the body be reassembled which the wind has blown away, and the water carried off? And how shall the resurrection take place?' Ahura Mazda replies: 'When I created the earth which bears all physical life . . . ; and when I created corn, that it might be scattered in the earth and grow again, giving back increase . . . ; and when I created the cloud, which bears water for the world and rains it down when it chooses; and when I created the wind . . . which blows as it pleases — then the creation of each of these was more difficult for me than the raising of the dead. For . . . consider, if I made that which is not, why cannot I make again that which was?'[47] Just as much as his original creation, the resurrection of the dead was to be a miraculous work of Ahura Mazda's, carried out as part of his plan for the perfecting of all things.

When the beginning of the cosmic struggle was revealed to Zoroaster, so was its outcome. At the end of 'limited time' — which will also be the end of 'the time of mixture' — the world is to undergo a sort of ordeal, through which it will be purged of all evil, including the wicked dead. All human beings who have ever lived will come together in a great assembly, where every individual will be confronted with his good and evil deeds, and the saved will be distinguished from the damned as clearly as a white sheep is from a black. Then Fire and the Spirit of Healing will together melt the metal in hills and mountains, the earth will be covered by a great stream of molten metal, and everyone will have to pass through the stream. To the righteous it will be like walking in warm milk, only the wicked will know that they are indeed in molten metal.[48]

In this notion Zoroaster probably fused tales of volcanic eruptions and streams of molten lava with his knowledge of a particular tribal practice. An accused person could be subjected to an ordeal in which molten copper was poured on to his breast; if he was innocent, the divine powers would intervene to save him, if guilty he would perish then and there.[49] The purpose of the universal ordeal at the end of 'limited time' was analogous: the wicked were to be destroyed in the molten metal. Zoroaster says as much in one of his hymns: 'That requital which Thou wilt assign to the two parties, O Mazda, by Thy bright blazing fire and molten metal, is a sign to be given among all living beings, to destroy the wicked man, to save the just...'[50] Admittedly, in latter-day Zoroastrian teaching the fiery flood is presented simply as a purgation: the wicked are to have their sins burned away, so that they become fit to join the righteous. But it seems that that interpretation was first thought of some two thousand years after Zoroaster's time. To the prophet such leniency would surely have been unimaginable.

Whereas the wicked dead will exchange their wretched sojourn in hell for an agonising annihilation, the righteous dead will exchange their blissful existence as disembodied souls in heaven for an incomparably more blissful existence on earth. More blissful because less one-sided: once more endowed with bodies, they will be able to experience the joys of the senses as well as those of the spirit.

The *Bundahishn* tells how existence will be utterly transformed. The divine beings whom Ahura Mazda created to be his allies, the Holy Immortals, will win a final victory over the forces created by Angra Mainyu. The truly spoken word will overcome the falsely spoken word. Wholeness and Immortality will defeat hunger and thirst. In every way *asha* will triumph over *druj*, the order intended by the supreme god will prevail against everything that would negate it. Finally Ahura Mazda himself will come to the world as celebrating priest, to perform one last sacrifice. All the righteous will partake of the fat of the fabulous bull and the supernatural 'white haoma' offered in that sacrifice, and as a result their bodies will become not only immortal but eternally young: those who have reached maturity will remain for ever as if they were forty years old, the bodies of the young will remain fixed at fifteen. So Angra Mainyu's seeming victory over that wonderful 'creation', man, will be undone.

Ahura Mazda's good world will be purified of all the evil that Angra Mainyu introduced into it. Angra Mainyu himself, 'helpless and with his power destroyed, will rush back to shadowy darkness through that way by which he entered. And the molten metal will flow into hell; and the stench and filth in the earth, where hell was, will be burnt by that metal, and it will become clean. The gap through which the Evil Spirit had entered will be closed by that metal...'[51]

The very appearance of the world will change. The earth will be flattened by the fiery flood, so that its surface will be a single level plain: the snow-covered mountains of Iran — first thrown up as a result of Angra Mainyu's onslaught — will be no more. In this perfect environment the surviving human beings will live in the most perfect harmony with one another. Husbands and wives and children, including of course the resurrected dead, will be re-united and will live together as they do in this present world — except that there will be no more begetting of children. All mankind will form a single community of devout Zoroastrians, all united in adoration of Ahura Mazda and the Holy Immortals, and all at one in thought, word and deed.

The great transformation is called 'the making wonderful' (*Frashokereti* in Avestan, *Frashegird* in Pahlavi); while in the Pahlavi books the eternity that is to follow it is called 'separation', to indicate the contrast with 'the time of mixture'. It is a promise which, however remote its fulfilment, has always meant a great deal to Zoroastrians. Each year the coming state of bliss is prefigured in the New Year festival called Nō Rōz: held at the spring equinox, this is experienced as a rebirth of nature and of society and of individuals, a making new of the world.

The 'making wonderful' will indeed change everything. What lies ahead, at the end of time, is a state from which every imperfection will have been eliminated; a world where everyone will live for ever in a peace that nothing could disturb; an eternity when history will have ceased and nothing more can happen; a changeless realm, over which the supreme god will reign with an authority which will be unchallenged for evermore.

9

How soon, when Zoroaster first foretold 'the making wonderful', did he expect that great consummation to come about? Certainly, in the near future. Admittedly, he cannot always have felt that all his contemporaries would live to see it, otherwise he would hardly have concerned himself with the fates awaiting those who died while the world was in its present condition — their adventures at the fateful bridge, their sojourn in heaven, hell or limbo. But the *Gathas* do convey a great sense of urgency. There is no mistaking the conviction that drove the prophet on: he clearly believed that he had been sent by Ahura Mazda at that particular moment to urge human beings to align themselves with the right side at once, in the short time remaining before the transformation of the world. In one passage he even seems to be asking the supreme god to permit him and his followers to take part in 'the making wonderful'.[52]

But Zoroaster died, his figure began to fade into the past, and still the world was not transformed. The first generations of Zoroastrians must have been as bitterly disappointed as the early Christians were to be, a thousand years later. Subsequent generations consoled themselves in ways that also recall the development of Christian belief. They came to see their prophet as a world-saviour sent by the supreme god — and they also elaborated the notion of a future saviour, in whom Zoroaster would be, as it were, reincarnated, and who would complete his work.

A nativity myth developed. It was said that when the time for Zoroaster's birth drew near Ahura Mazda created the prophet's fiery glory and sent it on its way, via the worlds of endless light, and the sun, and the moon, and the stars (imagined of course as nearer to the earth than the sun and moon), and the fire of the house of the prophet's grandparents, and so into the body of his grandmother, who thereupon gave birth to his mother — a child with a body as radiant as fire. Then, as though to set the prophet still further apart from the rest of mankind, Ahura Mazda instructed the Holy Immortals to place his soul in a miraculous haoma-stalk and his future body in the milk of miraculous cows. As in the age-old rite of sacrifice, Zoroaster's father mixed the haoma and the milk together and consecrated the mixture to Ahura Mazda; after which he and his wife drank it. Now the prophet could be conceived, in the certainty that he would come into the world filled with divine power, a unique embodiment of *asha*. And at his birth the whole 'good' creation rejoiced, while the demons, foreseeing their defeat, strove frantically to destroy the baby. They strove in vain: Zoroaster's coming represented a direct intervention by the supreme god in world history, and ensured the eventual fulfilment of the divine plan.[53]

As for the future saviour, the *Gathas* themselves gave a useful hint; for the prophet, when cast down by the thought that he might not live to see 'the making wonderful', had found consolation in imagining 'one greater than good' who would come after him.[54] On the basis of this hint the prodigious figure of the Saoshyant — meaning literally 'future benefactor' — was constructed.[55]

The coming of the Saoshyant will be preceded by a time when, so far from *asha* triumphing over *druj*, the triumph of *druj* over *asha* seems assured. Those days are described in a prophecy supposedly addressed to Zoroaster by Ahura Mazda himself: 'In that time . . . all men will become deceivers, and great covenants will be altered. Honour and affection and love for the soul will depart from the world. . . . The sun's rays will be very level and low-slanting, and year and month and day will be shorter. And the earth . . . will contract. . . . And people will be born very stunted, and will have little skill or energy. It will not be possible for an auspicious cloud and a just wind to bring rain at its due time and season. Sullen clouds will darken the whole sky. A hot wind and a cold wind will come and carry off all the fruits and grains of corn. The rain will not fall at its due time, and it will rain noxious creatures rather than water. And the water of the rivers and springs will shrink and have no increase. . . . Camel and ox and sheep will be born much smaller and less sturdy. . . . The draught-ox will have small strength, and the swift horse will have little power and be able to gallop but a small way. . . . That Evil Spirit will be very oppressive and tyrannical, then when it becomes needful to destroy him.'[56] The coming of the Saoshyant will launch that needful destruction.

The Saoshyant's birth will be even more miraculous than Zoroaster's. The prophet's seed, it is said, is preserved in a lake in south-eastern Iran, where it is watched over by 99,999 souls of the righteous dead. As 'limited time' draws to its tormented close a virgin called Vispa-taurari (meaning 'she who conquers all') will bathe in the lake, become pregnant with the prophet's seed, and bear his son Asvat-ereta (meaning 'he who embodies truth'). Asvat-ereta is the Saoshyant, and he will play the central role in every phase of the eschatological drama. He will wield the 'victorious weapon' with which Zoroaster's royal patron Vishtaspa once defended the faith against its foes — and with which still earlier, legendary heroes in the Iranian past slew the monsters and ogres of their day. And grouped around him will be certain 'deathless chieftains' — mighty warriors who once led the Iranian peoples in war, and who ever since have been waiting in remote places for the summons to the final battle; pre-eminent among these will be one of Vishtaspa's sons, the commander of the earliest Zoroastrian army. Alongside these comrades in arms, all of them 'thinking well, speaking well, acting well, of good conscience', Ahura Mazda's supernatural allies, the great Holy Immortals, will advance against Angra Mainyu and his hosts.

That is not all. For fifty-seven years before 'the making wonderful' the Saoshyant will be resurrecting the dead and giving them back their bodies; he will also assemble dead and living for the fiery ordeal. According to some versions he will even take over from Ahura Mazda the task of bestowing immortality on the righteous. Finally, by gazing on the world he will make it immortal and incorruptible — thereby completing 'the making wonderful', the final triumph of cosmos over chaos.

The prophecy about the Saoshyant is very ancient — it certainly antedates the Achaemenian era, and may well date back almost to Zoroaster's time. But its appeal has proved perennial: it has helped generation after generation of Zoroastrians, through all the misfortunes that befell them, to keep alive their faith in the eventual perfecting of the world. Indeed, belief in the coming of the Saoshyant has flourished on misfortune. There is evidence to suggest that it was clung to most tenaciously at the very times when the Zoroastrian community has suffered its greatest disasters — after Alexander's conquest, and again after the Arab conquest. It was a vital factor in sustaining Zoroastrians in their faith when they were being persecuted by their Muslim rulers; and latterly it has flourished more among the oppressed Zoroastrians in Iran than among their more fortunate brethren, the Parsis of India.[57]

But if expectation of a single *saoshyant*, whose coming will make all things perfect once and for all, has always bulked large in popular Zoroastrianism, Zoroastrianism as a state religion embedded that simple hope in a most complicated body of doctrine.

10

In the sixth century BC Zoroastrianism became the religion of the first Iranian empire. Whether or not it was adopted already by the founder of that empire, Cyrus the Great (549–529), there can be no doubt about his successors. Inscriptions on the tombs of Darius the Great (522–486), Xerxes (486–465) and Artaxerxes I (465–424) bear witness to the unchanging nature of the dynastic faith. But indeed every Achaemenian monarch saw himself as Lord Wisdom's representative on earth.

However, not everything in the religion of the *Gathas* was appropriate to a state religion. An institution endowed not only with great spiritual authority but also with great temporal power, possessed of temples, shrines and vast estates, served by a numerous priesthood, could hardly be impatient for a total transformation of the world. On the contrary, if Zoroastrianism was to function effectively as the dominant religion of a triumphant, firmly established empire, it was imperative that Zoroastrian eschatology should be modified. 'The making wonderful' had to be postponed, officially and definitively, to a remote future.

The necessary revision was achieved, not later than the first half of the fourth century BC, by certain scholar-priests who had abandoned orthodox Zoroastrianism in favour of the heresy known as Zurvanism.[58] This version of the religion, which was adopted by the later Achaemenian monarchs and again by the Sasanians, easily accommodated a scheme of successive world-ages. In that scheme, which was influenced by the speculations of Babylonian astronomers about the 'great year', 'limited time' was divided into a number of equal periods. In one of the versions that have come down to us the totality of 'limited time' comprises 9000 years, divided into three periods of 3000 years each; in another, it comprises 12,000 years, divided into four periods. But in the original version it was probably fixed at 6000 years; and even in the 9000- and 12,000-year versions, the last 6000 years include everything that happens on this earth.

According to the *Bundahishn*, which expounds the full 12,000-year scheme, the first 3000 years are occupied by preparations for the cosmic struggle. The supreme god — now called Ormazd — becomes aware of the Evil Spirit — now called Ahriman — and his destructive intentions, and brings his good world into being in a purely spiritual state. Ahriman responds by attacking the good world and, having failed, plunges back into his native darkness, where he creates the *daevas* as allies. During the next 3000 years Ormazd transforms his spiritual creation into a material one; and at the end of the period Ahriman attacks that — with more success, since he is able to introduce death, disease and destructiveness into it. Ormazd has however long since taken his counter-measure by creating the soul of Zoroaster; and after existing for 6000 years in a spiritual state this soul is given a body. In the year 9000 Zoroaster receives the revelation of the one true religion.

The remaining 3000 years of 'limited time' witness the final struggle, which is predestined to end with 'the making wonderful'. However, this concluding period is itself divided into three periods of a thousand years, each terminating with the appearance of a new saviour: the Saoshyant is triplicated. The full legend, as told for instance in the *Dinkard*, tells how the prophet, when approaching his third wife, three times spilled his semen on the ground. Instead of one lot of semen, three lots lie at the bottom of the lake — even now they can be seen glowing there, like lamps. Instead of one predestined virgin, three such will bathe there, one before the end of each millennium. And each of the three sons of Zoroaster who will be so conceived will have a redemptive task. By the end of each millennium, Zoroastrian teaching will have fallen into neglect; it is for each *saoshyant* in turn to give it new life — until the last-born, the supreme Saoshyant Asvat-ereta, brings about 'the making wonderful'.

In this scheme of world history the present moment had its place: it could only be some time before the appearance of the first *saoshyant*. But that meant that 'the making wonderful', which Zoroaster had expected to take place in his lifetime or shortly after it, and which later generations of Zoroastrians had still awaited with impatience, lost all immediacy. Between the time when Zoroastrianism first became a state religion and the final transformation of the world there was set a comfortable interval of more than 2000 years. Whatever their intentions may have been, and however purely philosophical their interests, the Zoroastrian priests had done something that had social and political implications: they had modified the prophet's original message in such a way that Achaemenian monarchs, and after them Parthian and Sasanian monarchs, could find in it an ideology perfectly suited to their needs.

In fact Zoroastrianism as the religion of the royal dynasties of Iran functioned in very much the same way as the religions of the royal houses of other Near Eastern lands.[59] This is shown, for instance, by the inscriptions in which Darius the Great recorded his aims and achievements. Darius was convinced that he had been appointed by Ahuramazda (as Lord Wisdom was called at that time) to rule an empire that was itself a manifestation of *asha*: 'Ahuramazda when he saw this earth in commotion, thereafter he bestowed it on me, he made me king. I am king. By the grace of Ahuramazda I set it in its place.' Evils of every kind — famine, injustice, oppression within the community, but also hostile powers and their armies, and any opposition to his own rule — all these were the work of the Lie, *drauga* (formerly *druj*). Darius called on Ahuramazda for help in defending the land against *drauga*. He also exhorted his successor: 'Thou shalt be king hereafter, protect thyself vigorously from *drauga*.'[60] And some thousand years after Darius a king of the Sasanian dynasty still saw his task as maintaining *asha* in its present state: '. . . I have sought the course of action most pleasing to God, and have found that it consists in that whereby sky and earth continue to exist, the mountains remain immovable, the rivers flow, the earth is kept pure; that is to say, in equity and justice'.[61]

As we have seen, all this can be matched by the pronouncements of Egyptian pharaohs and Near Eastern kings — monarchs who saw the divinely appointed order as constantly impaired and threatened yet essentially unchanging, and who could never have imagined a future consummation that would utterly transform the world.

But Zoroaster's proclamation lived on, and continued to exert its fascination, in circles far removed from courts and kings.

CHAPTER 5

From Combat Myth to Apocalyptic Faith

At the heart of Zoroaster's teaching is a sense of cosmic war: a conviction that a mighty spiritual power intent on maintaining and furthering life in an ordered world is locked in struggle with a spiritual power, scarcely less mighty, intent on destroying life and reducing the ordered world to chaos. Had this world-view a prehistory amongst the Iranians? Is it perhaps a novel version — thoroughly intellectualised and spiritualised — of the combat myth? Unfortunately, no god comparable with Indra figures in the *Avesta*, nor any combat comparable with Indra's fight with Vritra; and this silence has led even very eminent scholars to dismiss the possibility.[1] But the matter is of such importance to the argument of this book that it cannot be left there: one must look further afield.

From *c.*4500 to *c.*2500 the proto-Indo-Europeans, it seems, were living somewhere on the steppes of southern Russia, but by the second half of the third millennium various peoples were emerging amongst their descendants — peoples with distinctive identities and speaking languages which, though related, were also distinctive. These peoples were also moving further and further away from the original Indo-European homeland. The proto-Indo-Iranians and their descendants the Indo-Aryans and Iranians constituted only one branch of a mighty tree that was to spread its branches until they extended from the Indus valley to Scandinavia. And in Scandinavia one finds not only the combat myth but even a god whose kinship with Indra is unmistakable: Thor.

Most of what we know about Thor comes from an Icelandic text, the *Prose Edda*, which was composed by Snorri Sturluson in the early thirteenth century.[2] The late date, and the fact that by then Iceland had been Christian for more than two centuries, might make the *Prose Edda* a suspect source for ancient pagan beliefs — except that it can be shown to incorporate very ancient traditions: its cosmogony, for instance, is practically identical with one of the Vedic cosmogonies.

What the *Prose Edda* has to tell of Thor likewise derives from ancient traditions. The very name Thor — meaning 'thunder' — suggests that he was related to a lost proto-Indo-European god — for its German version, Donar, is clearly related to Tanaris, which was the name of the Celtic god of thunder and of war. In fact both names are derived from a common root, which is also to be found in the Latin, Greek and Sanskrit words for 'thunder'. However late the literary sources, when we approach Thor we are peering into the mists of a very remote past indeed.

In Scandinavia Thor increased in importance down the centuries, until he became the central figure in the Nordic pantheon, rivalling and even surpassing Odin, and presiding over every aspect of life. In the Viking period he was the most popular of the gods. His name was to be found embedded both in place-names and in the names of individuals, as a theophoric element. And wherever the Vikings went his cult went too: it flourished not only in the Scandinavian lands but in Dublin, probably even in Kiev.

In many lands temples were dedicated to Thor. There exists a description — dating from the second half of the eleventh century but reflecting an earlier state of affairs — of the Swedish national sanctuary. The sanctuary contained images of three gods: the senior god Odin, the goddess Freyr, and between them Thor, as the mightiest of the three. And the cult survived down to the final defeat of paganism by Christianity and beyond. Inscriptions dating from the very eve of the conversion still appeal to Thor to protect the dead in their graves, and long after that people were still wearing amulets representing Thor's hammer, instead of crosses.

Thor's resemblance to Indra is very striking. Thor too was a young god — often he is presented as Odin's son. Blond, with a red beard, and enormously strong, he was a prodigious eater and drinker: all characteristics of Indra. Above all, he was a warrior: in time of war he led the whole people. At such times he rode in a chariot drawn by two he-goats — which seems strange until one recalls that in India a doublet of Indra called Pusan likewise rode in a chariot drawn by goats. And like Indra Thor possessed irresistible weaponry: a belt of power, iron gloves, above all a wonderful hammer. Like Indra's mace, Thor's hammer was fashioned by a craftsman who specialised in making treasures for the gods — and both weapons resembled thunderbolts.

Thor's affinity to Indra did not stop there. If as warrior Thor was terrifying, to his own people he was benign: he cared for cattle and crops and harvests. He would act as patron to a settlement, both defending it against external enemies and ensuring its inner stability. Guardian of law, he was called to witness every oath. He also cared for individuals: he was the god to whom a person would most readily turn in the hour of need. And he watched over all the important events in a person's life: at wedding and at death-bed he was there, friendly and protective.

At all times and in every way Thor was the upholder of order. When the gods made the ordered world they created a space for themselves, called Asgard, and a space for human beings, called Midgard. Thanks to his great strenth Thor was able to sustain this whole creation. Only, the ordered world was never secure: it was constantly threatened by the giants from Jotunheimar, Giantland, which lay outside its boundaries. It was Thor's task to hold the giants at bay.

The giants were counterparts to the Vedic serpents and dragons: true embodiments of chaos, nullity, death. Once, in Thor's absence, the most fearsome of the giants, Hrungnir, threatened to kill all the gods and goddesses. Terrified, the gods called on Thor, who appeared amid thunder and lightning. Hrungnir had an assistant to help him — and that assistant was a three-headed monster, like the Vedic monsters Trisiras and Visvarupa, whom Indra and Trita Aptya fought. Thor fought and killed the giant nevertheless — and so saved the world of the gods. As for the world of men, Thor saved it again and again. He himself describes how he had to stay awhile in the east, fighting the host of giants; for if they had had their way, they would have devastated Midgard until it could no longer support human beings.

There are echoes of Vedic combats also in Snorri's account of Thor's fight with that vast sea-monster, the Midgard serpent, which lay coiled around the earth and was quite capable of destroying it. Out at sea Thor cast his line and hooked the monster. For frightfulness, we are told, nothing could compare with the way Thor's eyes blazed at the serpent and the serpent stared at Thor and blew out its poison. Thor would have smashed the serpent's skull with his hammer, if his companion had not taken fright and cut the line.

In the event the Midgard serpent, like Vritra, remains an enduring threat to the ordered world. For the threat of chaos is always there: the gods were as clear as human beings about that. Once, when the giants managed to steal Thor's hammer, panic spread among the gods — for who now could defend the world of gods and human beings against the forces that were forever threatening from the realm of chaos?

The affinity between Thor and Indra is generally accepted by scholars — indeed, it was recognised already at the first beginnings of comparative mythology as a serious discipline, in the mid-nineteenth century. Already then it was explained in terms of common descent from a forgotten proto-Indo-European god who must have possessed the same characteristics — and that explanation too is now generally accepted. Lately it has even been reinforced by the discovery of a Russian folktale that, for etymological reasons as well as in its content, is clearly related to the myth of Indra and Vritra.[3]

But if the Vedic god Indra is descended from a proto-Indo-European god, the line of descent must pass through a proto-Indo-Iranian god — and it would be very strange if there were no Iranian counterpart to Vedic Indra. So are there really no traces at all in the *Avesta* of a god or gods who, like Thor and Indra, fought chaos-monsters and so preserved the ordered world? It is worth a search.

2

The *Avesta* has much to tell of chaos-monsters and of the human heroes who fought and overthrew them.

One may start with the fate that was wished upon the whole demonic host. It is plain, in the *Rig Veda*, that the demons did not always inhabit the netherworld: Indra despatched them there. Ever since, though they can and do visit the earth's surface to cause havoc, their true abode has been in that dark realm. Zoroastrians held a similar view — indeed, one *yasht* tells how demons could be seen coming up to the earth's surface at a certain mountain col, which was the gate to the netherworld. Only, Zoroastrians were convinced that it was no god but Zoroaster himself who, by reciting a particularly potent prayer, with appropriate ritual, had originally sent the demons below.[4]

Then there were the dragons Svuvara, Gandarva and Snavidka. All were fearful monsters, yellow, poisonous, man-eating — but they were much more than that.[5] Of Sruvara it is said that if he had not been killed, the whole universe would have been destroyed, and Ahura Mazda himself would have found no defence against Angra Mainyu. It was the same with Gandarva, who lived in the depths of the sea: if he had not been slain, Angra Mainyu would have become master of Ahura Mazda's creation. As for Snavidka — fortunately he was killed at an early age; for he boasted that if once he reached adulthood he would make heaven and earth his chariot. Clearly these dragons symbolise a power that, if it is not contained, is capable of reducing the whole ordered world to chaos. But in that case who could master them if not a warrior-god? And must not the warrior Keresaspa, who destroys them in the stories we possess, be a humanised version of such a god?

One gets the same impression, even more strongly, from another legend included in the *Avesta*.[6] The Iranian Thraetaona, son of Athwya, is a purely human hero — yet he has much in common with the ancient god Trita Aptya, who in the *Rig Veda* is shown duplicating some of Indra's most prodigious feats. In Iran, Thraetaona defeats the three-headed, six-eyed, screaming dragon Azi Dahaka; while in India Trita Aptya likewise slays a three-headed, six-eyed, screaming dragon. And there are links between Thraetaona and Indra himself: the waters that Indra liberates by killing Vritra are also goddesses — and by killing Azi Dahaka, Thraetaona frees two maidens: a shift such as commonly takes place when a myth changes into a legend. It has even been suggested that the name Azi Dahaka meant 'dragon of the *dasas*' — i.e. of those native peoples who were conquered by the invading tribes — the Iranian counterparts of the Indians with whom Vritra was associated and whom Indra fought.[7]

But if these warriors are humanised versions of ancient, pre-Zoroastrian gods who fought chaos-monsters, who could those gods have been?

3

The *Avesta* itself does in fact tell of a god — albeit a lesser one — who fights and defeats a chaos-monster: he is called Tishtrya. *Yasht* 8, which is dedicated to Tishtrya, is thought to be of pre-Zoroastrian origin, though edited to fit with Zoroastrian doctrine.[8] It presents Tishtrya as a creation of Ahura Mazda — but that says nothing about the god's original status. Even in the *yasht* there are hints of a status that had once been very exalted indeed: Tishtrya is presented as endowed with the power of magic, a dominant ruler yet full of solicitude, for whom all creatures on earth or in the water or in the air incessantly yearn.

Tishtrya was an astral god. His name, in the form that we know, seems to derive from a proto-Indo-European word meaning 'belonging to the group of the three stars' — presumably Orion's belt; though at some stage he came to be associated instead with Sirius. From other Zoroastrian texts it is known that the fixed stars were imagined as being organised in five armies, under the command of five great stars, with the task of fighting against the demons. Tishtrya, at the head of the eastern army, was the most important of these commanders — he is described as god of 'the bright and radiant star', 'lord and overseer of all stars'. Yet Tishtrya is not at all remote from human beings. In particular, he is greatly concerned to ensure the survival and prosperity of the Iranian people: he gives them places where they can dwell in peace, with plenty of water. As a star at night he wards off the female demons who fall from the sky as shooting stars, intent on harming human beings. And he is not always in the sky — mostly he operates on earth, and in various guises. When he appears in the guise of a tall, strong youth, it is to grant plenty of sons. In the form of a bull he promises an abundance of cattle, as a stallion an abundance of horses.

Tishtrya's greatest achievement is as a champion of human beings against Apaosha, demon of drought and dearth and famine. Here too he appears as a stallion, white and beautiful, with golden ears and muzzle. He tries to make his way to the sea Vourukusha, the mythical water that is the source of all rivers and all rain, but the way is blocked by Apaosha — also in the form of a stallion, a black and hairless one. For three days and nights the white and black horses battle, hoof against hoof. In the first combat Tishtrya is defeated — and he knows why: he has received too little worship. He protests that, if only he were better worshipped, he would have the strength of ten stallions, ten camels, ten bulls, ten mountains, ten channelled streams. Thereupon Ahura Mazda himself worships Tishtrya, his example is followed by human beings, and that changes everything: Tishtrya becomes irresistible. In a second combat Apaosha is utterly overthrown. The combat was between sexual rivals — two supernatural stallions competing for a mare — for the sea Vourukusha is described as being like a horse. Now, as Tishtrya plunges into the sea the water goes into turmoil, clouds rise from it, bearing both water and seeds, rain pours down, plants sprout from the seeds, the land is saved. All this takes place each year.

The *yasht* we know is not of course a wholly reliable guide to the way Tishtrya was imagined in pre-Zoroastrian times, but it does at least show that this god had many of the traits we find in the Vedic Indra. Like Indra, Tishtrya is a releaser of the waters — not a rain-god but a god who, by overthrowing and destroying a chaos-monster, sets the waters free to fertilise the earth. He is friendly and helpful to his people, i.e. the tribes who worship him. He shows his goodwill not only in his annual combat but also in his constant war with lesser demons.

There are other similarities. There are good grounds for thinking that his combat was ritually re-enacted each year in a horse-race over one complete circuit of a race-course — why else should the *yasht* specify that each horse drives the other the length of a race-course, that is, half the circuit? Now, it has been argued that Indra's combats were likewise re-enacted through chariot-races.[9] Again, both Tishtrya and Indra are embodiments of sexual potency: Tishtrya's plunge into the waters cannot but recall Indra's marriage with the liberated waters. Which no doubt is why both gods have avatars as young man, as bull, as stallion.[10]

4

It seems clear that before Zoroaster Iranians did indeed, like Vedic Indians, have gods who were responsible for defending the ordered world against the ever-renewed assaults of the agents of chaos. Tishtrya was one of those gods — but one may reasonably suspect that there was a greater god, a warrior-god, who did so on a more massive scale.

Yasht 14, which is dedicated to the god of victory Verethraghna, shows him as sharing many traits with Vedic Indra.[11] Verethraghna, we learn, could be embodied in any one of ten incarnations, all expressive of his overwhelming vitality: as a rushing wind, a bull, a stallion, a rutting camel, a youth of fifteen, an eagle, a ram, a wild goat, a warrior. Indra was likewise able to take on all kinds of forms, some of them — ram, bull, stallion, eagle — identical with those assumed by Verethraghna.[12]

The kinship of the two gods goes deeper than that. The same *yasht* shows Verethraghna as much more than a god of victory in war. He grants victory not only in fighting but in eloquence, in disputation, in every kind of action. The enemies he overcomes are not only hostile armies but demons and those human associates of demons, the witches and sorcerers. He gives men strength of arm, health in every limb, well-covered bodies, inexhaustible testicles. In fact he is a guardian god who helps his people in every way. When he is worshipped in the proper manner, not only enemy chariots but famine and sickness are held at bay — whereas wrong or insufficient worship brings disasters on the land. All this recalls Indra. And if, as we are told, the rutting camel which was one of Verethraghna's avatars has the greatest passion and the most powerful ejaculation of any male creature, that too recalls the Indra's epithet 'he of the thousand testicles'.

But indeed Verethraghna's very name links him to Indra, whose commonest epithet in the *Rig Veda* is *vritrahan*. *Vritrahan* meant 'smasher of opposition'; but it could also have a more specific reference, to the slaying of that embodiment of opposition, the serpent Vritra. The name Verethraghna likewise meant 'smashing of opposition,' or simply 'victory.' It remains to determine whether it too could refer to the slaying of a serpent called (as it would be in

Avestan) Verethra. Nowhere in the *Avesta* is there a hint that Verethraghna ever performed such a feat. However, there are a couple of other sources which suggest that he did.

From the first century AD Armenia was a predominantly Zoroastrian land until it was gradually converted to Christianity from the third century onwards. Embedded in a Christian work from Armenia is a mention of a former god called Vahagn, who was believed to bestow valour on his worshippers.[13] His birth was miraculous: heaven and earth were in travail, a reed rose from the purple sea, from the reed came smoke which turned into flame, and out of the flame came a child with fiery hair and moustache of flame and eyes like suns. Now this Vahagn is certainly Verethraghna — and he is explicitly called 'dragon-slayer'. In another Armenian text the cosmic dragon is given a name, Vishap. That too is of Iranian origin: *vishapa* is a stock Avestan dragon-epithet meaning 'having poison as its juices'.[14]

These Armenian items add to the significance of a story now preserved only in a fragment of a Parsi work.[15] It concerns a mission that Ahura Mazda gave to the god Bahram, i.e. Verethraghna. As the god 'created victorious from the beginning' Bahram was entrusted with the task of capturing the evil demon Gannak Menok, who was devastating the world, and binding him and imprisoning him in hell for ever, head downwards. This was after the beings whom Ahura Mazda had specially created as his allies, the six Holy Immortals, had all attempted the task and failed. Bahram of course succeeded.

Much in this story is unclear. Though it is said that these great events are to take place at the great consummation, they are narrated as though they had already happened, some time in the remote past. Moreover, though Gannak Menok is of course Angra Mainyu, the way the combat is described makes him look more like a dragon than a purely spiritual being. These ambiguities are significant. Surely the whole story is simply an elaboration of the ancient myth of the warrior-god who fought and slew the chaos monster? Certainly the reward bestowed on Bahram suggests as much — for after his victory he was promoted to be a seventh Holy Immortal, and the greatest of them all. One recalls that Indra, after his victory over Vritra, was promoted to be king over the gods. No doubt Verethraghna was similarly honoured — and what the Parsi text records is a Zoroastrianised version of that singular event.

The similarities between Verethraghna and Indra are in fact so many and so striking that one is bound to ask: Were the two gods originally one and the same — and is the diminished Verethraghna of the *Avesta* simply Indra made acceptable to Zoroastrianism?[16]

5

The fact that in the *Avesta* Indra figures as the chief demon, the personification of *druj* itself, shows both that he had once been a major Indo-Iranian god and that he was unacceptable to Zoroastrians. But why was he unacceptable?

It has been argued that Indra was rejected by Zoroaster and by Zoroastrians because he was a patron of cattle-raiders. That may well have played a part — but is there no more to be said? Could it not be that in pre-Zoroastrian times Iranian Indra stood in much the same relation to Ahura Mazda as Vedic Indra to Varuna: the relation of a warrior, ceaselessly and actively engaged in holding the forces of chaos at bay, to the serenely majestic overseer of universal order; a partnership between equals? If so, that in itself would have been enough to damn him in Zoroastrian eyes. For Zoroaster and for Zoroastrians no god could be even approximately equal to Ahura Mazda. Tishtrya might be allowed to keep his highly specialised task — an Indra as mighty as that could only be turned into a demon.

However, even Zoroastrian Iranians needed a divine assistance in time of war. It seems that Indra's role as war-god was taken over by Mithra — a far more aggressive power than Vedic Mitra. And this Zoroastrianised Mithra is indeed strangely reminiscent of Indra as war-god — even to the precise details of the mighty mace 'with its hundred bosses and hundred blades, a feller of men as he brandishes it, cast of yellow metal, strong and golden, strongest of weapons, most victorious of weapons. . . .'[17] Moreover, Mithra has that diminished Indra, Verethraghna, as his assistant — and Verethraghna still does, on Mithra's behalf, what once Indra did on his own initiative: 'he cuts to pieces everything at once, mingling together on the ground the bones, the brains, the blood of men false to the contract',[18] — just as, in the *Rig Veda*, Indra 'like a stone hurled from the sky', with his burning strength strikes down those who are false to the contract. Verethraghna even retains his Indra-like avatar of wild boar. When Mithra becomes — as he eventually does, for Iranians — a sun-god, the boar Verethraghna is still there, fierce, strong, with sharp tusks, iron feet and iron jaws, rushing along in front of Mithra on his daily journey across the sky.[19]

So, it is suggested, Indra is still a presence in Zoroastrianism — partly as a demon, but also, it is suggested, reduced, fragmented, disguised, in Verethraghna and in Mithra. There was no place for him in his own original, magnificent form. For now Ahura Mazda — greater in Zoroastrian teaching than any god had ever been — combined the functions of the two greatest gods in the Vedic pantheon. He not only, like Varuna, watched over universal order —

he also, like Indra, ceaselessly fought the forces of chaos, now embodied in Angra Mainyu/Ahriman.

6

At this point one has to recognise what a vast gulf separates Zoroaster's teachings from the ancient combat myth.

What Ahura Mazda does goes far beyond anything known to the traditional myth. The war that he fights is a spiritual war, and its aim is not simply to ensure the fertility of the land and the military victory of his people, it is not even the mere maintenance of the ordered world. It is to remove every form of disorder from the world, wholly and for ever; to bring about a state in which cosmos will no longer be threatened by chaos. So in the end Angra Mainyu/Ahriman is annihilated once and for all, along with all his host of demons and all his human allies. In place of repeated but incomplete victories we are promised a final and total one.

Zoroaster, it is suggested, was inspired by the ancient and potent combat myth to create a different and even more potent combat myth.[20] And his creation survives to this day: the very core of Zoroastrianism has always been a combat myth — indeed, even the divine warrior himself is there, in the form of the future saviour, the *saoshyant* Asvat-ereta. But the traditional myth, as it was known to the Ancient Near East before Zoroaster, has been transformed into an apocalyptic faith.

It was a drastically new perception of the world, and it opened up new possibilities. World-views that knew only of cosmos forever threatened by chaos yet always surviving — and surviving unchanged — were essentially conservative. Though they might command the allegiance of a whole society, they served especially the interests of the established authorities. When integrated into an imperial ideology, Zoroastrian teachings could do the same. But they also had another and very different potentiality.

Originally, in the thought of the prophet himself, the conflict between Ahura Mazda and Angra Mainyu reflected a social conflict, and 'the making wonderful' meant, among other things, the resolution of that conflict. In the present world rich and powerful warriors were despoiling defenceless herdsmen and their herds, in the perfect world to come herdsmen would flourish and the predatory warriors would have been consumed by fire. Some echo from those distant times lingered on: Zoroastrian teachings retained their capacity, in certain circumstances, to inspire dissenting individuals or groups to look forward with confidence to the day when the established order would be abolished, the existing authorities exterminated, and they themselves vindicated and exalted. When Zoroastrian eschatology was assimilated and adapted by non-Zoroastrians, this happened — as we shall see — on a grandiose scale.

PART TWO

Syro-Palestinian Crucible

CHAPTER 6

Ugarit

Between those two great centres of civilisation, Egypt and Mesopotamia, lay the cultural-geographical entity that in the Bible is called the land of Canaan and now is known to historians as Syria-Palestine. Embracing approximately the area of modern Israel, Jordan, Lebanon and coastal-central Syria, it was inhabited by a mixture of Semitic peoples whom it is customary to call, down to *c.*1200, Canaanites.[1] From *c.*1200 onwards it was inhabited also by the people we know as Israelites.

In this land too people lived for centuries in what they perceived as a divinely appointed order that was essentially changeless, yet perpetually threatened by the forces of chaos. And here too a time came when prophetic spirits began to tell of a glorious consummation to come, when all things would be made new. These developments deserve to be examined in some detail, for their consequences have persisted down the centuries, right down to the present day.

In the second millennium the Canaanites lived in a number of city-states and engaged in agriculture and in trade. But, without great rivers such as had fostered the development of civilisation to east and west, Canaan was a relatively backward land. The urban communities were rather small — one of the largest cities is known to have measured less than 35 acres. They lived from season to season, very dependent on rainfall at the right time and in the right amounts, with drought and famine as a constant possibility.

Until fairly recently almost all our knowledge of the Canaanite world-view came from the polemical comments of the Hebrew prophets.[2] The situation was transformed by the discovery, in 1929, beneath a mound known as Ras Shamra, of the remains of the city-state of Ugarit. Situated on the Syrian coast, opposite the northern tip of Cyprus, Ugarit was the nexus of trade-routes between Mesopotamia, Egypt and the Mediterranean. It was a metropolis where people from all the great civilisations of the Late Bronze Age, Indo-European as well as Semitic, came in contact and exchanged ideas and stories. It was also strategically important both to the Egyptians and to their temporary rivals the Hittites. As a result it enjoyed exceptional wealth and prestige. The abundance, quality and variety of the writings found in the palace archives and in the library situated between the two main temples bear witness to a golden age lasting from *c.*1400 to *c.*1200.

Even though Ugarit lay beyond the northern limit of the land of Canaan, it shared in the common Canaanite culture of the Middle and Late Bronze Ages (*c.*1700–*c.*1200 BC). Politically the whole area was included in the larger fabric of empire, usually the Egyptian empire. Most of the city-states, large or small, were kingdoms, and their rulers, though vassals of far greater rulers, exercised great authority and enjoyed great prestige at home.

Ugaritic legends have much to tell about Canaanite kingship, or at least about the Canaanite ideal of kingship. The dynasty of the legendary King Keret was believed to have received divine sanction from the head of the pantheon. Like a Mesopotamian king, a king of Ugarit both represented the people before the gods and represented the gods to the community. There is evidence to suggest that after death he was himself accorded some sort of divine status.

In theory the king was responsible for justice and fair dealing within the community. Like greater monarchs, he was supposed to take special care of widows and orphans.[3] By maintaining good order in society he was also believed to exercise a benign influence on nature. Where justice and fair dealing prevailed, drought and famine were held at bay and the land was kept fertile — the stock epithet for King Daniel is 'dispenser of fertility'. And originally the king was also leader in war, whose victories further strengthened the ordered world. It is true that by the second half of the second millennium the functions that had once belonged to the king had devolved on professionals — priests, judges, soldiers. Nevertheless, the king was still the supreme authority in the state, and he was still perceived as responsible for sustaining the divinely appointed order.[4]

Not that either the monarchy or the divinely appointed order can have seemed very benign to the Canaanite peasantry. The task of supporting the luxurious life-style of the royal establishment, in a land as poor as Canaan, imposed a crushing burden on the peasants: in Ugarit some 6000–8000 city-dwellers, who were mostly dependants of the palace and economically unproductive, were supported by a mere 25,000 peasants in the surrounding countryside.[5] In the long run the system proved unworkable. In the thirteenth century the economy collapsed, the villages were deserted, and the city-states — no longer protected by an Egypt that was itself in a weakened state — proved unable to ward off invasions by the 'sea-peoples' from Anatolia and the Aegean islands.

The Canaanite world-view survived nevertheless and deeply influenced the world-view of a people that was only then achieving an identity, the Israelites.

2

It was apparently a certain Elimelek who gave the Ugaritic myths their present literary form, some time between 1380 and 1360, though they had probably been circulating, whether as oral or as written literature, for a good century before that.[6] The myths reveal a large and variegated pantheon dominated by three major deities: the gods El and Hadad (the latter commonly known as Ba'al, meaning 'lord') and the goddess Anat. El, whose very name meant 'god', was the creator god. Creator and procreator: overseer of conception and childbirth among human beings, El seems to have sired the gods in the most literal sense — which, no doubt, is why he was sometimes called 'Bull El'. He was also called 'Creator of Created Things', and there is good reason to think that — like An and Marduk — he was regarded as creator of heaven and earth. He had a consort, the goddess Athirat or Ashera, who had participated in the work of creation. A somewhat shadowy figure at Ugarit, Athirat is known to have been worshipped as a major deity in other parts of the land. El and Athirat were both primordial beings, they had been there always.

Father of the gods and head of the family of gods, El presided over the divine assembly.[7] He is called 'king', and he is indeed a kingly figure. Majestic, aloof, he is often described as sitting alone 'at the outflowing of the two streams' — meaning perhaps at the common source of the upper and lower waters of the cosmic ocean. This, it seems, was thought to be somewhere in the Amanus mountains, north of Ugarit. There El dwelt in a tent-shrine, and it was there that the assembly of gods gathered to receive his instructions. El's tent was at the very centre of the universe as the Canaanites imagined it, and from that centre El exercised his rule.

It was a benevolent rule. For if El was imperturbable, he was not uninvolved. He was frequently required to consider requests from his children the lesser gods. They were forever trying to influence him — yet they prostrated themselves before him, acknowledging his superior wisdom: 'Your decree, El, is wise, your wisdom is everlasting.'[8] El was the only god with the right to issue decrees — and his decrees had to be obeyed. He was in charge of the entire universe, and it was his responsibility to ensure that equilibrium was preserved among all the competing and conflicting powers within it.

El was also concerned with human society.[9] In the legend of King

Keret he is called the father of the king, and the king's role as guarantor and sustainer of justice in the community is clearly a reflection of El's own role. Just as he watched over order in the universe, so he watched over order in society — and that order included justice and fair dealing. It was not for nothing that El was called 'the kindly, the compassionate' — a designation strangely reminiscent of 'Allah the Merciful, the Compassionate' in Islam. Not that El was incapable of anger: transgressions in the community, witting or unwitting, ritual or 'ethical', could provoke him — and then he would prompt neighbouring powers to invade and conquer. To avert such calamities the king had to perform rites of expiation and offer sacrifices. But that too shows how much right order in society was thought to matter to the supreme god.

3

The god who bulks largest in Ugaritic myths is Ba'al.[10] He seems to have been a latecomer in the pantheon — maybe he was a god of foreign origin, introduced by immigrants. Certainly he was no son of El's consort Athirat, for he was feared and hated by her and by the many gods who were her offspring.

Originally Ba'al was a divine warrior — often he is depicted as armed with dagger, mace and spear. A young and vigorous god, his stock epithets are 'the mighty', 'the mightiest of heroes', 'the prince' — but also 'he who mounts the clouds', for, like many other divine warriors, he was a god of storm and rain. He manifested himself above all in the violent storms of autumn and of late winter. It was said of him that he appointed the due season for his rains and opened the clouds to discharge them when the time came to soften the hard-baked soil and prepare it for cultivation. He could also be terrifying: his darts as lightning, his voice as thunder made the mountains reel and quake and convulsed the earth.

Unlike El, Ba'al was not aloof, beyond the reach of destructive powers. On the contrary, he was always at risk. He is shown as incessantly active, for ever defending cosmos against the forces of chaos. Ba'al is the unresting power on whose exertions the proper course of nature and the very survival of life in the world have always depended and always will. If El created the world and still watches over it, it is Ba'al's responsibility to ensure that El's benevolent intention is realised.[11] And if the extant texts include no myth of El's original creative act, only myths about Ba'al's incessant activity, that no doubt reflects the relative importance that people attached to a happening in the remote past and to their own well-being in the present.

Ba'al's initial adventure has much in common with the exploit of that other youthful storm-god, Marduk of Babylon. Once upon a time El, disregarding dire warnings from various gods and goddesses, yielded to the demands of a god called Yam and allowed a palace to be built for him — thereby bestowing royal status on him. Yam's epithets include 'Lord of the Sea' and 'Sea and Ocean Current' — and if some translations give 'Sea and River', even 'Prince River', it seems that in fact that 'river' is simply an ocean-current. For Yam is clearly god of the sea — and of the sea imagined as an unruly power, perpetually on the move, perpetually threatening the solid land — in fact the eastern Mediterranean as the sailors and fishermen of Ugarit experienced it each winter. But that is not all: Yam's realm includes also that still more terrifying sea, the mythical ocean that encompasses the world and could at any moment overwhelm and obliterate it.[12]

No sooner has Yam acquired royal status than he proceeds to terrorise the assembly of gods, and so effectively that when he demands that they hand over Ba'al, they acquiesce. But Ba'al himself does not. Instead, he emerges as champion of the gods and embarks on a combat with the turbulent waters, with the prospect of kingship as his reward. The divine craftsman provides him with weapons, and at the same time defines what is at stake:

> Truly I tell you, O prince Ba'al,
> You shall take your everlasting kingdom,
> your dominion for ever and ever.
> . . .
> Chase away Yam from his throne . . .[13]

When Ba'al wins the gods fully acknowledge what he has achieved and what the consequences must be. Now El has a palace built for Ba'al; this was imagined as a heavenly residence above Mount Zaphon, some twenty miles north of Ugarit. The very full treatment of this theme suggests that it may have had a bearing on real life: was it perhaps intended to encourage or to explain the building of the great temple of Ba'al which has now been excavated at Ugarit? It is more than likely, for just as Ba'al could not rule over the gods without a palace, he could not dispense fertility to mankind without an earthly temple.

Once properly housed Ba'al becomes truly 'Lord'. He asserts his rule over 'eight and eighty towns, yea nine and ninety', and proclaims:

> [For] I alone am he that shall be king over the gods,
> [that] indeed fattens gods and men,
> that satisfies the multitudes of the earth.[14]

Like El, Ba'al is now king over the gods — but his kingship is different from El's. El has always been king, his rule is timeless, changeless. Ba'al, on the contrary, has not only to win his kingship but to defend it; his is an unstable, strenuous rule. Nor is he ever the supreme ruler. As El's vice-regent he rules over the earth and its human inhabitants. He never succeeds El as lord over the entire universe, as Marduk succeeded Anu and Enlil in Babylon. And, although it is possible, even probable, that the myth of Marduk and Tiamat owes something to the myth of Ba'al and Yam, the older, Canaanite myth is the less grandiose of the two: there is no suggestion that Ba'al makes heaven and earth out of Yam's body.

Nevertheless Yam is a chaos monster, and by defeating him Ba'al preserves the ordered world. Passages in other Ugaritic myths make the point even more clearly. Here the god of the sea is identified with a serpent or a dragon. In one passage Ba'al's sister Anat recalls how she assisted him in the fateful combat:

> Did I not destroy Yam the darling of El,
> . . .
> Was not the dragon captured [and] vanquished?
> I did destroy the wriggling serpent,
> the tyrant with seven heads.[15]

Elsewhere Ba'al himself is reminded of his victory:

> . . . you smote Leviathan the slippery serpent,
> and made an end of the slippery serpent,
> the tyrant with seven heads.[16]

Yet the chaos-monster Yam is not destroyed, only contained, held at bay — after all, he too is a god, 'beloved of El'. And in any case Ba'al has another, even more fearsome antagonist to face: the god Mot, who is also 'beloved of El'.[17] If Ba'al is the god of rain and helps the land to flourish, Mot is the god of drought and condemns the land to sterility. On earth his habitation is the sun-baked desert, he is the genius of the scorching summer heat. But he is much more than that. Just as Ba'al is lord of the living world, so Mot is the lord of death — indeed, his very name meant 'death'. Like Mesopotamian Nergal, he is death imagined as a voracious being, possessed by an insatiable craving for human flesh and blood.[18]

When Mot is abroad he turns every hill and dale to desolation and extinguishes the breath of life in every human being he meets. And there is no human being whom Mot does not meet sooner or later. When the goddess Anat tries to tempt a certain prince with promises of immortality, he knows better:

> Do not lie, o virgin;
> for to a hero your lying is unseemly.
> As [his] ultimate fate what does a man get?
> What does a man get as [his] final lot?
> . . .
> . . . the death of all men I shall die,
> even I shall surely die.[19]

Mot's home is the netherworld, where he reigns as king; his 'devouring' refers also to the descent of the dead into the netherworld. This dark realm, variously described as 'the earth', 'the Pit', 'the Abyss', is also described as a 'city' belonging to Mot. It is not a city that anyone enters willingly. For Canaanites as for Mesopotamians death was a miserable form of existence. Granted that regular offerings of food and drink by one's children and grandchildren could stave off hunger and thirst — not everyone had caring descendants, or indeed any descendants at all. The spirits of the desperate, starving dead were a perpetual danger to the living.[20]

When Mot challenges Ba'al, Ba'al has no choice but to fight him. The combat takes place on the edge of the netherworld, and there Ba'al dies. His death threatens such total catastrophe that El himself comes down from his throne, sits on the ground and performs all the rites of mourning. 'What will happen to the people?' he asks — and even plans to go down into the netherworld to rescue Ba'al. In the end it is Ba'al's sister and consort Anat who finds his body and gives it proper burial. Ba'al revives and the earth becomes fertile again. El sees in a dream how 'the skies rained oil, the wadis ran with honey' and in delight cries out:

> Even I may sit down and be at ease,
> And [my] soul within me may take its ease;
> for mightiest Ba'al is alive,
> the prince lord of earth exists.[21]

But untroubled security is not for this world. Mot in turn revives, and the two rivals face one another anew in a mighty struggle:

> They eyed each other like burning coals;
> Mot was strong, Ba'al was strong.
> They bit like serpents;
> Mot was strong, Ba'al was strong.
> They tugged like greyhounds;
> Mot fell down, Ba'al fell down on top of him.[22]

In the end El sends a messenger who orders Mot to give way and to let Ba'al live and to reign over the kingdom that is rightly his.

The Ba'al myths can be viewed in more than one way.[23] Ba'al, Yam and Mot are all of them gods, each sovereign in his own domain. At one level their conflicts symbolise the meteorological vicissitudes of the land of Canaan. That does not mean — though it has often been maintained[24] — that those conflicts should be interpreted in terms of the cycle of the seasons, let alone that Ba'al was a seasonally 'dying and rising god'. There is no reference to seasonal cycles in the text, and when Ba'al is absent it is not for a season but for seven or eight (meaning 'many') years. What the myth says is that Ba'al, the bringer of fertility, can hold sway only by subduing both Yam, the genius of the waters which are always capable of overwhelming the land, and Mot, the genius of drought which is always capable of plunging the land into famine. It has even been argued that the myths telling of Ba'al's victories were recited at an autumnal New Year festival, to ensure that the victories would be repeated, and lifegiving rain granted yet again — and it may well be true.

Nevertheless, the myths are not only fertility myths. Mot is not only drought, he is also death. Ba'al's fight with Mot symbolises the struggle of the forces of life against the forces of death. The very survival of the living world is at stake. And much the same can be said of Ba'al's combat with the waters; for the waters symbolise the destructive forces which are for ever threatening the ordered world and which, if they triumphed, would reduce that world to the primordial chaos from which it came. Moreover, it is equally true of both these mighty powers that, if neither can finally defeat Ba'al, neither can be finally defeated. Chaos is a perennial possibility, death the most certain of certainties, both are ineluctable parts of reality.[25]

4

Ba'al's sister and consort, the goddess Anat, was worshipped not only in Canaan but in Anatolia, Mesopotamia and Egypt — but it is the Ras Shamra texts that tell us most about her.[26] Like Ba'al, she is concerned with fostering fertility. Moulded clay plaques from Canaan show her nude and with sexual organs emphasised; probably they are amulets designed to promote childbirth. She is no less involved with the fertility of the land. When Ba'al is killed by Mot, Anat helps to bring him back to life. Moreover she tackles Mot himself and utterly destroys him:

> She seized divine Mot,
> with a sword she split him,

with a sieve she winnowed him,
with a fire she burnt him,
with mill-stones she ground him,
in a field she scattered him;
his flesh indeed the birds ate . . .[27]

Anat is indeed a doughty fighter. In one passage she reminds Ba'al that she was present at all his combats, and took an active part in them all, right back to the original fight with 'Sea and Ocean-Current'. This means that, like her brother, Anat is a defender of the divine assembly against an overweening, rebellious god, indeed a defender of cosmos against chaos. And that, surely, is the key to understanding a passage that has perplexed more than one commentator.[28]

The passage in question, which is embedded in the story of Ba'al, describes how Anat cut down people living in valleys, and in cities, and on the seashore, and in the land of sunrise, until the cut-off heads of soldiers reached to her belt and she was wading in blood. Not satisfied with this, she continued to massacre troops in her own palace (or temple?) — and rejoiced and laughed over it. After which she, 'the Progenitress of Nations', washed her hands in the blood of the slain, and in dew and rain supplied by her brother Ba'al, and in oil from the earth.

None of this appears strange if one bears in mind how large military victory and defeat bulked in the life of all Near Eastern societies, including the city-states of Canaan. Around 1200 BC Ugarit itself was to be conquered and utterly destroyed — but meanwhile it looked to its gods to defend it. Ba'al himself could be invoked as an ally in war: 'If a strong one attacks your gate, a warrior your walls, raise your eyes to Ba'alu [praying]: "O Ba'alu, please drive away the strong one from our gate, the warrior from our walls". . . And Ba'alu will hear your prayers . . .'[29]

Ugaritic society was a military society: the king was head of the army, and one of his chief officers was the military governor of the city. The city itself was well fortified, and protected by archers, slingers and chariot troops. No doubt victory in war had the same transcendent value for that small polity as it had for the great empires: it must have seemed as much part of the divinely appointed order, as much a manifestation of the rightness of the world, as was fertility of the land. And here, surely, lies the significance of Anat's orgy of killing. After all, multitudes of cut-off hands and heads can be seen in Assyrian bas-reliefs celebrating the victory of god and king, and in Egypt pharaoh could glorify the terror imposed on the vanquished as an affirmation of *ma'at*. Just as Anat sustained the ordered world by helping Ba'al to overthrow the gods of the unruly waters and of drought, so she sustained it by defeating and slaughtering the enemies of whatever state was worshipping her. It was not for nothing that in Egypt her cult was observed by the warrior pharaohs of the nineteenth dynasty, or that Rameses II named his sword 'Anat is victorious'. Anat was in fact a western counterpart of the Mesopotamian goddess of victory Inanna/Ishtar.

The overall picture is clear enough: in Ugarit, and presumably in other Canaanite city-states, the notion of a divinely appointed, all-embracing order was as familiar as it was in the great empires. In Ugarit as in the great empires that order was imagined as perennially threatened, yet always surviving. And there too it was taken for granted that that was the most that could be hoped for: that as things had been, so they would remain.

CHAPTER 7

Yahweh and the Jerusalem Monarchy

It might be thought that the history of the Israelites would be easy to summarise, and their world-view easy to define and to describe, since these things are documented in the Hebrew Bible, otherwise known as the Old Testament. Unfortunately that is by no means the case, for the relevant parts of the Bible were collected and edited very late, between 600 and 100 BC — and edited, moreover, to fit in with the beliefs and experiences of the redactors. It is often difficult, sometimes impossible, to disentangle what may have been experienced and expressed in earlier times from later accretions and interpretations. To choose between the arguments and conclusions of biblical scholars, who have been disagreeing with one another for well over a century, is no easier. But, with that *caveat lector*, one can try.[1]

As an identifiable people the Israelites were latecomers in the land of Canaan. The earliest area of settlement that can plausibly be regarded as Israelite dates, according to recent archaeological research, from around 1200, when a hundred unfortified villages sprang up in the hill-country, far from the Canaanite cities on the coast. These village communities were very small, and drew their livelihood from agriculture and the breeding of sheep, goats, sometimes also of oxen. Some scholars believe that they were founded by peasants who, at a time when the power of the city-states was declining, were able to escape from their control; while others hold that originally they consisted of nomadic immigrants from the east, from Edom and Moab.[2]

That need not imply that the story told in Exodus is purely fictional. It seems that in Egypt numbers of propertyless people, living on the fringes of urban society, and known as Hapiru, were forced to work on building the new capital of Rameses II (1304–1237). Some of them may well have escaped and joined the settlements in Canaan. The similarity of 'Hapiru' to 'Hebrew' makes it likely — even though the Hapiru themselves never were one single ethnic group.

During the following two centuries the Israelites, apparently organised in tribes, occupied large areas of Canaan — though even then the fertile and densely populated coastal regions, with their city-states, remained untouched. Towards 1000 BC a combination of economic and political factors led to the formation of a centralised Israelite state, under the rule of a king. Many scholars regard that as the point at which the history of Israel, in the sense of a credible story about a clearly identifiable people, begins.

Up to that point the Israelites had been divided into two main groups or 'houses', the northern and the southern. The second king, David, welded both 'houses' into a united kingdom; and he, and after him his son Solomon, ruled over both from their capital Jerusalem, which stood on neutral ground between the two. Indeed they ruled over more than that: the Canaanite city-states of the central and northern plains were subjugated and made into vassals. Whether neighbouring kingdoms were defeated and incorporated into the realm, is, again, a matter of dispute.

The Jerusalem monarchy owed much to older Near Eastern societies. Its political organisation was copied from the Egyptian New Kingdom, its bureaucracy was apparently recruited from Canaanite city-states, its ideology drew on Canaanite and Mesopotamian models. None of this brought it lasting prosperity or security. Not even the union of the two 'houses' under a single monarch lasted beyond Solomon's death, which took place in 926 or 922. The 'houses' survived as separate kingdoms — the northern kingdom was to last for a further two centuries, the southern for more than three. Sometimes the two kingdoms fought one another, frequently they fought other small powers within Syria-Palestine. But their power was slight, and was no match at all for the perils that faced them from the eighth century onwards.

The career of conquest which the Neo-Assyrian empire had been following for a good century took a leap forwards when, in 745, Tiglath-Pileser III came to the throne. In the course of the 730s and 720s the northern kingdom was first reduced to vassal status, then abolished, its territory being incorporated into the Assyrian system of provinces. In accordance with normal Neo-Assyrian practice, the upper class was deported to various distant parts of the empire, where it was absorbed into the local population and disappeared. The southern kingdom, the kingdom of Judah, became a vassal state under Assyrian domination and so remained — until, at the close of the seventh century, the Assyrian empire itself was overthrown by a coalition in which the Babylonians were dominant partners. Shortly afterwards the whole of Syria-Palestine came under Babylonian domination.

In 597 the Babylonian monarch Nebuchadnezzar or Nebuchadrezzar, being dissatisfied with the behaviour of the vassal king of Judah, occupied Jerusalem. Most of the inhabitants who possessed either influence or skill were deported to Babylon: the king and his family, the palace officials, the well-to-do and the educated, also smiths, metal-workers, craftsmen of all kinds. After a few years the new vassal king, who had been appointed by Nebuchadrezzar, tried to defect. The consequences were as might have been expected: in 586 the Babylonians again captured Jerusalem — and this time the city walls were razed and Solomon's temple burned to the ground. The same fate befell other towns in Judah. The Davidic monarchy, which had ruled for some four centuries, was eliminated: the last king, after being forced to watch the execution of his sons, was taken to Babylon blinded and in chains. The state collapsed, Judah lost the last remnant of political independence.

2

Though the northern kingdom, while it lasted, was far larger and more powerful, it was the southern kingdom that inherited and preserved the ideology of the Davidic and Solomonic empire. Most of our knowledge of Israelite religion — of what biblical scholars are accustomed to call Yahwism — comes from Judah.

In the Hebrew Bible Yahwism is portrayed as a unified and unchanging world-view, but it is no longer possible to accept that portrayal as historically valid. Modern scholarship has shown that Yahwism embraced two very different world-views. One of these always diverged markedly from the common Near Eastern pattern and ended by breaking right out of that pattern. The other form of Yahwism, which flourished under the Jerusalem monarchy, conformed pretty closely to that pattern.[3]

There are similarities between the world-view revealed by the Ugaritic material and the Yahwism of the Jerusalem monarchy. This cannot be due to direct influence: not only was the distance between Ugarit and Jerusalem very considerable by the standards of the time — the city-state of Ugarit was destroyed some two centuries before the Jerusalem monarchy was founded. But the world-view that we associate with Ugarit was not peculiar to that city-state. On the contrary, it was familiar throughout Syria-Palestine, and survived, as the world-view of those latter-day Canaanites, the Phoenicians, for a thousand years after the fall of Ugarit.[4]

It is becoming ever more difficult to say with any confidence when, where and how the Israelites first came to know the god Yahweh. It may be that, as Exodus says, he was originally a Midianite god, introduced into the land of Canaan by immigrants from Egypt; or he may have started as a minor member of the Canaanite pantheon. What is certain is that by the time they had become aware of themselves as a people the Israelites had adopted Yahweh as their patron god. With the establishment of the monarchy Yahweh became the patron god of the kingdom, and when the kingdom was divided into two kingdoms he remained the patron god of each — just as Chemosh was the patron god of the Moabites, Milkom of the Ammonites, Hadad of the Aramaeans, Melkart of the Tyrians.

That does not mean that from the start Yahweh was regarded as the greatest of all gods. Originally El was the supreme god for Israelites as he had always been for Canaanites. Even if one discounts the pronouncement of El in the Ba'al cycle, 'The name of my son is Yaw' — the import of which is still being debated[5] — one cannot ignore a passage in the Bible which shows Yahweh as subordinate to El. Deuteronomy 32: 8 tells how when El Elyon, i.e. El the Most High, parcelled out the nations between his sons, Yahweh received Israel as his portion. The suggestion, which has sometimes been advanced, that this means simply that El, 'God', under the name of Yahweh, took the Israelites for himself, is unconvincing. Besides, El always retained traces of his original dignity: whenever he is referred to in the Bible, it is with profound respect.

But if Yahweh was originally subordinate to El, could it be that the Israelites at first imagined him as a god of the same type as Canaanite Ba'al and Babylonian Marduk? It could indeed. In what is widely regarded as the oldest text in the Bible, the Song of Deborah (Judges 5), Yahweh appears as a storm-god at whose approach the earth trembles, heaven quakes and rain streams down in torrents. In another very ancient hymn he appears 'riding the clouds in his glory'.[6] And the parallelism goes much further than that — further, certainly, than one would expect in a work as severely edited as the Bible.

Ba'al first established his kingship over the world by subduing the unruly cosmic waters, symbolised by a serpent or dragon. There are psalms that show Yahweh subduing the waters along with the dragons Leviathan and Rahab — and those same psalms proclaim Yahweh's kingship:

> The voice of Yahweh
>   is upon the waters;
> the God of glory thunders,
>   Yahweh, upon many waters.
> Yahweh sits enthroned over the flood;
>   Yahweh sits enthroned as king for ever.[7]

There is strong evidence that these psalms were sung at the autumn festival that marked the beginning of the New Year, and that that festival included an affirmation and celebration of Yahweh's kingship. Eminent scholars have even argued that it included something more: a ritual symbolising the enthronement of Yahweh as king of the world — as Marduk was enthroned during the *akitu*; or else a celebration of Yahweh's triumphant return from victory over the forces of chaos.[8] However that may be, many such psalms (including this one) certainly date from the monarchic period, and so antedate the account of creation in Genesis 1, which is almost certainly a sixth-century work. Before he became the god who merely needed to make the firmament and separate 'the waters which were under the firmament from the waters which were above the firmament' and to say, 'Let the waters under the heavens be gathered in one place, and let the dry land appear',[9] Yahweh had been a god who, like Ba'al, had to fight the waters until they submitted to his will:

> Thou didst divide the sea by thy might;
> thou didst break the heads of the dragons on the waters.
> Thou didst crush the heads of Leviathan,
> thou didst give him as food for the creatures of the wilderness.[10]

Like Ba'al, Yahweh constantly sustained the ordered world. Thanks to his victory over Mot, Ba'al was able to ensure the fertility of the land and the survival and proliferation of life on earth. Yahweh's victory over the waters enabled him to do the same. From time to time he would release a little of the upper part of the cosmic sea, through window-like openings in the sky; what came out was rain. Psalm 65, after praising Yahweh as the god who calms the raging of the seas, hails him also as the god of rain and so the guarantor of abundant life:

> Thou visitest the earth and waterest it,
> thou greatly enrichest it;
> the river of God is full of water;
> thou providest their grain,
> for so thou hast prepared it.
> Thou waterest its furrows abundantly,
> settling its ridges,
> softening it with showers,
> and blessing its growth.
> Thou crownest the year with thy bounty;
> the tracks of thy chariot drip with fatness.
> The pastures of the wilderness drip,
> the hills gird themselves with joy,

the meadows clothe themselves with flocks,
 the valleys deck themselves with grain,
they shout and sing together for joy.[11]

3

If the divine warrior Ba'al left it to his sister Anat to wage war on human enemies, Yahweh carried out that task himself: he was a fearsome war-god.[12] Although it is no longer thought that there ever was an Israelite conquest of Canaan such as is described in Joshua 1–12, there is no good reason to doubt that some of the tribes were at times involved in military action against Canaanite forces. The 'Song of Deborah' describes a battle in which six tribes defeat a coalition of Canaanite city-states on the plain of Jezreel. Already here the struggle against political enemies is given a cosmic dimension: Yahweh is shown intervening directly in the battle with the assistance of the stars, perceived as lesser divine beings. The origin of the notion is not in doubt: Canaanite mythology knew of a heavenly assembly of 'sons of El', which included an assembly of stars. These beings were inherited by Yahweh. They are the myriads of holy ones, streaming along with flaming fire at his right hand[13] — and they assist him in fighting Israel's wars.

In other accounts of Yahweh's warlike deeds the influence of the Ba'al myth is obvious. When he launches himself against Israel's foes Yahweh is often pictured as a storm-god riding upon the clouds, his subjection of the raging nations is of a piece with his subjection of the roaring, foaming waters.

In a passage in Habakkuk, which was certainly intended to be sung in the Temple at the autumn festival, the unruly waters are wholly identified with an enemy people, presumably the Babylonians, and the divine warrior from the sky shatters both:

Why was thy wrath against the rivers, O Yahweh?
 Was thy anger against the rivers,
 or thy indignation against the sea,
When thou didst ride upon thy horses,
 upon thy chariot of victory?
. . .
Thou didst bestride the earth in fury,
 thou didst trample the nations in anger.
Thou wentest forth for the salvation of thy people,
. . .
Thou didst trample the sea with thy horses,
 the surging of mighty waters.[14]

It was above all through ever new victories over ever new enemies that Yahweh was expected to do, now and in future, what he had done at the beginning: overcome chaos, re-establish cosmos.

4

Yahweh did not — any more than Ba'al or Marduk — remain subordinate to the supreme god. It was normal for a people to exalt its patron god to a position of unique dignity, setting him above all other gods. This happened to Yahweh too: he came to be identified with El.

Some scholars believe that the two gods remained separate throughout the centuries of the monarchy and were fused for the first time during the exile, in the prophecies of Second Isaiah. However, some psalms that are thought to date from the early monarchy suggest that Yahweh was taking over El's attributes already then.[15]

A common epithet of El was Elyon, meaning 'the Most High'. In these psalms Yahweh is likewise called 'the Most High', and his dominance is as absolute as El's. 'Be still', he proclaims, 'and know that I am God. I am exalted among the nations, I am exalted in the earth.' Yahweh is 'most high over all the earth, . . . exalted far above all gods', he has 'established his throne in the heavens, and his kingdom rules over all'.[16] This is indeed the god whom the prophet Isaiah saw in a vision, 'seated on a throne, high and exalted', surrounded by seraphim ceaselessly calling, 'Holy, holy, holy is Yahweh of hosts: the whole earth is full of his glory.'[17]

Yahweh's authority is universal, for — again like El — he created the world, which therefore belongs wholly to him:

> For Yahweh is a great God,
>   and a great King over all gods.
> In his hand are the depths of the earth,
>   the heights of the mountains are his also.
> The sea is his, for he made it;
>   for his hands formed the dry land.[18]

In Psalm 82 Yahweh is even shown presiding over an assembly of lesser gods and holding judgment. He has harsh words for them all. They have neglected to defend the poor and downtrodden, they have sided with the oppressors. By their failure to uphold justice they are endangering the whole ordered world: the very foundations of the earth are shaken. Therefore, though they are 'sons of El', they must die.

Amongst the Canaanite gods it was always the father of the

gods El who was concerned that equity and justice be maintained amongst human beings — and Yahweh showed the same concern. Many psalms dwell on his compassion for the defenceless members of society: 'Father of the fatherless and protector of widows . . . is God in his holy habitation.'[19] The age-old Near Eastern notion of equity as an expression of cosmic order is vividly expressed in Psalm 72, for what is there asked for the king is what was normally expected of Yahweh as El:

> May he defend the cause of the poor of the people,
> give deliverance to the needy,
> and crush the oppressor![20]

The theme was taken up and developed by the prophets, from Amos and Hosea in the eighth century to Jeremiah at the beginning of the exile. Again and again these men voiced their concern for those archetypes of vulnerablity in the Ancient Near East, 'the widow, the orphan, the poor'. Again and again they insisted that in so far as society ignored the rights of such people, it was condemning itself to destruction:

> Ah, sinful nation,
> a people laden with iniquity,
> . . .
> Your country lies desolate,
> your cities are burned with fire;
> . . .
> cease to do evil,
> learn to do good,
> seek justice,
> correct oppression;
> defend the fatherless,
> plead for the widow.[21]

5

David and Solomon made Jerusalem the centre of the cult of Yahweh, and their successors, the Davidic kings of Judah, followed suit. An oracle proclaimed that 'For Yahweh has chosen Zion; he has desired it for his habitation: "This is my resting place for ever . . ."' Jerusalem was accordingly declared 'the holy dwelling of the Most High'.[22] It was a politically motivated innovation. In the older Israelite tradition there were many places of great religious significance — whereas Jerusalem had none. But now Jerusalem had become the royal capital, and that changed everything.

Yahweh dwelt among his people in Jerusalem. It was there that he revealed his will and there that he poured out blessing upon his people.[23] And he did so as king: victorious over the waters of chaos, 'enthroned over the flood', he ruled from Mount Zion as Ba'al ruled from Mount Zaphon.[24] And he continued to offer security and refuge, now as the defender of Israel against those other forces of chaos, the enemy peoples. Because it was his dwelling-place, Zion came to be seen as the 'holy rock'. It was the centre and foundation of the ordered world, the supreme expression of a divinely appointed order that had ceaselessly to be defended against the agents of chaos. If it were captured, the whole cosmos would be reduced to chaos.[25]

Following the example of other Near Eastern kings, David planned and Solomon built a temple in Jerusalem for the patron god. Like other Near Eastern temples, it was a place of mystery: ordinary folk were admitted only to the outer court, the temple itself was accessible only to priests. Nevertheless, the building had a propagandist purpose: it was designed to impress both the Israelite and the Canaanite population with a sense that the new royal dominance was indeed divinely sanctioned. It contained the ark, an object which in pre-monarchic days had probably been regarded as Yahweh's throne and which had served as Israel's palladium in the Philistine wars. On the other hand the building itself was constructed and decorated in the Canaanite mode — a visual declaration that could not fail to impress the Canaanite subjects of the Israelite kings.

The Jerusalem Temple had in fact much in common with the temples of the neighbouring peoples.[26] Its foundation was perceived as a divine act; indeed, its plan was supposed to have been revealed to David by God, and to correspond to that of the temple in heaven. Admittedly, in one respect it was unique: it contained no image of the god. But if Yahweh himself could not be portrayed, his throne — flanked by sculpted cherubim — and his footstool — perhaps identical with the ark — were enough to show that, like any other god, he had his earthly dwelling in his temple.

In its siting and furnishings the Temple was replete with cosmic symbolism.[27] It was built on a great rock — today the spot is marked by the Dome of the Rock — and this rock was imagined as the fixed point around which, in the beginning, God had formed the earth. Beneath the rock were the subterranean waters, those forces of chaos that were for ever threatening to engulf the ordered world. The Temple held those forces at bay. Within the building the primordial waters were represented by an enormous bronze basin, supported on twelve bronze bulls. The basin was half as wide as the building, which itself was designed to represent the ordered world. The bulls and the many carvings of palm trees and pomegranates symbolised the fertility of the ordered world, while the free-standing pillars in front of the porch may well have symbolised its permanence and durability. The Temple was indeed perceived as a source of divine power and life, which flowed out from it, to the immense benefit of the people, their herds and crops.

Like a Mesopotamian temple, the Temple united heaven and earth: Yahweh's heavenly rule was reflected in the sovereignty that he exercised from his earthly throne. The rites performed in the Temple were perceived as maintaining and reinforcing that correspondence. Nobody doubted that any interruption or error in the temple service would endanger cosmos — would indeed be a cosmic disaster, signalling victory for the forces of chaos. In all this the Temple resembled the temples of other Near Eastern societies.

Nor were the rites performed in it peculiar to Yahwism. As elsewhere, sacrifice was at the centre of the cult. People brought bulls or rams or goats or, if they were poor, doves or pigeons, and killed them there; these offerings were then burnt on the altar by the priest. Grain was also offered. Each morning there was a burnt offering, each evening a cereal offering. And as elsewhere, the purpose of sacrifice was to nourish the god. And if, in some of the Psalms, songs of thanksgiving are preferred to sacrifice, these too are intended to augment Yahweh's power.

There were also royal rites, in which the king represented Yahweh and even, it seems, sat on the divine throne. Certainly the relationship between the national god and the king was no less close than in other Near Eastern societies. Through the mouth of the court prophet Nathan, probably in the reign of Solomon, Yahweh made a promise to David: 'Your family shall be established and your kingdom shall stand for all time in my sight, and your throne shall be established forever.'[28] Psalms sung in the Temple itself drive the point home:

> I have sworn to David my servant:
> 'I will establish your descendants for ever,
> and build up your throne for all generations.
> . . .
> I will not lie to David.
> His line shall endure for ever,
> his throne as the sun before me.
> Like the moon it shall be established for ever,
> it shall stand firm while the skies endure.'[29]

Imagery drawn from the myth of Ba'al's kingship, which doubtless figured in Canaanite royal ideology, figures here too: 'I set his hand on Sea, his right hand over River.'[30] Enthroned on Mount Zion, Yahweh's holy mountain, next to a royal temple where such words were sung, a Davidic king could well feel himself to be the earthly representative of his patron god, who was also the supreme god.[31]

6

All in all, the Israelite world-view in the days of the monarchy had much in common with the world-views of the Canaanites, the Mesopotamians, even the Egyptians. Israelites too thought of themselves as living within a divinely appointed order which had been established for their benefit and which would never basically change. What that order meant to them is indicated by three Hebrew words: *mishpat*, *tsedeq*, *shalom*.

Mishpat, often translated as 'judgment', meant more than that. It denoted the regular rule or government of Yahweh as king, and so the divinely appointed order itself. *Tsedeq* was the principle underlying the divinely appointed order. Usually translated, in English versions of the Bible, as 'righteousness', it would be better rendered as 'rightness'. For Canaanites *tsedeq* was the beneficent manifestation of the sun god — that mighty deity who in Canaan, as in so many other societies, watched over the world as judge, bringing hidden crimes to light and righting wrongs done to the innocent. When the Canaanite gods were merged into Yahweh *tsedeq* became his attribute, and the visible manifestation of his activity was called *tsedaqah*. Everything that was right and proper, from Yahweh's bestowal of the right amount of rain at the right season to his furious smiting of the foes of Israel, was included in *tsedaqah*.

When Mesopotamians sought for an Akkadian equivalent of *tsedeq* they chose *kettu*. And just as the deities Kettu and Mesharu supported the throne of the great god of the sun and of justice Shamash, so *tsedeq* and *mishpat* supported Yahweh's throne. Moreover *tsedeq* always kept something from its original association with the sun. At home in the sky as well as in the Jerusalem Temple, it shone out over the world. For Isaiah it was the antithesis of darkness and chaos.[32]

As for *shalom*, it included well-being and good fortune in all its aspects: prosperity in a fertile land, victory in war, peace. *Shalom* was not to be had for nothing. The order that Yahweh had established in the world of nature and the world of international politics was interwoven with the moral order that he looked for in his people. *Shalom* was the fruit of *tsedeq*: if *tsedeq* was maintained in the land, the land would enjoy *shalom*.

But was that how things really were? Israelites were no less aware than other peoples that the divinely appointed order was seldom tranquil, that cosmos was always liable to be disturbed by the forces of chaos.[33] There was the desert, which existed in patches inside the land and as a boundless expanse to the east and south of it. In Israelite eyes the desert was the demonic land, terrible, lawless, inhabited by vile creatures such as serpents, scorpions, jackals, vultures, hyenas. It was the abode of demons and monsters, a realm of confusion and chaos, such as had existed before the ordered world was made. And that waterless waste, where nourishing plants could not grow, was felt as an enduring threat to the cultivated land.

Then there were the hostile nations, some of them so powerful that the kingdom of Judah lay helpless before them. As we have seen, invading armies were perceived as chaos-monsters, akin to the unruly waters or to the scorching wind coming out of the desert. Invasion was experienced as a resurgence of primordial chaos.

And if life was full of uncertainty, death offered no encouraging prospect. What Israelites expected of the afterlife was no better than what Mesopotamians or Canaanites expected of it.[34] The common fate of all alike, rich and poor, righteous and unrighteous, was to go down to Sheol, the netherworld, 'the pit', never to return. Sheol was thought of as deep down under the earth, 'in dark places, in the depths'. Some sort of existence continued there and, as in other Near Eastern societies, the descendants of the dead could ameliorate it by offerings of food and drink. Nevertheless, Sheol was 'the land of oblivion'. The righteous man might console himself with the thought that he would leave behind him a good reputation, perhaps also that his name would survive in his sons. Beyond that the future held little promise for even the most righteous Israelite.

Nor, in the days of the monarchy, had Israelites any grandiose hopes for future generations. Most of the promises contained in the older prophetical books are now generally regarded as interpolations of much later date, and the few that are not are of very modest scope. Despite all the arguments that have been advanced to the contrary, it is hard to see that the Israelites, in the days of the monarchy, had any more expectation of a glorious future consummation than other Near Eastern peoples.

CHAPTER 8

Exile and After

If there had been no more to the Israelite world-view than what has been described in the previous chapter it would now be as dead as the world-views of the other small peoples of Syria-Palestine — or, for that matter, as the Egyptian and Mesopotamian world-views. But in fact there was more: there was the tradition known to historians as 'Yahweh alone'.[1]

On the evidence both of the Bible and of archaeology, polytheism must have been widespread at every level of Israelite society, from peasant hut to royal palace and to the Temple itself. Of course all were agreed that Yahweh was the patron god of Israel, and a mighty god, and a god to be devoutly worshipped — only, many held that other gods could and should be worshipped as well. These people did not regard worship of those ancient Canaanite deities Ba'al and Asherah, or of lesser divine beings in Yahweh's suite — often called 'the host of heaven' and identified with the stars — as derogating in any way from the unique dignity of Yahweh.[2] All this was normal enough in an ancient Near Eastern society. What was exceptional was the denunciation of polytheism by a whole series of prophets, their insistence that Israelites should worship Yahweh alone.

Such a requirement was unique at that time. Of course the patron gods of other peoples too demanded assiduous attention — but they never demanded exclusive attention. And this demand of Yahweh's was to have prodigious consequences. It was out of the tradition of 'Yahweh alone' that monotheism developed, and it is from that tradition that Judaism and, through Judaism, Christianity and Islam are descended.

The Book of Hosea is the oldest document of the Yahweh-alone movement. The prophet Hosea himself was active from 750 onwards, and though the book that bears his name includes later additions, these are the work of men who shared his convictions — and who probably also lived in the eighth century. And what the Book of Hosea portrays is an official religion that is polytheistic, and which is therefore abominated by Yahweh:

they kept sacrificing to the Baals
  and burning incense to idols.
. . .
I am Yahweh your God since
  your days in Egypt
you know no God but me,
  and besides me there is no saviour.[3]

To the present-day reader the words may seem to echo the first of the Ten Commandments, but in fact that commandment echoes Hosea: the Decalogue dates from much later. It was Hosea, too, who first portrayed Yahweh's relationship with Israel as having all the emotional intensity, and all the ambivalence, of marriage at its most passionate. For him, and still for Jeremiah and Ezekiel, polytheistic Israel was like an unfaithful wife, even like a prostitute.[4] In using such language these men were speaking on Yahweh's behalf: 'Yahweh said . . . You shall not prostrate yourself to any other god, for Yahweh's name is the Jealous God, and a jealous god he is.'[5]

In the southern kingdom the Yahweh-alone movement seems to have developed later than in the north. It is only in the reign of King Josiah (641–609) that we find the movement unmistakably at work there. At the beginning of that reign the prophet Zephaniah appears as the spokesman:

I will stretch my hand against Judah
and against all the inhabitants of Jerusalem,
and I will cut off from this place the remnant of Baal
and the name of the idolatrous priests,
those who bow down and swear to Yahweh,
and yet swear by Milcom.[6]

Perhaps under Zephaniah's influence, the movement found supporters among the priests of the Temple, including the high priest Hilkiah. In 622 Hilkiah presented the King with a book which was supposed to have been found during restoration work on the Temple. Genuine find or — as seems more likely — forgery, the book had an overwhelming impact on the king. Its contents are widely believed to have been identical with the nucleus of Deuteronomy 12–26. However that may be, the book prompted Josiah to order the removal from the Temple of all objects devoted to Ba'al, to Asherah or to 'the host of heaven', and the closure of all provincial shrines.

When Josiah was killed in battle in 609 his reform had not produced any mass conversion: the final triumph of the Yahweh-alone movement still lay ahead. But already a process had begun which in the end was radically to transform the traditional Israelite world-view.

2

The Yahweh-alone movement can be understood as a particularly ingenious response to a situation of permanent insecurity.

As the effects of political decline made themselves ever more severely felt and as final defeat and humiliation loomed, an explanation was called for. The notion of Yahweh-alone suggested an explanation: what if the patron god Yahweh was punishing his people for failing to give him exclusive devotion? To some the thought was irresistibly convincing, indeed it opened the way to a whole new theodicy. Yahweh was such a great god that he could shape the destiny of nations — and he was using his power to chastise his people. The kings of Assyria and Babylonia, who appeared so overwhelmingly powerful, were but instruments that he was using to punish the Israelites. Moreover, the Israelites deserved it all: no matter what disaster befell them, it was presented as further proof of Yahweh's righteousness as well as of his power. This was something new. Constantly repeated divine punishment inflicted, quite explicitly, for constantly recurring national apostasy — such an interpretation of political events and of the course of history is without parallel in any other culture in the ancient world.

As portrayed in the Bible, Yahweh's status is indeed quite different from that of any other Near Eastern god. In other Near Eastern societies political misfortunes might be interpreted as signs of divine displeasure — but not such misfortunes as descended on the people of Israel in the period of Assyrian domination. When a people experienced such overwhelming military defeats and such total political subjugation, the obvious conclusion was drawn: its patron deity was recognised as weaker than the patron deity of the conqueror. And once discredited, a god or goddess was soon neglected and forgotten. Nothing of the kind happened to Yahweh. On the contrary: the very magnitude of the disasters was offered as conclusive evidence both of Yahweh's justice and of his power.

In the literature of the Deuteronomistic movement, which belongs to the seventh and the first half of the sixth century, this view of Yahweh and his role is elaborated into a coherent theology. In the Book of Deuteronomy itself the concept of election is made more explicit than ever before: 'for you are a people holy to Yahweh your God; Yahweh your God chose you to be a people for his possession, out of all nations on the face of the earth. It was not because you were more in number than any other people that Yahweh set his love upon you and chose you, for you were the smallest of all nations; it was because Yahweh loves you . . .' At the same time a new emphasis is placed on the notion of the agreement, or 'covenant', that Yahweh was supposed to have made with his people on Mount Horeb: 'You shall have no other gods before me . . . for I, Yahweh your God, am a jealous god, visiting the iniquity of the fathers upon the children to the third and fourth generation of those that hate me, but showing steadfast love to thousands of those who love me and keep my commandments.'[7] In the so-called 'Deuteronomistic History', which comprises the Book of Joshua, the Book of Judges, the two books of Samuel and the two books of Kings, some seven centuries of Israelite history are interpreted in terms of the twin concepts of election and covenant. Each disaster is portrayed as a punishment inflicted by Yahweh on his chosen people for transgressing the covenant, each recovery as a reward for renewed fidelity.

3

'Keeping God's commandments' took on a new meaning. As presented by the Deuteronomist, the covenant included a number of laws that the people were required to observe. There were the 41 laws of the Covenant Code (Exodus 20:23–23:33), and the 68 laws of the Deuteronomic Code (Deuteronomy chapters 12–26), and the innumerable regulations of the Holiness Code (Leviticus chapters 17–26) — and the number of commandments and prohibitions kept growing, until it totalled 613.

All these laws were attributed to Moses, or rather, to God speaking through Moses. In reality they were of diverse orgin. Those cast as judicial cases are probably very old — many of them have parallels in Mesopotamian legal collections. This is true of the laws dealing with such matters as the penalties for murder, rape, theft and other crimes; the damages for harm done to person or property; rules for agriculture and commerce; the financial arrangements involved in matrimony. But there are also many laws that reflect the ideology of the Deuteronomistic movement.

Yahweh had called the Israelites his 'kingdom of priests', his 'holy nation', and stipulations such as circumcision and sabbath observance were designed specially for such a people. Much was even taken directly from priestly law: prescriptions about purity, sacrificial practices, marriage, and many other matters, which hitherto had affected only priests, now became obligatory for the population as a whole. Thanks to this body of religiously sanctioned law an exclusively Israelite and Yahwist way of life came into being: the Israelites became a separate and peculiar people.

If all this had little effect in Judah before the kingdom was destroyed, it had an enormous effect among the exiles in Babylon. There the commandment to learn and teach the Law became all-important for the preservation both of the religion and of the community. As observance of the sabbath and synagogue worship were instituted, the Law became of central importance. It was at the heart of a tradition that each generation was required to master and to pass on to the next generation. By their adherence to that tradition Jews showed their exclusive devotion to Yahweh.

After the exile this new kind of religion was established also in Judah, thanks to the efforts of two men, Nehemiah and Ezra — both of whom belonged to the community in Babylon. Nehemiah, a Jew who held high office at the Persian court, was appointed governor of Judah, which was now incorporated into the Persian empire. Ezra 'the scribe' was empowered by the Persian monarch to teach the Law to all those in Syria-Palestine who called themselves Jews, and to establish an administrative system to ensure that within Judah the Law was obeyed. Both men owed their authority to the fact that, despite its minute size, Judah was strategically important to the Persian empire, and stability within it desirable for military reasons. Both used their authority to strengthen the sense of identity and dignity of the Jews of Judah.

A thorough-going religious reform was introduced. The 'Law of Ezra' was drawn up — a code which by its stipulations and prohibitions ensured that Jews would remain effectively separated from all other peoples. Imposed with the sanction of the Persian government, this body of law also gave Jews a legal status within the empire: no longer a nation, they at least became a community which was licensed to regulate internal affairs in accordance with the law of its god. Some time later the Pentateuch was given its definitive form and, as the Torah, became central to Jewish religion.

At the time of its establishment and exaltation the Law bestowed on individual Jews benefits comparable with those which Zoroastrians received from their own complicated religious code. Now ordinary people could help to sustain and strengthen the divinely appointed order. Moreover, they could be certain that order would never fail. Psalm 119 conveys admirably what the Law had come to mean:

> Eternal is thy word, O Lord
>   planted firm in heaven.
> Thy promise endures for all time,

stable as the earth which thou hast fixed.
This day, as ever, thy decrees stand fast;
for all things serve thee.
. . .
I see that all things come to an end,
but thy commandment has no limit.[8]

It was an encouraging message for a people desperately in need of encouragement. In the past Yahweh had indeed often showed himself wrathful and punitive — but that was because the Jews had not fulfilled the demands of the Law. If they fufilled them in future, all would be well.

4

The Law was not the only source of encouragement uncovered by the intellectuals grouped in the Deuteronomistic movement: it was they who endowed the tradition of the Exodus with the unique significance that it still possesses for practising Jews today.[9] That is not to deny that the tradition had ancient roots. Scholars who accept the historicity of the Exodus usually place the event itself in the thirteenth century, and the tradition was certainly familiar in the northern kingdom by the eighth century.

However, a story of how an enslaved people was liberated, and triumphed over its oppressors, and set out on a journey that in the end was to bring it into a land of its own — such a story can hardly have had much appeal to kings or courtiers. It was a different matter with people who had witnessed the destruction of the kingdom of Judah and who now faced the anguish of exile: to them it must have spoken intimately. And still today the version of the story that they produced, in the Book of Exodus, is the part of the Hebrew Bible that means most to the enslaved and the oppressed.[10]

It was shortly before or during the Babylonian exile that the ancient autumn festival, with its celebration of Yahweh's mastery of the waters, yielded in importance to the spring festival of Passover, with its commemoration and celebration of the Exodus. Nothing could show more clearly how radically the traditional world-view was being transformed. In place of an essentially changeless world order, always threatened yet always surviving, history began to move into the centre of interest.

Not that Yahweh was the only ancient god who was imagined as 'acting in history'. As we have seen, many other gods — Egyptian, Sumerian, Assyrian, Babylonian, even Canaanite — were imagined as taking a very active part in international politics, especially wars.[11]

Nor was it unusual to interpret military victory or defeat, the success or the ruin of a dynasty, as manifestations of divine approval or displeasure: the Canaanite Amarna letters of the fourteenth century, the Moabite Mesha inscription of the ninth, show how widespread the notion was. These parallels are real, and they ought not to have been overlooked as they commonly have been. And nevertheless when all this has been taken into account it is true that, as presented by the Deuteronomistic writers, Yahweh's operation in the field of history is more constant, purposeful and consistent than anything that was attributed to any other god.[12]

It was this view of their god as 'lord of history' that led certain adherents of the Yahweh-alone movement, around 600 BC, to break out of an age-old world-view in which both order and disorder were accepted as permanent realities and to look forward, impatiently, to a glorious consummation when all things would be set to rights.[13]

5

The destruction of the kingdom of Judah by the Babylonians took place while the work of the Deuteronomistic writers was in progress, and it affected its course. Even more profoundly, it affected the thinking of certain prophets.

What is commonly called 'classical prophecy' — meaning the sayings and writings of prophets, and disciples of prophets, that are preserved in the Hebrew Bible — began around the middle of the eighth century, just as the effects of political decline were beginning to make themselves felt, and continued as an accompaniment to the long series of defeats, humiliations and disillusionments that followed. 'Ah, the thunder of many peoples, they thunder like the thundering of the sea! Ah, the roar of nations, they roar like the roaring of mighty waters!'[14] — the traditional symbolism of chaos is wholly appropriate to the age in which 'classical prophecy' flourished. Sometimes the prophets forecast disasters which were about to occur, sometimes they commented on disasters which had already taken place — but above all they proclaimed, ostensibly as a message from Yahweh himself, that these events were judgments by the god of Israel upon the people of Israel. But that too changed with the final collapse of the kingdom of Judah.

That crowning disaster went beyond anything that prophecy had had to explain and justify in the past. It was experienced as a collapse of the ordered world itself. With the destruction of the Temple the divinely appointed order had lost its centre, the correspondence between heaven and earth had been disrupted. As he contemplated the ruins of Jerusalem the prophet Jeremiah felt that he was witnessing a return to primordial chaos:

> I saw the earth, and it was without form and void;
> the heavens, and their light was gone.
> I saw the mountains, and they reeled;
> all the hills rocked to and fro.
> I saw, and there was no man,
> and the very birds had taken flight.[15]

The very desperateness of the situation impelled a new generation of prophets to ask a new question — and to answer it. Granted that Israel had, by its infidelity and disobedience, earned a fearsome punishment — it was still Yahweh's people. Surely, then, Yahweh must relent in the end, must become once more the helpful god he had shown himself at the beginning of Israel's history? If he had once liberated his people from foreign slavery, surely he could and would do so again, and this time permanently?

Yahweh would do more than that. At the very moment when the fortunes of the Israelites were at their lowest ebb, prophecy began to tell of a new, wholly glorious order of things that was shortly to be brought about. The order that Yahweh had always willed was to be re-established — but in a new form, and at a higher level. And it was to be re-established for the sole benefit of those who, like the prophets themselves, were utterly devoted to Yahweh alone.[16]

This reorientation was a product of the exile: the prophets who achieved it, and the people to whom they addressed their prophecies, belonged to the élite that had been deported to Babylon. Materially the situation of that élite — a few thousand nobles, officials, priests and skilled artisans, with their families — was by no means intolerable. They had their own villages, where they were permitted to build houses, plant gardens, buy land. They were also allowed to engage in trade, to employ workers, even to own slaves. Nor were they restricted in their social or family life, or subjected to religious persecution. Nevertheless they were unhappy people: exile was perceived as a state of chaos, comparable with death itself. Moreover, whereas the Israelites left in Judah at least continued to live in familiar surroundings, the deportees found themselves in a strange and perplexing environment.[17]

It was not only that the nation-state of Judah had ceased to exist, that the Davidic dynasty had been deposed, that Yahweh's representative on earth had been brought, blinded and in chains, to die in captivity — the conquerors who had done these terrible things were flourishing. In Babylon the deportees found a vastly more developed and sophisticated civilisation than they were accustomed to.

Moreover this strange land apparently had superior gods. Marduk seemed to have shown himself stronger than Yahweh, for with his Babylonians he had overthrown Judah: the splendid pomp with which he and his fellow-gods were worshipped seemed appropriate to their dignity and power. No wonder that some of the deportees took to worshipping Babylonian gods alongside Yahweh, or that others abandoned Yahweh altogether.

But that was not the only possible reaction. It is not uncommon for a minority of foreign origin to bring intensified devotion to whatever it feels to be peculiarly its own — to emphasise and glorify whatever seems to set it most clearly apart from, and above, the surrounding, indigenous population. The unique inheritance of the deportees was the knowledge and worship of Yahweh. And even while some turned away, in disillusionment and bitterness, from the god who had watched over Israel from its first beginnings, others turned to him with greater confidence than ever. The experience of the Babylonian exile ensured the final victory of the adherents of 'Yahweh alone'.

The emergence of a new hope can be traced in the Book of Ezekiel.[18] Trained as a priest of the Temple in Jerusalem, Ezekiel was deported to Babylon in 597, as a young man, and for the rest of his life devoted himself to the spiritual care of the exiled Israelites. Disciples gathered round him, collated and copied his writings and also altered and added to them. The Book of Ezekiel, though it unmistakably bears the imprint of a single dominant personality, speaks for a whole community — the adherents of 'Yahweh alone' in the first generation of deportees. And if much of the work is devoted to explaining the conquest of Judah and the fall of Jerusalem as a just retribution for polytheistic worship, it also contains a message of hope, likewise uttered by Yahweh himself.

The present crisis, we are assured, will be the final crisis. The community of deportees will make it so — for the deportees are repenting, they are turning to Yahweh without reservation, abandoning all other gods. So the exiled Israelites will become the true Israel, Yahweh's own people, the one and only group with a claim to his support. And Yahweh in return will bring them back to Judah where, in the Temple rebuilt on Mount Zion, they will establish his worship as the one and only cult: 'For on my holy mountain, the mountain height of Israel, says Yahweh, there all the house of Israel, all of them, shall serve me in the land; there I will accept them.'[19]

Ezekiel foresees a miraculous transformation of the Israelite character. This too is described by Yahweh himself: 'And I will give them one heart, and put a new spirit within them; and I will take the stony heart out of their flesh and give them a heart of flesh; that they may walk in my statutes and keep my ordinances and obey them . . . and they shall be my people, and I will be their God.'[20] The time will be ripe for a great ingathering of the exiles. Not only the deportees in Babylon but all the dispersed Israelites, including the descendants of those deported from the northern Kingdom by the Assyrians, more than a century before, will be brought back to the land of Israel. The long-vanished kingdoms will rise again, now indissolubly united, and centred on Jerusalem.

Above the reconstituted nation will rise the rebuilt Temple, endowed with cosmic significance. It is to be Yahweh's house and when he enters it, it will be filled with radiant glory. It will be set upon Mount Zion, which is exalted as the chief mountain of the world. To guard the nation Yahweh will appoint his servant, a new David: he will be the royal shepherd of the reassembled flock — the metaphor so familiar in Mesopotamia and Egypt recurs here. And ordinary mortals too will be required to observe the same norms of social conduct as were accepted, in theory, throughout the Near East. In Ezekiel's view the righteous man, he who lives according to *tsedeq*, oppresses nobody, and especially not the weak — aliens, widows, orphans. He gives bread to the hungry and clothes to those who have none. He does not commit adultery, shuns injustice, deals fairly between man and man.[21]

Yahweh for his part shows himself a thoroughly benevolent patron god. 'And I will make them a covenant of peace and banish wild beasts from the land, so that they may dwell securely in the wilderness and sleep in the woods. And I will make them and the places round about my hill a blessing; and I will send down the showers in their season; and they shall be showers of blessing. And the trees of the field shall yield their fruit, and the earth shall yield its increase, and they shall be secure in their land; and they shall know that I am Yahweh, when I break the bars of their yokes, and deliver them from the hand of those who enslaved them . . .'[22] And Yahweh proceeds to describe the fate of the nations that have been hostile to the people of Israel: they will become 'a waste of desolation', their hills and valleys full of the slain.

In all this the bulk of the population, which never left Judah, is to have little or no part. The exiles for whom Ezekiel and his disciples wrote constituted both a social and an intellectual elite, and it is not difficult to detect, in his prophecies and those ascribed to him, their awareness of their special status, their contempt for the peasantry of the homeland. It is of those still in Judah that Yahweh says, 'surely those who are in the waste places shall fall by the sword; and him that is in the open field I will give to the beasts to be devoured; and those who are in strongholds and caves shall die by the pestilence.... Then they will know that I am Yahweh, when I have made the land a desolation and a waste because of all their abominations which they have committed'.[23] Extermination, no less, is to be the fate of all who refuse to adhere to Yahweh alone and remain obstinately polytheistic.

When Ezekiel and his followers looked to the future, then, they saw themselves establishing the exclusive worship of Yahweh in the land of Judah; and Judah as a nation-state where the common Near Eastern ideal of a divinely appointed, all-embracing order would be realised in every respect, and the most impressive manner imaginable: everything that might impair that order would have been eliminated. But there was to be another prophet among the deportees in Babylon who would go much further, and tell of a future that would be far more radically novel: the anonymous prophet known as Deutero-Isaiah or Second Isaiah.

6

The prophet Isaiah lived in the eighth century, but it is generally accepted that at least half of the book that goes under his name in the Hebrew Bible was composed much later. How, when and where it was composed and redacted is still being debated by biblical scholars, and it is unlikely that agreement will be reached soon. The account given here represents what is still the majority view.[24]

According to that view, by far the greater part of chapters 40–55 is the work of a single prophet, 'Second Isaiah,' who was active half a century after Ezekiel's time. His prophecies seem to belong to the period 547–538. During that period he will have seen the Medo-Persian monarch Cyrus II build by far the greatest empire ever known, and witnessed collisions of empires on a scale never before imagined. Compelled to ask himself what part there could be in those colossal happenings for Yahweh, the patron god of a small and powerless people, he was able to find an answer appropriate to the hour: all those upheavals were the work of Yahweh, and their purpose was the total salvation of his faithful followers.

For Second Isaiah, as for Ezekiel before him, Yahweh's faithful followers are to be found amongst the exiles. The relationship that Yahweh now has with these people is quite different from the relationship he has had with Israelites down the ages. So far as the exiles are concerned, the chastisement so often fiercely threatened by earlier prophets belongs wholly to the past, it has been realised in the fact of the exile itself. And Second Isaiah knows, too, just how Yahweh will prove to his people that they are indeed forgiven and restored to favour: Babylon is about to be overthrown by the Persians.

Pre-exilic prophets had often presented the great conquerors of their day as mere instruments in the hands of Yahweh — but then those instruments were to be used for the chastisement of the Israelites. Cyrus, as presented by Second Isaiah, has a very different role: this pagan monarch is to be the saviour of the Israelites. Yahweh himself has commissioned him: 'I have called you by name and given you your title, though you have not known me.' — 'You shall be my shepherd, to carry out all my purpose, so that Jerusalem may be rebuilt and the foundations of the temple may be laid.'[25] The capture of Babylon will mean the end of exile for the deportees, Cyrus will set them free to return to their homeland.

But if Second Isaiah is first and foremost the prophet of the return, he does not stop there. If one excludes the case of Zoroaster, which is debatable and much debated, Second Isaiah is the first monotheist we know of.[26] Traditionally, even those who insisted that Israelites must worship Yahweh alone accepted that the gods of other peoples were real gods, with real powers, and deserving of worship. The eighth-century prophet Micah summarised the situation with admirable concision: 'All the peoples may walk, each in the name of its god, but we will walk in the name of Yahweh our God for ever and ever.'[27] The Book of Judges was written in the sixth century — and it still has an Israelite warrior say to the king of a neighbouring people: 'Will you not possess what Chemosh your god gives you to possess? And all that Yahweh our God has dispossessed before us, we will possess.'[28]

Second Isaiah will have none of this. Again and again, through his mouth, Yahweh denies all reality to the gods of the heathen nations — challenging them to show their powers, mocking them because they have no powers to show. No doubt this was directed largely at those Israelites who had taken to worshipping Babylonian gods — but beneath the polemical intention one senses concern with a far deeper problem. The Israelites were scattered far and wide, they had no political power left at all — how then could their god save them unless he were omnipotent, in fact the one and only god? 'I am Yahweh, and there is no other, besides me there is no God.' — 'My counsel shall stand, and I will accomplish all my purpose.'[29]

In the days of Second Isaiah the notion that Yahweh created the world was also taking on more importance than it had possessed for the pre-exilic prophets. In Psalm 74, which is apparently a lament for the destruction of the temple in 586 BC, the ancient imagery of the combat myth is given a truly cosmogonic significance. Here Yahweh's victory over the unruly waters becomes an essential part of the original ordering of the world:

Thou didst divide the sea by thy might,
  thou didst break the heads of the dragons in the waters.
Thou didst crush the heads of Leviathan,
  thou didst give him as food for the creatures of the wilderness.
Thou didst cleave open springs and brooks;
  thou didst dry up ever-flowing streams.[30]

For Second Isaiah too Yahweh was the creator god. Through his mouth Yahweh proclaims: 'My hand laid the foundation of the earth, and my right hand spread out the heavens. When I call to them, they stand forth together.'[31] The rationale is clear enough. The collapse of the kingdom of Judah, the capture of Jerusalem, the exile itself — these things represented a victory of chaos over cosmos. Only a god who in the beginning had converted primordial chaos into the ordered world could re-establish such a world.

But in that case Yahweh could certainly do more than merely restore Israel to its former status. Second Isaiah was positive: the love which Yahweh bore to his chosen people was about to be manifested in the most impressive manner conceivable. By an act as wondrous as its original creation, the world was about to be transformed — and the people of Israel were about to be given a most glorious position in the transformed world.

The prophesied overthrow of Babylon, already, is presented as much more than a political event, however momentous: it is an affirmation of right order in the world. For Second Isaiah Babylon represents all the heathen nations that have ever oppressed Israel, and as such it is a concentrated embodiment of the forces of chaos. In the subjugation of Babylon by his instrument Cyrus, Yahweh will be giving a truly shattering demonstration of his power: 'I will make your oppressors eat their own flesh, and they shall be drunk with their own blood as with wine. Then all flesh shall know that I am Yahweh your Saviour.'[32]

Next will come the liberation of the exiles, and their return to Palestine. The return is foretold in terms designed to recall the exodus from Egypt — and the exodus not as it was, or may have been, in reality, but the exodus as it had come to be imagined by the sixth century. For Second Isaiah the way Yahweh had made a path through the sea for the fleeing Israelites was a further manifestation of his power over the forces of chaos — and that same power was now about to accomplish another saving miracle:

Awake, awake, put on your strength, O arm of Yahweh,
  awake as you did long ago, in days gone by.
    Was it not you

who hacked the Rahab in pieces and ran the dragon through?
Was it not you
who dried up the sea, the waters of the great abyss,
and made the ocean depths a path for the ransomed?
So Yahweh's people shall come back, set free,
and enter Zion with shouts of triumph . . .[33]

Like the waters, the desert had always symbolised chaos. When Second Isaiah tells how Yahweh is about to turn the desert into an orderly and fertile place, it is another way of foretelling the triumph of cosmos over chaos. A highway will run from Babylon to Jerusalem, and the countryside will be flattened to ease the way: 'Every valley shall be lifted up, and every mountain and hill be made low.'[34] And though the highway will lie across the desert it will form a sort of oasis, planted with forest trees and supplied with abundant water. The exiles will march along it in triumph. Not only towns and villages but wild beasts and birds will welcome them, and so even will inanimate nature: 'The mountains and the hills before you shall break forth into singing, and all the trees of the field shall clap their hands.'[35]

As the exiles return, so will Yahweh himself. Like Ezekiel before him, Second Isaiah sees the exile as a time when Yahweh has abandoned his rightful home in Jerusalem. Now he will return, like a king, to take up residence in his city. 'The glory of Yahweh shall be revealed, and all flesh shall see it together.'[36] Nor is the glory that of a transcendental king only, it is also the glory of the divine warrior who in olden time led the Israelite tribes into battle, and who is now once again rising in his wrath:

Yahweh goes forth like a mighty man,
like a man of war he stirs up his fury;
he cries out, he shouts aloud,
he shows himself mighty against his foes.[37]

The return of the deportees from Babylon will be only the first stage of a great ingathering of Israelites from all the lands where they are scattered, north, south, east, west. They will be so numerous that the boundaries of Jerusalem will have to be enlarged: the city will be rebuilt, and in greater splendour than ever. All the other cities of Judah will likewise be rebuilt and re-populated. The population will multiply, and the land will enjoy blessings beyond anything it knew before the exile.

Yahweh will establish a new covenant with his people. The love and fidelity that he formerly showed to David and the Davidic dynasty will now go to his faithful people as a whole. *Shalom* —

welfare, harmony, prosperity, peace — will be theirs as never before. And this new dispensation will last for ever:

> For the mountains may depart,
> and the hills be removed,
> but my steadfast love shall not depart from you,
> and my covenant of peace shall not be removed . . .[38]

And again: 'Yahweh has indeed comforted Zion, comforted all her ruined homes, turning her wilderness into an Eden, her thirsty plains into a garden of Yahweh . . . my deliverance is everlasting and my saving power shall never wane.'[39] Clearly Second Isaiah sees the end of the Babylonian exile as inaugurating an age in which Yahweh's sovereignty will be made manifest, unchallenged and unchallengeable, once and for all.

But Yahweh's rehabilitation of his chosen people will not stop there. In the eyes of the heathen nations, the misfortunes that have come upon that people have seemed to reflect on Yahweh himself. Now the time has come for him to show how mistaken they were, how unjustified their scorn: Yahweh is about to demonstrate to all nations that he is indeed the one and only true god — and in so doing he will give the people of Israel a unique position among the nations of the world.

Much has been written about Second Isaiah's 'universalism'; it has even been argued that his work marks the beginning of missionary enterprise. Such a perception is possible only if one assumes that the so-called 'servant songs' are by the same author as the rest of chapters 40–55 — something that has been much contested — and then interprets two lines in one of the 'songs' to fit universalist preconceptions. The main thrust of Second Isaiah's argument leads in a very different direction.[40] All nations that oppose the people of Israel are to be destroyed:

> You shall seek those who contend with you,
> but you shall not find them:
> those who war against you
> shall be as nothing at all.
> You shall winnow them and the wind shall carry them away,
> and the tempest shall scatter them.[41]

Other nations will be permitted to serve the Israelites by bringing them back to their homeland:

> Behold, I will lift up my hand to the nations,
> and raise my signal to the peoples;
> and they shall bring forth your sons in their bosom,

and your daughters shall be carried on their shoulders.
Kings shall be your foster fathers,
  and their queens your nursing mothers.
With their faces to the ground,
  they shall bow down to you,
and lick the dust of your feet.[42]

Nowhere does Second Isaiah advocate proselytism, not once does he recommend that Israelites should travel the world, calling the heathen to conversion. The 'mission' of the chosen people is simply to demonstrate to the whole world, by the way it is rescued from a position of total impotence and deep humiliation, the unique power of Yahweh:

Break forth together in singing,
  you waste places of Jerusalem;
for Yahweh has comforted his people,
  he has redeemed Jerusalem.
Yahweh has bared his holy arm
  before the eyes of all the nations;
and all the ends of the earth shall see
  the salvation of our God.[43]

Again and again the prophet tells how the nations will watch, dazzled, dumbfounded, Yahweh's deliverance and exaltation of the people of Israel. Some will even become slaves of the Israelites, marching behind them in chains, bowing down in supplication, saying, 'God is with you only, and there is no other, no god beside him.'[44] Only in this way will Yahweh achieve his aim 'that men may know, from the rising of the sun and from the west, that there is none beside me. I am Yahweh, there is no other'.[45] Mankind as a whole is of little interest to the prophet: along with the mountains and forests, it is a mere spectator at the prodigious drama. What Yahweh will do for Israel — that matters; and only that.

Less is known about Second Isaiah than about any other Hebrew prophet. In some respects he resembles his pre-exilic predecessors: like them, he claims to have been commissioned by Yahweh and to be speaking in Yahweh's name. But he draws more heavily than they on the language and imagery of the Hebrew liturgy — indeed, his message may well have been delivered to groups of exiles assembled for public worship, before it was incorporated in the literary work we know. He had followers, but there are no grounds for thinking them numerous. And if, as is more than likely, the fourth of the 'servant songs' is about him, he paid for his prophetic role by being scourged and killed — whether by the Babylonian authorities, alarmed by the political implications of his message, or by the deportees, disillusioned when Cyrus failed to carry out the prophesied destruction of Babylon.

The kind of prophecy inaugurated by the prophet of the exile and the return was nevertheless to continue, and to flourish more vigorously than ever, after the exile had ended and the return had taken place.

7

The exile lasted only a couple of generations, for in 538 the Neo-Babylonian empire was indeed overthrown by Cyrus. The policy of this remarkable ruler allowed subject peoples far more autonomy than had been allowed in earlier empires. While political control remained of course firmly in the hands of the Persian conquerors, the various peoples within the Achaemenian empire were encouraged to keep and develop their own ways of life, under their own cultural elites. In accordance with this policy, the Israelite deportees in Babylon were allowed to return to Judah. Funds were even allocated from the imperial treasury for rebuilding the Temple in Jerusalem.

For a moment it must have seemed as though the prophecy of Second Isaiah was about to be fulfilled — but only for a moment. Not only did the nations not stream to Jerusalem — the descendants of the Israelites deported by the Assyrians failed to reappear. The majority even of the deportees in Babylon elected to remain there. The diaspora had come to stay — and that, no doubt, is why it is customary at this point to drop the term 'Israelites', with its territorial associations, in favour of the term 'Jews.'

So far from being the centre of the cosmos the land of Judah, a mere 25 miles long and with a population of perhaps 20,000, rising over a century to perhaps 50,000, became and remained a tiny sub-province in an empire so gigantic that it must have seemed world-wide. Politically impotent, without an army or any means of defence, the population of Judah was forced to abandon all hope of regaining national independence in the foreseeable future. Moreover it was still an impoverished population, scraping an existence from a land that had been repeatedly devastated by war, conquest, taxation.

Prophets continued to foretell a glorious consummation. Many of these prophecies are embedded in the Book of Isaiah: not only all the prophecies contained in the closing chapters, 56 to 66, but also many scattered through earlier chapters are usually accepted as post-exilic.[46] In all probability most of this material belongs to the half-century or so after the end of the exile, but concerning some of it scholarly speculation ranges from the sixth to the third century. Other prophecies of future salvation are to be found in two post-exilic books, Zechariah and Joel; and in the view of many scholars, as post-exilic insertions into the books of the pre-exilic prophets Amos, Hosea, Micah and Zephaniah. In none of these cases can context and date be established with certainty.

On the other hand, there is no doubt as to the general gist of these prophecies. Themes first adumbrated by one or other of the prophets of the exile, Ezekiel and Second Isaiah, recur again and again and are developed further.[47] In the additions to and insertions into the Book of Isaiah, past and present are viewed as an age of sin — but a new age is at hand. There is no suggestion that the former could possibly merge into the latter by gradual improvement: the change can only be brought about by the direct intervention of Yahweh, and it will be total. Yahweh himself speaks of a new creation: 'For behold, I create new heavens and a new earth. Former things shall no more be remembered nor shall they be called to mind. Rejoice and be filled with delight, you boundless realms which I create . . .'[48] It is a prophecy not of a destruction of the universe but of a radical transformation of the world: the present order of the world, imperfect and precarious as it is, is to be suddenly replaced by a perfect and indestructible order.

The supernatural essence of that order is revealed in the famous passage telling how it extends even to the animal kingdom:

> Then the wolf shall dwell with the lamb,
> and the leopard lie down with the kid;
> and the calf and the lion and the fatling together,
> and a little child shall lead them.
> The cow and the bear shall feed;
> their young shall lie down together;
> and the lion shall eat straw like the ox.
> The sucking child shall play over the hole of the asp,
> and the weaned child shall put his hand on the adder's den.
> They shall not hurt or destroy in all my holy mountain;
> for the earth shall be full of the knowledge of Yahweh
> as the waters cover the sea.[49]

The holy mountain is Mount Zion, imagined — as already in Ezekiel — as a huge mountain on which Jerusalem and the Temple are raised high above the world. It is the abode of Yahweh as king, just as Jerusalem will be called Yahweh's city. In the 'night-visions' ascribed to Zechariah Yahweh even announces that the rebuilt Jerusalem will need no walls, as he himself will be as a wall of fire surrounding it on all sides, as well as a glory in its midst.[50]

Radiating from this centre, Yahweh's spirit will transform the inner lives of his people. In oracles, of uncertain date and origin, but included in Joel, this transformation is described with extraordinary vividness. The coming age will be an age of visionary ecstasy:

> You shall know that I am in the midst of Israel,
> and that I, Yahweh, am your God and there is none else . . .
> And it shall come to pass afterward,
> that I will pour out my spirit on all flesh;
> your sons and your daughters shall prophesy,
> your old men shall dream dreams,
> and your young men shall see visions.
> Even upon the menservants and maidservants,
> in those days, I will pour out my spirit.[51]

An addition to Isaiah describes how bodily life too will be transformed. Death in infancy or youth will be unknown: it will be an exceptional misfortune to die before the age of a hundred.[52] Even the gravest infirmities will be cured: 'Then shall blind men's eyes be opened, the ears of the deaf unstopped. Then shall the lame leap like a deer, and the tongue of the dumb shout aloud.'[53] The coming age is, of course, what is often called 'the messianic age', but the term is a misleading one. The designation 'messiah' — which in Hebrew and Aramaic means simply 'anointed one' — figures only rarely in the Hebrew Bible; and when it does appear, it is simply a title given to the king or, when the monarchy no longer existed, to the high priest. The expected future king, of David's line, is never referred to as 'messiah'. Nor is that future king ever portrayed as a supernatural figure. He will be, at most, a great military leader and a wise and just ruler, guided by Yahweh and appointed by him to rule over his people in Judah. The notion of a transcendental saviour in human form, so important in Zoroastrianism and so central to Christianity, is totally unknown to the Hebrew Bible.

In exilic and post-exilic prophecy the future Davidic king plays only a minor part. The reason is obvious: as the chances of a restoration of the dynasty dwindled to nothing, Yahweh assumed direct rule. Yahweh is the real ruler over the coming age of bliss. And that age is imagined as, above all, a time when his kingly rule will be finally and unshakably established, made manifest, and acknowledged. It is also imagined as the time when Yahweh will impose his 'rightness' on the world as never before. Second Isaiah and his post-exilic successors still use the term *tsedeq*, but for them *tsedeq* is something which, though inherent in the world ever since creation, is only now about to be realised:

> For, as the earth puts forth her blossom
> or bushes in the garden burst into flower,
> so shall Yahweh make [*tsedeq*] and praise
> blossom before all the nations.[54]

8

Future bliss is of course reserved for Yahweh's faithful followers. The radiant glory of the coming age has its shadow in the fate that awaits the heathen. It is true that occasionally post-exilic prophecy admits that some of the heathen may be converted to the worship of Yahweh. Those who are will automatically acquire the right to share in the Temple cult, some will even be accepted as priests.[55] Such thoughts reflect the widening of intellectual horizons that had resulted first from exile in Babylon, then from membership of the Persian empire. In the corpus of post-exilic prophecy they constitute a very minor theme.

The main theme is different: Israel's enemies are Yahweh's enemies, and the vengeance that Yahweh will take upon such people will be ruthless. The lightest punishment is servitude: the heathen will be condemned to serve Yahweh's people as shepherds or agricultural labourers.[56] They will also be compelled to contribute to the glorification of Jerusalem, with its rebuilt Temple:

> Foreigners shall build up your walls,
> and their kings shall minister to you;
> your gates shall be open continually;
> day and night they shall not be shut;
> that men may bring you the wealth of the nations,
> with their kings led in procession.
> For the nation and kingdom
> that will not serve you shall perish;
> those nations shall be utterly laid waste.
> . . .
> The sons of those who oppressed you
> shall come bending low to you;
> and all who despised you
> shall bow down at your feet;
> they shall call you the City of Yahweh.[57] . . .

A far worse fate awaits the nations that have oppressed or fought against Yahweh's people. While the stars are darkened in the heavens and the fruits of the earth are blasted these people are given over to slaughter and destruction: 'Their slain shall be cast out, and the stench of their corpses shall rise, and the mountains shall flow with their blood.'[58] Edom — a traditional enemy of Judah, and moreover one which had taken advantage of Judah's weakness in the years following the Babylonian conquest — will be fearfully chastised: 'For Yahweh has a day of vengeance, a year of recompense for the cause of Zion. And the streams of Edom shall be turned into pitch, and her soil into brimstone; and her land shall become burning pitch. Night and day it shall not be quenched; its smoke shall go up for ever. From generation to generation it shall lie waste; none shall pass through it for ever.'[59]

Yahweh's involvement is indicated with the utmost vividness: he is imagined in his ancient guise of the divine warrior, marching victoriously cross-country, and more terrible than ever — trampling Edom and suchlike nations in his fury, so that his garments are drenched in blood.[60] And this fulfils his intention for the world: just as the coming age represents the consummation of history, so the casting down of the heathen represents the final triumph of cosmos over chaos. The core of chapters 38 and 39 of Ezekiel may have been provided by the prophet himself, but in their present form those chapters date mostly from post-exilic times. They tell how the prince Gog, of the land of Magog, will lead a vast army, drawn from many nations, to invade and plunder the land where the Israelites are at last living in peace. Yahweh has planned this — so that by overthrowing Gog and his hosts he may force all nations to acknowledge that his power is indeed boundless. His fury will express itself in an upheaval of cosmic dimensions: 'The fish in the sea and the birds in the air, the wild animals and all the reptiles that move on the ground, all mankind on the face of the earth, all shall be shaken before me. Mountains shall be torn up, the terraced hills collapse, and every wall crash to the ground. I will summon universal terror against Gog . . . and his men shall turn their swords against one another. I will bring him to judgment with pestilence and bloodshed; I will pour down teeming rain, hailstones hard as rock, and fire and brimstone, upon him, upon his squadrons, upon the whole concourse of peoples with him . . . For seven months the Israelites shall bury them and purify the land . . . I will show my glory among the nations; all shall see the judgment that I execute and the heavy hand that I lay upon them. From that day forwards the Israelites shall know that I am Yahweh their God.'[61]

Clearly the mythical Gog and his mythical armies do not stand for specific political entities: what they represent is an evil power which is incarnate in the heathen yet is itself universal in scope, absolute in character. The extermination of the heathen is tantamount to the elimination of the forces of chaos — which in turn is an indispensable prelude to the final triumph of Yahweh and the final vindication of his people. Joel says much the same: Yahweh will pour out his spirit, and the age of visionary ecstasy will dawn, only after Yahweh has brought all the heathen nations to judgment 'on behalf of Israel'. Then 'Jerusalem shall be holy . . . Egypt shall become a desert and Edom a desolate wilderness'.[62]

Yet not every Jew who is alive at the time of the great consummation will share in its blessings. It is perfectly possible to be born into Yahweh's people and still to forfeit one's privileged status: no doubt the prophets were thinking of those who remained obstinately polytheistic.[63] When the new age dawns, such Jews — 'the wicked', 'the lawless', 'the ungodly' — will be destroyed. Indeed, before describing the delights of the coming age Yahweh passes sentence on these miscreants — as though their elimination, no less than that of the heathen nations, were a necessary first step in the great renewal: 'I will deliver you to your fate, to execution, and you shall all bend the neck to the sword . . . For behold, I create new heavens and a new earth.'[64]

Polytheism declined, and so did the tradition of prophecy. But what had been said could not be unsaid. Thanks to its incorporation into the Bible, what the exilic and post-exilic prophets had foretold was to have vast influence, and not only amongst Jews. Confronted with the destruction of temple, nation and monarchy, Ezekiel and Second Isaiah and their followers had found a highly effective response. Shaken by events that seemed to call in question the very existence of an ordered world, wrestling with a sense of utter disorientation and frustration, they had produced imaginings of a glorious future, to be enjoyed by an elite, that were to remain a living force centuries after the situation which originally inspired them had lost all actuality.

CHAPTER 9

Jewish Apocalypses (I)

Some two centuries after the overthrow of the Babylonian empire by the Persians the Persian empire was overthrown by Alexander. Alexander's victories over the Persian armies, between 334 and 331, effectively brought the history of the Ancient Near East to a close and inaugurated the Hellenistic period in the eastern Mediterranean world. Where Alexander's armies penetrated, Greek colonists followed, new, purely Greek cities were founded, old cities acquired Greek inhabitants. And after Alexander's death the vast empire he had founded was divided amongst dynasties of Greek descent. In the third century Palestine — or rather, that part of Palestine which was called Judaea, and which corresponded roughly to the former kingdom of Judah — was under the rule of one such dynasty, the Ptolemaic, based on Egypt. At the beginning of the second century it came under another, the Seleucid, which was based on Syria.[1]

The earliest of the writings to which modern scholars have attached the label of 'Jewish apocalypses' were produced in Palestine in the third and second centuries.[2] They are difficult works, full of strange learning and sophisticated symbolism. And though there is no convincing evidence that they were composed for the benefit of particular sects, the notions about chaos, cosmos and the world to come that they express had no place in official Judaism as it had developed since the days of the Deuteronomists.

The modern label is appropriate enough. The Greek *apokalypsis* means 'unveiling', 'uncovering' — and the one feature common to all the apocalypses is that they purport to unveil to human beings secrets hitherto known only in heaven. Sometimes that secret knowledge is about the heavenly world, but chiefly it is about the destiny of this our world. Indeed, the two kinds of secret are intimately connected, for what happens on earth is perceived as reflecting what happens in heaven. If the world now stands on the brink of a total and final transformation, that is because it has been so decreed in heaven.

The original unveilings were supposed to have taken place long before. The apocalypses are usually pseudonymous: they bear the names of authors, but those authors are holy men who lived, or were believed to have lived, in a past that was already very distant. Of the three apocalypses to be considered here, the Book of Daniel is ascribed to a man who was supposed to have lived during the Babylonian exile of the sixth century; while *Jubilees* is attributed to Moses and *1 Enoch* to a patriarch from the very dawn of time.

The device of pseudonymity reflected the archaising tendency that was characteristic of the Hellenistic age, but above all it served to enhance the authority of a writing. The apocalyptists passionately wanted their productions to be taken seriously, as true, divinely inspired pronouncements. They achieved this by claiming that when God had orginally made these revelations, he had stipulated that they were to be kept secret, locked away, 'sealed', until the time was ripe for them to be published. Such fictions did more than merely authenticate the apocalypses. Not only was the centuries-long delay accounted for — the revelations themselves seemed all the more precious for having waited so long.

The apocalyptists certainly did their utmost to make their books look genuine — for instance, they took care never to mention by name any individual who lived after the time of the supposed authors. There is no mistaking the element of conscious contrivance, of deliberate pretence. Nevertheless — when one reads these works it seems clear that their authors regarded them as in some sense genuine.[3] More: these men seem to have thought of their writings not only as supplementing biblical prophecy but as surpassing it, and of themselves not merely as successors of but as superior to the prophets. Behind the pronouncements of the prophets, they imply, lay a hidden meaning, which was understood only imperfectly by the prophets themselves. Only to a few sages had God revealed that meaning fully — and only now, with the unsealing of the writings of those sages, would the true import of biblical prophecy be made plain.

To a much greater extent than the prophets, an apocalyptist commonly received his revelations in visual form, whether as dreams or as ecstatic visions — sometimes he even felt himself transported to some distant region of the earth, or of the heavens. Often the events that were revealed to him were disguised in symbols and allegories, so that animals would stand for men or nations, good angels be represented by men and fallen angels by stars. Admittedly, it is not at all obvious how far the mass of symbolic material that one finds in the apocalypses reflects first-hand visionary experience. The symbolic language is traditional, in fact it is largely derived from ancient myths; unlike biblical prophecy, apocalyptic is a learned genre, and the smell of midnight oil pervades it. Yet when every qualification is made, it seems inconceivable that without some real, compelling visions the apocalypses would ever have been written down at all.

The revelations that the apocalyptist received from God were very different from the revelations received by the biblical prophets. There is no suggestion in the apocalypses that human beings can, by their obedience or disobedience, affect the shape of things to come. The future is already determined, in fact its course is already inscribed in a heavenly book. And its outcome will be different from anything foretold in classical prophecy. There will be a final judgment. There will be an afterlife when human beings, including the resurrected dead, will receive their just rewards and punishments. And if some human beings will be transformed into angels, some angels will be condemned to everlasting torment.

Apocalyptic differs from biblical prophecy in other respects. To the prophets God had spoken directly — but since their time God had become more remote, futher removed from human beings and their concerns. When he communicated with an apocalyptist it was almost invariably through an intermediary, an angel. Though angels are not unknown to the Hebrew Bible, it is only in the apocalypses that they become major actors. There they accompany and guide the apocalyptists on their visionary excursions, they elucidate the meaning of the visions, the truth of the visions is guaranteed by them. The relationship between angel and apocalyptist is vividly indicated in Daniel: 'I found myself on the bank of the great river, that is the Tigris: I looked up and saw a man clothed in linen with a belt of gold from Ophir round his waist. His body gleamed like topaz, his face shone like lightning, his eyes flamed like torches, his arms and feet sparkled like a disc of bronze; and when he spoke his voice sounded like the voice of a multitude. I, Daniel, alone saw the vision, while those who were near me did not see it . . . I heard the sound of his words and, when I did so, I fell prone to the ground in a trance . . . When he addressed me, I stood up trembling and he said, "Do not be afraid, Daniel . . . I have come to explain to you what will happen to your people in days to come; for this too is a vision for those days." '[4]

The mention of the Tigris is significant. For if one of the roots of Jewish apocalyptic leads back to biblical prophecy, another leads back to the civilisation of Mesopotamia. Ever since the days of Sumer, Mesopotamia had been renowned for its professional class of 'wise men'. In Babylon some of these sages specialised in 'cosmological wisdom' — astronomy, meteorology, the geography of the known world and the mythical geography of paradise; while others specialised in 'mantic wisdom', the art of interpreting dreams. Thanks no doubt to the Babylonian diaspora, the men who first created and established the genre of Jewish apocalyptic were able to draw on these traditions.[5] It is surely no coincidence that — as we shall see — both the dream-interpreter Daniel and the encyclopaedic Enoch have strong Babylonian associations.

In fact the apocalyptists cast their nets wide.[6] Ancient myths, which the Israelites once shared with the Canaanites, come alive again in their writings. And Zoroastrian influence was also at work — how strongly will be considered in a later chapter.

2

In the Hellenistic world there was widespread resentment against foreign rule, and it sometimes found expression in pseudonymous prophecy.[7] In Egypt the *Demotic Chronicle* and the *Oracle of the Potter*, two prophecies of political emancipation composed under Greek rule, were both dressed up to look as though they dated from the reigns of long-dead pharaohs. The Persian *Oracle of Hystaspes* likewise foretells political emancipation, this time from the Roman rule which had succeeded the Greek — and the Hystaspes to whom it is ascribed is none other than Zoroaster's patron Vishtaspa. It is as though people in the conquered nations turned to a distant past for strength to face a present and a future that they had no way of influencing.

Some of the Jewish apocalypses fulfilled the same function, but on a far grander scale. Whereas the Egyptian and Persian oracles deal with limited periods of time and promise improvements that are similarly limited, those Jewish works aim to interpret history itself and to tell of what lies beyond the end of history. The world-view they offer is both dualistic and eschatological. Throughout history the divine intention has been constantly opposed and thwarted by demonic powers, but now God is about to assert his absolute authority: he will bring history to a close and inaugurate the final, everlasting age of salvation.

The earliest of these works were produced in response to a sudden crisis in the 160s. In general governments in the Greek-speaking world did not interfere with ancestral religions, but in the 160s, for reasons about which historians are by no means agreed, the Seleucid monarch Antiochus IV Ephiphanes made an exception for Judaism. It is true that the power of the dynasty was very shaky: Antiochus had been conducting a successful war against Egypt, and was robbed of his victory by Roman intervention. It seems, too, that Antiochus was an unbalanced personality. Whatever the reason, he was more than ready to turn against the Jews of Jerusalem. When a deposed high priest tried to oust his successor, who was favoured by the king and had paid handsomely for that favour, Antiochus had his excuse for intervention.

He proceeded with singular brutality. In 169 he entered the Temple, stole cultic ornaments and stripped the building of its gold decoration. As perceived by the Jews these acts already constituted an unforgivable offence — but worse was to come. In 167, having been forced by the Romans, in a most humiliating fashion, to terminate a renewed campaign against Egypt and to abandon all his designs on that country, Antiochus turned on Jerusalem. The city was pillaged and burned, many of its inhabitants were killed, many fled to the desert, many women and children were taken as slaves. Finally the city walls were demolished. A new fortified city was created and settled with Seleucid troops.

All the observances of the Jewish religion were prohibited: the customary sacrifices were not to be offered, the sabbath was not to be observed, circumcision was not be carried out, the sacred scrolls were to be destroyed — and infringement of any one of these prescriptions was punishable by death. Worst of all, in the Temple the cult of Yahweh was replaced by the cult of a Syrian god, Baal Shamen, a new altar was superimposed on the old, and sacrifices of those tabu animals, pigs, were carried out on it. In the provinces too altars to pagan gods were set up — and everywhere the cult involved, in addition, offerings in honour of the king. Throughout the land everyone was required to take part in this foreign cult, and the royal officials were required to ensure that this was done. The guaranteed right that the Jewish community had always enjoyed, to live according to its own religious laws, was thereby abolished.

But what was Israel if not a community bound together by 'zeal for the Law', as defined by Torah? Many were prepared to fight, if need be to die, rather than transgress it. The priestly family of the Hasmonaeans — a father and five sons — supplied the leaders; and one of the sons, Judas, nicknamed Maccabaeus (perhaps 'Mallethead') proved such an outstanding commander that the war is known to history as the Maccabaean rising. The generalship of Judas and the readiness of his followers to risk their lives in the cause, combined with the internal and external difficulties besetting the Seleucid state, brought victory after victory. In 164 the Temple was liberated and the rightful cult restored, a couple of years later the Jewish community was again granted its traditional rights.

3

In the Hebrew Bible the last book to be composed was the Book of Daniel, which in its present form is a product of the Antiochan persecution.[8] Ostensibly that book is concerned with the doings and experiences of a Jew called Daniel — a legendary embodiment of wisdom and righteousness — at the Babylonian court during and after the exile. The first six of its twelve chapters contain stories about Daniel: they probably originated in the Babylonian diaspora, though they may well have been redacted during the Antiochan crisis. The last six chapters are made to look as though they were written by Daniel himself: in four interlinked apocalypses he describes a series of visions in which the shape of things to come has been revealed to him. But this is all fiction: in reality these chapters were written between 169 and 165 BC, and probably by more than one author.

Alone amongst the first six chapters, chapter 2 contains an apocalypse. It tells how King Nebuchadnezzar dreamed of a huge and fearsome image, with head of gold, breast and arms of silver, belly and thighs of bronze, legs of iron, and feet part iron and part terracotta. While he watched, a stone hewn from a mountain — but 'not by human hands' — struck the feet of the image and shattered them; whereupon all the other parts of the image disintegrated and disappeared, leaving no trace behind. But the stone grew into a great mountain, filling the whole earth. What none of the wise men of Babylon could do, God enabled Daniel to do: in a vision the sage was shown not only what the king had dreamed but also what the dream meant.

The golden head, Daniel explained to Nebuchadnezzar, was the king himself, while the silver and bronze parts of the image stood for future kingdoms, inferior to the Babylonian. But Daniel's main interest was reserved for the fourth kingdom, represented by the iron legs and the feet of iron and terracotta. As iron shatters and destroys all things, so, he foretold, that kingdom would break and shatter the whole earth: he was of course foreseeing the history of Alexander's empire and its successor states. Nevertheless, that kingdom would suffer from internal weaknesses: attempts to bind its several parts together by means of dynastic marriages would fail, for those parts would be as incompatible as iron and terracotta — clearly a reference to the troubled relationship between the Seleucids and the Ptolemies. Finally God himself would intervene: 'In the period of those kings the God of Heaven will establish a kingdom which shall never be destroyed; that kingdom shall never pass to another people; it shall shatter and make an end of all these kingdoms, while it shall itself endure for ever. This is the meaning . . . of the stone being hewn from a mountain, not by human hands, and then shattering the iron, the bronze, the clay, the silver, and the gold.' The stone in fact represents a kingdom which God is to establish 'at the end of this age'.[9] That kingdom will be universal and everlasting. Moreover, it will be terrestrial — why else the assurance that it can never pass to 'another people'? But indeed, what else could be meant by a stone that fills 'the whole earth'?

The schema of four successive world empires, or 'kingdoms', was well known to the Ancient Near East,[10] but in the hands of the compiler of Daniel, working at the height of the Antiochan persecution and the Maccabaean rising, it took on a new significance. This is still more apparent in chapter 7. For chapter 7 foretells much the same future as chapter 2 — only it presents the story in quite a different symbolic guise, of far greater imaginative power; and it carries it further on in time. It also explains things far more precisely. Here Daniel figures not as an interpreter of dreams but as the dreamer, while the task of interpretation is taken over by an angel.

In his dream, or nocturnal vision, Daniel sees four beasts come up out of a tumultuous sea, one after another — each beast different, and each bizarre. A lion with eagle's wings, a bear-like creature, a four-headed winged leopard are followed by a more fearsome beast. Again it is the fourth item that claims Daniel's attention: 'I saw a fourth beast, dreadful and grisly, exceedingly strong, with great iron teeth and bronze claws. It crunched and devoured, and trampled underfoot all that was left. It differed from all the beasts which preceded it in having ten horns. While I was considering the horns I saw another horn, a little one, springing up among them . . . And in that horn were eyes like the eyes of a man, and a mouth that spoke proud words.'[11] The emergence of the little horn is the signal for the consummation of history. God himself appears, as 'the Ancient of Days' or 'Ancient of Years' — a title perhaps borrowed from Canaanite El, who had meanwhile become the chief god of the Syrian pantheon, and who was sometimes called 'Father of Years'. White-robed, white-haired, God is seated on a throne of fire, attended by myriads of beings who make up the heavenly host. The court sits and — as in a contemporaneous court of law — the books are opened. At the command of the divine judge the fourth beast is destroyed and its carcase given to the flames. Then 'one like a son of man' appears 'with the clouds of heaven.' He is presented to the Ancient of Days, who bestows on him a sovereignty which will never pass away, a kingly power such that all peoples and nations in the world will serve him.

Although it is commonly assumed that all this takes place in heaven, there are abundant indications that the author imagined it as taking place on earth. The beasts emerge from the sea, that symbol of chaos, hostile to God and for ever threatening the ordered world. The land on to which they emerge is the same as the land which the fourth beast tramples — and that surely can only be

Palestine. And when the thrones are set in place and the Ancient of Years, attended by myriads of angels, takes his seat, surely that too takes place in Palestine. One recalls other theophanies foretold in the Hebrew Bible — how in Psalm 96 'all the trees of the wood sing for joy before Yahweh, for he comes, for he comes to judge the earth'; how in Zechariah 'Yahweh your God will appear, and all the holy ones with him' in a miraculously created valley by Jerusalem; how in Joel Yahweh himself proclaims that in that same valley 'I will sit to judge all the nations round about.'[12]

What the symbol of the four beasts is meant to convey is explained in the same chapter 7: like the four parts of the image in chapter 2, they stand for the imperial powers that have ruled over the Jews. The fourth beast, so much more terrible than its predecessors, is identified as Alexander's empire and its successor states; the ten horns being various monarchs, with Antiochus represented both by the tenth horn and by the 'little horn'. But there is certainly much more to the symbolism than that.

4

It is known that the ancient myths about chaos-monsters were still familiar in the second century, and they certainly provided the author of chapter 7 of Daniel with his symbolism.[13] In the beasts emerging from the turbulent sea those monsters rise to new life, endowed with a new meaning. Like those primordial beings, the pagan empires war against the divinely appointed order, they strive to replace cosmos by chaos. This is especially true of the fourth and last empire, above all it is true of Antiochus himself. Chapter 7 foretells how the tyrant will hinder pious Jews — 'the saints of the Most High' — in their observance of the Law and will try to alter the times of religious festivals — observances on which the maintenance of the divinely appointed order depended. In chapters 8 and 11, which must have been written later, he appears as a chaos-monster in human form. He will set up 'the abomination of desolation' (*siqus shomen* — an intentional deformation of the divine name Baal Shamen) in the Temple itself. He will exalt himself above every god, including the one true God, he will hurl defiance at the Most High. In visions and by angelic communications all these things are revealed to Daniel — and so is God's revenge: within three and a half years the tyrant's kingdom will be destroyed and the tyrant himself will perish.

Neither Antiochus' rule nor its overthrow is imagined in ordinary political terms. Jews might no longer accept the patron gods of the nations as real gods, but they had replaced them by patron angels — and these angels could take part, alongside human beings, in international conflicts. In Daniel the guardian angel of Israel, Michael, is referred to as 'the great prince,' 'one of the chief princes'; and the fact that Israel has such a powerful protector at the heavenly court means that, however insignificant the Chosen People may appear in purely political terms, it can never be destroyed by any other nation.[14]

On occasion, the patron angels of the nations fight one another in heaven — just as, in Mesopotamian myths, the gods used to fight one another in battles which decided the outcome of battles being fought on earth. In Daniel the notion is presupposed: we hear of future struggles of Gabriel and Michael against the patron angel of Persia, and later — when the Achaemenian empire comes to an end and the Ptolemaic and Seleucid kingdoms arise — against the patron angel of Greece.[15] It is the outcome of this last battle in the heavens that decides the outcome of the Maccabaean war. In the final deliverance and salvation of the Jews Michael is directly involved: '[Antiochus] will meet his end with no one to help him. At that moment Michael shall appear, Michael the great captain, who stands guard over your fellow-countrymen; and there will be a time of distress such as has never been since they became a nation till that moment. But at that moment your people will be delivered . . .'[16]

Given this context, one can understand the cryptic statement that 'the little horn' 'aspired to be as great as the host of heaven, and . . . cast down to the earth some of the host and some of the stars and trod them underfoot. It aspired to be as great as the Prince of the host.'[17] Stars and angels were closely associated; indeed, both in the Bible and in the apocalypses angels are often symbolised by stars.[18] Stars and angels alike were fiery beings, and both were intelligent and responsible agents of their creator; together they made up 'the hosts of heaven'. From 169 onwards Antiochus had in fact had coins minted showing his own image with the title of Antiochus Theos Epiphanes — 'Antiochus God-made-manifest'; and that image was sometimes surmounted by a star.[19] To the devout Jew who was the author of chapter 7 of Daniel, the tyrant must indeed have seemed to be placing himself on a level with the heavenly host and their leader, the archangel Michael, and pitting himself against them.

The Book of Daniel is not a Maccabaean manifesto. Its aim is not to recruit troops but to encourage the civilian population — or rather, an élite within the civilian population — to stand firm under persecution. It is this underlying purpose that links the first half of the book to the second, to form a coherent whole. For the moral conveyed by the stories is the same as the assumption underlying the prophecies. Shadrach, Meshach and Abednego, when they refuse to worship the golden image and are thrown into the white-hot furnace; Daniel himself, when he persists in praying to his god despite the royal prohibition and is cast into the lions' den — such figures are offered as exemplars to the Jews on whom Antiochus was forcing a no less appalling choice. And if Yahweh had rescued those heroes of long ago, how could he fail his faithful followers now? The individual deliverances recounted in the stories foreshadow the mass deliverance promised in the apocalyptic prophecies.

For the deliverance was to be God's work: the Maccabaean forces were but instruments in his hand, their victory, when it came, would really be his victory. In the great vision of 'the Ancient of Days' it is God himself who judges the Seleucid kingdom symbolised by the fourth beast and sentences it to destruction. And it is God himself who bestows everlasting sovereignty over the whole world on 'the one like a son of man'.

5

What are we to make of 'the one like a son of man' who appears 'with the clouds of heaven'? Although in itself the phrase meant no more than 'one like a human being', 'one in human likeness', the figure in Daniel's dream clearly has a special significance. But just what it signifies is open to discussion — and has indeed been endlessly discussed.[20]

Some scholars have claimed that the one like a human being is in fact a human being, a historical personage: Moses, or Judas Maccabaeus, or even Daniel himself. Yet when two passages in chapter 7 are brought together a different answer, or choice of answers, would seem to impose itself. Of the man-like figure it is said that 'sovereignty and glory and kingly power are given to him, so that all peoples and nations of every language should serve him; his sovereignty was to be an everlasting sovereignty which should not pass away, and his kingly power such as should never be impaired.'[21] Of the 'saints of the Most High' it is said that 'the kingly power, sovereignty, and greatness of all the kingdoms under heaven shall be given to [them]. Their kingly power is an everlasting power and all sovereignties shall serve and obey them.' Surely there are only two possibilities: either the 'one like a son of man' is simply a symbol for 'the saints of the Most High', or else he is their representative — the angel Michael or maybe the future messianic king. In either case he embodies the sense of election, the certainty of future vindication and exaltation, of the Jews — or rather, of the Jews for whom the author of Daniel wrote.

For the 'saints (or holy ones) of the Most High' are surely Jews.[22] And the promise which Daniel makes to them in chapter 7 echoes a phrase which, in chapter 5, he addressed to Belshazzar, king of Babylon: 'My lord king, the Most High God gave your father Nebuchadnezzar a kingdom and power and glory and majesty; and, because of this power which he gave him, all peoples and nations of every language trembled before him and were afraid.'[23] All that ever belonged to the great pagan empires will pass to the Jews whom Daniel has in mind. All, and more: for whereas each of those empires exercised its dominion only until it was replaced by another empire, no such fate is in store for the dominion exercised by these Jews: 'Their kingly power is an everlasting power' — or, in the even more explicit words of chapter 2, 'their kingdom shall never pass to another people; it shall shatter and make an end of all these kingdoms, while it shall itself endure for ever.'[24]

All this will happen on this earth. The future empire, which will also be the kingdom of God, will be as purely terrestrial as the pagan empires of the past — indeed, its beginning will be marked by the reconsecration of the Jerusalem Temple, desecrated by Antiochus. Yet the future empire will be utterly different from any previous empire, in fact it will stand in total opposition to everything that has happened in history. Hitherto rightness has been largely absent from the earth, only in heaven has it obtained fully. With the realisation of the kingdom of God rightness will obtain on earth also, the divinely appointed order will have become all-embracing. The Jews who preside over the kingdom will likewise be different from the Jews of the past. The very phrase 'people of the saints of the Most High' hints at a people wholly without sin and wholly reconciled with God; and so does the association with the awe-inspiring figure of 'one like a son of man'.

It is possible to be rather more precise. There are indications in Daniel that these people are the Jews who have followed the teachings of 'the wise' — i.e. of visionaries such as the author of Daniel. From them they will have learned the technique of non-violent resistance; by standing firm under persecution they will have undergone an inner refinement and purification, so that they will become 'shining white'.[25] They will also have learned the technique of eschatological interpretation — how to relate both Torah and visionary experiences to the 'end-time'. Inwardly changed and endowed with esoteric wisdom, they will constitute an élite raised far above the normal condition of mankind. More: as a community of 'holy ones' on earth, they will correspond to the angelic 'holy ones' in heaven. And whereas the kingdoms symbolised by the beasts were in their day so many embodiments of purely human, political power, so these denizens of the coming kingdom will be vehicles of divine power.

6

The establishment of the empire of the saints, or holy ones, as the final and everlasting empire will be preceded by a divine judgment — and this will determine the fate not only of the Seleucid empire but of each individual Jew. After the overthrow and death of Antiochus all the faithful Jews — 'everyone who is written in the book' — will be saved from further suffering. And there was to be an even more marvellous benefaction. Chapter 12 — the last in the book — closes with a remarkable prophecy: '. . . many of those who sleep in the dust of the earth will wake, some to everlasting life and some to the reproach of eternal abhorrence.' This passage has no parallel in the Hebrew Bible: it marks a decisive break with the traditional Israelite notion of death. The prospect of Sheol, 'the pit', 'the land of oblivion', that lay before righteous and unrighteous alike, is replaced by a very different prospect: at the great consummation the dead are to be resurrected, judged and either rewarded or punished.[26]

Who were those dead? This again is a matter on which scholars have expressed widely differing opinions. On the whole it seems likely that the apocalyptist was thinking not of the mass of mankind, nor even of Jews as such, but of two categories of Jews. On the one hand there were the martyrs who, under the Antiochan persecution, had perished rather than betray their god. On the other hand there were those who had capitulated and who were now secure in the tyrant's favour. For why should the pious perish, not so much despite as because of their piety? And why should apostasy be rewarded with life, and often with a prosperous life at that? The prophecy in Daniel 12 affirms that a state of affairs which offended monstrously against Israelite and Jewish standards of justice would not last. Daniel 12 was written while the persecution was still raging — what more natural than that it should have offered a solution to a problem that was all too real to its readers?

The state of the apostates and the martyrs after their resurrection is indicated clearly enough. As in Third Isaiah, the bodies of the apostates are to be exposed to vilification — no doubt in the valley of Hinnom. The martyrs, on the other hand, are to live for ever. It would seem, too, that they are to live a bodily life on this earth. There is a passage in 2 Maccabees which tells how during the persecution a pious Jew, rather than commit idolatry, impaled himself on his sword and threw his entrails at the crowd of onlookers — and as he did so, cried out that God, as lord of life, would in due course give him back his entrails.[27] Truth or fiction, the story shows that the notion that martyrs would be resurrected to live again in the flesh was a very familiar one. But indeed — to return to the Book of Daniel — how else could they participate in the joys of the Jewish world-empire? And if they were to live for ever in the body, would not that body have to be incorruptible and unageing? The revelation that was supposed to have been granted to the sage Daniel, four centuries in advance, would seem to imply all this.

The fate that awaited the 'wise leaders' was more wonderful still. It is indicated in chapter 12: 'The wise leaders shall shine like the bright vault of heaven, and those who have guided the people in the true path shall be like stars for ever and ever'. Admittedly, some scholars have interpreted these images as mere metaphors, signifying no more than that the glory of these men's achievements will remain for evermore. Yet there is abundant evidence, from the following three centuries, in Jewish and Christian sources, that exceptionally holy individuals expected, at the End, to receive garments of glory that would make them resplendent and fiery. The apocalyptist is surely foretelling that he and his fellows will exist for ever as superhuman beings, angel-like, star-like.

CHAPTER 10

Jewish Apocalypses (II)

Two apocalyptic works, *1 Enoch* and the *Book of Jubilees*, deal explicitly with the divinely appointed order and the forces that threaten it.

Although *1 Enoch* does not figure in the Bible, not even in the Apocrypha, in the centuries immediately before and after Jesus it was widely known and enjoyed great prestige. During the second and first centuries BC no less than eleven manuscripts of it were produced for the Qumran community alone, and it was certainly known in far wider circles than that: the authors of later apocalypses were still familiar with it at the close of the first century AD. And if the rabbis, when they came to finalise the Hebrew canon — also towards the end of the first century AD — excluded *1 Enoch*, early Christians were much more favourably disposed. The New Testament and its Apocrypha contain references to the work: in the first century Jude quotes from it, and in the second century Barnabas refers to it as though it belonged to the Scriptures. Indeed, throughout the first three centuries AD it continued to carry all the authority of a canonical book with Christian writers, including such major Fathers as Clement of Alexandria, Irenaeus and Tertullian. It was only in the fourth century, under the influence of Jerome and Augustine, that it fell into discredit, and then only in the western church. In the eastern church it continued to be treated with respect down to the ninth century.

Thanks to the rabbis' veto, no complete version of the work in its original language or languages has survived. The Qumran fragments suggest that the greater part of the work was composed in Aramaic, though some may have been in Hebrew. Our main source, however, is an Ethiopic translation which was made, some time between the fourth and sixth century, for the Christian church in Ethiopia.[1] This version is based mainly on a Greek translation, parts of which survive. Irrespective of language the work is known as *1 Enoch*, to distinguish it from the very different work which is variously known as *2 Enoch*, *The Secrets of Enoch*, and *Slavonic Enoch*.

In reality *1 Enoch* is not the work of any one individual but a collection of works composed between the third century BC and the first century AD; parts of it, like the Book of Daniel, reflect the stresses and strains of the Antiochan persecution. But that is not how the book is presented: ostensibly it was all composed by the Enoch who is mentioned briefly in Genesis, as the seventh patriarch in a genealogy that runs from Adam to Noah. There we are told that he was the father of Methuselah, and a man of exceptional piety: of him alone it is said that he 'walked with God'. His reward was likewise exceptional, for he never died: having reached the age of 365 'Enoch was seen no more, because God has taken him away'.[2]

It has long been recognised that behind the passage in Genesis there lies a more complex tradition. Enoch, the seventh patriarch, has features in common both with the seventh king in the Sumerian King List and with the seventh Sumerian sage — two figures from the remote past about whom Babylonians had much to tell. The Enoch legend seems in fact to have originated in the eastern diaspora, and to have been developed partly in emulation of Mesopotamian models. Certainly by the second century BC Enoch had become a quasi-superhuman figure, enjoying close contact with celestial beings, and endowed with unique knowledge both about the cosmos and about the future. One of the authors of *1 Enoch* has him say, 'I looked at everything in the tablets of heaven, and I read everything which was written . . . all the deeds of men, and all who will be born of flesh on earth for the generations of eternity.' And the *Book of Jubilees* singles him out as the one man chosen by God to foresee and foretell the future, right down to the Last Judgment.[3]

At first glance *Jubilees* seems to be simply an elaboration of the story told in Genesis and Exodus, from the creation of the world down to the escape from Egypt.[4] However, the book is a true apocalypse. It has the form of an apocalypse, in that the story is presented as a secret revelation originally transmitted by angels to Moses on Mount Sinai. Moreover — as in *1 Enoch* — the narrative is interspersed with prophecies of the great consummation; while the way past events such as the Flood are recounted makes them too look prophetic — foreshadowings of the final cataclysm.

Jubilees seems to have been composed by a single author some time between *c.*175 and 140 BC. The author was familiar with the older parts of *1 Enoch* and makes explicit much that those writings only hint at. The fate of the book, too, has paralleled that of *1 Enoch.* Composed in Hebrew, it was translated into Greek and from Greek into Ethiopic; and Ethiopic is the only language in which the complete work survives (it is still printed in versions of the Ethiopic Bible). Again like *1 Enoch*, it was taken very seriously by the Qumran sect. One of the sect's writings, known as the Damascus Document, cites it as authoritative,[5] and twelve fragmentary manuscripts of the work have been found at Qumran — one more, even, than the manuscripts of *1 Enoch*.

Also, the messages of the two apocalypses have much in common.

2

Both *1 Enoch* and *Jubilees* are unmistakably products of Hellenistic civilisation. A world-view so encyclopaedic that it embraced the geography of heaven and earth, astronomy, meteorology, medicine was no part of Jewish tradition — but was very familiar to educated Greeks. In Greek eyes rational comprehension of the working of the universe, and rational speculation about the force behind that working, were the highest of human privileges and achievements. *1 Enoch* and *Jubilees* show that Jewish 'wise men' knew a great deal about Greek wisdom — but they also show them engaged, implicitly, in controversy with that wisdom. These men were concerned not to accept that alien wisdom as it stood but, rather, to point to what it lacked: knowledge of the divine plan — knowledge, above all, of the impending fulfilment of that plan. The authors of *1 Enoch* and of *Jubilees* never doubted that they possessed an understanding of the world that was superior to that of the Greeks — and they were intent on proving it. Those works are not so much attempts at imitating Greek wisdom as exercises in emulating and surpassing it.

Both works are pervaded by a sense of universal order, and in both that order is presented as a expression of God's will. God created heaven and earth and now rules over both like a king. Enoch sees him in the heights of heaven, sitting on a radiant throne, with ten thousand times ten thousand angels in attendance. There lies the source of all order: the cosmos is governed by ordinances decreed by God. In this world-view, which knows nothing of impersonal 'laws', the regularity of nature springs from obedience. Human beings, plants, winds and stars are all creatures of God, and as such, in duty bound to obey him.[6]

The angels are responsible for ensuring that they do indeed obey. Everything in the world is in the care of an angel, and all the angels are under the command of God, 'the Lord of Spirits' as *1 Enoch* calls him. *Jubilees* shows God, on the very first day of the creation, ensuring its stability by creating and appointing angels to look after the winds and clouds, hail and frost, thunder and lightning, cold and heat, winter, spring, summer, harvest-time, the light of dawn and of the morning, the dusk of evening, in fact all things in the heavens and on earth.[7] And *1 Enoch* tells how the angel Uriel 'has power in heaven over night and day to cause light to shine on men: the sun, the moon, and the stars, all the powers of heaven which rotate in their orbits', while lesser angels keep watch over individual stars to ensure that they appear at their proper times and in their proper places.[8]

One of the oldest sections of *1 Enoch* (chapters 72–82) consists of a treatise on cosmic and astronomical phenomena; it is a shortened version of a work that is known to have existed independently, and to date from at least as early as the third century. In the Enochic version the sage is guided through the heavens by the angel Uriel. As he watches the celestial luminaries appearing and disappearing through their 'gates' he learns to appreciate the uniformity and order that God has established throughout his creation and which will continue, unchanged, 'for each year of the world . . . until the new creation shall be made which will last for ever'. He also sees the 'gates' through which the winds blow, and the winds themselves: 'I saw the four winds which turn heaven and cause the disk of the sun and all the stars to set.'[9] Elsewhere the blowing of the winds is presented as symmetrical, and this too is intended as an illustration of all-embracing order.

More clearly than any passage in the Hebrew Bible, *Jubilees* and *1 Enoch* tell of a Last Judgment which is to come at the consummation of time. The splendid opening chapters (1–5) of *1 Enoch*, which are generally thought to date from the third century, tell how human beings will be judged by their submission or otherwise to the divine will which regulates all things in heaven and on earth. The sage sees in a vision how at that time God will come down from heaven, accompanied by his ten thousand angels, take his stand on Mount Sinai, and pronounce judgment. The norm by which he will judge is made perfectly plain:

> Contemplate all the events in heaven, how the lights of heaven do not change their courses, how each rises and sets in order, each at its proper time, and they do not transgress their law. Consider the earth . . . Consider the summer and the winter, how the whole earth is full of water, and clouds and dew and rain rest upon it. . . . Contemplate how the trees are covered with green leaves, and bear fruit. And understand in respect of everything and perceive how He who lives for ever made all these things for you and [how] his works [are] before him in each succeeding year, and all his works serve him and do not change, but as God decreed, so everything is done. And consider how the seas and rivers together complete their tasks. But you have not persevered, nor obeyed the Law of the Lord. But you have transgressed . . . you will not have peace![10]

Within the order that God has established there is a right way for each creature to behave, a proper role for each creature to fulfil. Straying from the way prescribed — that is what will bring condemnation.[11] As *Jubilees* puts it: '[On] the day of the great condemnation . . . judgment is executed on all those who have corrupted their ways and their works before the Lord . . . all who depart from the path which is ordained for them to walk in; and if they walk not therein, judgment is written down for every creature and for every kind.'[12] God is a king — and as on earth, royal wisdom and royal power are correlated. Just like a Near Eastern king, God affirms his authority by displaying both the splendours of his realm and the mercilessness with which he punishes rebellion.[13] It is altogether appropriate that after Enoch, in the course of his heavenly journey, has viewed the wonderful order of the universe controlled by God, he should find himself at the edge of the abyss where rebellious stars, which disobeyed the divine command by failing to rise at their appointed times, are rolling in anguish over fire for 10,000 years.

Though the 'Law of the Lord' described here is not obviously at variance with the Law that is described in the Bible as having been laid down at Sinai, it is different. It is, after all, supposed to be far older, and it is intended not simply for Israelites — who of course did not yet exist in Enoch's day — but for all mankind. The sinfulness of human beings is presented as a form of disorder, an offence against the divinely appointed order of the universe.

In *Jubilees* the Law is indeed revealed to Moses — yet even here, it carries implications which are unknown to Mosaic Law as laid down in the Bible. Its commandments and prescriptions are written on heavenly tablets, and they are promulgated by an angel. They reflect an all-embracing order, and in observing them Jews and angels are united in a common endeavour. Circumcision was a case in point. All angels were male, and God had created the two highest ranks of angels already circumcised. Now Jewish males were required to follow that example. A Jewish boy who was not circumcised on the eighth day after birth had transgressed the order that God had established and was fit only to be 'rooted out of the earth'.[14]

There was another way in which Jews were expected to collaborate with angels: both were supposed to observe the sabbath and the various annual feasts. And of course they were supposed to observe them on the same days — were not the calendrical regulations laid down in heaven and inscribed on the heavenly tablets? Unfortunately, not all Jews accepted the same calendar: the official Jewish calendar of that time was quite different from the calendar expounded in *1 Enoch* and *Jubilees*.[15] But the apocalyptists were not the only ones to know that the latter had been ordained and revealed by God: the Qumran community observed it too.

The official Jewish calendar, sanctioned by the priesthood of the Temple and observed by the great majority of Jews, was in effect a lunar calendar; it gave a 354-day year, plus an intercalated month every three years. The cosmic-astronomical treatise in *1 Enoch*, on the other hand, expounds a solar calendar. Unlike the lunar calendar this was characterised by its regularity. It consisted of 364 days or precisely 52 weeks; or twelve months of thirty days each, plus four intercalated days. Thanks to this regularity, the first day of the year and of each of the four seasons fell always on the same day of the week, which was Wednesday; and all the yearly feasts, such as Passover or the Day of Atonement, also always fell on the same day of the week. Those who advocated this calendar credited the patriarch Enoch with its discovery. Doubtless the age of 365 attributed to him in Genesis has a symbolic value and reflects the same tradition.

Both *Jubilees* and *1 Enoch* claim that the divinely ordained 364-day calendar was originally observed by all Israel but abandoned during the Babylonian exile, so that since that time all the Jews have gone astray. In reality the calendar seems to have been designed in the mid-third century. No doubt it will have appealed to the forerunners of the Qumran community, and later to the community itself, as a means both of affirming their separate — or separatist — identity — and staking their claim to be the one true Israel, the only ones who had preserved the pristine rightness of things.

For *1 Enoch* it is 'the great eternal light which for ever and ever is named the sun', running faultlessly through days and nights in its chariot, as God has commanded, — it is the sun alone that dictates the proper days for sabbaths and feasts.[16] The righteous know this very well — but sinners number the days incorrectly. *Jubilees* is more explicit. At the creation, we are told, 'God appointed the sun to be a great sign on the earth for days and for sabbaths and for months and for feasts and for years . . .'[17] And when the angel Uriel transmits God's instructions to Moses he stresses how all-important it is for Jews to adhere to the solar calendar. If they fail to obey that commandment, 'then they will disturb all their seasons, and years will be dislodged . . .'[18] In the end the true times of sabbaths and the feasts will be forgotten.

Uriel foretells that this will indeed happen. Thanks to exponents of the lunar calendar, holy days will be confounded with 'unclean' days. The implication is clear: in the eyes of the author of *Jubilees*, and of those who took him seriously, those who followed the lunar calendar were disturbing the divinely appointed order of the cosmos.

And this had a bearing on the Last Judgment and its outcome. In the age that will follow the Judgment only the solar calendar will be observed — and only those who observe it now can hope to share in that blissful future.

3

If the ordered world was imperfect, if cosmos was somehow out of joint, that was not the fault of human beings alone: an evil power was at work, intent on thwarting the divine intention.

Such a notion had no place in the Israelite world-view. The '*satan*' who appears from time to time in the Hebrew Bible — most notably in the prologue to Job — is clearly an angel in good standing at the heavenly court. Counsellor and emissary of Yahweh, he owes his title of *satan* — meaning 'adversary' or 'accuser' — solely to the fact that on occasion he takes on the role of prosecuting counsel against this or that human being. Though various attempts have been made to link him with the Satan of later times, these have now been shown to be misguided.[19]

It is more fruitful to set one rather strange passage in the Bible alongside the related passage in *Jubilees*. From Exodus we learn that when Moses, at Yahweh's command, was making his way to Egypt to rescue the enslaved Israelites, Yahweh decided to kill him — and would have done so but for the intervention of a woman who claimed Moses as her bridegroom.[20] In *Jubilees* the narrative that angels dictate to Moses on Mount Sinai is based on Genesis and Exodus — and when it comes to foretell Yahweh's attempted murder of Moses, it completely rewrites the story.[21] The notion that Yahweh could act capriciously and maliciously — that he could even act against the interests of his people — has become unacceptable: now the attempted murder of Moses is attributed not to him but to a spirit called Mastema (the name means 'hostility' or 'animosity'). Mastema will try to kill Moses because he is an enemy of the Israelites and a most active ally of the Egyptians. Fortunately God will be able to circumvent him at every turn and to save both Moses and the Israelites.

In this Mastema one meets, for the first time in a Jewish context, with a supernatural being who is a personification of enmity to God and of active opposition to God's plan for the world — in fact with that terrible power who, as the Devil, was to play so large a part in Christian experience.[22] The few scattered phrases in *Jubilees* stand at the head of a mighty tradition that was to subsist for some two thousand years, and still subsists today.

In *Jubilees* Prince Mastema, as he is called, does not operate alone: he has an army of demons to assist him. To learn who these demons were, and how they came into existence, one must turn to the first part of *1 Enoch*, known as the *Book of Watchers*,[23] which is presupposed by *Jubilees*. Chapters 6–16, plus 19, tell how, as mankind multiplied, some of the angels were so overcome by the beauty of the daughters of men that they came down to earth, took on human form, and acquired a wife each. By so doing they polluted themselves and forfeited the spiritual quality with which God had endowed them. They also taught human beings much that they ought never to have known: how to make weapons, how to dress seductively, how to practise magic — which in turn involved sacrificing to false gods. As a result 'there was great impiety and much fornication, and they went astray, and all their ways became corrupt'.[24] Worse: the illicit intercourse between angels and women produced a race of giants — a most destructive breed, who set about devouring everything on earth, including human beings and even one another.

From the devastated earth the cries of the murdered rose to heaven, where they were heard by the archangels. At their request, God intervened. He sent the Flood, from which only Noah and his offspring would be saved. He had the giants fight one another until all were killed. As for the fallen angels — having witnessed the slaughter of their progeny, they were imprisoned beneath the hills; the angel Azazel, who had taught weapon-making, being shut up in the very depths of the earth, bound hand and foot.

Most of this is a recapitulation of a well-known myth — which, incidentally, can be traced in the opening verses of Genesis 6. In its original form the story will have had no bearing on the present state of the world — and indeed, if the fallen angels are all imprisoned and the giants all dead, what bearing could it have? However, some time during the period of Greek domination the story was adapted to explain the parlous condition in which the Jews now found themselves. The *Book of Watchers* explains that although the fallen angels are held captive inside the earth, their spirits remain active on its surface, leading Jews to transgress the purity laws, and seducing them to sacrifice to pagan gods.[25] Or else — as an alternative — it is the spirits of the angels' offspring, the giants, that remain active. Invisible as spirits, yet capable of assuming many forms, they continue to attack and harass human beings. Whatever their origin, these spirits are the demons who make up Mastema's host.

Jubilees offers a more detailed explanation. Some time after the Flood Noah learned that evil spirits, born of the fallen angels, were leading his own grandchildren astray from the paths of righteousness and were even killing some of them. In answer to his prayer, God ordered the archangels to imprison all these spirits, or demons, inside the earth, in 'the place of condemnation' where their fathers already were. But the demons had a chief, Mastema — and he asked God a favour: that some of the demons should remain on earth, under his command, for the purpose of corrupting human beings and leading them astray. Impressed by Mastema's argument that 'great is the wickedness of the sons of men', God agreed to let them be tempted in this way. A tenth of the demons was spared, to be subject to their chief until the day of judgment.[26] And ever since, Mastema, or Satan, or Beliar (in *Jubilees* he is called by all these names) has been deploying his army of demons to do 'all manner of wrong and sin, and all manner of transgression, to corrupt and destroy, and to shed blood upon the earth'[27] — and moreover to seduce human beings into doing likewise.

This notion too was to haunt Christians down the centuries.

4

In Jewish thinking sin and sickness were closely connected. That the demons were imagined as causing both sickness and sin is clear from the archangels' counter-measures: 'And we explained to Noah all the medicines of their diseases, together with their seductions, and how he might heal them with herbs of the earth. And Noah wrote all things in a book as we instructed him concerning every kind of medicine'[28] — a stratagem which may have protected Noah's immediate descendants, but which clearly had little effect on the fate of later generations.

The author of *Jubilees* is persuaded that ever since the Flood people's health and vitality have been deteriorating, generation by generation.[29] Once people lived almost a thousand years, and all those years were good. Before the end the normal lifespan will have shrunk to seventy or at most eighty years, and all of them fraught with sorrow. In this way transgressions are punished — and especially the transgressions of the Jews who neglect God's commandments and ordinances. Yet the ultimate responsibility for those ever-repeated transgressions and that long, relentless degeneration lies with the demonic hosts under Mastema's command. Abraham recognises it when he prays, 'Deliver me from the hands of evil spirits who hold sway over the thoughts of men's hearts, And let them not lead me astray from Thee, my God',[30] and when he blesses his son Jacob with the words, 'The spirits of Mastema shall not rule over thee . . . to turn thee from the Lord.'[31]

Mercifully, the demons are not unopposed: there are also angelic beings sent by God to protect human beings from their influence. The world is in fact divided into two hostile camps, one consisting of God's obedient angels and an elect minority of Jews, the other of demons — themselves descended from disobedient angels — and of the multitudes of human beings who have fallen under their sway. And while the elect few, fortified by the obedient angels, steadfastly observe the divine commandments, the rest of mankind, constantly lured on by demons, plunges from transgression to transgression.

This state of affairs will not continue for ever. For the author of *Jubilees* the 'great judgment' is close at hand. After recounting, in the guise of prophecy, the evils that had flourished in Palestine in the recent past — the oppression and persecution of pious Jews by Seleucids, conflicts amongst the Jews themselves, such misery in the land that children were grey-haired and looked like little old men[32] — he foretells a great change. First will come a religious revival: 'And in those days the children will begin to study the laws, And to seek the commandments, And to return to the paths of righteousness.'[33] Then the oppressors will be overthrown.

No doubt the prophecy that the righteous will rise against their oppressors and drive them out should not be understood in purely military terms — any more than similar prophecies in the writings of the Qumran community. Rather, the author must have been expecting a judgment such as is described in *1 Enoch* — which tells how God will come down from heaven with the angelic host and the earth will be convulsed, while the elect ones will be kept in safety. Then the unrighteous will be judged and punished. And if the heathen are to disappear into the depths of the earth, Jews who have been seduced by demons into worshipping them are to be 'bound for ever' in the valley of Hinnom outside Jerusalem.[34]

At the same time the fallen angels will meet their final doom. And if their punishment is appalling, that — the *Book of Watchers* reminds us — is because they introduced chaos into the ordered world. An archangel conducts Enoch to a place where he sees a chasm with colossal pillars of fire falling from heaven; and beyond it, a place which has 'neither the firmament of heaven above it, nor the foundation of earth below it'. This fiery desert beyond earth and sky is the place of punishment for superhuman beings who have transgressed the divinely appointed order, including stars which failed to appear at their appointed times. Enoch learns that on the day of judgment the fallen angels themselves will be brought from their present prison beneath the earth's surface to be cast into that fiery abyss, there to remain, in perpetual torment, for all eternity.[35]

The world will be cleansed of every destructive power, human and demonic, it will be for ever healed and at peace: 'there will be no more a Satan nor any evil one, and the land will be clean from that time for evermore.'[36] In such a world the elect can look forward to a glorious destiny. *Jubilees* tells how the long process of degeneration will be put into reverse:

> And the days will begin to grow many and increase amongst the children of men,
> Till their days draw nigh to one thousand years,
> And to a greater numbers of years than [before] was the number of days.
> And there will be no old man
> Nor one who is full of days
> For all will be as children and youths.[37]

On a renewed earth, under a renewed heaven, the elect will dwell in safety, while the heavenly luminaries, endowed with fresh power, pour healing upon them. So far *Jubilees*: *1 Enoch* is more explicit. At 'the great judgment [which] will bring everything to its consummation for ever' the elect will inherit the earth, they will be blessed with prosperity and peace and joy. A wonderful tree, uniquely fragrant, with leaves and flowers that never wither, and bearing abundant fruit, will stand in their midst. They will draw its fragrance into their very bones and this will guarantee to each a long life on earth, free from all sorrow, toil or pain. Above all, God, 'the Holy and Great One, the Lord of Glory, the Eternal King', will reside amongst them, on a high mountain which will be his throne: they will be at one with him, his light will shine upon them.[38]

In another section of *1 Enoch*, comprising chapters 85–90 and known as the *Animal Apocalypse*, the theme of degeneration and regeneration is presented as involving all mankind. Here the various nations are symbolised by animals — the first generations of human beings as bulls and cows, the Israelites as sheep, the enemies of Israel at different historical periods as various kinds of wild beast which are given to attacking and devouring sheep, the Maccabees as powerful rams which turn on the wild beasts and rend them.

The fallen angels figure here too, and so do other maleficent angels — the guardian angels of the hostile, heathen nations. At the Last Judgment — which for the author lies in the immediate future — all these are to be thrown into the fiery abyss, along with all the peoples who have ever oppressed Israel. Now the rest of mankind embarks on a process of regeneration. The heathen nations are so filled with awe by the revelation of the power of the one true God that they are converted. Then God removes the existing Jerusalem and sets in its place a new Jerusalem. The existing Temple too is removed and replaced by a new Temple, larger, higher, more splendidly decorated — and to this all nations stream. God gladly accepts them all.

A profound transformation is set in motion. The first generations of mankind were appropriately represented by bulls and cows. It was only after the intervention of the fallen angels that the various peoples could be appropriately represented by such creatures as lions, tigers, wolves, dogs, hyenas, wild boars, foxes, badgers, pigs, falcons, vultures, kites, eagles, ravens: many of them fierce and dangerous to man, all of them unclean by Jewish standards and all, certainly, inferior to the original bulls and cows. And the sheep, too, are inferior: in the allegorical narrative they are generally shown as mere victims of the wild beasts, for ever crying out, but unable to protect themselves. Even the ram — Judas Maccabaeus — who emerges from their midst, and uses its horns to such good effect, is obviously a lesser creature than a bull. But all this changes when God has established his kingdom on earth.

First there is born a single white bull, with such big horns that all animals are afraid of it. But then the animals themselves are changed: 'And I looked until all their species were transformed, and they all became white bulls; and the first among them was a wild-ox, and that wild-ox was a large animal and had black horns on its head.'[39] God rejoices over these new creatures — and with cause. The degeneration that has taken place since the fall of the angels is reversed, the grandeur of the first generations after creation is restored. Indeed, it is exceeded. For if Adam was represented simply by a white bull, the wild-ox with strikingly large horns clearly represents a new Adam, more glorious than the first — and perhaps a messianic figure too. And again — in the beginning there were only a few human beings in the world, but in that future and final time there will be multitudes, and each individual will be as fine as were those original few.

Admittedly, these happy people will not be immortal, nor will they include the righteous dead. When the righteous dead are mentioned at all in *1 Enoch* or in *Jubilees*, they seem destined for a blissful existence as disembodied souls — a notion so un-Jewish that scholars commonly attribute it to Greek influence. What these works most certainly promise is that generation after generation, succeeding one another endlessly, will enjoy long, healthy and peaceful lives, lived in perfect fellowship with God, in a world from which every agent of chaos, human or supernatural, will have been eliminated.

5

The authors of the Book of Daniel and of the Enochic writings certainly thought of themselves as men set apart by God, endowed with a wisdom not available to ordinary mortals, the only ones to understand the past and to foresee the future. They were also convinced that they were destined for a uniquely glorious place in that future. Yet there is no convincing evidence that they were sectarians in the sense of belonging to an identifiable group. In fact only two apocalyptic sects are known to have existed between, say, 200 BC and 100 AD: the Qumran sect and the early Christians.

A good deal is known about the sect that produced the 'Dead Sea Scrolls' found at Qumran, in the Judaean desert, between 1947 and 1956.[40] In the opinion of most scholars it was identical with the Essene sect described by the Jews Josephus and Philo of Alexandria and more briefly mentioned by the Roman Pliny the Elder. It probably came into being in the early second century BC, during the Antiochan crisis; its end came in 68 AD, during the first Jewish war against Rome. Some of its members, male and female, lived an ordinary lay existence within Palestinian society. Other, more strictly observant members — probably all of them men — joined the community at Qumran; this originated between 150 and 140 BC. Numerically the sect was insignificant: it has been estimated, on the strength of archaeological evidence, that the population of Qumran can never have exceeded 200 at any one time; while the total number of Essenes is believed to have been about 4000. On the other hand these people were all voluntary and committed members of the sect: one became an Essene not by virtue of one's birth (as a Jew became a Jew) but by virtue of a personal, adult choice.

The sect was rigidly exclusive and supremely self-confident. Small as it was, it regarded itself as the true Israel, the one and only custodian of the authentic religious tradition. Its founder — a priest referred to only as 'the Teacher of Righteousness' — had been sent to establish a 'new convenant', a new and final form of the eternal alliance between God and the people of Israel. And this covenant existed for the benefit of the members of the sect, and for theirs alone. If members of the sect were encouraged by their spiritual leaders to bear in mind their frailty and unworthiness, their need for God's help and support, they were also assured that faithfulness to the new covenant would be marvellously rewarded. Already in this present life they were raised to an 'everlasting height', and united with the angels in heaven: God had 'joined their assembly to the Sons of Heaven.'[41]

The brotherhood at Qumran followed a way of life that was peculiar to itself. The purpose of these 'men of perfect holiness', as they called themselves, was 'to seek God with a whole heart and soul'. This of course meant that they must observe every single one of the 613 positive and negative commandments of the Law, but that was not all. Like the Christian monks of later times, they were required to sink themselves in the community — eating in common, praying in common, holding their possessions in common. And the structure of the community was hierarchical. The priests came first, and chief amongst the priests was the Guardian or Master: it was his responsibility to teach the community not only how it should live but what it should believe.

Doctrinal instruction was very necessary, for God had revealed to the Teacher of Righteousness a wisdom so esoteric that it was otherwise enjoyed only by the angels:

> My eyes have gazed
>   on that which is eternal,
> on wisdom concealed from men,
>   on knowledge and wise design
>   [hidden] from the sons of men;
> on a fountain of righteousness
>   and on a storehouse of power,
> on a spring of glory
>   [hidden] from the assembly of flesh.
> God has given them to His chosen ones
>   as an everlasting possession,
> and has caused them to inherit
>   the lot of the Holy Ones.[42]

At the heart of 'the wisdom concealed from men' was the conviction that all things in heaven and earth are ordered according to 'the mysteries of God'. Implicit in the term *raz*, 'mystery' — which is found also in Daniel — is the notion that everything that exists or ever has existed or ever will exist does so because in the very beginning the God of knowledge established its design and destiny. Human beings and angels alike are involved, the course of history and the vicissitudes of the heavenly host are all graven before God: all things must run their appointed course and accomplish their appointed tasks. Suffering and sin too are in accordance with 'the mysteries of God', and they too must continue until the end that God has appointed. The workings of the universe are no less predetermined: the stars must follow their prescribed paths, snow and hail must fulfil their prescribed purposes. It is, essentially, the world-view of *1 Enoch* and of *Jubilees*.

'The wisdom concealed from men' included calendrical lore. Every ritual act had to be performed not only in the right manner but also at the right time. As the Community Rule puts it, members of the sect were not to 'depart from any command of God concerning their appointed times; they shall be neither early nor late for any of their appointed times.'[43] This was a demand not only for exact punctuality in making the two daily prayers, at sunrise and sunset, but also for a strict observance of the sect's liturgical calendar. Many references in the scrolls show this to have been based on the same solar calendar as is described in *1 Enoch* and *Jubilees*. Only by keeping in harmony with 'the laws of the Great Light of heaven'[44] — which were also God's laws — and not with the 'festivals of the nations', could the liturgy be made to correspond with the liturgy sung by the angelic choirs in the heavenly temple.

No less important was the doctrine of the 'two spirits'. The clearest account of this is also to be found in the Community Rule:

> [The God of Knowledge] has created man to govern the world, and has appointed for him two spirits in which to walk until the time of His visitation: the spirits of truth and falsehood.
>
> Those born of truth spring from a fountain of light, but those born of falsehood spring from a source of darkness. All the children of righteousness are ruled by the Prince of Light and walk in the ways of light, but all the children of falsehood are ruled by the Angel of Darkness and walk in the ways of darkness.
>
> The Angel of Darkness leads all the children of righteousness astray, and until his end, all their sins, iniquities, wickednesses, and all their unlawful deeds are caused by his dominion in accordance with the mysteries of God . . .
>
> But the God of Israel and His Angel of Truth will succour all the sons of light. For it is He who created the spirits of Light and Darkness and founded every action upon them and established every deed [upon] their ways.
>
> And he loves the one everlastingly and delights in its works for ever; but the counsel of the other he loathes and for ever hates its ways.[45]

'The sons of light', 'those born of truth', were of course the members of the sect. They were the ones in whose hearts the Prince of Light had triumphed over the Angel of Darkness, and the fruits of that victory were supposed to be such qualities as humility, patience, goodness. Those in whose hearts the Angel of Darkness reigned were characterised by pride, haughtiness, impiety — qualities which it was easy enough to perceive in the great of this world.

At first 'the children of darkness', 'those born of falsehood', were identified with the Jerusalem priesthood, with the high priest as the supreme embodiment of evil. For many centuries, in fact ever since the time of Solomon and his chief priest Zadok, the Zadokite family had monopolised the office of high priest — but during the Hellenistic crisis of the early second century it lost that monopoly. In the eyes of traditionalist Jews the Hasmoneans who succeeded them were usurpers. The individual whom the so-called 'Damascus Rule' identifies as 'the wicked priest', 'the liar', 'the spouter', was certainly one of the Hasmonean high priests — probably the first of them, Jonathan. It was in protest against his usurpation that the sect first took refuge in a 'place of exile', its settlement by the Dead Sea. And some Essenes always insisted that so long as the Temple remained in Hasmonean hands they would take no part in its rites: God could be truly worshipped only by and in the sect itself.

Later, for instance in the scroll known as the War Rule, the most passionate denunciations are directed against the Romans — here called by the name traditionally used by Jewish writers to denote the greatest world power of the day: Kittim. The Romans, who ruled directly over Judaea from 6 AD onwards (save for one three-year interlude), were generally hated by the Jews. When the corruption and ineptitude of their procurators resulted in war, they found the sectaries of Qumran so intransigent that in the summer of 68 they destroyed the settlement and exterminated its occupants. On the assumption that the Qumran sect was indeed Essene, it is worth quoting the account that Josephus gives of the conduct of Essenes when tortured by their last enemies:

> The war with the Romans tried their souls through and through by every variety of test. Racked and twisted, burned and broken, and made to pass through every instrument of torture in order to induce them to blaspheme their lawgiver or to eat some forbidden thing, they refused to yield to either demand, nor ever once did they cringe to their persecutors or shed a tear. Smiling in their agonies and mildly deriding their tormentors, they cheerfully resigned their souls, confident that they would receive them back again.[46]

What gave these men such extraordinary strength was the interpretation they put on biblical prophecy. Like the apocalyptists, they were convinced that only they understood what the prophets had proclaimed; even the prophets themselves had not appreciated its full significance. Thanks to divine inspiration, the Teacher of Righteousness had been able to grasp and expound the real import of the teaching of Isaiah, Hosea and the rest. To him God had made known 'when time would come to an end', and what would then befall the righteous and the unrighteous. As is normal with such groups, the value that the Qumran community attached to humility and patience did not prevent it from harbouring fantasies of a very different nature. That all who had rebelled against God were about to be annihilated, that 'the House of Judah', i.e. the sect, was about to triumph once and for all, that the righteous dead would be resurrected to share in their glory — all this belonged to the secret knowledge that the Teacher had decoded from biblical prophecy and passed on to his disciples, the sages of the community. And this was the knowledge that, in the hour of trial, enabled members of the sect not only to accept but to rejoice in martyrdom.

The Teacher of Righteousness and the sages who followed him always had looked forward to a final struggle, in which a central role would be reserved for the sect itself. Under the command of 'the Prince of the Congregation' the 'sons of light' would attack the 'army of Satan' — first the ungodly Jews and their allies amongst the neighbouring peoples, next the Romans occupying the land. Then they would move on to Jerusalem and restore the right kind of Temple worship there. From this base they would again wage war against various Near Eastern peoples. Victory over all these would be followed by victory over the Romans. With the totality of the hosts of Beliar utterly defeated, the sons of light would celebrate their 'hero', God himself. The hymn in which they would do so recalls post-exilic prophecy:

> Rise up, O Hero!
> . . .
> Smite the nations, Thine adversaries,
> and devour flesh with Thy sword!
> Fill Thy land with glory
> and Thine inheritance with blessing!
> Let there be a multitude of cattle in Thy fields,
> and in Thy palaces silver and gold and precious stones!
> O Zion, rejoice greatly!
> Rejoice all you cities of Judah!
> Keep your gates ever open
> that the host of the nations may be brought in!
> Their kings shall serve you
> and all your oppressors shall bow down before you;
> they shall lick the dust of your feet.
> Shout for joy, O daughters of my people!
> Deck yourselves with glorious jewels
> and rule over the kingdoms of the nations!
> Sovereignty shall be to the Lord
> and everlasting dominion to Israel.[47]

The earthly war was to last no less than forty years, with a sabbatical interlude every seventh year — and, as in Daniel, it was to have a cosmic dimension, or heavenly conterpart. Angelic armies under the command of Israel's patron angel Michael — here called also the Prince of Light and Melchizedek ('my king is righteousness') — would fight demonic forces led by Beliar, also called Melkiresha ('my king is unrighteousness'). The two hosts would be so evenly matched that victory would go three times to the angelic hosts, three times to the demonic. In the end God himself would intervene to annihilate all evil.[48] Or else — an alternative version — there would be a Last Judgment, when Michael/Melchizedek would recompense the 'holy ones of God' and execute vengeance on Satan and his lot.[49]

The sect expected its final victory to be immediately followed by the messianic age. In some scrolls the 'Prince of the Congregation' is identified as the Davidic Messiah: he is to rule over Israel as king, under the guidance of a priest-Messiah, 'interpreter of the Law', 'who shall teach righteousness at the end of days'.[50] This was little more than a magnified projection on to the future of what already existed in the institutions of the sect. In any case, the messianic age is not the final age: there are hints of a more fundamental transformation, sometimes called 'the Renewal'.[51] When that comes about sinners will be plunged into 'eternal torment and endless disgrace . . . in the fire of the dark regions'.[52] The righteous, on the other hand, will be rewarded with 'healing, great peace in a long life, and fruitfulness, together with every everlasting blessing and eternal joy in life without end, a crown of glory and a garment of majesty in unending light'.[53]

There is no suggestion here — any more than in Daniel — that the righteous will exist as immaterial souls in an immaterial realm: those crowns of joy and garments of majesty will be bestowed on bodies, which will then become — as in Daniel — radiant, angel-like. And there are passages that confirm — what one would in any case have assumed — that the righteous dead will be resurrected to share in that final, everlasting state of glory: 'Hoist a banner, O you who lie in the dust! O bodies gnawed by worms, Raise up an ensign . . . !'[54] Life in fellowship with the angels, which they have enjoyed already in this present life,[55] will be the lot of all the righteous for evermore.

Such was the world-view of the Qumran community. Much in it recalls those works so treasured by the community: the Book of Daniel, *1 Enoch*, *Jubilees*. In its thorough-going dualism, on the other hand, it is reminiscent of another body of teaching. The two warring spirits, at work both in the world and in the heart of every human being; the eschatological battle between the prince of light and the prince of darkness, with victory going first to one, then to the other; the final intervention of God to annihilate the forces of evil; 'the Renewal', inaugurating, for the elect, an eternity of bliss on a purified earth — all this is strangely similar — more so than anything in the apocalypses — to the expectations propounded and propagated by Zoroastrianism, especially in its Zurvanite version.[56]

Coincidence or influence? We shall be returning to the question.

CHAPTER 11

The Jesus Sect

Although for hundreds of years Jews had been united in their devotion to Yahweh and in their acceptance of the obligations enshrined in the Torah, there the unity ended. Until the fall of Jerusalem in 70 AD and the ensuing council at Yavneh there was no Jewish orthodoxy: Judaism embraced a number of groups and sects. Christians constituted one of these, alongside Sadducees, Pharisees, Essenes, 'Zealots' (resistance fighters), and other less well known. Christians, including Gentile converts, regarded themselves as Jews — and until well into the second century other Jews also regarded them as Jews, albeit Jews with strange beliefs about the prophet Jesus of Nazareth.[1]

Almost all that we know about Jesus and his first followers comes from the Greek writings by the unknown authors who took the names of Matthew, Mark and Luke, and which we know as the synoptic gospels. The oldest gospel, Mark, was probably composed around 70 AD, but older material is to be found embedded in Matthew and Luke. This material, not known to Mark, is commonly credited to a lost source known as Q, which is thought to have been composed around 50 AD.

It is thought that Mark and Q reflect the beliefs and expectations of charismatics who, like Jesus and the original disciples, wandered from village to village in Syria-Palestine, establishing communities of converts as they went.[2] Both sources draw on traditions reaching back to the time of Jesus himself. The Jesus they portray is first and foremost a proclaimer of the kingdom of God (we stay with the customary term, though 'reign of God' might be a more accurate translation). He is obsessed with the coming of the kingdom and the elimination of the forces that obstruct it.[3]

But what did Jesus mean by the kingdom and its coming? Did he think of it as a gradual process of ethical improvement, extending into the remote future? Or as something that exists here and now, and into which individuals can enter if they so choose? Or as an individual's sense of fellowship with God? All these views have been maintained, with much learning and firm conviction, by serious scholars. But other scholars have offered interpretations which, however they may differ on particular points, are at one in taking full account of the historical context in which Jesus lived and thought and taught.[4] They maintain that Jesus expected a total transformation of the world in the very near future. That interpretation — which is powerfully supported both by Mark and by Q — will be adopted here.

2

Why did the kingdom or reign of God lie in the future at all, why had it not always been present? Mark's answer is clear enough, though many present-day Christians find it difficult to accept. Various Jewish sectarians, such as the Qumran community and the author of *Jubilees*, believed and taught that a supernatural being of terrifying power was at work in the world, constantly striving to thwart God's intentions — and would continue to do so until, in the last days, he was overthrown and destroyed.[5] Mark shows Jesus and his disciples as deeply imbued with the same conviction: a dualist eschatology was central to their world-view too.

At the very beginning of his ministry, after his baptism by John, the Spirit descends on Jesus and immediately drives him into the wilderness, there to be tempted by Belial (or Satan) for forty days. In Jewish tradition temptation was thought of not as seduction but as a trial of strength: Jesus is locked in combat with Satan — a Satan so powerful that he has possession of all the kingdoms of the world. And the setting of the contest, or combat, is significant: 'Jesus was among the wild beasts, and the angels waited upon him'. The images were very familiar from the Bible: as, according to Genesis, Adam lived in peace among the wild animals in the Garden of Eden, so, according to Isaiah, in the age to come animals of all kinds will live in peace with one another and with human beings. Now that Satan is being vanquished, paradise is being regained — and if angels serve a human being, that is a sign that communion between God and mankind is being restored.[6]

In earlier versions of the combat myth the forces of chaos that the hero — Marduk or Ba'al — fought and defeated were symbolised by the tempestuous sea. Perhaps echoes of that linger in the stories of how Jesus rebuked and calmed the stormy waters of the Lake of Genesareth, and walked upon them? More certainly Jesus fights Belial by means of his exorcisms.[7] In the northern territories 'men of God' always had been credited with healing powers: already in the ninth century Elijah and Elisha were famous healers. But the powers ascribed to Jesus (also a northerner) had a new and deeper meaning. It was generally believed that physical and mental sickness alike were manifestations of Satan's power. Physical illness was God's punishment for sin — but it was Satan who seduced human beings to sin in the first place. Mental disorder was the result of demonic possession — but again, the demons were Satan's assistants.

God had given Jesus power over demons — as they themselves recognised, crying, 'What do you want with us, Jesus of Nazareth? Have you come to destroy us?'[8] And because demons belonged to the Satanic hosts, each casting out of a demon was seen as a successful assault on Satan's realm. That is how, in the gospels, Jesus presents his exorcisms to those who criticised them: his debates with his opponents make it plain that he regarded these acts as part of a mighty struggle which he and his followers were waging, on God's behalf and with God's help, against God's enemies.[9] He even compares himself to a robber who breaks into the house of a strong man, binds him and steals his belongings — the strong man being, of course, Satan.[10]

The same significance is ascribed to the activity of Jesus and his disciples as preachers. When Jesus sends out his followers to preach the coming of the kingdom he also bids them, at the same time and as part of the same mission, to cast out demons, to heal the sick, and to offer forgiveness of sins — three ways of saying the same thing, since the words meaning 'to heal', 'to expel demons', 'to forgive sins' were interchangeable synonyms.[11] Exorcism, healing, telling of the kingdom — these were all ways of extricating people from the dominion of Satan.

Winning people away from Satan by preaching, defeating demons by exorcism and healing, were all part of the eschatological drama. Although Jesus' miracles have sometimes been compared with the feats of Hellenistic or rabbinical magicians, their original significance was quite distinctive: they were all intended to prepare the way for the coming of the kingdom, indeed they were all signs that the kingdom was at hand. When the disciples return from their mission, rejoicing in its success, the report evokes a vision in Jesus: he sees Satan fall like lightning from heaven.[12] The meaning is surely plain enough: Satan, who once had possessed all the kingdoms of the world, is losing his power, his dominion is ending, his ruin is assured.

Not that Satan's reign will end peacefully, gradually yielding to the kingdom of God. Before cosmos can be made perfect, the forces of chaos will rage as never before. Apocalyptic writings had long foretold a period of terrible tribulation which would precede the final age of salvation: the war of the fourth beast against the people of

God, in Daniel, is an example. The so-called 'Marcan apocalypse' tells how wars and rumours of wars, earthquakes and famines, persecutions and flights, darkening of sun and moon, disturbances of the stars will usher in the great consummation[13] — and even if this particular prophecy was constructed by the early Church, the dread it reflects may well have been shared by Jesus. The wording of the Lord's prayer suggests as much: for originally 'lead us not into temptation' or 'do not put us to the test' referred to the tribulation planned by Satan as a last, desperate stratagem to subvert the faithful and to retain his power on earth.[14] That is why, in the Matthean version, the appeal is reinforced by another: 'Save us from the evil one', i.e. Satan. As we shall see, the Book of Revelation has much to say about all this.

The kingdom would come when God wished it to come, its coming would be a breaking into history of a divine force, destroying and transforming. But human beings could prepare the way, the number of those who would be eligible to participate in the kingdom could be increased. Jesus and his disciples are shown as aiming at that.

3

In the coming kingdom God's original intention, no longer thwarted by Beliar/Satan, would be fully realised.

Jesus shared the view of the world that was normal in his time. There was the earth with its human inhabitants, and there was heaven with the angelic hosts — and the two were not only related, they were meant to correspond exactly. That was now about to happen: God, in a supreme manifestation of his sovereign authority, was about to restore the order that he had originally intended for heaven and earth, but which now obtained only in heaven. 'Thy kingdom come, Thy will be done, On earth as it is in heaven' — viewed in such a context the words take on a new meaning. They speak of the restoration on earth of what had been there in the beginning. The Garden of Eden had indeed been heaven on earth. Now that primordial perfection was about to be re-created — on a massive scale, involving multitudes instead of only Adam and Eve, and this time irreversibly.

There would be a new relationship between human beings and God — a relationship in which trusting, filial submission would be answered by boundless paternal love. And that love would manifest itself in a transformation of the human condition. All the blessings that the prophets had foretold would be granted. In Isaiah it is said,

'Then shall the blind man's eyes be opened, and the ears of the deaf unstopped'.[15] For Jesus this could only mean that the power that Satan and his demons had exercised over human beings would be broken — and that was already happening. In the words of Matthew: 'Great was the amazement of the people when they saw the dumb speaking, the crippled strong, the lame walking, and sight restored to the blind; and they gave praise to the God of Israel.'[16]

There would be no more hunger either. Here too the Book of Isaiah pointed the way:

> On this mountain Yahweh of Hosts will make
> for all peoples a feast of fat things,
> a feast of wine on the lees, of fat things
> full of marrow, of wine on the lees well refined.[17]

Jesus too sometimes compares the kingdom to a banquet — and it seems that this was no mere comparison, for at the Last Supper he is reported to have said, 'I tell you this: never again shall I drink from the fruit of the vine until that day when I drink it new in the kingdom of God.'[18] This need not imply that Jesus expected to return from the dead — it could equally well indicate that he expected the next few days to bring not his death but the kingdom. And there is also the story of the fig-tree that Jesus is supposed to have cursed for not bearing figs when he wanted them, though it was out of season: it has been plausibly argued that he was in fact praying for the coming of the kingdom, when the primordial curse on the ground would be lifted and nature would pour forth its fruit in unceasing abundance.[19]

However we choose to interpret such passages, there is no doubt that some early Christians did look foward to an age of boundless fertility and plenty. An echo of such expectations is preserved in the writings of the 'Apostolic Father' Papias, which date from around 110 AD.[20] A man of learning, and bishop of Hieropolis in Phrygia, he was a Jewish Christian who shared the outlook of the Jewish Christians who had fled from Palestine to Asia Minor after the catastrophe of 70 AD. He devoted himself to preserving the accounts of Jesus' teaching that were circulating — and this is what he believed Jesus to have foretold about the millennium which was to follow his return to earth:

> The days will come in which vines shall appear, having each ten thousand shoots, and on every shoot ten thousand twigs, and on each true twig ten thousand stems, and on every stem ten thousand bunches, and in every bunch ten thousand grapes, and every grape will give five-and-twenty metretes of wine. And when any one of the Saints shall take hold of a

bunch, another bunch shall cry out, 'I am a better bunch, take me; bless the Lord through me'. Likewise [the Lord] said that a grain of wheat would bear ten thousand ears, and every ear would have ten thousand grains and every grain would give ten pounds of the finest flour, clear and pure; and apples and seeds and grass would produce in similar proportions; and all animals, feeding only on what they received from the earth, would become peaceable and friendly to each other, and completely subject to man. Now these things are credible to believers. And Judas, being a disbelieving traitor, asked, 'How shall such growth be brought about by the Lord?' But the Lord answered, 'They shall see who shall come to those times'.[21]

Such expectations were traditional. Sanctioned by much in post-exilic prophecy, they found a place also in Jewish apocalyptic: the apocalypse known as *2 Baruch*, which dates from around 100 AD, contains a prophecy very similar to the one in Papias.[22] Still in the late second century Irenaeus, who was both bishop of Lyons and a distinguished theologian, could quote Papias along with passages from the Scriptures — and even insist that it was an indispensable part of orthodoxy to believe that these things would come to pass.[23] That Jesus himself should have shared the same expectations must have seemed a matter of course.

As presented in the Gospels, Jesus expected the denizens of the kingdom to be very different from ordinary mortals. His comment on John the Baptist indicates as much: nobody greater than John had ever been born of woman, yet the least in the kingdom would be greater than he.[24] Elsewhere Jesus makes it plain that he regards John the Baptist as the reincarnation of Elijah — that more-than-prophet whose return to earth was expected, traditionally, to herald the coming of the kingdom. So if John is inferior to the denizens of the future kingdom, these will have become something more than those 'born of woman'.

The hint can be pursued. Again one recalls the phrase in the Lord's Prayer, 'on earth as it is in heaven'. With the coming of the kingdom, the state of this world will mirror what has always obtained in heaven. Perhaps, then, heaven and earth will be fused, and all those dwelling in that single realm will be equally glorious? Sometimes Jesus seems to suggest just that: in the kingdom, he says, men and women will be 'like angels in heaven', and will not marry. Elsewhere he is reported as saying that in the kingdom the righteous 'will shine like the sun'.[25]

Paul, admittedly, expected a purely spiritual kingdom, 'in the air'. Jesus himself seems, rather, to have looked forward to a transformed earth. If so, he was true to a tradition which went back to such apocalypses as *1 Enoch*, and beyond that to Second Isaiah. Nor — contrary to a widespread opinion — was that tradition to be quickly rejected by Christianity: not everyone agreed with Paul. The greatest of the Fathers, Augustine, has this to say in *The City of God*, composed between 413 and 427: '. . . this heaven and this earth shall cease, and a new world shall begin. But the old one shall not be utterly consumed; it shall only pass through a universal change . . . Then (as I said) shall the world's corruptible qualities be burnt away, and all those that held correspondence with our corruption shall be made fit for immortality, that the world, being so substantially renewed, may be fitly adapted unto the men whose substances are renewed also.'[26]

A dispensation in which human beings were rescued from the tyranny of the demons, relieved of the burden of sin, relieved also of those physical and mental disorders which were the outward sign of sin or of demonic possession, situated in an incorruptible and infinitely fertile earth, endowed with glorious, unageing and immortal bodies, above all reconciled with a loving and forgiving father-god — that, it would seem, is what many early Christians understood Jesus to have promised.

But he had promised it only to a minority.

4

The Galilee in which Jesus operated was a fertile land, cultivated by prosperous farmers. Still, even in Galilee there were the unprivileged and the marginalised — and Jesus concerned himself with them. They did not have to be deserving, let alone pious: the fact that they were usually excluded was commendation enough. The physically sick and the mentally disturbed; people who followed despised trades, such as tax-collectors and prostitutes; the poor and ignorant; women and children, who normally counted for nothing — these were given priority by Jesus in his personal dealings.

These were also the people to whom Jesus chiefly addressed his proclamation. When Jesus summarises the miraculous healings that he has performed in preparation for the coming of the kingdom he does so in words that combine three passages from Isaiah — and two of those three refer specifically to the coming salvation of the lowly, the humble, the poorest of the poor, captives, prisoners. Then he adds, as a further sign of the impending consummation: 'the poor are hearing the good news'.[27] And it was indeed good news for them, for they were the ones best qualified to enter the kingdom: 'But many who are first will be last, and the last first.'[28] The Beatitudes point in the same direction: 'Blessed are you poor; for yours is the kingdom of God. Blessed are you that hunger now, for you shall be satisfied.'[29]

The kingdom will be open also to those who care for the poor — who give food to the hungry, drink to the thirsty, clothing to the naked, help to the sick and to prisoners.[30] 'Go, sell what you have, and give to the poor, and you will have treasure in heaven.'[31] — 'When you give a feast, invite the poor, the maimed, the blind ... You will be repaid at the resurrection of the just':[32] Jesus was no social reformer, let alone a revolutionary, nor did he regard anyone as automatically excluded from the kingdom by his social position in this world — but clearly the kingdom which he expected was not for those who clung to their power, prestige or wealth.

There was another limitation. Jesus was Jewish through and through — and if his followers were all Jews, that corresponded to what he believed about his own mission: like any prophet before him, he felt that he was sent to Israel alone.[33] Of the evangelists only Luke shows Jesus as sometimes preaching to the Gentiles as well as to Jews — and Luke, who was also the author of the Acts of the Apostles, had every reason to suggest that the mission to the Gentiles corresponded with the original intentions of Jesus. The other two synoptic gospels present a different picture: according to them, the ministry of Jesus and his disciples was wholly confined, during his lifetime, to the Jewish people. Indeed, to judge by Mark one would think that the mission of 'the twelve' never was expected to extend beyond Jesus' own country, Galilee, before the kingdom came.

The Gentiles were of little concern to Jesus. If on occasion he could use his power as exorcist for the benefit of a Gentile, it was an act of great condescension. The story of the Syro-Phoenician no doubt represents his attitude fairly. This Gentile begged him to drive a demon out of her daughter. 'He said to her, "Let the children be satisfied first; it is not fair to take the children's bread and throw it to the dogs." "Sir," she answered, "even the dogs under the table eat the children's scraps." He said to her, "For saying that, you may go home content; the unclean spirit has gone out of your daughter."'[34] And the Gentiles whom he imagines as streaming to the new Temple do so — as in *1 Enoch* — because they have been converted to Judaism. For the nations the way to salvation could only lie through assimilation to a saved Israel.

As proclaimer of the kingdom Jesus thought only of Jews. What is more, he was himself a strict observer of the Law. The widespread notion that he substituted for the Law a new dispensation of grace is based on the sayings of the Diaspora Hellenist Paul. Jesus himself spoke differently: 'It is easier for heaven and earth to come to an end than for one dot or stroke of the Law to lose its force.'[35] If, as seems likely, he foretold that the existing Temple would be destroyed and replaced by a new Temple, that will no doubt have earned him the hostility of the priestly establishment — but it in no sense implied an abrogation of the Law: *1 Enoch* and *Jubilees* also foretell these things, and there they usher in the consummation of time.[36] The denizens of the kingdom of God were to be strictly observant Jews.

5

Why did Jesus' disciples wonder whether he was, perhaps, the Messiah? And did Jesus, perhaps, regard himself as the Messiah? No aspect of his life and teaching has been more hotly debated than this, and no answer is ever likely to find general acceptance.

On the one hand there is not a word in the gospels to suggest that Jesus ever claimed to be the Davidic Messiah, i.e. a military leader who would defeat Israel's enemies, re-establish the nation as a political power, and install himself as king. On the other hand he does seem to have expected that, at the coming of the kingdom, God would reassemble the scattered tribes of Israel in a purified Zion, around a new Temple.[37] Moreover, his decision to choose twelve disciples seems to have originated in his expectation of ruling over all the twelve tribes. His promise to 'the twelve' certainly suggests as much: 'I vest in you the kingship which my Father vested in me; you shall eat and drink at my table in my kingdom and sit on thrones as judges of the twelve tribes of Israel.'[38] Indeed, some of his followers are even shown staking claims for themselves in the future kingdom — as when they ask who will be the greatest in the kingdom,[39] or when the mother of Zebedee's sons' requests, 'I want you to give orders that in your kingdom my two sons here may sit next to you, one on your right, and the other on your left.'[40]

Perhaps the contradiction is more apparent than real. 'Messiah', after all, meant no more than 'the anointed one': it did not necessarily refer to a Davidic monarch.[41] We are told that when Jesus read the lesson in the synagogue at Nazareth he chose a passage from Isaiah:

> The spirit of the Lord is upon me because he has anointed me;
> He has sent me to announce good news to the poor,
> To proclaim release for prisoners and recovery of sight for the blind;
> To let the broken victims go free,
> To proclaim the year of the Lord's favour.[42]

He added, 'Today, in your very hearing this text has come true' — and both he and his listeners must have recalled the threat with which the Isaianic text continues: 'a day of vengeance of our God.'

It would seem, then, that Jesus thought of himself as the Messiah of the poor; and that he expected Roman rule in Palestine to be overthrown in the very near future, not indeed by an armed rising but by the direct intervention of God, and to be replaced by a regime in which he would rule as god's vice-regent. So the mocking notice that the Romans nailed to the cross seems to have been more appropriate than is usually thought.

Yet there was something paradoxical in the situation. None of the changes that were expected to accompany the appearance of the Messiah took place: the kingdom did not come, and Jesus was executed. That the sect did not disappear but, on the contrary, began to prosper, was due to the development that figures in the gospels as the resurrection. As has been observed in a scholarly study by a Christian writer, the resurrection cannot be established by the methods of historical enquiry:[43] the accounts of the appearances of the risen Jesus in Galilee and in and around Jerusalem differ too widely to count as historical evidence for a physical occurrence. But there is no doubt that stories of a resurrected Jesus soon began to circulate, and to be believed. And that changed everything.

Belief in the resurrection of Jesus was the very core of the faith of the early Church: without it that Church would probably never have come into existence, certainly it would never have flourished as it did. On this we have the evidence of Paul, who had clearly heard more about these appearances than is recorded in the gospels or in Acts: '. . . he was raised to life on the third day, according to the scriptures . . . he appeared to Cephas, and afterwards to the Twelve. Then he appeared to over five hundred of our brothers at once, most of whom are still alive, though some have died. Then he appeared to James, and afterwards to all the apostles. In the end he appeared even to me . . . This is what we all proclaim, and this is what you believed. . . . Now if this is what we proclaim, that Christ was raised from the dead, how can some of you say there is no resurrection of the dead? If there be no resurrection, then Christ was not raised; and if Christ was not raised, then our gospel is null and void, and so is your faith; and we turn out to be lying witnesses for God . . .'[44]

At first the resurrected Jesus was still thought of as the Messiah who was to bring salvation to the Jewish people. Indeed, the resurrection seemed to make sense of a fate which otherwise ought certainly not have befallen the Messiah. If Jesus had failed to carry out the messianic task in his lifetime, that must simply mean that his messiahship had become effective only after his death. Thanks to this interpretation the original expectations not only survived the crucifixion but were reinforced. Luke sees nothing incongruous in making the apostles ask Jesus, as a final question before his ascension into heaven: 'Lord, is this the time when you are to establish once again the sovereignty of Israel?'[45] In fact it was because Jesus continued to be identified with the expected Messiah of Judaism that, within a few years of his death, the term 'Christian' was coined in the Greek-speaking Judaeo-Christian community of Antioch: for 'Christos' is simply the Greek equivalent of the Semitic 'Messiah', meaning 'the Anointed One'.

But the concept of the Messiah, as applied to Jesus, soon began to be transformed.

6

Traditionally, the Messiah had been thought of as a human being. But by the first century AD certain groups were elaborating a concept of the Messiah as a transcendent, supernatural being — manlike in appearance, yet in effect a second divine figure.

One classic account of this figure is to be found in the part of *1 Enoch* commonly known as the *Parables or Similitudes* but described by the author, more appropriately, as the *Second Vision.*[46] The *Similitudes* form a substantial portion of the whole work — chapters 37 to 71, out of a total of 104 chapters; but its relation to the rest has been, and continues to be, hotly debated. It is absent both from the Aramaic fragments of *1 Enoch* found at Qumran and from the fragmentary Greek translation, and this has led some scholars to regard it as a late work, dating from the second or even the third century AD, and much influenced by the Gospels. However, prevalent opinion at present is that it is a Jewish work, originally composed in Hebrew or Aramaic some time in the Roman period; and it has been plausibly argued, from internal evidence, that this was either during or shortly after the ministry of Jesus.[47]

In the *Similitudes* the Messiah, i.e. the Anointed One, is called also 'the Son of Man' — perhaps a reminiscence of Daniel 7 — and 'the Elect One'; and we are told that he was chosen, designated for his unique destiny, before sun or stars or earth were created. God, called here 'the Lord of Spirits' — a title found nowhere outside *1 Enoch* — has kept him hidden until the time comes for him to be revealed. That time will be the Day of Judgment.

The Day of Judgment will come when a predetermined number of the elect has been reached. Then the Lord of Spirits will take his place on the throne of his glory, surrounded by the angelic hosts and with his council of angels standing before him. The 'books of the living' — the records of the good and evil deeds done by each individual — will be opened, and judgment will be passed. That will be the task of the Son of Man: seated, like the Lord of Spirits, on a throne of glory, he will pronounce sentence on the living and the dead.[48]

Especially he will condemn the great ones of the earth. Confident in their wealth and trusting in their heathen gods, 'the kings and the mighty and the exalted, and those who possess the earth' have denied the Lord of Spirits — and denied, too, the Son of Man.[49] Now they will gaze in terror and despair on the Son of Man. They will beg him for a respite in which to confess their wrongdoing and to praise the one true God — but, unmoved, the Son of Man will hand them over to the angels of punishment. The righteous will watch with delight as their oppressors are driven from the face of the earth, to dwell for ever in darkness underground, among the worms, with no hope of resurrection — or else to be tormented in the fiery Valley of Hinnom.[50]

By the judgments he pronounces the Son of Man will effect a purification of the earth. Not only human sinners but also the fallen angels, 'those who led the world astray', will be disposed of once and for all — 'and all their works will pass away from the face of the earth'. Everything evil will pass away, vanquished by the power of the enthroned Messiah — 'and from then on there will be nothing corruptible'.[51] Finally the Lord of Spirits will transform heaven and earth into 'an eternal blessing and light'.[52]

On the transformed earth, under the transformed heaven, the righteous — including the righteous dead, now resurrected — will enjoy unchanging bliss. From being oppressed they will triumph 'in the name of the Lord of Spirits', and glory and honour will be theirs. More: 'the earth will rejoice, and the righteous will dwell on it, and the chosen will go and walk upon it'.[53] In them, the elect of the new Israel, the ancient prophecy about possessing the land of Palestine will be fulfilled, finally and for evermore.

Although the righteous will live on earth, their lives will altogether transcend the normal limitations of human life. The Son of Man will live in their midst, and with him they will dwell, and eat, and lie down, and rise up, for ever.[54] They themselves will be transformed. The Lord of Spirits will provide them with 'garments of life', so that they become like angels. And they will be immortal: 'the chosen [will be] in the light of eternal life; and there will be no end to the days of their life . . .'[55]

The end of the *Similitudes* is astonishing. Enoch describes how he was translated in spirit into the heavens where, in the presence of the

Lord of Spirits and myriads of angels, the archangel Michael assured him: 'You are the Son of Man who was born to righteousness.' The Messiah who is to preside over the transformed world and its transformed denizens turns out to be none other than Enoch himself. Michael's promise could not be clearer or more absolute: 'And all . . . will walk according to your way . . . and with you will be their dwelling, and with you their lot, and they will not be separated from you for ever and for ever and ever . . . And so there will be length of days with that Son of Man, and the righteous will have peace . . .'[56]

The significance of the term 'Son of Man' in *1 Enoch* has been, and still is, a subject of much philological debate. It seems that it was not a title, either there or in the passages of the gospels where Jesus applied it to himself; in fact it seems to have had no more than its basic meaning of 'one like a man', or simply 'a man'. No matter: in *1 Enoch* the figure called 'the Son of Man' is clearly a very extraordinary one.

The Son of Man in some of the sayings ascribed to Jesus in the gospels is no less extaordinary. He too will be sent down from heaven to judge mankind, accompanied by angels, and those who have denied him will be condemned as surely as those who have denied God himself. Not every scholar accepts those sayings as authentic, and even amongst those who do accept them, some believe that Jesus was referring not to his own destiny but to a divine being who was yet to come. For our purpose it is enough that the early Church laid much store by those sayings, and so ensured that later generations would do so also.[57]

7

Applied to Jesus, the notion of a transcendent, supernatural Messiah was indeed well adapted to explain and justify the paradox of his wretched death. Primarily, the Jesus who stood at the centre of the teaching of the early Church was neither the exorcist, healer and preacher who lived in Palestine, nor the expected political leader, but Jesus the transcendent Messiah, whose earthly life and death had been above all the prelude to his resurrection and glorification. Extraordinary as this notion must have seemed to most Jews, and little as it attracted them, it proved satisfying to some. The suffering, humiliation and death of Jesus ceased to present a problem if they could be understood as preconditions for an exaltation far beyond any known to mere mortals: 'Was the Messiah not bound to suffer thus before entering upon his glory?'[58]

What the *Similitudes* foretells of Enoch, the New Testament repeatedly foretells of Jesus: he is to come down from heaven to earth as the transcendent Messiah. As Paul puts it in his epistle to the Philippians, 'Therefore God raised him to the heights and bestowed on him the name above all names, that at the name of Jesus every knee should bow — in heaven, on earth, and in the depths . . .'[59] In one passage after another, in the synoptic gospels, in Acts, in the Pauline epistles, Jesus appears as judge of the world — alongside God or even in God's place. Above all he was expected to act as God's plenipotentiary at the Last Judgment. In the words of Acts, God 'has fixed the day on which he will have the world judged, and justly judged, by a man of his choosing; of this he has given assurance to all by raising him from the dead'[60] — and again and again Jesus is referred to as the one who is to judge the living and the dead. Nor was all this imagined as lying in some remote, unpredictable future — the early Christians were certain that Jesus would return very soon indeed: 'The time we live in will not last long.' — 'It is far on in the night; day is near.' — 'The end of all things is upon us.'[61] The same certainty is reflected in the promise which Jesus is supposed to have made to his disciples — whether he really made it or not: 'I tell you this: there are some of those standing here who will not taste death before they have seen the kingdom of God already come in power.'[62]

Not that it mattered if one died before. For some two centuries Jews had been familiar with the notion that at the great consummation the righteous would be resurrected and given immortal bodies — and though some Jews, such as the Sadducees, rejected the notion, others, such as the Pharisees, had long accepted it. The first Christians not only accepted the notion, they saw the resurrection as already beginning. Although the resurrection of Jesus has always been central to the faith of the Church, its original significance is largely forgotten. The first Christians understood it not simply as a dramatic intervention by God to vindicate his son but as a sign and guarantee that every true follower of Jesus, including those who had already died, would be able to dwell for ever in the kingdom.

The implications are developed in 1 Thessalonians, which is the earliest Christian document in existence — it dates from around 50 AD, considerably earlier than the oldest gospel. Paul is concerned to assure the Christians of Thessalonica that those of them who live to see the Second Coming will not be separated from their dear ones who have died before:

> We want you not to remain in ignorance, brothers, about those who sleep in death . . . God will bring them to life with Jesus. For this we tell you as the Lord's word: we who are left alive until the Lord comes shall

not forestall those who have died; because at the word of command, at the sound of the archangel's voice and God's trumpet-call, the Lord himself will descend from heaven; first the Christian dead will rise, then we who are left alive shall join them, caught up in the clouds to meet the Lord in the air. Thus we shall always be with the Lord. Console one another, then, with these words.[63]

8

Such was the faith of the early Christians, and it shaped their view of themselves. They did not think of themselves as launching a new religion. They were all Jews who continued to observe the Law — and any Gentiles who joined their number had to become Jews too. Even in their preaching amongst the Gentiles they carried on what the propaganda of Hellenistic Judaism had begun. Just like other Jews, they set up, against the polytheism of the heathen, the doctrine of the one God who was both creator and judge. More specifically, their mental world was still largely that of the Jewish apocalyptists: the notion of the Last Judgment, which was at the heart of their thinking, was also at the heart of Jewish apocalyptic. But in one vital respect they stood apart from all other Jews: they regarded themselves as entrusted by God with the task of proclaiming that Jesus had been crucified, had been resurrected and would shortly return in glory to bring the present age to a close and to inaugurate 'the age to come'. As the Jesus sect gradually changed into the Christian Church, this conviction remained central to its sense of identity.

The primitive Church saw itself as the congregation of the last days — a prototype, as it were, of the kingdom of God which was shortly to appear.[64] It was well aware that, as part of the 'woes' which would usher in the age to come, hostile powers would strive to overwhelm the congregation — but it also knew that those efforts would be in vain: 'Have no fear, little flock; for your Father has chosen to give you the Kingdom.'[65] The very titles which the members of the Church bestowed on themselves — 'the chosen', 'the saints' — were traditional in Judaism as eschatological titles. The title 'congregation of God', adopted by the Church itself, had similar overtones, for it was the traditional term for the 'saving remnant' which was to be revealed at the coming of the kingdom. The term *ekklesia* too denoted, at that time, the fellowship of the chosen at the moment when 'this age' was about to give place to 'the age to come'.

The rites and practices of the Church likewise possessed eschatological significance. Baptism was a bath of purification in preparation for the coming of the kingdom, a rite by which the proselyte was initiated into the congregation of the last days. The common meals (the 'breaking of bread') were held in a mood of eschatological expectation, echoes of which can be heard in a eucharistic prayer which was still being recited in an isolated community around 120 AD: 'Remember, Lord, thy Church, to deliver it from evil and make it perfect in thy love, and gather it together in its holiness from the four winds of thy kingdom which thou hast prepared for it! . . . Let the Lord come, let this world pass away!'[66] Again, according to the Jewish view the spirit of prophecy had departed from Israel for a time, but would be imparted again at the end of days. The early Church was convinced that that was indeed happening, that there were once more prophets about, who could foresee the future.[67] And missionary work, preaching, healing, exorcism — all these retained the same meaning, and were carried out with the same sense of urgency, as in the days of Jesus. In all their doings first-century Christians declared, as clearly and emphatically as could be, that in them the hopes of the apocalyptists were being fulfilled.

Collective salvation for God's chosen people was, of course, a profoundly Jewish notion — and the early Church did indeed feel great solidarity with Israel, it did indeed see itself as carrying on Israel's history. On the other hand, the continuity was not unbroken; the appearance of Jesus, his resurrection, his glorification, the promise of his return — these eschatological events marked a total break. By failing to recognise Jesus as the Messiah, Israel had missed the chance of bringing to realisation God's age-old promise of salvation, it had forfeited its position as the elect people of God, it had in fact caused itself to be rejected by God. It was not Israel but the Christian Church that would inherit the fruits of the divine promise.

Meanwhile the Church had the duty to keep itself apart from the world, the realm of sin which was about to be abolished. The ethical ideal which the early Christians set themselves — unworldliness, purity, asceticism — symbolised the separateness of the eschatological community, its fitness and readiness to enter into the kingdom at any moment. 'For you know perfectly well that the Day of the Lord comes like a thief in the night . . . we must not sleep like the rest, but keep awake and sober.'[68] By withdrawing from 'this age' Christians prepared themselves for the transformation which they would undergo when the kingdom came.

9

What the early Church offered was not simply membership of a divinely chosen élite, it was the assurance of belonging, in the very near future, to a community of immortal, transfigured beings.

Christ himself, returning in glory as judge of the living and the dead, would allot this eternal joy to some, while to others he would allot eternal torment — and the test would be, whether they have accepted or rejected him and his teaching. Already John the Baptist is supposed to have prophesied this: 'His shovel is ready in his hand and he will winnow his threshing-floor; the wheat he will gather into his granary, but he will burn the chaff on a fire that can never go out.'[69] Inevitably, Jesus himself is also supposed to have foretold it. Sayings ascribed to him by Matthew make this abundantly plain: 'Whoever then will acknowledge me before men, I will acknowledge him before my Father in heaven; and whoever disowns me before men, I will disown him before my Father in heaven.'[70] And again: 'When the Son of Man comes in his glory and all the angels with him, he will sit in state on his throne, with all the nations gathered before him. He will separate men into two groups, as a shepherd separates the sheep from the goats, and he will place the sheep on his right hand and the goats on his left. Then the king will say to those on his right hand, "You have my Father's blessing; come, enter and possess the kingdom that has been ready for you since the world was made."' These are the people who gave food, drink, shelter and succour of every kind to those whom Jesus calls his 'brothers'.

The fate of those who refused to support Jesus' followers, and who now stand at his left hand, is terrible. To them Jesus says, 'The curse is upon you; go from my sight to the eternal fire that is ready for the devil and his angels.'[71] These angels are of course the fallen angels whom one meets in *Jubilees* and *1 Enoch*. The angels who did not fall will also have a part to play in those days: '. . . at the end of time the Son of Man will send out his angels, who will gather out of his kingdom everything that causes offence, and all whose deeds are evil, and these will be thrown into the blazing furnace, the place of wailing and grinding of teeth. And then the righteous will shine as brightly as the sun in the kingdom of their Father'.[72]

Whatever doubts there may be about the authenticity of such passages, there can be no doubt that they faithfully mirror the expectations of the first generations of Christians. Precisely the same view of the future is to be found in 2 Thessalonians — which, though now known not to be by Paul, is still approximately as old as the oldest gospel. It too tells how, when Jesus appears in the sky, it will be to bring not only salvation to his faithful followers but perdition to his and their opponents:

> It is surely just that God should balance the account by sending trouble to those who trouble you, and relief to you who are troubled, and to us as well, when our Lord Jesus Christ is revealed from heaven with his

> mighty angels in blazing fire. Then he will do justice upon those who refuse to acknowledge God and upon those who will not obey the gospel of our Lord Jesus. They will suffer the punishment of eternal ruin, cut off from the presence of our Lord and the splendour of his might, when on that great Day he comes to be glorified among his own and adored among all believers . . .[73]

The apotheosis of Jesus, as a heavenly being and as the supreme agent of God, was to be carried a step further in the Book of Revelation.

CHAPTER 12

The Book of Revelation

The many millions of Christians who today regard the Book of Revelation as uniquely important can claim a notable precedent: in second-century writings the book is more frequently cited than any other book in the New Testament.[1]

The work was probably composed towards the end of the reign of the emperor Domitian, around 95–96 AD. The author was clearly a Christian of Jewish and Palestinian origin; moreover, his strange and ungrammatical Greek suggests that he normally thought in Hebrew or Aramaic. He calls himself John, and traditionally he has been identified with the apostle John, son of Zebedee. This attribution, which was accepted by various first and second-century Fathers of the Church, was partly responsible for the inclusion of Revelation in the New Testament canon, and even today it is defended by some scholars. Yet it is almost certainly false. Apostolic authorship is not even hinted at in the work itself; moreover, it would presuppose that the apostle composed this intensely emotional work when he was eighty-five or more. It is more likely that the John in question was an itinerant prophet — perhaps a charismatic akin to the prophets who, somewhat earlier, and in Syria-Palestine, had produced Q and Mark. He himself seems to have circulated among the churches of the Roman province of Asia — which comprised, approximately, the western coast of what is today Turkey.

The book was written for Christians who still felt themselves to be Jews — indeed, the only true Jews, the rest being 'the synagogue of Satan'. The Jewishness of the work is everywhere apparent. Not only is it influenced by Jewish apocalypses — many passages are simply translated from the Hebrew Bible, and in addition there are more than 300 references to Daniel, Isaiah, Second Isaiah, Jeremiah, Ezekiel and Zechariah.

The seer's acute sense of the continuity of Israel and the Christian branch of Judaism explains much that would otherwise be quite mysterious. The 144,000 'servants of God' who have seals set upon their foreheads, to protect them from the catastrophes visited upon the rest of mankind, are certainly Christians — yet they are described as belonging to the twelve tribes of Israel. To indicate the Christian Church, persecuted by the heathen yet secure in God's protection, the seer uses the image of the earthly Jerusalem or Mount Zion. And when, after the Last Judgment, the New Jerusalem comes down from heaven, the names of the twelve tribes are found to be inscribed over its twelve gates, just as the names of the twelve apostles are inscribed on the twelve foundation stones of the city wall.

Revelation is nevertheless a profoundly Christian work throughout. Whatever is taken over from the Hebrew Bible is reinterpreted in a Christian sense and integrated into a Christian world-view. Jewish prophecies and oracles are invoked precisely in order to show that the history of the Church is faithfully following the course foretold in Scripture — and conversely, that what Scripture foretold is now coming to pass. The prophets and the Book of Daniel are made to testify to the imminent victory of the Christian Church — while Revelation itself takes on the appearance of a Christian conclusion to the prophetic tradition of Israel.

Above all, the role that had hitherto been assumed by Jews in general is now assumed by the Christian branch of Judaism. It is in the Church that the divinely appointed order finds its supreme expression on earth. The affirmation of that order which, traditionally, Jews had performed by their obedience to the Law, Christians now performed by their adherence to Jesus.

2

The Book of Revelation opens with a statement of its nature and purpose. God has revealed to Jesus what must shortly happen, at 'the hour of fulfilment'. Jesus in turn has conveyed the revelation to 'his servant John', who now comes forward as a prophet, charged with the task of passing on the message to the Church, represented by seven churches in the neighbourhood of Ephesus. The whole work has the form of a letter, and there are signs that it was intended for liturgical reading.

John received the message on the island of Patmos, in a series of visions of overwhelming power. Already the first vision presents the risen Jesus as a transcendent being of inconceivable majesty, source and lord of the seven churches and of the Church as a whole:

> It was on the Lord's day, and I was caught up by the Spirit; and behind me I heard a loud voice, like the sound of a trumpet . . . I turned to see whose voice it was that spoke to me; and when I turned I saw seven standing lamps of gold, and among the lamps one like a son of man,

robed down to his feet, with a golden girdle round his breast. The hair of his head was white as snow-white wool, and his eyes flamed like fire; his feet gleamed like burnished brass refined in a furnace, and his voice was like the sound of rushing waters. In his right hand he held seven stars, and out of his mouth came a sharp two-edged sword; and his face shone like the sun in full strength.

When I saw him, I fell at his feet as though dead. But he laid his right hand upon me and said, 'Do not be afraid. I am the first and the last, and I am the living one: for I was dead and now I am alive for evermore . . .'[2]

There follow seven letters which Jesus has dictated to John, praising and blaming the various churches for their respective merits and shortcomings and promising them appropriate rewards and punishments. Faithful Christians can look forward to a glorious future: '. . . They shall walk with me in white, for so they deserve. He who is victorious shall be robed all in white; his name I will never strike off the roll of the living, for in the presence of my Father I will acknowledge him as mine . . .'[3] — 'Because you have kept my command and stood fast, I will also keep you from the ordeal that is to fall upon the whole world and test its inhabitants . . .'[4] — 'To him who is victorious, to him who perseveres in doing my will to the end, I will give authority over the nations — that same authority which I received from my Father — and he shall rule them with an iron rod, smashing them to bits like earthenware . . .'[5]

With their promise of boundless exaltation for an élite, these letters set the tone.

3

Chapters 12 and 13 of Revelation offer a Christian — and most impressive — version of the ancient combat myth.[6]

In the form of a great red dragon with seven heads and ten horns Satan appears in heaven and sets about reducing the ordered world to chaos. With its tail the dragon attacks the stars, those supreme symbols and guardians of the divinely appointed order, and flings a third of them down from their proper places on to the earth. Then he confronts the 'woman clothed with the sun' as she is about to give birth — and when her son is born, he tries to devour it. But God snatches up the child to himself and to his throne, and for the woman he prepares a place of refuge in the wilderness, where she can hide — for the critical period (inherited from the Book of Daniel) of three and a half years.

The providential rescue of the child is the signal for war in heaven. The archangel Michael — the same who in Daniel and other apocalypses figures as the patron angel of Israel — emerges as the champion of the Christian Church. With a host of angels he fights Satan, who likewise commands a host of angels. Michael is victorious, and Satan and his host are thrown down from heaven to earth.

As usual in Near Eastern belief, what happens in heaven determines what happens on earth. Almost certainly, the 'woman clothed with the sun' represents Israel and the child symbolises the Christian community — heavenly counterparts of the real Israel and its Christian offspring on earth. Now the persecution and rescue of the Church must be played out in the world of human beings, where the dragon-Satan, expelled from heaven, is frantically active. It is the fated, final tribulation foretold in the Jewish apocalypses and indeed by Jesus: 'But woe to you, earth and sea, for the Devil has come down to you in great fury, knowing that his time is short!'

In his pursuit of 'those who keep God's commandments and maintain their testimony to Jesus',[7] Satan has allies. He is aided by two beasts, one coming from the sea, the other from the depths of the earth. On the first beast Satan confers 'power and rule' and 'authority over every tribe and people, language and nation'.[8] As for the second beast, it is wholly devoted to strengthening the power of the first beast: it makes men erect an image in its honour, it causes all who will not honour the image to be put to death. There is no doubt either about the sources of these images or about what they symbolise in Revelation. The first beast is modelled on the four beasts in Daniel, amalgamated, and its role too is akin to that of the blasphemous world-tyrant in Daniel — only, the symbol that once stood for the Seleucid monarchy stands here for the Roman empire. The second beast, otherwise called 'the false prophet', owes much to the prophecy in 2 Thessalonians of 'the wicked man' whose coming 'will be attended by all the powerful signs and miracles of the Lie' — but here it stands for the priesthood of the official Roman religion.

In Revelation the Roman empire and its agents are indeed despised and hated — and there is a standard explanation of why this is so. It is widely agreed that Revelation was written in the reign of Domitian — and until quite recently it was believed that Domitian was the first Roman emperor to regard himself as a living god, and to demand that sacrifices be offered to him already in his lifetime; that Christians regarded such sacrifices as idolatrous and refused to make them; and that Domitian accordingly launched a persecution of Christians, resulting in a number of executions. However, recent research suggests that this explanation is mistaken at every point: Domitian made no special claim to worship, and he did not persecute

Christians.[9] In fact the Christians in the cities of Asia — most of them Jewish Christians — led quiet lives and, like other Jews, participated fully in urban society. Nor are there any good grounds for the common assumption that the reason why John wrote Revelation on the island of Patmos was that he had been banished there for preaching Christian doctrine.

It seems, rather, that John was intent on encouraging Christians to see themselves in conflict with the larger society. Like other apocalyptists, he had a notion of cosmic order which was in total contrast with the notions sanctioned by the Hellenistic world in general and by the Roman empire in particular. So far from reflecting divine government, the rule of kings and emperors was an expression of Satan's power. This was not because that rule was 'objectively' oppressive but because John was obsessed by his vision of the church and the world as radically antagonistic.[10] That was enough to sustain his enthusiasm for the overthrow of the established order.

4

In the synoptic gospels Jesus fights Satan by reducing his servants, the demons, to impotence. In Revelation he fights Satan by destroying his creation, the Roman empire.

In a vision the seer sees Jesus as a fierce warrior on a white horse, at the head of a host of angels: 'His eyes flamed with fire, and on his head were many diadems . . . He was called the Word of God, and the armies of heaven followed him on white horses, clothed in fine linen, clean and shining. From his mouth there went a sharp sword with which to smite the nations: for he it is who shall rule them with an iron rod, and tread the winepress of the wrath and retribution of God the sovereign Lord. And on his robe and on his leg there was written the name: "King of kings and Lord of lords".[11]

The first beast and his assistant — the latter now called 'the false prophet' — and the kings of the earth and their armies muster to do battle with Jesus. This battle of Armageddon ends in total defeat for the demonic powers and their human allies. The beast and the false prophet are captured and thrown alive into a lake of fire. As for the kings and their armies, they are killed by the sword issuing from Jesus' mouth. An angel summons the birds: 'Come and gather for God's great supper, to eat the flesh of kings and commanders and fighting men, the flesh of horses and their riders, the flesh of all men, slave and free, great and small!' — and the birds duly gorge themselves. The glory of Rome is at an end: voices from heaven proclaim,

'Fallen, fallen is Babylon the Great! She has become a dwelling for demons, a haunt for every unclean spirit, for every foul and loathsome bird.'[13] And while that fall will be greeted with lamentation by the merchants and sea-traders of the earth, the followers of Jesus will rejoice: 'But let heaven exult over her; exult, apostles and people of God; for in the judgment against her he has vindicated your cause!'[14]

All who have served the empire are similarly doomed. Their fate is announced by an angel: 'Whoever worships the beast and its image and receives its mark on his forehead or hand, he shall drink the wine of God's wrath, poured undiluted into the cup of his vengeance.'[15] Those wicked ones will be afflicted with malignant sores, their drinking-water will turn to blood, they will be fearfully burned. Imprisoned in perpetual darkness, they will gnaw their tongues in agony. And their torment will last, without respite by day or night, for ever and ever.[16]

5

The fate of the Devil himself is less final. An angel comes down from heaven, chains him, throws him into an abyss and shuts and seals it over him — not however for all eternity but for a thousand years, after which 'he must be let loose for a short while'.[17] During the thousand years — the original 'Millennium' — the Christian martyrs, those who have preferred to be executed rather than worship the beast, receive their special rewards: they are resurrected and reign with Christ on earth, before passing to their eternal blessedness. Nor are they the earth's only inhabitants: it is made clear that in this intermediate period the nations of the world are required to submit to the authority of Christ and his saints, who rule them with an iron rod.

After his thousand-year imprisonment, Satan summons 'the nations in the four corners of the earth' to besiege 'the camp of God's people and the city that he loves'. These armies are described as 'the hosts of Gog and Magog, countless as the sand of the sea' — a reference to the prophecy in Ezekiel.[18] It seems likely that in the seer's imagination these legions consisted not of human beings but of demons — true companions of Satan, who would rise with him from the depths of the earth in a last effort to destroy the Church.[19] When these last, supernatural enemies are destroyed by fire from heaven, the way lies open for the Last Judgment. All the dead are resurrected, and judged according to their records. While those whose names do not appear in 'the roll of the living' are cast into the lake of fire, there to suffer torment for ever and ever, all the righteous — and not simply the martyrs — pass into a realm of bliss, where they dwell for ever with God, as his children, free from death and from suffering and grief of every kind: 'All this is the victor's heritage.'[20] Time has reached its consummation.

The realm of bliss is something wholly new, a fresh creation that will replace the old:

> Then I saw a new heaven and a new earth, for the first heaven and the first earth had vanished, and there was no longer any sea. I saw the holy city, new Jerusalem, coming down out of heaven from God, made ready like a bride adorned for her husband. I heard a loud voice proclaiming from the throne: 'Now at last God has his dwelling among men! He will dwell among them and they shall be his people, and God himself will be with them. He will wipe every tear from their eyes; there shall be an end of death, and to mourning and crying and pain; for the old order has passed away!' Then he who sat upon the throne said: 'Behold! I am making all things new!'[21]

By the descent of the heavenly Jerusalem earth and heaven are made indissolubly one, a realm where human beings will share the bliss of the angels. The new Jerusalem is portrayed in imagery of great concreteness. The city is built as a square, with each side 12,000 furlongs in length, and its walls of jasper 144 cubits in height. The city itself is of pure gold, 'bright as clear glass', and the foundations of its walls are adorned with jewels of every kind. The kings and the nations bring their wealth and splendour to it. It becomes a source of salvation for the whole earth: 'The leaves of the trees shall serve for the healing nations, and every accursed thing shall disappear.'[22] The miraculous fertility of the trees is a sign that the divinely ordained order is now unimpaired, and a world in which there is no longer any sea is a world for ever immune from the threat of chaos.

The work ends as it began, with an assurance that the stupendous drama which is its theme is about to open: '. . . the hour of fulfilment is near'. Jesus himself confirms it: 'Yes, I am coming soon, and bringing my recompense with me, to requite everyone according to his deeds! . . . Yes. I am coming soon!' And the seer replies: 'Amen. Come, Lord Jesus.'[23]

6

The Book of Revelation is not the only Christian apocalypse — the *Apocalypse of Peter* and the *Shepherd of Hermas*, for instance, are also Christian through and through. But it is the only full-length apocalypse to have been received into the canon, where it forms as it were a Christian counterpart to the Book of Daniel. This distinction may not be wholly due to its supposedly apostolic authorship. It is a splendidly imaginative prose-poem, full of arresting imagery, passing from songs of praise to cries of distress and back again, alternating between dazzling light and terrifying darkness. The dragon's pursuit of 'the woman clothed with the sun', the reign and overthrow of the many-headed beast, the fall of 'Babylon the Great' — these are powerful symbols, and all the more powerful for being so enigmatic.

The specific forecasts which the seer was trying to convey to his fellow-Christians all proved mistaken: not one of the events which were supposed to happen around the year 100 came to pass. And nevertheless, the prophecies in Revelation lived on: reinterpreted again and again to fit ever-changing circumstances, they were to affect the perceptions of generation after generation of Christians.

In these prophecies the ancient myth of the assault of the forces of chaos upon the divinely appointed order, and of the victory of the young divine warrior over those forces, is radically reinterpreted. No longer concerned with a regularly recurring repetition of primordial happenings, it is transformed into a prophecy of the coming kingdom — of a world transfigured, for ever immune from the threat of chaos, and inhabited by an elect community of transformed human beings, for ever immune from ageing, disease and death.

Again one is reminded of Zoroaster — and again one wonders: coincidence or influence?

CHAPTER 13

Jews, Zoroastrians and Christians

1 Enoch, *Jubilees*, the *Community Rule* from Qumran, the synoptic gospels, the Book of Revelation are very different works — but an eschatological preoccupation is evident in all of them, while the world is viewed in ever more dualistic terms with the passing generations. In varying degrees, the authors of all these works were conscious of a destructive supernatural power which had been working to frustrate the divine intention down the ages, and was still doing so. They were also convinced that in the very near future that power and its human agents would be overthrown by the angels of God and reduced to nullity. A universal judgment would be held — with, in some versions, a transcendent Messiah as judge. Time and history would come to an end, to be succeeded by the eternal kingdom of God, established on this earth. The true servants of God, endowed with immortal and unageing bodies, would live as denizens of that kingdom for evermore, while the rest would be cast into a fiery abyss. These contrasting fates would befall also the dead, who would be resurrected for the purpose.

These notions flourished most vigorously in relatively small sects, and the contrast they present with ancient Israelite religion is startling. The Hebrew Bible knows of foreign powers which threaten the people of Israel, and which in that sense are enemies of Israel's god — but it does not know of a supernatural power devoted to frustrating the divine intention. Genesis never suggests that the serpent which tempts Eve is a demon, or indeed anything more than 'the most subtle of all the wild beasts Yahweh God has made'; and the only 'satan' to appear is a member of Yahweh's court. Again, the exilic and post-exilic prophets look forward to a time when the enemies of the chosen people will be cast down, and the chosen people itself will flourish in a wonderfully fertile and peaceful land. But there is no suggestion that in that time individual Jews will live for ever: like all previous generations, each future generation will go down to Sheol, there to exist as pale disembodied shades. With the exception of Daniel the Hebrew Bible offers no assurance that the dead will be resurrected, let alone that they will all be resurrected together, to face a universal Last Judgment. Nor has it anything to say about a transcendent Messiah who is to carry out that judgment, and so bring time and history to their consummation. But indeed, the very notion of a new, eternal world, lying beyond time and history, is foreign to the Hebrew Bible.

These notions were in fact such major innovations that, though adopted in their entirety by relatively few Jews, the controversy they caused in the Jewish community lasted for generations. They were also clearly of foreign origin — for if some Jewish thinker had been responsible for such radical rethinking we would surely know something about him, if only his name. So what of possible Zoroastrian influence?[1]

Zoroastrians had always believed in a future glorious consummation, when the world would be transformed, and all the righteous, including the righteous dead, would be endowed with immortal and unageing bodies. They had also always believed in a destructive, supernatural power at work in the world. To appreciate how much Jewish and Christian Beliar/Satan owes to Zoroastrian notions one has only to recall what the *Avesta* has to tell of Angra Mainyu.[2] For Angra Mainyu too brought death into the world and is the cause of bodily deformities and afflictions; he too is called the father of lies; he too is the leader of a host of demons. And he too will eventually be utterly defeated by the supreme god.

Moreover, the one great difference between Angra Mainyu and the Judaeo-Christian Devil had disappeared by the time that any Jews could have experienced the full impact of Zoroastrian thinking. For if originally Angra Mainyu had been imagined as coeval with the supreme god, and almost his equal, he had ceased to be so in the version of Zoroastrianism known in the West in Hellenistic times, Zurvanism.[3] That heterodoxy seems to have evolved under the late Achaemenians in their western lands, notably Babylonia, and to have been adopted by those monarchs as orthodox. Zurvanism was a monism: it postulated a high god, Zurvan (meaning 'Time'), who created both Ahura Mazda and Angra Mainyu. Such a doctrine could be more easily harmonised with Jewish belief than could the original Zoroastrianism. In the apocalypses and the Qumran writings the Devil is likewise a creature of God and subject to him. The Community Rule of the Qumran community, for instance, tells how the spirits of truth and falsehood, of light and darkness, compete for mastery over human beings — but God is above them both. In *Jubilees* too the destructive spirit, Mastema or Beliar or Satan, and his host of demons are creatures of God and operate only by his permission.

The similarities between Zoroastrian beliefs and beliefs that flourished in apocalyptically minded groups of Jews extended to lesser matters. The protective angels who assist God in governing the world recall the Amesha Spentas: in *Jubilees* they are even charged, like Ahura Mazda's assistants, with supervising particular aspects of the cosmos. When, in *1 Enoch*, the archangels Raphael and Michael defeat, respectively, the archdemons Azazel and Semyaza, they bind them and bury them underground, beneath great piles of rocks, there to await the day of judgment: in Zoroastrian legend exactly the same fate befell the archdemon Azi Dahaka. Above all, the periodisation of time into a series of world-ages, which is characteristic of Zurvanism, is found also in various apocalypses. The parallelism is particularly striking in the case of the Book of Daniel: the symbolism of the four metals, representing four world-ages, has a counterpart in the Zoroastrian apocalypse known as the *Vahman Yasht*, which dates from the time of the Macedonian conquest.[4] Even the curious detail that the fourth and last age is symbolised by 'iron mixed with clay' is present also in the Persian work — and nowhere else: the Greek source of the whole tradition, Hesiod's *Works and Days*, knows nothing of it.

That is not to say that there are no differences between Zoroastrian (or Zurvanite) expectations and Jewish expectations. Neither the fate of individuals after death nor the fate of the world after the great consummation is imagined in quite the same way. For Zoroastrians, pending the final judgment individual souls existed in heaven or hell, experiencing the reward or punishment earned during life on earth. After the universal judgment they would be reunited with their bodies — after which the righteous would live for evermore on the perfected earth, while the sinners would simply be annihilated. In the Jewish apocalypses the dead sleep until the Last Judgment — but then the sinners will be condemned to eternal punishment. The Zoroastrian vision of a future world wholly good and happy, wholly cleansed of evil and suffering, has therefore no precise Jewish counterpart: in the apocalypses hell subsists, a fearful imperfection in an otherwise perfect world. It is as though the apocalyptists were trying to reconcile Zoroastrian notions with the ancient Israelite/Jewish notions of Sheol.

Nevertheless, the similarities between Zoroastrianism and the notions that one finds in the Jewish apocalypses are too remarkable to be explained by coincidence.

2

It has often been objected — and continues to be objected right down to the present day — that Jews cannot have known much about Zoroastrianism, as the *Avesta* was not written down before the fifth or sixth century AD. However, the argument is not valid: in fact Jews had ample opportunity to familiarise themselves with the essentials of Zoroastrianism.[5]

For some two centuries Judaea formed part of the vast Achaemenian empire, while the large Jewish diaspora also lived within the bounds of that empire. Achaemenian rule was relatively benign, and was recognised by the Jews to be so: whereas there is plenty of Jewish propaganda against Babylon and Greece and Rome, there is not a single Jewish text, biblical or rabbinic, directed against the Persians. Moreover, already in Achaemenian times there was a certain affinity between Jewish and Iranian religion. It was not simply that, like Zoroastrians, Jews saw themselves as a people chosen by God to implement his intention for the world — Second Isaiah and his successors had taught them to look forward with confidence to a time when, under God, they would be lords of a fertile, prosperous and peaceful world, and when their enemies would be finally subdued, never to rise again. Relatively modest though it was, this prospect will have prepared at least some Jews to sympathise with the far more grandiose Zoroastrian notions about the 'making wonderful'.

Nor need Jews have had any difficulty in learning about those notions. In Achaemenian times Jews employed by wealthy Zoroastrian families as scribes or business agents or household servants or outdoor workers could easily have been exposed to the religion of their masters. The process could have continued for generations on end, until the Jewish employees came to know as much about the Zoroastrian as about the Jewish faith — in modern India, Hindus and Moslems working for Zoroastrians have had just such an experience.

More solid evidence is available about contacts after the fall of the Achaemenian empire. In the Hellenistic period the descendants of Iranian colonists of Achaemenian times are known to have dwelt side by side with Jewish settlers in many towns in Babylonia, in the area around Damascus, in Lydia and Phrygia. Both groups produced distinguished citizens, who served together on town or provincial councils — and, as Greek was now a common language of the educated, they will have communicated with one another more easily than before. And wherever Iranians lived there were Zoroastrian priests, many of whom will have been impressively devout and zealous. A Jew who talked with such men and enquired after their beliefs, and set about harmonising those beliefs with his own, need not have felt that he was being false to the faith that he treasured above all things. But if Jewish understanding of Zoroastrianism grew in the diaspora, it did not stop there: whatever emerged from such contacts will soon have become known in Palestine also — for, through pilgrimages and the remission of dues to the Temple, Jews of all regions kept in touch with Jerusalem.

By that time what Zoroastrian priests had to tell will have been very much what some Jews wanted to hear. The overthrow of the Achaemenian empire was a truly traumatic experience for Iranians. It was not simply that a dispensation that had been perceived as divinely ordained and everlasting was abruptly and totally obliterated — it was replaced first by the miseries of defeat, then by generations of warfare between the successor states. Iranians and Jews were no longer rulers and ruled but fellow-sufferers in an uncertain and tormented world.

In such circumstances the eschatological promises enshrined in Zoroastrian teaching must have taken on a new urgency. Faced with the horrors of the Antiochan tyranny, when for the first time they were persecuted for fidelity to their religion, and again when they were faced with the brutalities of Roman rule, some Jews could find in that teaching an assurance that evil came not from God but from a great adversary of God, working through human agents. They could also find there assurance that evil would not go unpunished. So great was the wickedness of the foreign rulers, so overwhelming the power of the forces of chaos, that cosmos was impaired — but not for long: God, acting through his angels and his Messiah, was about to put all things to rights.

Zoroastrian teaching was all the more effective because it had found a new vehicle. Whereas the *Avesta* was still being transmitted orally, and in archaic Iranian, there now came into being a Zoroastrian literature — and one intended to be read by non-Iranians. Persian Sibylline oracles, modelled upon Greek prototypes and written in Greek, were probably in circulation already in late Achaemenian times. After Alexander's overthrow of the empire more extended prophecies were produced — prophecies that foretold how Greek rule would in turn be overthrown by the Saoshyant, and how the eternal kingdom of Ahura Mazda would be established on a perfect earth. Fragments of such works have been preserved, embedded in the writings of Christian apologists; and one, the *Oracles of Hystaspes* (named after Zoroaster's patron Vishtaspa), is known in some detail.[6] These works will certainly have been studied by learned Jews long before there were any Christians: we have seen the influence that the closely related *Vahman Yasht* had on the author(s) of the Book of Daniel.

The attraction of Zoroastrianism will have been reinforced when, in the second century BC, Iranian power revived under the Parthians. When, in the first century, Judaea came under the harsh rule of

Rome, Jews looked to Parthia as Rome's most formidable enemy. Pompey and, after him, Crassus made themselves very unpopular by invading the Temple: Crassus even despoiled it. In 53 BC Crassus marched against the Parthians — and, despite great numerical superiority, his forces were decimated and he himself was killed. The Parthians became more popular than ever with the Jews; and when, in 40 BC, they invaded Syria-Palestine, entered Jerusalem, and installed a Jewish king in place of the hated Roman nominee Herod, they could be regarded as champions of the Jews against the Romans. And though Herod was reinstated by the Romans two years later, the Parthians persisted with their efforts to move west and to oust the Romans. These developments can only have made Zoroastrian prophecies of salvation from tyranny and of the coming of the kingdom of God sound still more convincing.[7]

Contacts between Parthians and Jews — including, later, Christian Jews — continued also outside Palestine. Babylon, with its important Jewish community, was under Parthian rule. In Syria, Armenia and Anatolia, too, the two cultures remained in contact for generations on end.

3

Some Zoroastrian notions were widely accepted amongst Jews. Thus the Pharisees, though they belonged to mainstream Judaism, felt no difficulty in 'interpreting' the scriptures in the light of new doctrines which they believed to be truly Jewish, but which were really of Zoroastrian origin. And some of the early rabbis in turn adopted those doctrines. Around the time of Jesus, the important rabbinical school headed by Bet Hillel was maintaining that after death all souls are rewarded or punished in heaven or hell until the end of time, when they will be reunited with their bodies for a final judgment — a notion unknown to the Hebrew Bible, but central to Zoroaster's teaching. And this Pharisaic legacy has endured: it is preserved in normative Judaism as it exists today — even though in practice it has far less importance for Jews than for Christians.

On the other hand, the Pharisees never accepted the notion of a great supernatural power hostile to God — they had no use for even a qualified dualism, any more than present-day Judaism has. Belief in the Devil, his power and his eventual overthrow, remained the preserve of certain groups which deviated more widely from the central tradition of Judaism. Two of these groups are known to history: the Qumran sect and the Jesus sect.

Already while the Scrolls were first coming to light, between 1947 and 1956, scholars were struck by the affinity between the Community Rule, with its doctrine of the two great antagonistic spirits, and Zoroastrian doctrine, especially in its Zurvanite form.[8] And if the Qumran sect was annihilated already before the fall of Jerusalem, the Jesus sect, transformed into the Christian Church and later into the Christian churches, was to keep a very similar blend of dualism and eschatology alive down the centuries.

Then there is the matter of God's agent in the last days. The Messiah of the Book of Revelation has far less in common with any messianic figure in the Hebrew Bible than with the divine warriors in the various versions of the combat myth — and amongst them, neither Indra, nor Marduk, nor Ba'al, nor the early Yahweh offer as close a parallel as the Zoroastrian Saoshyant. For Zoroaster is expected to return, resurrected and glorified, in the Saoshyant miraculously born of his seed, to fight and defeat the demonic hosts, resurrect the dead and carry out the eschatological judgment — and Revelation tells us to expect the very same deeds of the resurrected and glorified Christ when he returns. Moreover, in both cases the return of the saviour marks the end of time and the beginning of the world beyond time, the kingdom of God on earth.[9]

All in all, it would seem that amongst the fringe groups in Judaism the Jesus sect was the one that was most exposed to Zoroastrian influence. There is nothing mysterious about that. The Iranian culture is now known to have been long and firmly established in areas into which early Christians moved.[10] There was, for instance, a strong Zoroastrian influence in Anatolia — and Anatolia had great importance in the early development of Christianity. The author of the Book of Revelation knew the region well.

Soon, of course, Christianity was to change out of all recognition into something that was quite remote from both Judaism and Zoroastrianism. That Jesus' death on the cross was a redemptive act, by which God offered mankind the possibility of salvation from the consequences of sin — this was something wholly new, and it has remained central to the creeds of the major Christian churches to this day. However, what Christianity had taken over from Zoroastrianism has also lasted, and that too has been carried across the continents and down the centuries and into the modern world.

Afterword

This book is concerned with a major turning-point in the history of human consciousness: it tries to describe how the destiny of the world and of human beings came to be imagined in a new way, and how these new expectations began to spread abroad. A brief recapitulation of the main argument may not come amiss.

Until around 1500 BC peoples as diverse as Egyptians, Sumerians, Babylonians, Indo-Iranians and their Indian and Iranian descendants, Canaanites, pre-exilic Israelites were all agreed that in the beginning the world had been organised, set in order, by a god or by several gods, and that in essentials it was immutable. For each people, security — meaning fertility of the land, victory in war, stable social relations sanctioned by custom and law — was the outward and visible sign that a divinely ordained order did indeed exist.

However, that order was never untroubled, it was always threatened by evil, destructive forces — sometimes identified as flood or drought, famine or plague, inertia or death itself — but sometimes also as hostile peoples or tyrannical conquerors. In the combat myth, in its various formulations, the conflict between universal order and the forces that threatened and invaded and impaired it — between cosmos and chaos — was given symbolic expression. A young hero god, or divine warrior, was charged by the gods with the task of keeping the forces of chaos at bay; and in return he was awarded kingship over the world.

Some time between 1500 and 1200 BC Zoroaster broke out of that static yet anxious world-view. He did so by reinterpreting, radically, the Iranian version of the combat myth. In Zoroaster's view the world was not static, nor would it always be troubled. Even now the world was moving, through incessant conflict, towards a conflictless state. The time would come when, in a prodigious final battle, the supreme god and his supernatural allies would defeat the forces of chaos and their human allies and eliminate them once and for all.

From then on the divinely appointed order would obtain absolutely: physical distress and want would be unknown, no enemy would threaten, within the community of the saved there would be absolute unanimity; in a word, the world would be for ever untroubled, totally secure.

Unheard of before Zoroaster, that expectation deeply influenced certain Jewish groups — as witness some of the apocalypses and some of the writings found at Qumran. Above all it influenced the Jesus sect, with incalculable consequences.

In this book the story is carried only to the close of the first century AD — but the story itself has continued down the ages. And what a story it has become! Much theological speculation; innumerable millenarian movements, including those now flourishing so vigorously in the United States; even the appeal once exercised by Marxist-Leninist ideology — all this belongs to it.[1] Nor is there any reason to think that the story is nearing its end. The tradition whose origins are studied in this book is still alive and potent. Who can tell what fantasies, religious or secular, it may generate in the unforeseeable future?

Notes

The notes include both bibliographical references and matters of academic rather than of general interest. Works are in general listed in the chronological order of their first publication. At the first mention of a work the full title and place and date of publication are given. In subsequent mentions which are not too widely separated from the first mention, but where *op. cit.* would not suffice, a brief title is given. Journals and translations of texts are indicated in the same manner. Frequently cited journals and collections are indicated by abbreviations.

Abbreviations

ANET *Ancient Near Eastern Texts Relating to the Old Testament*, ed. J.B. Pritchard, 2nd edn., Princeton, 1955
BSOAS *Bulletin of the School of Oriental and African Studies*, London
CBQ *Catholic Biblical Quarterly*, Washington
ET English translation
HELLHOLM *Apocalypticism in the Mediterranean World and the Near East*, Tübingen, 1983 (Proceedings of the International Colloquium of Apocalypticism, Uppsala, 1979)
HR *History of Religions*, Chicago
HTR *Harvard Theological Review*, Cambridge, Mass.
HUCA *Hebrew Union College Annual*, Cincinnati
IIJ *Indo-Iranian Journal*, The Hague
JAOS *Journal of the American Oriental Society*, Baltimore
JBL *Journal of Biblical Literature*, Philadelphia, later Cambridge, Mass., and Missoula
JJS *Journal of Jewish Studies*, London
JSOT *Journal for the Study of the Old Testament*, Sheffield
JSS *Journal of Semitic Studies*, Manchester
LA *Lexikon der Ägyptologie*, W. Helck and E. Otto (later W. Helck and W. Westendorf) (eds.), 6 vols., Wiesbaden, 1975–86
RHPR *Revue d'Histoire et de Philosophie religieuses*, Strasbourg
RHR *Revue de l'histoire des religions*, Paris
RQ *Revue de Qumran*, Paris

UF *Ugarit-Forschungen*, Neukirchen-Vluyn
VT *Vetus Testamentum*, Leiden
VTS *Vetus Testamentum, Supplement*
ZAW *Zeitschrift für die alttestamentliche Wissenschaft*, Giessen

Chapter 1: Egyptians

1 On the civilisation and world-view of Ancient Egypt: J.H. Breasted, *The Development of Religion and Thought in Ancient Egypt*, New York, 1912, repr. 1972; J. Baillet, *Le régime pharaonique dans ses rapports avec l'évolution de la morale en Égypte*, 2 vols., Blois, 1912, 1913; J.A. Wilson, 'Egypt' in H. Frankfort *et al.*, *The Intellectual Adventure of Ancient Man*, Chicago, 1946, repr. 1977 (British title: *Before Philosophy*, Harmondsworth, now out of print); H. Frankfort, *Kingship and the Gods: a Study of Near Eastern Religion as the Integration of Society and Nature*, Chicago, 1948, repr. 1978; Frankfort, *Ancient Egyptian Religion: an Interpretation*, New York, 1949; John A. Wilson, *The Burden of Egypt*, Chicago, 1951, repr. 1956 as *The Culture of Ancient Egypt*; J. Cerny, *Ancient Egyptian Religion*, London etc., 1952; W.C. Hayes, *The Scepter of Egypt*, 2 vols., New York, 1953, 1959; S. Morenz, *Egyptian Religion*, London and Ithaca, N.Y., 1973 (trans. from the German of 1960); A.H. Gardiner, *Egypt of the Pharaohs*, London, 1961; C.J. Bleeker, 'The Religion of Ancient Egypt' in C.J. Bleeker and G. Widengren (eds.), *Historia Religionum* 1, Leiden, 1969; Ph. Derchain, 'La religion égyptienne', in H.-C. Puech (ed.), *Histoire des religions* 1, Paris, 1970, pp. 63–104; W.W. Hallo and W.K. Simpson, *The Ancient Near East: a History*, New York, 1971, Part 2; E. Hornung, *Conceptions of God in Ancient Egypt: The One and the Many*, 1982 (trans. from the German of 1971); *id.*, 'Verfall und Regeneration der Schöpfung', in *Eranos* 46 (1977), publ. Frankfurt a.M., 1981, pp. 411–49; A.R. David, *Cult of the Sun: Myth and Magic in Ancient Egypt*, London etc., 1980; *id. The Ancient Egyptians: Religious Beliefs and Practices*, London, Boston, etc., 1982; B.G. Trigger, B.J. Kemp, D. O'Connor and A.B. Lloyd, *Ancient Egypt: a Social History*, Cambridge, 1983; B.J. Kemp, *Ancient Egypt: Anatomy of a Civilization*, London and New York, 1989; D.B. Redford, *Egypt, Canaan and Israel in Ancient Times*, Princeton, 1992.

2 This and the following dates are as given in Kemp, *op. cit.* 1989, p. 14.

3 Trans. R.O. Faulkner, *The Ancient Egyptian Pyramid Texts*, Oxford, 1969, p. 226, para 1466 b. On the primordial chaos *cf.* Hornung, *op. cit.*, pp. 174–7; H. Grapow, 'Die Welt vor der Schöpfung', in *Zeitschrift für ägyptische Sprache und Altertumskunde*, Leipzig, 67 (1931), pp. 34–8.

4 *Cf.* J. Assmann, *Zeit und Ewigkeit im Alten Ägypten*, Heidelberg, 1975, pp. 21–2, 30; Hornung, 'Licht und Finsternis in der Vorstellungswelt Altägyptens', in *Studium Generale*, Berlin, 18 (1965), pp. 73–83, esp. p. 78.

5 *Cf.* Hornung, *Conceptions of God*, p. 170, with references in note 105. A variant of the cosmogonic myth is described in Hornung, *Der ägyptische Mythos von der Himmelskuh. Eine Ätiologie des Unvollkommenen*, Göttingen, 1982 (with summary at pp. 96 sq.)

6 On the demiurge and cosmogony: S. Sauneron and J. Yoyotte, 'La Naissance du Monde selon l'Égypte Ancienne', in *La Naissance du Monde*, Paris, 1959 (*Sources Orientales 1*), pp. 19–91; and more briefly, David, *Ancient Egyptians*, pp. 46–9.

7 Trans. Bleeker, *op. cit.*, p. 52.

8 On the concept of *ma'at*: Morenz, *op. cit.*, chapter 6; Bleeker, 'L'idée de l'ordre cosmique dans l'ancienne Égypte', in *RHPR*, Strasbourg, 42 (1962), pp. 193–200; W. Westendorf, 'Ursprung und Wesen der Maat', in F. Cornelius (ed.), *Festgabe für Walter Will*, Munich, 1966, pp. 201–225; Hans Heinrich Schmid, *Gerechtigkeit als Weltordnung*, Tübingen, 1968, pp. 46–61; J. Bergman, 'Zum "Mythus vom Staat" im Alten Ägypten', in H. Biezais (ed.), *The Myth of the State*, Stockholm, 1972, pp. 80–101; L.G. Perdue, *Wisdom and Cult. A Critical Analysis of the Views of Cult in the Wisdom Literature of Israel and the Ancient Near East*, Missoula, 1977, pp. 19–28; A. Brodie and J. Macdonald, 'The concept of cosmic order in Ancient Egypt in Dynastic and Roman times', in *L'Antiquité Classique*, Brussels, 47 (1978), pp. 106–28; L. Epsztein, *La justice sociale dans le Proche-Orient Ancien et le Peuple de la Bible*, Paris, 1983, pp. 421–78; article 'Maat' in LA 3, cols 1110–19.

9 *Cf.* Bleeker, *Egyptian Festivals: Enactments of Religious Renewal*, Leiden, 1967, pp. 54–5.

10 Trans. Bleeker, *Hathor and Thoth: Two Key Figures in Ancient Egyptian Religion*, Leiden, 1973, p. 122.

11 *Cf.* J. Spiegel, 'Der Sonnengott in der Barke als Richter', in *Mitteilungen des deutschen archäologischen Instituts, Abteilung Kairo*, Berlin, 8 (1939), pp. 201–206.

12 *Cf.* p. 15 [p. 28 in MS]

13 *Book of the Dead*, chapter 26. (For translations see note 57.) *Cf.* on the relevant passage: J. Assmann, *Der König als Sonnenpriester*, Glückstadt, 1970, pp. 60–4.

14 On Thoth: Bleeker, *Hathor and Thoth.*

15 *Ibid.*, p. 119.

16 *Ibid.*, p. 122.

17 On the nature of Egyptian monarchy see, in addition to the relevant passages in the works listed under Note 1: A. Moret, *Du caractère de la royauté pharaonique*, Paris, 1902; H. Goedicke, *Die Stellung des Königs im Alten Reich*, Wiesbaden, 1960; G. Posener, *De la divinité du Pharaon*, Paris, 1960.

18 On Seth: Herman te Velde, *Seth, God of Confusion: A Study of his Role in Egyptian Mythology and Religion*, Leiden, 1967; E. Hornung, 'Seth: Geschichte und Bedeutung eines ägyptischen Gottes', in *Symbolon. Jahrbuch für Symbolforschung*, n.s. 2, Cologne, 1974. The fullest account of the myth of Seth and Osiris is that by Plutarch in *De Iside et Osiride*; but the myth itself is certainly ancient.

19 Trans. Kemp, *op. cit.*, p. 198. *Cf.* H. Brunner, *Die Geburt des Gottkönigs*, Wiesbaden, 1964.

20 Trans. Kemp in B.G. Trigger *et al.*, *Ancient Egypt: a Social History*, p. 74.

21 Both trans. Morenz, *op. cit.*, pp. 120–21.

22 Both trans. Bleeker, 'The Religion of Ancient Egypt', p. 79.

23 Trans. J.H. Breasted, *Ancient Records of Egypt*, (5 vols., Chicago, 1906–7) 4, p. 228.

24 *Ibid.*, 3, p. 119.

25 *Ibid.*, 4, p. 26.

26 Trans. A. Erman and A.M. Blackman, *The Literature of the Ancient Egyptians*, London, 1927, pp. 278–9.

27 Both trans. in ANET, pp. 415, 417. On the historical context: R.J. Williams, 'Literature as a medium of political propaganda in Ancient Egypt', in W.S. McCullough (ed.), *The Seed of Wisdom: Essays in Honour of T.J. Meek*, Toronto, 1964, pp. 14–30, esp. pp. 14–19.

28 *Cf.* Perdue, *op. cit.* (see note 8), pp. 26–7.

29 Trans. Morenz, *op. cit.*, p. 115.

30 *Cf.* Baillet, *op. cit.*, vol. 1, pp. 276–8.

31 *Cf.* Bleeker, *loc. cit.*

32 Trans. Morenz, *op. cit.*, p. 50.

33 Trans. Breasted, *op. cit.*, 3, p. 79.

34 *Ibid.*, 2, pp. 263–6.

35 *Cf.* Hornung, *Geschichte als Fest*, Darmstadt, 1966, pp. 14–15, with

references p. 55, notes 13, 15. Text trans. A.H. Gardiner, *The Kadesh Inscriptions of Rameses II*, Oxford, 1960, pp. 7–14.

36 See e.g. W. Helck, 'Die Ägypter und die Fremden', in *Saeculum*, Freiburg and Munich, 15 (1964), pp. 103–15, esp. p. 105.

37 The theme is present already in the Narmer Palette, which is predynastic; see the reproductions and comments in Kemp, *Ancient Egypt: Anatomy of a Civilization*, p. 42.

38 *Cf.* articles 'Feindsymbolik' in LA 2, cols. 146–8, and 'Vernichtungsrituale', *ibid.*, 6, cols. 1010–12; Hornung, *loc. cit.*, p. 17; Kemp, *loc. cit.*, p. 47.

39 On this literature: F. Junge, 'Die Welt der Klagen', in *Fragen altägyptischer Literatur*, Wiesbaden, 1977, pp. 275–8, esp. pp. 283–4; J. Assmann, 'Königsdogma und Heilserwartung. Politische und kultische Chaosbeschreibungen in ägyptischen Texten', in HELLHOLM, pp. 345–77.

40 Trans. M. Lichtheim, *Ancient Egyptian Literature*, 3 vols., Berkeley etc., 1973–8, 1, pp. 140–44.

41 Full translation *ibid.*, pp. 150–61.

42 *Ibid.*, pp. 134–5.

43 *Cf.* p. 21 [p. 48 in MS]

44 On Apophis: E.A.W. Budge, *Legends of the Gods, edited with translations*, London, 1912, pp. 12 sq.; Hornung, *op. cit.*, pp. 158–9; article in LA 1, cols. 350–52.

45 Trans. A.J. Wilson in ANET, p. 7.

46 The extant text (in the Papyrus Bremner-Rhind, British Museum) dates only from the third century BC, but the material is some two thousand years older. For a translation of the entire work: R.O. Faulkner, in *Journal of Egyptian Archaeology*, London, 22 (1936), pp. 221 sq.; 23 (1937), pp. 10 sq.; 26 (1938), pp. 41 sq. For a brief account, with extracts: Budge, *From Fetish to God in Ancient Egypt*, Oxford, 1934, pp. 516–21.

47 *Cf.* Hornung, 'Chaotische Bereiche in der geordneten Welt', in *Zeitschrift für ägyptische Sprache* 81 (1956), pp. 28–32.

48 *Cf.* David, *Ancient Egyptians*, pp. 127–32; *id.*, *Cult of the Sun*, pp. 67–70.

49 *Cf.* Derchain, 'La religion égyptienne', pp. 91 sq.

50 *Cf.* Derchain, *Le Papyrus Salt 825: Rituel pour la conservation de la vie en Égypte*, Brussels, 1965, *passim*, esp. pp. 17, 125; J. Leclant, 'Espace et temps, ordre et chaos dans l'Égypte pharaonique', in *Revue de Synthèse*, Paris, 90 (1969), pp. 217–39, esp. pp. 214–15.

51 *Cf.* Hornung, *Conceptions of God*, pp. 214–15, with reproduction of relief at Karnak; Bergman, *op. cit.* (see note 8), esp. pp. 83–93, with reproduction of relief at Kom Ombo.

52 *Cf.* D. Meeks, 'Génies, anges et démons en Egypte', in *Génies, anges et démons*, Paris, 1971, (*Sources Orientales* 8), pp. 19–84.

53 *Cf.* Hornung, *Geschichte als Fest*, p. 15.

54 *Cf.* Westendorf, 'Ursprung und Wesen der Maat' (see note 8), p. 223; Derchain, 'La religion égyptienne', p. 100. All studies of Egyptian religion deal with Osiris and his cult. For further bibliography: David, *Ancient Egyptians*, p. 242.

55 *Cf.* Assmann, *Zeit und Ewigkeit*, p. 47.

56 *Cf.* Hornung, 'Licht und Finsternis . . .', p. 80.

57 *Cf.* Hornung, *Conceptions of God*, pp. 93, 95.

58 *Cf.* Leclant, *op. cit.*, p. 235.

59 *Cf.* *The Book of the Dead*, chapter 175. (For translations see below, note 65); also Hornung, *Der ägyptische Mythos von der Himmelskuh*, p. 104.

60 *Cf.* C.C. McConn, 'Egyptian apocalyptic literature', in *Harvard Theological Review*, 18 (1925), pp. 357–411; G. Lanczkowski, *Altägyptischer Prophetismus*, Wiesbaden, 1960; Jonathan Z. Smith, *Map is not Territory*, Leiden, 1978, pp. 74–87,

esp. the concise summary of the characteristic features of Egyptian prophecy at p. 76; Assmann, 'Königsdogma und Heilserwartung. Politische und kultische Chaosbeschreibungen in ägyptischen Texten', in HELLHOLM, pp. 345–78. Not even the 'eschatological prophecy' at the end of Lanczkowski's work speaks of a future without parallel in the past.

61 Notions about the afterlife figure prominently in most works on the Egyptian world-view; a particularly thorough treatment is to be found in David, *Ancient Egyptians*. For detailed studies see A.H. Gardiner, *The Attitude of the Ancient Egyptians to Death and the Dead*, Cambridge, 1935 (Frazer Lecture); H. Kees, *Totenglaube und Jenseitsvorstellungen der alten Ägypter*, 2nd edn., Berlin, 1956; A.J. Spencer, *Death in Ancient Egypt*, Harmondsworth, 1982, esp. chapter 6. E. Hornung, *The Valley of the Kings. Horizon of Eternity*, New York, 1990 (trans. from the German edn. of 1982), illumines much more than its ostensible subject, the royal tombs of the New Kingdom. Valuable collections of texts, in translation, illustrating notions about the afterlife are, for the Old Kingdom and the First Intermediate Period: S.A.B. Mercer, *The Pyramid Texts in Translation and Commentary*, 4 vols., London and New York etc, 1952, and R.O. Faulkner, *The Ancient Egyptian Pyramid Texts*, Oxford, 1969; for the Middle Kingdom: Faulkner, *The Ancient Egyptian Coffin Texts*, 3 vols., Warminster, 1973–8; for the New Kingdom: E.A.W. Budge, *The Book of the Dead*, 3 vols., London, 1898; T.G. Allen, *The Book of the Dead or Going Forth by Day*, Chicago, 1974; Faulkner, *The Ancient Egyptian Book of the Dead*, London, 1972, rev. edn. 1985.

62 *Cf.* the inscription on the tomb of a New Kingdom prince trans. in part in Gardiner, *The Attitude of the Ancient Egyptians*, pp. 29–30, and in part in K. Sethe, *Urkunden der 18. Dynastie*, Leipzig, 1914, p. 58.

63 *Cf.* Westendorf, 'Ursprung und Wesen der Maat' (see note 8), esp. p. 216.

64 *Cf.* Hornung, *Altägyptische Höllenvorstellungen*, Berlin, 1968 (*Abhandlungen der sächsichen Akademie der Wissenschaften, Philologisch-historische Klasse* 59, 3). For a more general account: J. Zandee, *Death as an Enemy*, Leiden, 1960, esp. pp. 14–41.

65 Trans. Gardiner, *op. cit.*, p. 32.

Chapter 2: Mesopotamians

1 On the civilisation and world-view of Sumer: S.N. Kramer, *Sumerian Mythology*, Philadelphia, 1944 (*Memoirs of the American Philosophical Society* 21); Kramer, *History Begins at Sumer*, London, 1958; Kramer, *The Sumerians: their History, Culture and Character*, Chicago, 1963. On the civilisation and world-view of Ancient Mesopotamia in general: T. Jacobsen, 'Mesopotamia', in H. Frankfort *et al.*, *The Intellectual Adventure of Ancient Man*; Frankfort, *Kingship and the Gods* (for both these see note 1 to Chapter 1); E. Dhorme, *Les religions de Babylonie et d'Assyrie*, Paris, 1949 (vol. 2 of collection *Mana*); J. Bottéro, *La religion babylonienne*, Paris, 1952; H.W.F. Saggs, *The Greatness that was Babylon*, London, 1962, rev. edn. 1988; A.L. Oppenheim, *Ancient Mesopotamia: Portrait of a Dead Civilization*, Chicago, 1964; J. Nougayrol, 'La religion babylonienne', in H.-C. Puech (ed.) *Histoire des religions*, 1, Paris, 1970; W.W. Hallo and W.K. Simpson, *The Ancient Near East: a History*, New York, etc., 1971, Part 1; H. Ringgren, *Religions of the Ancient Near East*, ET London, 1973; T. Jacobsen, *The Treasures of Darkness: a History of Mesopotamian Religion*, New Haven and London, 1976; Saggs, *The Encounter with the Divine in Meso-*

potamia and Israel, London, 1978; Joan Oates, *Babylon*, London, 1979, rev. edn. 1986; G. Roux, *Ancient Iraq*, rev. edn. Harmondsworth, 1980; John Gray, *Near Eastern Mythology*, 2nd edn. London, 1982, pp. 6–105; Saggs, *The Might that was Assyria*, London, 1984; J. Bottéro, *Mésopotamie: L'écriture, la raison et les dieux*, Paris, 1987.

See also the articles by Kramer 'Mythology in Sumer and Akkad', in Kramer (ed.), *Mythologies of the Ancient World*, New York, 1961; Jacobsen, 'Ancient Mesopotamian religion: the central concerns', in *Proceedings of the American Philosophical Society*, Philadelphia, 107, No. 6 (1963), pp. 473–84; W.G. Lambert, 'Destiny and divine intervention in Babylon and Israel', in A.S. Van der Woude (ed.), *The Witness of Tradition*, Leiden, 1972, pp. 65–72; S.N. Kramer and J. Maier, *Myths of Enki, The Crafty God*, New York and Oxford, 1989, esp. chapter 3, 'Enki and Inanna: the organization of the earth and the cultural processes'.

2 Trans. Jacobsen, *Treasures of Darkness*, p. 57.

3 Trans. Kramer, *History Begins at Sumer*, p. 143.

4 On the principle of straightness/rightness/truth/justice in Mesopotamia: B. Geiger, *Die Amesha Spentas, ihr Wesen und ihre ursprüngliche Bedeutung*, in *Sitzungsberichte der kaiserlichen Akademie der Wissenschaften in Wien*, 176, Vienna, 1916, esp. pp. 144–7; Benno Landsberger, 'The conceptual autonomy of the Babylonian world', originally Inaugural Lecture, Leipzig, 1926, now trans. Jacobsen *et al.* in *Monographs on the Ancient Near East*, 1, fasc. 4, Malibu, California, 1976, esp. p. 13; E.A. Speiser, 'Authority and Law in Mesopotamia' in JAOS Supp. 17 (1954) (*Authority and Law in the Ancient Orient*), pp. 10–15; J. Van Dijk, 'Einige Bemerkungen zu sumerischen religionsgeschichtlichen Problemen', in *Orientalische Literaturzeitung*, Berlin, 62 (1967), cols. 229–47, esp. col. 231; H. Ringgren, *Religions of the Ancient Near East*, pp. 43, 103, 112–13. On the relationship of the sun, or the sun-god, with that principle: Geiger, *loc. cit.*; R. Labat, *Le caractère religieux de la royauté assyro-babylonienne*, Paris, 1939, pp. 228–33; Hans Heinrich Schmid, *Gerechtigkeit als Weltordnung*, Tübingen, 1968, pp. 61–5; Ringgren, *op. cit.*, pp. 9, 39, 44, 58–9. For the Hittites see O.R. Gurney, *The Hittites*, London, 1952, p. 139. For other cultures R. Pettazoni, *The All-knowing God*, ET London, 1956, *passim*; and chapter I of the present work.

5 On the concept of *me*: J. Van Dijk, *La Sagesse suméro-accadienne*, Leiden, 1953, p. 19; H.H. Schmid, *Wesen und Geschichte der Weisheit: Eine Untersuchung zur altorientalischen und israelitischen Weisheitsliteratur*, Berlin, 1966, pp. 115–8; *id.*, *Gerechtigkeit als Weltordnung*, pp. 61–5; G. Farber-Flügge, *Der Mythos 'Inanna und Enki' unter besonderer Berücksichtigung der Liste der me*, Rome, 1973, esp. pp. 118–22, 197–9; L.G. Perdue, *Wisdom and Cult: a Critical Analysis of the Views of Cult in the Wisdom Literature of Israel and the Ancient Near East*, Missoula, 1977, pp. 85–94.

6 For the following *cf.* Labat, *op. cit.*, pp. 234–5; Saggs, *The Greatness that was Babylon*, pp. 364–9.

7 On the role of the king see, in addition to the relevant passages in the works listed in note 1 above: Labat, *op. cit.*, *passim*; W.G. Lambert, 'The seed of kingship', in P. Garelli (ed.), *Le palais et la royauté (Archéologie et civilisation)*, Paris, 1974, pp. 427–40.

8 *Cf.* Labat, *op. cit.*, p. 280.

9 From the German translation in A. Falkenstein, 'Sumerische religiöse Texte', in *Zeitschrift für Assyriologie*, n.s. 16, Berlin, 1952, pp. 79–80.

10 *Cf.* Labat, *op. cit.*, pp. 232–3.

11 Trans. T.J. Meek, in ANET, p. 164.

12 Trans. Meek, *ibid.*, p. 178. *Cf.* the royal hymns translated in Jacobsen,

Treasures of Darkness, p. 98, and in W.H.P. Römer, *Sumerische Königshymnen der Isin-Zeit*, Leiden, 1965, p. 11.

13 Trans. Jacobsen, *op. cit.*, p. 79.

14 Trans. Jacobsen, *ibid.*, p. 231.

15 Trans. Jacobsen, *ibid.*, p. 137.

16 Trans. Jacobsen, *ibid.*, p. 238.

17 On the theme of hero-god versus chaos-monster — the so-called 'combat-myth' — in Antiquity see J. Fontenrose, *Python: a Study in Delphic Myth and its Origins*, Berkeley, 1959; N. Forsyth, *The Old Enemy: Satan and the Combat Myth*, Princeton, 1987; and at more popular level, U. Steffen, *Drachenkampf: Der Mythos vom Bösen*, Stuttgart, 1984. Also relevant to the present chapter: M. Wakeman, *The Battle of God against the Monster*, Leiden, 1973, esp. pp. 7–22.

18 *Cf.* J. Bottéro, 'Le mythe d'Anzu', in *Annuaire de la IVe Section de l'École Pratique des Hautes Études*, 1970–71, pp. 116–29; and, for a different interpretation, Jacobsen, *op. cit.*, pp. 132–3. See also B. Hruška, *Der Mythenadler Anzu in Literatur und Vorstellungen des alten Mesopotamien*, Budapest, 1975. For a new translation of this and the other Akkadian myths considered here see Stephanie Dalley, *Myths from Mesopotamia*, Oxford and New York, 1989. For a poem dealing with Ninurta, the assembled gods, and Enlil: J.C. Cooper, *The Return of Ninurta to Nippur*, Rome (Pontificium Institutum Biblicum), 1978, and esp. the editor's introduction, pp. 2–12.

19 The definitive edition of this myth is now J. Van Dijk, *Lugal Ud Me-Lam-bi Nir-Gal*, Leiden, 1983, which includes a lengthy introduction and a translation into French. For earlier interpretations: Kramer, 'Mythologies of Sumer and Akkad', p. 105; and Jacobsen, *op. cit.*, pp. 130–1. On the dispute between these two scholars see G.S. Kirk, *Myth: its Meaning and Functions in Ancient and Other Cultures*, Cambridge (England), Berkeley and Los Angeles, pp. 90–1. On the antiquity of the myth see, in addition to Van Dijk, W.G. Lambert, 'A new look at the Babylonian background of Genesis', in *Journal of Theological Studies*, Oxford, n.s. 16 (1965), pp. 285–300, esp. p. 296.

20 Trans. Kramer, *Sumerian Mythology*, p. 81; and *cf.* Van Dijk, pp. 96–7.

21 English translations of *Enuma elish* include S. Langdon, *The Babylonian Epic of Creation*, Oxford, 1923; A.S. Heidel, *The Babylonian Genesis: The Story of Creation*, Chicago, 1946; E.A. Speiser in ANET, pp. 60–72. For full analyses of the work: Jacobsen, *op. cit.*, pp. 167–91; Bottéro, *Mythes et rites de Babylone*, Paris, 1985, pp. 113–62. On the probable date of composition: W.G. Lambert, 'The reign of Nebuchadnezzar I', in W.S. McCullough (ed.), *The Seed of Wisdom*, Toronto, 1966; W. Sommerfeld, *Der Aufstieg Marduks. Die Stellung Marduks in der babylonischen Religion des zweiten Jahrtausends v. Chr.*, Neukirchen/Vluyn, 1982, esp. p. 175.

22 Trans. Jacobsen, *op. cit.*, p. 182.

23 Trans. Frankfort, *Kingship and the Gods*, p. 327.

24 *Cf.* Lambert, 'The great battle of the Mesopotamian religious year: the conflict in the Akitu house', in *Iraq*, London, 25 (1963), pp. 189–90.

25 *Cf.* Roux, *Ancient Iraq*, pp. 104–105, 365–9. There is an extensive literature on the *akitu*; for an account which disposes of various erroneous interpretations see J.A. Black, 'The New Year ceremonies in Ancient Babylon: "Taking Bel by the hand"', in *Religion*, London, 11 (1981), pp. 39–59.

26 Trans. Jacobsen, *op. cit.*, pp. 102–103.

27 Trans. W.G. Lambert, *Babylonian Wisdom Literature*, Oxford, 1960, p. 41.

28 On the myth of Atrahasis: Jacobsen, *op. cit.*, pp. 116–21.

29 Trans. Jacobsen, *op. cit.*, pp. 87–8.

30 ET: L. Cagni, *The Poem of Erra: Translated with an Introduction*, Malibu, California, 1977. For a full account of the work: Bottéro, *Mythes et rites*, pp. 221–61; and *cf.* Kramer, 'Mythology of Sumer and Akkad', pp. 127–35; J. Roberts, 'Erra — Scorched Earth', in *Journal of Cuneiform Studies*, 24, Cambridge, Mass., 1971, pp. 11–16; D. Bodi, *The Book of Ezekiel and the Poem of Erra*, Fribourg and Göttingen, 1991, esp. pp. 52–68. According to Bodi, the Babylonians are shown as having brought calamity on themselves by neglecting the cult of Erra; but he accepts that the indiscriminate slaughter carried out by Erra springs from the god's violent nature.

31 On good and bad spirits: M. Leibovici, 'Génies et démons en Babylonie', in *Génies, anges et démons*, Paris, 1971 (*Sources Orientales 8*). On demons in particular: G. Contenau, *La magie chez les Babyloniens et les Assyriens*, Paris, 1947, pp. 84–224; Saggs, *The Greatness that was Babylon*, pp. 306 sq.

32 *Cf.* Reginald C. Thompson, *The Devils and Evil Spirits of Babylon*, London, 2 vols., 1903, 1904, for translations of incantations against various demons.

33 *Cf.* Bottéro, *La religion babylonienne*, pp. 88–9.

34 On Mesopotamian attitudes to death: Bottéro, 'La mythologie de la mort en Mesopotamie', in B. Alster (ed.), *Death in Mesopotamia*, Copenhagen, 1980.

35 Trans. Jacobsen, *op. cit.*, pp. 202–203.

36 *Ibid.*, p. 207.

37 Trans. A. Heidel, *The Gilgamesh Epic and Old Testament Parallels*, 2nd edn., Chicago, 1949, p. 121.

38 *Cf.* A. Tsukimoto, *Untersuchungen zur Totenpflege (kispum) im alten Mesopotamien*, Kevelaer and Neukirchen-Vluyn, 1985.

39 *Cf.* A.H. Gardiner, *The Attitude of the Ancient Egyptians to Death and the Dead*, Cambridge, 1935, pp. 16–22.

40 The nearest approach to such an expectation is perhaps to be found in the document described in P. Hoffken, 'Heilszeitherrschererwartungen im babylonischen Raum', in *Die Welt des Orients* 9, Göttingen, 1977, pp. 57–71. This patriotic fantasy, stemming from Uruk, and probably directed against Persian rule, is of very limited scope. The suggestion of W. Hallo, 'Akkadian apocalypses', in *Israel Exploration Journal*, Jerusalem, 16 (1966), pp. 231–42, that Text D in W.G. Lambert and A.K. Grayson, 'Akkadian prophecies', in *Journal of Cuneiform Studies*, New Haven, 18 (1964), pp. 7–30, may point to 'a final and permanent *Heilzeit* under the aegis of a saviour-king' is not supported by evidence. Nor is the 'Marduk prophetic speech' referred to by Grayson in *Babylonian Historical-literary Texts*, Toronto and Buffalo, 1975, pp. 13 sq., and which includes Text D, more than a prophecy *ex eventu*, with no eschatological import.

Chapter 3: Vedic Indians

1 A fuller account of life on the steppes and its vicissitudes is given in Chapter 4.

2 On the Indo-Aryans and their arrival in the Indus valley: A.L. Basham, *The Wonder that was India*, 3rd edn., New York, 1967, pp. 1–34 sq.; S. Wolpert, *A New History of India*, New York and Oxford, 1982, pp. 10–38.

3 *Cf.* B. Schlerath, *Das Königtum in Rig- und Arthavaveda*, Wiesbaden, 1960, pp. 122–6.

4 On the *Rig Veda*: J. Gonda, *Vedic Literature*, Wiesbaden, 1975 (vol. I., fasc. 1 of *A History of Indian Literature*, ed. J. Gonda). For a remarkable translation of a selection of Rigvedic hymns: Wendy D. O'Flaherty, *The*

Rig Veda: An Anthology, Harmondsworth, 1981. Complete (but not necessarily reliable) English translations are: R.T.H. Griffith, *The Hymns of the Rig Veda*, London, 1889; H.H. Wilson, *Rig-Veda-Sanhita: A Collection of Ancient Hindu Hymns*, 6 vols., London, 1850–1888. A complete and reliable translation into German is: K.F. Geldner, *Der Rig-Veda*, 4 vols., Cambridge, Mass., 1951–57.

5 On the Vedic world-view: H. Oldenberg, *Die Religion des Veda*, 2nd edn., Berlin 1917, repr. 1970; A.A. Macdonnell, *Vedic Mythology*, Strassburg, 1897; H.D. Griswold, *The Religion of the Rigveda*, London, 1923; A.B. Keith, *The Religion and Philosophy of the Veda and Upanishads*, 2 vols., Cambridge, Mass., 1925; A.D. Pusalker, *The Vedic Age*, London, 1951 (vol. I of *History and Culture of the Indian People*, ed. R.C. Majundar); W. Norman Brown, *Man in the Universe*, Berkeley, 1966, Chapter 1; S. Bhattacharji, *The Indian Theogony*, Cambridge, England, 1970.

6 For brief surveys of Vedic cosmogonies: W. Norman Brown, 'Theories of creation in the Rig Veda', in JAOS, 85 (1) (1965), pp. 23–34; F.B.J. Kuiper, 'Cosmogony and conception: a query', in HR, 10 (2) (1970), pp. 91–138, esp. pp. 99 sq.; M. Eliade, *A History of Religious Ideas*, 1, ET London, 1979, pp. 223–7; O'Flaherty, *op. cit.*, pp. 25–40 (translated hymns with commentaries). A particularly interesting cosmogony, of proto-Indo-European origin, concerns the sacrifice and dismemberment of the primal man. The Vedic version is given in the *Purusha-Sukta* (RV 10.90); for translation and commentary see O'Flaherty, *op. cit.*, pp. 30–31. See also O'Flaherty, *The Origins of Evil in Hindu Mythology*, Berkeley, 1976, pp. 139–140; Bruce Lincoln, *Myth, Cosmos and Society: Indo-European Themes of Creation and Destruction*, Cambridge, Mass., and London, 1986, esp. Chapter 1; *id.*, 'The Indo-European Myth of Creation', in HR 15 (2) (1975), pp. 121–45; and W. Norman Brown, 'Theories of creation'.

7 On Indra see, in addition to the relevant passages in the works listed in note 5 above: Usna Choudhuri, *Indra and Varuna in Indian Mythology*, Delhi, 1981; M. Paliwahadana, *The Indra Cult as Ideology: a Clue to Power Struggle in an Ancient Society*. Repr. from *Vidoyana Journal of Arts, Science and Letters*, 9 (1981) and 10 (1982). For Indra as fertility-god: E.W. Hopkins, 'Indra as god of fertility', in JAOS 36 (1917), pp. 243–68; J. Gonda, *Aspects of Early Viṣṇuism*, Utrecht, 1934, pp. 32–55.

8 Paliwahadana, *op. cit.*, esp. pp. 43 sq.

9 *Ibid.*, p. 84 (trans. of RV 10.103. 4–8).

10 For the Vala myth see Hanns-Peter Schmidt, *Bṛhaspati und Indra: Untersuchungen zur vedischen Mythologie und Kulturgeschichte*, Wiesbaden, 1968, *passim*; Paliwahadana, *op. cit.*, pp. 89–90, 95–9. For a brief account: Oldenberg, *Religion des Veda*, pp. 143 sq. For a translation, with commentary, of the most important source (RV 3.31): O'Flaherty, *op. cit.*, pp. 151. Other relevant passages are RV 4.3.11; 10.62.2; 10.67, 2,3.

11 *Cf.* W. Norman Brown, 'The creation myth of the Rig Veda', in JAOS 62 (1942), pp. 85–98; *id.*, 'Mythology of India', in S.N. Kramer (ed.), *Mythologies of the Ancient World*, New York, 1961, pp. 281–6.

For a translation, with commentary, of the most relevant Rigvedic text (RV 1.32): O'Flaherty, *The Rig Veda*, pp. 148–51.

12 RV 10.124. 2,4.

13 On *rita* and its Iranian equivalent: H. Lüders, *Varuṇa* (ed. L. Alsdorf), Göttingen, 11, 1959, esp. pp. 568–84 (the fullest account, though marred by an excessively narrow equating of

rita with 'truth' only); J. Duchesne-Guillemin, *La religion de l'Iran ancien*, Paris, 1962, pp. 191–6 (includes a critique of Lüders); M. Boyce, *A History of Zoroastrianism*, 1, Leiden, 1975, p. 27 (in the series *Handbuch der Orientalistik*, ed. B. Spuler); J. Gonda, *Die Religionen Indiens*, 1, pp. 77–9.

14 *Cf.* Lüders, *op. cit.*, I, 1951, pp. 13–40; I. Gershevitch (ed. and trans.), *The Avestan Hymn to Mithra*, Cambridge, 1959, esp. pp. 26–54 in the Introduction; P. Thieme, 'The "Aryan" gods of the Mitanni treaties', in JAOS 80 (1960), pp. 301–17, esp. p. 308; Gonda, *op. cit.*, pp. 73–82; Boyce, *op. cit.*, pp. 22–37.

15 *Cf.* Boyce, *op. cit.*, pp. 34–5.

16 RV 2.35.2.

17 *Cf.* Gonda, *The Vedic God Mitra*, Leiden, 1972, pp. 91, 109–110.

18 *Cf.* V.N. Toporov, 'Indo-Iranian social and mythological concepts', in J.C. Heersterman *et al.* (eds.), *Pratidānam: Studies Presented to F.B.J. Kuiper*, The Hague and Paris, 1968, pp. 108–20 (Mitra at pp. 108–13); W.B. Kristensen, 'Het Mysterie van Mithra', in *Mededeelingen der Koninklijke Akademie van Wettenschappen*, Amsterdam, Aft. Letterkunde 9 (1946), pp. 25–38, esp. pp. 3–5.

19 *Cf.* Choudhuri, *op. cit.*, pp. 12–14, where many of the relevant passages from the *Rig Veda* are translated.

20 On Soma (drink and god): Macdonnell, *op. cit.*, pp. 104–14; Keith, *op. cit.*, 1, pp. 166–72; Gonda, *Religionen Indiens*, pp. 62–6 (see note 5 above for complete references); Boyce, *op. cit.*, pp. 157–62.

21 *Cf.* D.S. Flattery and M. Schwarz, 'Haoma and Harmeline', in *University of California Publications in Near Eastern Studies*, Berkeley, 21 (1984).

22 On Agni: Macdonnell, *op. cit.*, pp. 88–100; Keith, *op. cit.*, pp. 154–62; Gonda, *op. cit.*, pp. 67–73; Boyce, *op. cit.*, pp. 69–70.

23 *Cf.* Gonda, *op. cit.*, pp. 68–9. For an alternative explanation: Oldenberg, *op. cit.* pp. 108 sq. (summarised in Boyce, *op. cit.*, pp. 45–6).

24 *Cf.* W. Norman Brown, *Man in the Universe*, pp. 58–64.

25 RV 8.101: 15–16 (trans. Brown, *ibid.*, p. 62).

26 On Vedic sacrifices: S. Lévi, *La doctrine du sacrifice dans les brahmanas*, Paris, 1898, repr. 1966; Keith, *op. cit.*, 2, pp. 313–66; Gonda, *op. cit.*, pp. 104–73; M. Biardeau and Ch. Malamoud, *Le sacrifice dans l'Inde anciennne*, Paris, 1976.

27 *Cf.* Biardeau, *op. cit.*, pp. 7–57.

28 On Rudra: Gonda, *op. cit.*, pp. 85–9.

29 *Cf.* Biardeau, *op. cit.*, p. 25; O'Flaherty, *The Origins of Evil*, p. 79.

30 *Cf.* Macdonnell, *op. cit.*, pp. 162–4.

31 RV 7.104.

32 *Cf.* W. Norman Brown, 'The Rigvedic equivalent of hell', in JAOS 61 (1941), pp. 76–80, esp. at p. 79.

33 *Cf.* E. Arbman, 'Tod und Unsterblichkeit im vedischen Glauben', in *Archiv für Religionswissenschaft*, Leipzig and Berlin, 25 (1927) pp. 339–87 and 26 (1928) pp. 152–238; Macdonnell, *op. cit.*, p. 166.

34 *Ibid.*, p. 168.

Chapter 4: Zoroastrians

1 On Zoroaster, and on Zoroastrianism in the ancient world: H. Lommel, *Die Religion Zarathustras nach dem Awesta dargestellt*, Tübingen, 1930, repr. 1971; R.C. Zaehner, *The Dawn and Twilight of Zoroastrianism*, London, 1961, repr. 1975; J. Duchesne-Guillemin, *La religion de l'Iran ancien*, Paris, 1962 (includes an excellent bibliography); B. Schlerath (ed.), *Zarathustra, Wege der Forschung*, Darmstadt, 1970 (an anthology of essays covering the previous half-century); G. Gnoli, *Zoroaster's Time and Homeland*, Naples, 1980; *id.*, *De Zoroastre à Mani*, Paris, 1985; M. Boyce, *A History of Zoroastrianism*, vols. 1, 2, 3, Leiden, 1975, 1981, 1991 (in the

series *Handbuch der Orientalistik*, ed. B. Spuler); *id.*, *Zoroastrians: Their Religious Beliefs and Practices*, London, 1979; *id.*, *Zoroastrianism: Its Antiquity and Constant Vigour*, Costa Mesa, California, 1993. Parts of J.R. Hinnells, *Persian Mythology*, London etc., 1973 (an illustrated introduction) and of G. Widengren, *Die Religionen Irans*, Stuttgart, 1965, are also relevant.

For a bibliography of the best translations of Zoroastrian texts see Boyce, *Zoroastrians*, pp. 229–31. Zaehner, *The Teachings of the Magi*, London, 1956, is an anthology of Zoroastrian sources from the Sasanian period, translated, with commentary. Boyce, *Textual Sources for the Study of Zoroastrianism*, Manchester, 1984, is an anthology of sources from all periods, translated, with commentary; except where otherwise stated, the quotations in the present chapter are taken from this work. Another useful anthology of translated passages, with commentary, is W.W. Malandra, *An Introduction to Ancient Iranian Religion: Readings from the Avesta and the Achaemenid Inscriptions*, Minneapolis, 1983.

For the history of ancient Iran down to the Sasanian period and beyond: R.N. Frye, *The History of Ancient Iran*, Munich, 1984 (in the series *Handbuch der Altertumswissenschaft*, ed. H. Bengton).

2 The sixth-century dating was still accepted by W.B. Henning, *Zoroaster, Politician or Witch-Doctor?*, Oxford, 1951, pp. 35 sq., and Zaehner, *Dawn and Twilight*, p. 33. For its erroneous basis see P. Kingsley, 'The Greek origin of the sixth-century dating of Zoroaster', in BSOAS 53 (1990), pp. 245–64.

3 *Cf.* Boyce, 'Persian religion of the Achemenid age', in *The Cambridge History of Judaism*, Cambridge, etc., 1 (1984) pp. 275–6; *id.*, *Zoroastrianism*, chapter 2. *id.*, *History*, 2, pp. 1–3; Gnoli, *op. cit.*, pp. 159 sq.; H.E. Eduljee, 'The date of Zoroaster', in *Journal of the K.R. Cama Oriental Institute*, Bombay, 48 (1980), pp. 103–60.

4 Yasna 44.18. The Yasna is that part of the *Avesta* which contains the texts recited during the act of worship (*yasna*); it consists of some 72 numbered sections.

5 On the constitution of the Zoroastrian canon: H.S. Nyberg, *Die Religionen des Alten Irans* (trans. from the Swedish), Leipzig, 1983, chapter 8, esp. pp. 415–19.

6 *Cf.* p. 66.

7 The only complete English translation of the *yashts* is that in J. Darmesteter, *The Zend-Avesta*, part 2, Oxford, 1883 (repr. Delhi, 1965), which forms vol. 23 in the series *Sacred Books of the East*. It is out of date in many respects. Malandra's *Introduction* (see note 1 above) includes a liberal selection of *yashts*, with valuable notes. For a good German translation of the complete set, also with valuable notes: H. Lommel, *Die Yašts des Awesta*, Göttingen and Leipzig, 1927.

8 Certain passages in the *Rig Veda* (notably RV 5.63.3d and 7b,c, RV 5.83.6d) have sometimes been cited as referring to this god; see P. Thieme, 'The "Aryan" gods of the Mitanni treaties', in JAOS 80, (1960), pp. 301–17, esp. p. 309. But those passages are given quite a different interpretation by Geldner in his translation and commentary, and the same can be said of the only one of the three passages (the last) which is included in O'Flaherty's translation. For fuller references to these works see note 4 to Chapter 3.

9 Yasna 44. 3–5, 7.

10 Yasna 30.3.

11 Yasna 45.2.

12 Text and translation: B.T. Anklesaria, *Zand-Ākāsīh, Iranian or Greater Bundahishn*, Bombay, 1964. Selected passages in translation are

given in Boyce, *Textual Sources.*

13 *Cf.* note 6 to Chapter 3.

14 On Ahura Mazda's creation of the Holy Immortals and of the physical world see Boyce, *History*, 1, pp. 192–5, 202–203, 220–21, 229–31. On the physical world as a trap for Angra Mainyu see also Zaehner, *Teachings of the Magi*, p. 18, and *Dawn and Twilight*, p. 265 (though Zaehner associates the notions exclusively with Sasanian Zoroastrianism).

15 On Iranian sacrificial ritual: Boyce, *History*, chapter 6; and *cf. ibid.*, pp. 219–20.

16 From the German translation of Yasht 10.6 in H. Lommel, *Yašts*, p. 192.

17 On the soteriological role of human beings: N. Söderblom, *La vie future d'après le mazdéisme*, Paris, 1901, pp. 240, 255–7; M. Molé, *Culte, mythe et cosmologie dans l'Iran ancien*, Paris, 1963, p. 395.

18 Trans. Boyce, *Textual Sources*, p. 100.

19 *Vendidad* 3. 23–35, quoted and trans. in M. Schwarz, 'The religion of Achaemenian Iran', in *The Cambridge History of Iran*, vol. 2, Cambridge etc., 1985, p. 662.

20 *Cf.* Lommel, *Religion Zarathustras*, p. 238; Boyce, *History*, 1, pp. 210–11.

21 On the *daevic* creation: Lommel, *op. cit.*, pp. 113–20; Boyce, *op. cit.*, pp. 294–307.

22 Yasna 29.

23 *Vendidad* 33.39. The only complete English translation of the *Vendidad* is part 1 of Darmesteter, *The Zend-Avesta.* It forms vol. 4 of *Sacred Books of the East*, Oxford, 1880.

24 This and the two preceding quotations are from Yasht 13, verses 15, 23, 65; trans. Boyce, *History*, 1, pp. 125, 126.

25 Yasna 13. 12–13.

26 Louis H. Gray, *The Foundations of the Iranian Religions*, Bombay, 1929 (K.R. Cama Oriental Institute Publications No. 5) and A. Christensen, *Essai sur la démonologie iranienne*, Copenhagen, 1941, though dated, give comprehensive surveys of Iranian and Zoroastrian beliefs about demons.

27 Yasna 30.7.

28 Malandra, *op. cit.*, p. 162.

28 *Vendidad* 17. 7–10.

29 From the German translation of Yasht 13.57 in Lommel, *Yašts*, p. 119.

30 *Vendidad* 10. 9–10 and 19.43; *cf. Bundahishn* 1.55 and 34.27.

31 *Cf.* T. Burrow, 'The Proto-Indoaryans', in *Journal of the Royal Asiatic Society*, London, 1973, pp. 123–40, and Gnoli, *op. cit.*, pp. 73 sq.

32 *Cf.* Boyce, *History*, 1, pp. 201, 251–2.

33 Relevant passages in the *Bundahishn*: 1.55 and 34.27; in the *Dinkard*: 9.9.1. See also Gray, *op. cit.*, pp. 181–4; and, amongst earlier authors, J. Darmesteter, *Ormazd and Ahriman*, Paris, 1877, pp. 259–65; A.V.W. Jackson, 'Die iranische Religion', in *Grundriss der iranischen Philologie* (ed. W. Geiger and E. Kuhn), Strassburg, 1896–1904, 2, pp. 655–7.

34 Yasna 46.2 and Y.50.1.

35 For this and the preceding quotation: Yasna 29.9.

36 Yasna 44.18.

37 *Cf.* Boyce, *op. cit.*, p. 252. Some scholars see the conflict as one between different social strata rather than between different kinds of society; see Kai Barr, 'Avest. *dragu, drigu*', in *Studia Orientalia Ioanni Pedersen dicata*, Copenhagen, 1953, pp. 21–40; Bruce Lincoln, *Priests, Warriors and Cattle: a Study in the Ecology of Religion*, Berkeley, etc., 1981, esp. chapters 5 and 6; Gnoli, *op. cit.*, p. 185. These scholars do not, however, take into account the transformation of warfare considered below. For a rejoinder to Lincoln's argument see Boyce, 'Priests, cattle and men', in BSOAS 50, (1987), pp. 508–26.

38 *Cf.* A. Kammenhuber, *Die Arier im Vorderen Orient*, Heidelberg, 1968;

Boyce, *Zoroastrians*, pp. 2–3, 18.; *id.*, *Zoroastrianism*, pp. 37–9.

39 *Cf.* P. Friedrich, *Proto-Indo-European Syntax*, Butto, Montana, 1975, pp. 44–6; Boyce, 'The bipartite society of the ancient Iranians', in M.A. Dandamayev *et al.* (eds.), *Societies and Languages in the Ancient Near East: Studies in Honour of I.M. Diakonoff*, Warminster, 1982, pp. 33–7. The view propounded by Stig Wikander in *Der arische Männerbund* (Lund, 1938), and developed by Georges Dumézil in many of his works, that proto-Indo-Iranian and even proto-Indo-European society already possessed a class of professional warriors, can no longer be seriously maintained. It overlooks the chronology of the Neolithic and Early Bronze Ages in the relevant area.

40 *Cf.* Boyce, *Zoroastrians*, p. 3.

41 Yasna 32. 11–12.

42 Yasna 49.4.

43 *Cf.* Yasna 46.4.

44 *Cf.* N. Cohn, *The Pursuit of the Millennium*, London and New York, 1957 etc., *passim.*

45 For Zoroastrian teaching concerning the afterlife: Lommel, *Religion Zarathustras*, pp. 185–204; Zaehner, *Teachings of the Magi*, p. 25; *id.*, *Dawn and Twilight*, pp. 55–7, 304–307; Boyce, *History*, 1, pp. 109–17, 198, 236–41. For a detailed survey of Zoroastrian writings on the theme: Jal Dastur Cursetji Pavry, *The Zoroastrian Doctrine of a Future Life from Death to the Individual Judgment*, New York, 1926. For Zoroastrian teaching concerning the final state of the world see, in addition to the relevant passages in the general works listed under note 1 above: N. Söderblom, *op. cit.* (see note 17); G. Widengren, 'Leitende Ideen und Quellen der iranischen Apokalyptik' in HELLHOLM, pp. 77–162. Chapter 34 of the *Bundahishn* is especially relevant, and the following account of the great consummation is based on it (see note 12).

46 The same two contrasting expectations persisted for a time amongst the Indo-Aryans after their arrival in India; *cf.* E. Arbman, 'Tod und Unsterblichkeit im vedischen Glauben', in *Archiv für Religionswissenschaft*, Leipzig and Berlin, 25, (1927), pp. 339–89, and 26 (1928), pp. 187–240.

47 *Bundahishn*, chapter 34: 4–5.

48 *Cf.* Yasna 44.15 and Yasna 51.9; Söderblom, *op. cit.*, p. 224; Boyce, *History*, 1, pp. 242–4 (with footnotes giving references to fuller accounts in the *Bundahishn* and other Pahlavi books).

49 *Cf.* Lommel, *op. cit.*, pp. 219 sq.

50 Yasna 51.9.

51 *Bundahishn*, chapter 34: 27.

52 Yasna 30.9; and *cf.* Yasna 34.15. Also *cf.* Zaehner, *Dawn and Twilight*, pp. 58–9; Boyce, *History*, 1, p. 233.

53 *Cf. Dinkard* 7, chapter 2 (relevant extracts translated in Boyce, *Textual Sources*, pp. 72–4).

54 *Cf.* Yasna 43.3.

55 The *Avesta* describes the Saoshyant and his role in Yashts 13 and 19.

56 From *Zand i Vahman Yasht*, chapter 4. For comments on the origin of the prophecy see Boyce, 'On the antiquity of Zoroastrian apocalyptic', in BSOAS 47 (1984), pp. 57–75.

57 On the influence of Alexander's conquest: S.K. Eddy, *The King is Dead*, Lincoln, Nebraska, 1961, pp. 10 sq.; and for later periods: Boyce, *History*, 1, p. 293.

58 On the possible role of the 'Zurvanite heresy' in the revision see Boyce, *History*, 2, pp. 234–5.

59 *Cf.* G. Gnoli, 'Politique religieuse et conception de la royauté sous les Achéménides', in *Acta Iranica*, 2, Leiden, 1974, pp. 118–90, esp. pp. 162–9; K. Koch, 'Weltordnung und Reichsidee im alten Iran', in P. Frei and K. Koch, *Reichsidee und Reichsorganisation im Perserreich*, Göttingen, 1984.

60 Quotations in Boyce, *Zoroastrians*, p. 55. *Cf.* Boyce, 'Persian religion in

the Achaemenid age', pp. 286–7.

61 Trans. Boyce, *Textual Sources*, p. 115.

Chapter 5: From Combat Myth to Apocalyptic Faith

1 That Verethraghna ever was a dragon-slayer has been denied by e.g. E. Benveniste and L. Renou, *Vrtra et Vrthragna: étude de mythologie indo-iranienne*, Paris, 1934, esp. pp. 81 sq.; Boyce, *History*, 1, p. 64, with note 280. For early critiques of Benveniste/Renou: A.B. Keith, 'Indra and Vrtra', in *Indian Culture*, 1, Calcutta, 1934; Lommel, *op. cit.*

2 On Thor: Jan de Vries, *Altgermanische Religion*, 2nd edn., 2, Berlin, 1957, pp. 107–52; E.O.G. Turville-Petre, *Myth and Religion of the North*, London, 1964, pp. 75–105. There is a recent translation of the relevant parts of the *Prose Edda* by Jean I. Young, Cambridge, 1954, and Berkeley, 1964.

3 On Indra and Thor: After a brief indication by J. Grimm in his *Teutonic Mythology*, written in 1844, the theme was developed at length in Wilhelm Mannhardt, *Germanische Mythen*, Berlin, 1858, pp. 1–242. For a more recent treatment: F.R. Schröder, 'Indra, Thor und Herakles', in *Zeitschrift für deutsche Philologie*, 76, Berlin, 1957, pp. 1–41; and for a brief but cogent summary: Turville-Petre, *op. cit.* pp. 103–105. For the Russian folktale: Toporov, *op. cit.* (see note 18 to Chapter 3), pp. 113–20.

4 Yt. 19.81; and *cf.* Yt. 9.11.

5 The following passages in the *yashts* refer to the monsters slain by Keresaspa: 19.40; 9.11 (Sruvara); 15.28–9; 5.38–9 (Gandarva); 19.43–4 (Snavidka).

6 On Thraetona and Aži Dahaka: H. Lommel, *Der arische Kriegsgott*, Frankfort, 1939, pp. 59–60; Boyce, *History*, vol. 1, pp. 97–100.

7 *Cf.* S.E. Greenebaum, 'Vrtrahan — Verethraghna: Indian and Iranian', in G.L. Larson *et al.* (eds.), *Myth in Indo-European Antiquity*, Berkeley etc, 1974, pp. 93–7, at p. 96.

8 For an English translation of extracts from *Yasht* 8: Boyce, *Textual Sources*, p. 32; for a German translation of the whole: Lommel, *Yašts*, pp. 46–57. For the implication of the names: B. Forssman, 'Apaosha, der Gegner des Tishtriia', in *Zeitschrift für vergleichende Sprachforschung*, Göttingen, 82 (1968), pp. 37–61, esp. pp. 42–9.

9 On the chariot-races: F.B.J. Kuiper, 'The ancient Aryan verbal contest', in IIJ 4 (1960), at pp. 220–22; W.W. Malandra, *Introduction to Ancient Iranian Religion*, pp. 141–2. On the original ecological background of the Tishtrya myth: E.C. Polomé, 'Indo-European culture, with special attention to religion', in Polomé (ed.), *The Indo-Europeans in the Fourth and Third Millennia*, Ann Arbor, 1982, p. 165.

10 The affinity between the Tishtrya and Indra myths was noted already by A. Goetze in *Zeitschrift für vergleichende Sprachforschung*, 51 (1923), p. 153. J. Darmesteter, *Ormazd et Ahriman*, Paris, 1877, p. 126, went so far as to equate Tishtrya with Verethraghna. That is too far.

11 On Verethraghna: B. Geiger, *Die Amesha Spentas*, *Sitzungsbericht der Kaiserlichen Akademie der Wissenschaften*, Philosophisch-historische Klasse, Vienna, 176 (1916), pp. 56–83, esp. pp. 66–83; H. Lommel, *Der arische Kriegsgott*, pp. 46–76. For an English translation of extracts from Yasht 14: Boyce, *Textual Sources*, pp. 30–31; for a German translation of the whole: Lommel, *Yašts*, pp. 130–43.

12 *Cf.* Geiger, *op. cit.*, pp. 69–70.

13 On Vahagn: Geiger, *op. cit.*, p. 65; Lommel, *op. cit.* p. 52; G. Dumézil, 'Vahagn', in RHR 117 (1938), pp. 152–70; *id.*, *Heur et malheur du guerrier*, Paris, 1969, pp. 116–20.

14 *Cf.* Geiger, *op. cit.*, p. 65.

15 *Cf.* J. de Menasce, 'La promotion de Vahram', in RHR 133 (1947), pp. 5–18.

16 *Cf.*, in addition to Lommel, *Der arische Kriegsgott*, H.W. Bailey, 'The second stratum of the Indo-Iranian gods', in J. R. Hinnells (ed.) *Mithraic Studies*, 1, Manchester 1975, pp. 1–20, esp. p. 18.

17 Trans. Boyce, *Textual Sources*, pp. 29.

18 *Yasht* 10.72, trans. I. Gershevitch, *The Avestan Hymn to Mithra*, Cambridge, 1959.

19 *Yasht* 10.70.

20 Habent sua fata libelli! It was after I had laboriously arrived at the same conclusion that I came across the following passage in a work published more than a century ago: 'Le démon qui retient les eaux du ciel fut regardé comme un type de méchanceté et de perversité. C'est ce côté religieux . . . qui frappa surtout les Perses, donnant au myth de Vritra un développement extraordinaire: ils en firent le cadre de leur religion. Le *vritra* védique devint chez eux Ahriman, et la lutte des deux êtres merveilleux se prolongea pour les Perses à travers l'immensité du temps et de l'espace: lutte morale avant tout, où chaque homme doit prendre parti, et dont l'avenir de tous et de chacun est le prix.' — Michel Bréal, *Hercule et Cacus. Étude de mythologie comparée*, Paris, 1863, pp. 124–5.

Chapter 6: Ugarit

1 On the civilisation and world-view of the Canaanites: John Gray, *The Canaanites*, London, 1964, esp. chapters 4 and 5; *id.*, *The Legacy of Canaan*, 2nd edn., Leiden, 1965; and more briefly: A.F. Rainey, 'The Kingdom of Ugarit', in *The Biblical Archaeologist*, New Haven, 28 (1965); D. Kinet, *Ugarit — Geschichte und Kultur einer Stadt in der Umwelt des Alten Testaments*, Stuttgart, 1981; A. Curtis, *Ugarit (Ras Shamra)*, Cambridge, 1985. On the state of knowledge after a half-century of exploration and debate: G.D. Young (ed.), *Ugarit in Retrospect: Fifty Years of Ugarit and Ugaritic*, Winona Lake, Indiana, 1981. On Canaanite mythology in particular: C.H. Gordon, 'Canaanite Mythology', in S.N. Kramer (ed.), *Mythologies of the Ancient World*, New York, 1961, pp. 183–217; E.T. Mullen, *The Divine Council in Canaanite and Early Hebrew Literature*, Chico, California, 1980, Part I, pp. 1–112; the introduction to A. Caquot and M. Sznycer, *Ugaritic Religion*, (in series *Iconography of Religions*), Leiden, 1980; Gregorio del Olmo Lete, *Mitos y Leyendas de Canaan*, Madrid, 1981; Gray, *Near Eastern Mythology*, 2nd edn., London, 1982, pp. 68–102.

2 On the irrelevance of what has often been regarded as a second source of information see A.I. Baumgarten, *The Phoenician History of Philo of Byblos: A Commentary*, Leiden, 1981.

3 *Cf.* John C.L. Gibson, *Canaanite Myths and Legends*, Edinburgh, 1978, pp. 102, 107.

4 Gray, 'Sacral kingship in Ugarit', in *Ugaritica*, Paris, 6 (1969), pp. 289–302, esp. pp. 295–8; M. Heltzer, *The Internal Organization of the Kingdom of Ugarit*, Wiesbaden, 1982, esp. pp. 178–81.

5 *Cf.* M. Liverani, 'Ville et campagne dans le royaume d'Ugarit. Essai d'analyse économique', in *Societies and Languages* (see note 39 to Chapter 4), pp. 250–8.

6 *Cf.* Kinet, *op. cit.*, p. 67. The translated quotations from the myths in the present chapter are taken from Gibson, *Canaanite Myths and Legends*, which is partly based on G.R. Driver, *Canaanite Myths and Legends*, Edinburgh, 1956. C.H. Gordon, *Ugaritic Literature*, Rome (Pontificium Institutum Biblicum), 1949, contains, in addition to the legends and myths, administrative, medical

and religious texts. For particulars of other translations see Curtis, *op. cit.*, p. 82. On the possible role of temple singers: Gibson, *op. cit.*, Introduction, p. 6.

7 El's role as supreme god is described in all accounts of Canaanite mythology. See also: J.C. de Moor, 'El, the Creator', in G. Rendsburg *et al.* (ed.), *The Bible World*, New York, 1980, pp. 171–87; Gibson, 'The theology of the Ugaritic Baal cycle', in *Orientalia*, Rome, 53 (1984), pp. 202–19. Several scholars have argued that in the Ugaritic texts El is shown as effectively ousted by Ba'al, but this view no longer enjoys much favour; see Gibson, *loc. cit.*, p. 209; del Olmo Lete, *op. cit.*, pp. 68 sq.

8 Trans. Gibson, *Canaanite Myths*, p. 60.

9 *Cf.* Gray, 'Social aspects of Canaanite religion', in VTS 15 (1966), pp. 170–92.

10 On the Ba'al cycle see, in addition to the relevant passages in the works listed under note 1: A.S. Kapelrud, *Baal in the Ras Shamra Texts*, Copenhagen, 1952; T.H. Gaster, *Thespis. Ritual, Myth and Drama in the Ancient Near East*, New York, 1961, pp. 114–29: 'The Canaanite Poem of Baal'; J.C. de Moor, *The Seasonal Pattern in the Ugarit Myth of Ba'lu according to the Version of Ilimiliku*, Neukirchen-Vluyn, 1971; Gibson, 'The theology of the Ugaritic Baal cycle' (see note 7). The present account owes much to Gibson's article.

11 On the distinction between the creative roles of El and Ba'al: L.R. Fisher, 'Creation at Ugarit and in the Old Testament', in VT 15 (1965) pp. 313–24; Gray, 'Social aspects of Canaanite religion', esp. pp. 178, 192; Werner H. Schmidt, *Königtum Gottes in Ugarit und Israel*, 2nd edn., Berlin, 1966, p. 31; Kapelrud, 'Ba'al, Schöpfung und Chaos', in UF 11, (1979), pp. 407–12; R.J. Clifford, 'Cosmogonies in the Ugaritic Texts and in the Bible', in *Orientalia* (1984), pp. 183–201.

12 *Cf.* de Moor, *The Seasonal Pattern*, p. 141; Gibson, 'The Last Enemy', in *Scottish Journal of Theology*, Cambridge, 32 (1979), pp. 151–69, esp. p. 155; Kapelrud, 'Ba'al, Schöpfung und Chaos'.

13 Trans. Gibson, *Canaanite Myths*, pp. 43–4.

14 *Ibid.*, p. 66.

15 *Ibid.*, p. 50.

16 *Ibid.*, p. 68.

17 On Mot see, in addition to the relevant passages in the works listed in note 9: Gibson, 'The Last Enemy'; B. Margalit, *A Matter of 'Life' and 'Death'. A Study of the Baal-Mot Epic*, Kevelaer and Neukirchen-Vluyn, 1980, esp. pp. 201–205; and more briefly Margalit, 'Death and dying in the Ugaritic epics', in B. Alster, *Death in Mesopotamia*, Copenhagen, 1980; N. Wyatt, 'Cosmic entropy in Ugaritic religious thought', in UF 17 (1986) pp. 383–6.

18 *Cf.* Gibson, *op. cit.*, pp. 68–9.

19 Trans. Gibson, *op. cit.*, p. 109.

20 K. Spronk, *Beatific Afterlife in Ancient Israel and in the Ancient Near East*, Kevelaer and Neukirchen-Vluyn, 1986, pp. 139, 204–205.

21 Trans. Gibson, *op. cit.*, p. 78.

22 *Ibid.*, p. 80.

23 For a comprehensive survey of the various interpretations: Mark S. Smith, 'Interpreting the Baal cycle', UF 18, 1986, pp. 313–39; and *cf.* note 10.

24 Most effectively by J.C. de Moor, *The Seasonal Pattern*.

25 *Cf.* Margalit, *A Matter of 'Life' and 'Death'*, pp. 202–203; Gibson, 'The Last Enemy', pp. 164–5.

26 On Anat: article 'Anat', by M.H. Pope, in H.W. Haussig (ed.), *Götter und Mythen im Vorderen Orient* (vol. 1 of *Wörterbuch der Mythologie*), Stuttgart, 1965, pp. 235–41; W.F. Albright, *Yahweh and the Gods of Canaan*, London, 1968, pp. 112–18; Kapelrud, *The Violent Goddess. Anat in the Ras Shamra Texts*, Oslo, 1969.

In the Jewish military colony at Elephantine Anat was apparently worshipped as Yahweh's consort; for references see note 2 to Chapter 8.

27 Trans. Gibson, Canaanite Myths, p. 77. Some scholars have interpreted this passage as meaning that Mot is, in addition, a corn-god who is winnowed, but this view seems to be based on a mistranslation; see S.E. Loewenstamm, 'The Ugaritic Fertility Myth', two articles of 1962 and 1963, reprinted in his *Comparative Studies in Biblical and Ancient Oriental Literature*, Kevelaer and Neukirchen-Vluyn, 1980.

28 The passage is at p. 47 in Gibson, *op. cit.* For a summary of the interpretations advanced by various scholars: Pope in Haussig, *loc. cit.*, p. 239.

29 Quoted by J.C. de Moor in UF 7 (1975) p. 610.

Chapter 7: Yahweh and the Jerusalem Monarchy

1 J.A. Soggin, *A History of Israel. From the Beginning to the Bar Kochba Revolt*, London, 1984 (trans. from the Italian) contains bibliographies for every phase and aspect of Israelite and Jewish history in the relevant period. Soggin's history itself is exceptional for the fairness with which it presents conflicting opinions on matters of dispute. G. Garbini, *History and Ideology in Ancient Israel*, London, 1988 (trans. from the Italian) and N.P. Lemche, *Ancient Israel. A New History of Israelite Society*, Sheffield, 1988, offer a radically new approach, in which the biblical version of Israelite history is practically discounted.

2 The two opinions are exemplified by N.K. Gottwald, *The Tribes of Israel*, New York, 1979, and D.B. Redford, *Egypt, Cannaan and Israel in Ancient Times*, Princeton, 1992, pp. 271–5. See also D. Conrad, 'An introduction to the archaeology of Syria and Palestine on the basis of Israelite settlement', Appendix 1 to Soggin, *op. cit.*, pp. 357–67, esp. 362–4; R.B. Coote and K.W. Whitelam, *The Emergence of Israel in Historical Perspective*, Sheffield, 1987, chapter 4; W.G. Dever, 'The contribution of archaeology to the study of Canaanite and Early Israelite religion', in *Ancient Israelite Religion*, pp. 208–47, esp. pp. 234–6 (see next note).

3 The standard general studies of Israelite and Jewish religion, e.g. by Kaufmann, von Rad, Eichrodt, Ringgren, Fohrer, Clements, and the introductions to the Hebrew Bible or Old Testament, e.g. by Eissfeldt, Fohrer, Kaiser, Soggin, W.H. Schmidt, Rendtorff are well-known and easily available, also in translation. For a conspectus of the present state of scholarship, with due attention to divergent opinions, see Patrick D. Miller *et al.* (eds.), *Ancient Israelite Religion. Essays in Honor of Frank Moore Cross*, Philadelphia, 1987. On the two forms of Yahwism: E.W. Nicholson, *God and His People: Covenant and Theology in the Old Testament*, Oxford, 1986, esp. pp. 191 sq.; and the works listed under note 45 below.

On Israelite notions of a divinely appointed order: Hans Heinrich Schmid, *Gerechtigkeit als Weltordnung. Hintergrund und Geschichte des alttestamentlichen Gerechtigkeitsbegriffs*, Tübingen, 1968, esp. pp. 3–22, 65–9; *id.*, *Altorientalische Welt in der alttestamentlicher Theologie*, Zurich, 1974, and esp. the essay 'Jahweglaube, altorientalisches Denken' (pp. 31–47). Also relevant: S. Niditch, *Chaos to Cosmos: Studies in Biblical Patterns of Creation*, Chico, Cal., 1985. For the Israelite world-view in its Near Eastern context: O. Keel, *The Symbolism of the Biblical World. Ancient Near Eastern Iconography and the Book of Psalms*, London, 1978 (trans. of *Die Welt der altorientalischen*

Bildsymbolik and das Alte Testament: Am Beispiel der Psalmen, Neukirchen, 1972).

4 *Cf.* W.F. Albright, *Archaeology and the Religion of Israel,* 2nd edn., Baltimore, 1966, pp. 71–2; M.J. Dahood, 'Ancient Semitic deities in Syria and Palestine', in S. Moscati (ed.), *Antiche Divinità Semitiche,* Rome, 1958, pp. 65–94 esp. p. 70; R.A. Oden, 'The persistence of Canaanite religion', in *Biblical Archaeologist,* 39 (1976), pp. 31–6; P.C. Craigie, 'Ugarit, Canaan and Israel', in *Tyndale Bulletin,* Cambridge, 34 (1983), pp. 145–67.

5 For two opposing views see John Gray, 'The god Yaw in the religion of Canaan', in *Journal of Near Eastern Studies,* Chicago, 12 (1953), pp. 278–83, and Garbini, *op. cit.,* pp. 57–8. Gray cites the scholars who originally identified Yaw with Yahweh but rejects the identification, Garbini reaffirms it. Redford, *op. cit.,* p. 272, holds that Yahweh was first worshipped by proto-Israelites in Edom.

6 Deuteronomy 33: 26.

7 Psalm 29: 3, 10; and *cf.* Psalm 93. On the relationship between Ba'al and Yahweh and on Yahweh's battle with the waters of chaos: H.G. May, 'Some cosmic connotations of Mayim Rabbim, "Many Waters"', in JBL 74 (1955), pp. 9–21; R. Rendtorff, in his *Gesammelte Studien zum Alten Testament,* Munich, 1975: 'Kult, Mythos und Geschichte im alten Israel' (1958), at pp. 121–9, and 'El, Ba'al und Yahwe' (1966), at pp. 277–92; O. Eissfeldt, in vol. 2 of his *Kleine Schriften,* Tübingen, 1963: 'Das Chaos in der biblischen und in der phönizischen Kosmogonie', at pp. 258–62, and in vol. 3, 1966, 'Gott und das Meer', at pp. 256–64; B.W. Anderson, *Creation versus Chaos: The Reinterpretation of Mythical Symbolism in the Bible,* New York, 1967 (repr. 1987), esp. pp. 99 sq; M. Wakeman, *God's Battle with the Monster,* Leiden, 1973, pp. 56–138; A. Lelièvre, 'YHWH et la mer dans les Psaumes', in RHPR 56 (1976), pp. 253–75; A.H.W. Curtis, 'The "Subjugation of the Waters" motif in the Psalms: imagery or polemic?' in JSS 23 (1978), pp. 245–56; John Gray, *The Biblical Doctrine of the Kingdom of God,* Edinburgh, 1979, esp. pp. 39 sq.; J. Day, *God's Conflict with the Dragon and the Sea: Echoes of a Canaanite Myth in the Old Testament,* Cambridge, 1985, esp. pp. 18 sq.; and for Psalm 29 in particular: Carola Kloos, *Yahweh's Combat with the Sea: a Canaanite Tradition in the Religion of Ancient Israel,* Amsterdam and Leiden, 1986. J. Jeremias, *Das Königtum Gottes,* Göttingen, 1987, esp. pp. 15–45, deals with Israelite adaptations of the Ba'al myth.

8 For a good summary of the arguments about the ritual enthronement of Yahweh, from S. Mowinckel, *Psalmenstudien II, Das Thronbesteigungsfest Jahwäs,* Kristiana, 1922, onwards, see Gray, *op. cit.,* pp. 7–38. W.R. Millar, *Isaiah 24–27 and the Origin of Apocalyptic,* Missoula, 1976, esp. pp. 91 sq. detects a celebration of Yahweh's victory over hostile forces.

9 Genesis 1: 7, 9.

10 Psalm 74: 13–14.

11 Psalm 65: 9–13.

12 On Yahweh as war-god: G. von Rad, *Der heilige Krieg im alten Israel,* Zurich, 1951 (ET Grand Rapids, U.S.A., and Leominster, G.B., 1991); R. Smend, *Jahwekrieg und Stämmebund. Erwägungen zur ältesten Geschichte Israels,* Göttingen, 1963; F. Stolz, *Jahwes und Israels Kriege. Kriegstheorien und Kriegserfahrungen des alten Israel,* Zurich, 1972; M. Weippert, '"Heiliger Krieg" in Israel und Assyrien: kritische Anmerkungen zu Gerhard von Rads Konzept des "Heiligen Krieges" im alten Israel', in ZAW 84 (1972), pp. 460–93, esp. pp. 488–90; F.M. Cross, *Canaanite Myth and Hebrew Epic: Essays on the History of the Religion*

of Israel, Cambridge, Mass., 1973, pp. 91–111 ('The Divine Warrior'); P.D. Miller, *The Divine Warrior in Early Israel*, Cambridge, Mass., 1973; Hans Heinrich Schmid, 'Heiliger Krieg und Gottesfrieden im Alten Testament', in *Altorientalische Welt in der alttestamentlicher Theologie*, Zurich, 1974, pp. 91–120; Sa-Moon Kang, *Divine War in the Old Testament and the Ancient Near East*, Berlin, 1987. A. van der Lingen, *Les guerres de Yahvé*, Paris, 1990, argues that the terminology of holy war dates not from the early history of Israel but from the Exile and was inspired by hopes of liberation. This radical reinterpretation has still to be evaluated, but may well prove fruitful.

13 Deuteronomy 33: 2.

14 Habakkuk 3: 8 sq.; *cf.* Ezekiel 29: 3–5; also Day, *op. cit.*, pp. 105–109.

15 On El in various Near Eastern cultures: F. Stolz, *Strukturen und Figuren im Kult von Jerusalem*, Berlin, 1970, pp. 126–80. For various views on the relationship between El and Yahweh: O. Eissfeldt, 'El and Yahweh', in JSS 1 (1956), pp. 25–37; the same, 'Jahwe, der Gott der Väter', in *Theologische Literaturzeitung*, Leipzig, 88 (1963), cols. 482–90; F.M. Cross, 'Yahweh and the god of the patriarchs', in HTR 55 (1962), pp. 225–59; R. Rendtorff, 'El, Ba'al und Jahwe', in ZAW 78 (1966), pp. 277–92; J.J.M. Roberts, 'The Davidic origin of the Zion tradition', in JBL 92 (1973), pp. 329–44; E. Otto, 'El und Jhwh in Jerusalem. Historische und theologische Aspekte einer Religionsintegration', in VT 30 (1980), pp. 316–29; J. Van Seters, 'The religion of the patriarchs in Genesis', in *Biblica*, Rome, 61 (1980), pp. 220–23; M. Barker, *The Great Angel. A Study of Israel's Second God*, London, 1992, argues powerfully that El and Yahweh were first fused during the Exile, in the prophecies of Second Isaiah. If this is correct, the view expressed here would have to be modified, and the psalms on which it is based would have to be redated. The general argument of the chapter would not be affected.

16 Psalms 46: 10; 97: 9; 103: 19.

17 Isaiah 6: 3.

18 Psalm 95: 3, 5.

19 Psalm 68: 5; and *cf.* Psalm 10.

20 Psalm 72: 4.

21 Isaiah 1: 4, 7, 17.

22 Psalms 132: 13–14; 46: 4.

23 *Cf.* R.E. Clements, *God and Temple*, Oxford, 1965, p. 76.

24 Psalm 29: 10. On Yahweh as king on Mount Zion: J.J. Roberts, 'Zion in the theology of the Davidic-Solomonic empire', in T. Ishida (ed.), *Studies in the Period of David and Solomon*, Tokyo, 1982; B.C. Ollenburger, *Zion the City of the Great King*, Sheffield, 1987. On the relationship between Mount Zion and Mount Zaphon: R.J. Clifford, *The Cosmic Mountain in Canaan and the Old Testament*, Cambridge, Mass., 1972, pp. 141 sq.

25 *Cf.* Ollenburger, *op. cit.*, pp. 53–80; D.G. Johnson, *From Chaos to Restoration. An Integrative Reading of Isaiah 24–7*, Sheffield, 1988, p. 45.

26 On Solomon's Temple: Clements, *op. cit.*; Jonathan Z. Smith, 'Earth and Gods', in *Journal of Religion*, Chicago, 49 (1969), pp. 103–27, esp. pp. 111 sq.; Keel, *op. cit.*, chapter 3 (pp. 112–76); M. Barker, *The Gate of Heaven. The History and Symbolism of the Temple in Jerusalem*, London, 1991. M. Haran, *Temples and Temple-Service in Ancient Israel*, Oxford, 1978, is chiefly concerned with the post-exilic period and the Second Temple, but chapter 13, pp. 246–59, has some relevance to Solomon's Temple.

27 *Cf.* Clements, *op. cit.*, pp. 65 sq.; H.H. Rowley, *Worship in Ancient Israel*, London, 1967, p. 82.

28 2 Samuel 7: 16. (NEB)

29 Psalm 89: 4, 36.

30 Psalm 89: 25, trans. Cross, with comments, in *Canaanite Myth and*

Hebrew Epic, pp. 261–2.

31 On the relationship between Israelite and other Near Eastern perceptions of monarchy and temple see M. Weinfeld, 'Zion and Jerusalem as religious and political capital', in R.E. Friedman (ed.), *The Poet and the Historian*, Chico, Cal., 1983. On the king of Judah as Yahweh's representative: S. Mowinckel, *The Psalms in Israel's Worship*, 1, Oxford, 1962, pp. 50–55, 67–8; A.R. Johnson, *Sacral Kingship in Ancient Israel*, Cardiff, 1967, esp. pp. 4–29, 103 sq.; *id.*, *The Cultic Prophet and Israel's Psalmody*, Cardiff, 1979, esp. pp. 65, 76, 83; J.H. Eaton, *Kingship and the Psalms*, London, 1976, esp. pp. 135–8, 141–9, 155–68; Keel, *op. cit.*, chapter 5 (pp. 244–306).

32 For the above see R.A. Rosenberg, 'The god Ṣedeq', in HUCA 3 (1965) pp. 161–77. Relevant biblical passages: Psalm 89: 14; Isaiah 45: 8, 19.

33 For the following see Deuteronomy 8: 15; Numbers 20: 5; Isaiah 34: 9–15; Isaiah 27: 1; Psalms 46 and 89; Jeremiah 4: 11 sq.; and *cf.* Joh. Pedersen, *Israel, its Life and Culture*, 2, London, 1926, chapter 'The world of life and death' (pp. 453 sq.); Keel, *op. cit.*, chapter 2 (pp. 62–109); Robert Murray, 'Prophecy and cult', in R. Coggins *et al.*, *Israel's Prophetic Tradition: Essays in Honour of Peter R. Ackroyd*, Cambridge, 1982, pp. 200–16, esp. pp. 210–14.

34 *Cf.* K. Spronk, *Beatific Afterlife in Ancient Israel and the Ancient Near East*, Kevelaer and Neukirchen-Vluyn, 1986.

Chapter 8: Exile and After

1 On the tradition of 'Yahweh alone': Morton Smith, *Palestinian Parties and Politics that Shaped the Old Testament*, New York and London, 1971 (repr. London 1987), esp. chapter 2; M. Rose, *Der Ausschliesslichkeitsanspruch Jahwes: Deuteronomistische Schultheologie und die Volksfrömmigkeit der späten Königszeit*, Stuttgart, 1975; F. Stolz, 'Monotheismus in Israel', in O. Keel (ed.), *Monotheismus im alten Israel und seiner Umwelt*, Fribourg (Switzerland), 1980, esp. pp. 163–72; the essays by B. Lang and H. Vorländer in B. Lang (ed.), *Der einzige Gott: Die Geburt des biblischen Monotheismus*, Munich, 1981, entitled respectively 'Die Jahwe-Allein-Bewegung' (esp. pp. 55–7, 73), and 'Der Monotheismus Israels als Antwort auf die Krise des Exils' (esp. pp. 98–102).

2 On Israelite polytheism in general see e.g. G.W. Ahlström, *Aspects of Syncretism in Israelite Religion*, Lund, 1963; *id.*, *Royal Administration and National Religion in Palestine*, Leiden, 1982, pp. 82–3; J.A. Soggin, 'Der offiziell geförderte Synkretismus in Israel während des zehnten Jahrhunderts', in ZAW 78 (1966) pp. 179–204; Mark S. Smith, *The Early History of God: Yahweh and Other Deities in Ancient Israel*, San Francisco, 1990. For the Israelite cult of Ashera in particular see S.M. Olyan, *Asherah and the Cult of Yahweh in Israel*, Atlanta, 1988; K. Koch, 'Aschera als Himmelskönigin in Jerusalem', in UF 20 (1988) pp. 97–120. For the Yahweh's suite of lesser divine beings — 'the hosts of heaven' — see W. Herrmann, 'Die Gottersöhne', in *Zeitschrift für Religions- und Geistesgeschichte* 12, Cologne, 1960, pp. 247–51, and E.T. Mullen, *The Divine Council in Canaanite and Early Hebrew Literature*, Chico, Cal. 1980. esp. pp. 186 sq. The papyri from the Judaean military colony at Elephantine in Upper Egypt also contain evidence of polytheism; see E. Meyer, *Der Papyrusfund von Elephantine*, 3rd edn., Leipzig, 1912, esp. pp. 38 sq.; A. Vincent, *La religion des judéo-araméens à Elephantine*, Paris, 1937, esp. pp. 562 sq.; B. Porten, *Archives from Elephantine; the Life of an Ancient Jewish Military Colony*, Berkeley,

1968. However, just how widespread polytheism was remains a matter of debate. Some scholars argue that the onomastic evidence shows it to have been less important than the Bible suggests; see J.H. Tigay, *You Shall Have No Other Gods*, Atlanta, 1986; J.D. Fowler, *Theophoric Personal Names in Ancient Hebrew*, Sheffield, 1988 (JSOT Suppl. 49). But again, the significance of onomastic evidence has been questioned; see Olyan, *op. cit.*, pp. 35 sq.

3 Hosea 11: 2; 13: 4. (RSV and NEB combined)

4 *Cf.* R.C. Dentan, *The Knowledge of God in Ancient Israel*, New York, 1968, pp. 46, 147, 179; Morton Smith, *Palestinian Parties*, pp. 43–4.

5 Exodus 34: 14. (NEB)

6 Zephaniah 1: 4–6.

7 Deuteronomy 7: 6–8 and 5: 7–10. On the relatively late, Deuteronomistic origin of the covenant idea: L. Perlitt, *Bundestheologie im Alten Testament*, Neukirchen-Vluyn, 1969; E. Kutsch, *Verheissung und Gnade. Untersuchungen zum sogenannten 'Bund' im Alten Testament*, Berlin and New York, 1973.

8 Psalm 119: 89–91, 96. (NEB)

9 *Cf.* W. Johnstone, *Exodus*, Sheffield, 1990, esp. pp. 76 sq.

10 *Cf.* B. van Iersel, A. Weiler (eds.), *The Exodus — A Lasting Paradigm*, Edinburgh, 1987, Part 3, esp. pp. 83–92: Enrique Dussel, 'Exodus as a paradigm in Liberation Theology'.

11 And *cf.* B. Albrektson, *History and the Gods: an essay on the idea of historical events as divine manifestations in the Ancient Near East and in Israel*, Lund, 1967; R. Labat, *Le caractère religieux de la royauté assyro-babylonienne*, Paris, 1939, esp. pp. 253–74: 'La guerre sainte'. On this and other points of resemblance between Yahweh and other Near Eastern gods see also Morton Smith, 'The common theology of the Ancient Near East', in JBL 71 (1952), pp. 135–47, esp. pp. 144–5; H. Ringgren, 'Prophecy in the Ancient Near Eeast', in R. Coggins, A. Phillips and M. Knibb (eds.), *Israel's Prophetic Tradition: Essays in Honour of Peter R. Ackroyd*, London, 1982, pp. 1–11.

12 *Cf.* W.G. Lambert, review article of Albrektson, *History and the Gods*, in *Orientalia*, NS 39 (1970), pp. 170–7.

13 For Israelite and Jewish expectations of a glorious consummation see, in addition to works on prophecy (see next note): R.H. Charles, *Eschatology*, New York, 1963 (reprint of *The Doctrine of a Future Life in Israel, in Judaism and in Christianity: a Critical History*, first published in 1898–9); H. Gressmann, *Der Messias*, Göttingen, 1929; J. Klausner, *The Messianic Idea in Israel* (trans. from the third Hebrew edn. (1950)), London, 1956; S. Mowinckel, *He That Cometh* (trans. from the Swedish (1951)), Oxford, 1956; C. Ryder Smith, *The Biblical Doctrine of the Hereafter*, London, 1958; S. Herrmann, *Die prophetischen Heilserwartungen im Alten Testament*, Stuttgart, 1965; Hans-Peter Müller, *Ursprünge und Strukturen alttestamentlicher Eschatologie*, Berlin, 1969; H.D. Preuss (ed.), *Eschatologie im Alten Testament*, Darmstadt, 1978 (an anthology of essays); John Gray, *The Biblical Doctrine of the Reign of God*, Edinburgh, 1979; J. Becker, *Messianic Expectation in the Old Testament*, Edinburgh, 1980 (trans. from the German (1977); C. Westermann, *Prophetische Heilsworte im Alten Testament*, Göttingen, 1987. (ET *Basic Forms of Prophetic Speech*, London, 1991). D.E. Gowan, *Eschatology in the Old Testament*, Edinburgh, 1987, is concerned to relate that eschatology to the expectations of later times, including our own. H.D. Preuss, *Jahweglaube und Zukunftserwartung*, Stuttgart etc., 1968, offers an interpretation diametrically opposed to that offered in the present work.

14 A comprehensive bibliography of works on prophecy is given in J.

Blenkinsopp, *A History of Prophecy in Israel. From the Settlement in the Land to the Hellenistic Period*, London, 1984. Important recent studies include R.R. Wilson, *Prophecy and Society in Ancient Israel*, Philadelphia, 1980; R. Coggins *et al.* (eds.), *Israel's Prophetic Tradition*, Cambridge, 1982; and, on the reception and rejection of prophecy, R.P. Carroll, *When Prophecy Failed: Reactions and Responses to Failure in the Old Testament Prophetic* Traditions, London, 1979. For the passage on the peoples and the sea: Isaiah 17: 12.

15 Jeremiah 4: 23–5. (NEB)

16 On exilic prophecy in general see, in addition to the relevant passages in the works listed above: S.B. Frost, *Old Testament Apocalyptic*, London, 1952; P.R. Ackroyd, *Exile and Restoration: a study of Hebrew thought in the sixth century BC*, London, 1968, esp. chapters 5, 7, 8.

17 On conditions during the exile: Ackroyd, *op. cit.*, chapters 2 and 3; E.J. Bickerman, 'The generation of Ezra and Nehemiah', in *Proceedings of the American Academy for Jewish Research*, Philadelphia, 45 (1978), pp. 1–18, and esp. pp. 17–18. On exile perceived as chaos: Jonathan Z. Smith, *op. cit.* (see note 26 to chapter 7), pp. 118 sq.; A.J. Wensinck, in *Verhandelingen der Koninklijke Akademie van Wetenschapen*, Afd. Letterkunde, Amsterdam, n.s. 19 (1919), esp. pp. 51 sq.

18 Relatively recent commentaries on Ezekiel include those by D.M.G. Stalker (London, 1968); W. Zimmerli (Neukirchen-Vluyn, 1969); J.W. Wevers (London, 1969, New Century Bible); W. Eichrodt (trans. from the German edn. of 1965/66, London, 1970); K.M. Carley (Cambridge, 1974). For a briefer commentary: J. Muilenberg, in Peake's *Commentary on the Bible*, revised edn., 1962, pp. 568–90. Particularly relevant to the present argument are: D. Baltzer, *Ezechiel und Deuterojesaja. Berührungen in der Heilserwartung der beiden grossen Exilspropheten*, Berlin, 1971; and T.M. Raitt, *A Theology of Exile: Judgment/Deliverance in Jeremiah and Ezekiel*, Philadelphia, 1977.

19 Ezekiel 20: 40.

20 Ezekiel 11: 19–20; *cf.* 36: 26–8.

21 *Cf.* Ezekiel 18: 7–9; 22: 7.

22 Ezekiel 34: 25–8.

23 Ezekiel 33: 27, 29.

24 Relatively recent commentaries on Isaiah 40–55 and 40–66 include those by C.R. North (Oxford, 1964); G.A.F. Knight (New York and Nashville, 1965); C. Westermann (ET London, 1966); R.N. Whybray (London, 1967, New Century Bible); J. McKenzie, (Garden City, New York, 1968, Anchor Bible); A.S. Herbert, Cambridge, 1975 (Cambridge Commentary to the New English Bible); H.D. Preuss, Neukirchen-Vluyn, 1976. Not every scholar accepts that Isaiah 44–55 was originally concerned with the return of the deportees at all; *cf.* C.C. Torrey, *The Second Isaiah. A New Interpretation*, Edinburgh, 1928; and J.D. Smart, *History and Theology in Second Isaiah*, London, 1965; J.M. Vincent, *Studien zur literarischen Eigenart und zur geistigen Heimat von Jesaja, Kap. 40–50*, Frankfort; J.H. Eaton, *Festal Drama in Deutero-Isaiah*, London, 1979. Their doubts may prove justified; but whatever the origin of the text, it is still true that the interpretation now generally accepted was accepted already in early post-exilic times.

25 Isaiah 45: 4 (and *cf.* the preceding three verses); 44: 28. (NEB) Two interesting though controversial interpretations of the immediate political context of the composition of Isaiah 40–55 are: Sydney Smith, *Isaiah XL–LV: Literary Criticism and History*, London, 1944; and Morton Smith, 'II Isaiah and the Persians', in JAOS 83, Boston, 1963, pp. 415–21. On the other hand, the sceptics listed in note 24 regard the references to Cyrus as interpolations.

26 *Cf.* H. Wildberger, 'Der Monotheismus Deuterojesjas', in H. Donner *et al.* (eds.), *Beiträge zur alttestamentlichen Theologie: Festschrift für Walther Zimmerli*, Göttingen, 1977, pp. 506–30; and H. Vorländer, *op. cit.* (see note 1 above), pp. 93 sq. Even Margaret Barker, who has done so much to demonstrate the importance of polytheism in Israelite religion, accepts Second Isaiah's monotheism; in her view, he achieved it by identifying Yahweh with El (*cf. The Older Testament*, pp. 167 sq.; *The Great Angel*, pp. 17 sq.).

27 Micah 4: 5.

28 Judges 11: 24.

29 Isaiah 45: 5; 46: 10–11; *cf.* 43: 10 and 44: 6, 8.

30 Psalm 74: 13–17.

31 Isaiah 48: 13; *cf.* 51: 13, 16.

32 Isaiah 49: 26.

33 Isaiah 51: 9–11. (NEB)

34 Isaiah 40: 4. *Cf.* Wensinck, *op. cit.*, pp. 52–3. (See note 17 above).

35 Isaiah 55: 12.

36 Isaiah 40: 5. For similarities and differences between the expectations of Ezekiel and Second Isaiah see Baltzer, *op. cit.* (see note 18 above).

37 Isaiah 42: 13. *Cf.* F.M. Cross, *Canaanite Myth and Hebrew Epic: Essays in the history of the religion of Israel*, Cambridge, Mass., 1973, pp. 105–10 (in chapter 'The divine warrior'); P.D. Miller, *The Divine Warrior in Early Israel*, Cambridge, Mass., 1973, pp. 135–42.

38 Isaiah 54: 10.

39 Isaiah 51: 3, 6. (NEB)

40 For an uncompromising exposition of the traditional view see P.-E. Bonnard, *Le Second Isaïe, son disciples et leurs éditeurs*, Paris, 1972. The view adopted in the present chapter, i.e. that Second Isaiah had no universalist aims or interests, is far from original. It has been argued by, e.g., N.H. Snaith, 'The servant of the Lord in Deutero-Isaiah', in H.H. Rowley (ed.), *Studies in Old Testament Prophecy, presented to Professor Theodore H. Robinson*, Edinburgh, 1950, pp. 186–200; P.A. de Boer, *Second Isaiah's Message*, Leiden, 1956, pp. 92–110; R. Martin-Achard, *Israël et les nations, la perspective missionnaire de l'Ancien Testament*, Paris, 1959, pp. 8–31 (ET *A Light to the Nations*, London and Edinburgh, 1962); N.F. Snaith, *Isaiah 40–66, a Study in the Teaching of Second Isaiah and its Consequences*, and H.M. Orlinsky, *Studies on the Second Part of the Book of Isaiah*, both in VTS 14, (1967); R.N. Whybray, *Isaiah 40–66*, London, 1967, Introduction, pp. 31–2, and in the commentary *passim*; D.E. Hollenberg, 'Nationalism and "the Nations" in Isaiah XL–LV', in VT 19 (1969), pp. 23–36; A. Schoors, *I Am God Your Saviour; a Form-critical Study of the Main Genres in Isaiah XL-LV*, Leiden, 1973 (VTS 24); F. Holmgren, *With Wings As Eagles. Isaiah 40–55. An Interpretation*, New York, 1973. The two lines referred to in the present text are the last two in Isaiah 49: 6.

41 Isaiah 41: 12, 16; *cf.* 51: 23.

42 Isaiah 49: 22–3.

43 Isaiah 52: 9–10.

44 Isaiah 45: 14.

45 Isaiah 45: 6.

46 On the dating of additions to and interpolations into the Book of Isaiah other than chapters 40–50 see O. Eissfeldt, *The Old Testament: an Introduction* (trans. from the third German edn.), Oxford, 1965, pp. 318–19, 323–7, 342–6; and G. Fohrer, *Introduction to the Old Testament* (trans. from the German), London, 1970, pp. 369, 372, 385, 388. Snaith, *Isaiah 40–66*, pp. 139–46, argues that chapters 60–62 are by Second Isaiah. For commentaries on Isaiah 56–66 see Westermann, Whybray, Herbert (note 24 above).

47 On post-exilic prophecy in general see, in addition to the works listed in note 13 above: O. Plöger, *Theocracy and Eschatology*, Oxford, 1968 (the first German edition was published in 1959); P.D. Hanson, *The*

Dawn of Apocalyptic: the Historical and Sociological Roots of Jewish Apocalyptic Eschatology, Philadelphia, 1975; R.P. Carroll, 'Second Isaiah and the failure of prophecy', in *Studia Theologica*, Lund, 32 (1978), pp. 119–31.

48 Isaiah 65: 17–18. (NEB)

49 Isaiah 11: 6–9. Some scholars continue to ascribe this passage to the eighth-century prophet Isaiah, but the view taken here, that it is a post-exilic interpolation, is becoming ever more widely accepted; see, e.g. O. Kaiser, *Das Buch des Propheten Jesaja Kapitel 1–12*, 5th edn., Göttingen, 1981, pp. 240–7 (vol. 17 of *Das Alte Testament Deutsch*; ET *Isaiah 1–12,* London, 1983), and Eissfeldt, *The Old Testament*, pp. 317–18.

50 Zechariah 2: 5.

51 Joel 2: 27–9.

52 Isaiah 65: 20.

53 Isaiah 35: 5–6.

54 Isaiah 61: 11. (NEB)

55 *Cf.* Isaiah 56: 3 sq.; 66: 21.

56 *Cf.* Isaiah 61: 5–6; cf. 60: 12.

57 Isaiah 60: 10–12, 14.

58 Isaiah 34: 3.

59 Isaiah 34: 8–10.

60 *Cf.* Isaiah 63: 1–6.

61 Ezekiel 38: 20–22; 39: 12, 21–2. (NEB)

62 Joel 3: 17, 19.

63 Another view is that 'the ungodly' were, on the contrary, the returning exiles as perceived by those who had never left Judah — whether the exiles in general, as argued by M. Barker, *The Older Testament*, London, 1987, pp. 212 sq., or the Zadokite priests in particular, as argued by Hanson in *The Dawn of Apocalyptic.* For an endorsement of Hanson's argument, albeit with certain reservations, see the review-article by R.P. Carroll. 'Twilight of prophecy or dawn of apocalyptic?' in JSOT 14 (1979), pp. 3–39. The view expressed in the present chapter, on the other hand, coincides with that expressed by Ina Willi-Plein in her review of Hanson in VT 29 (1979), pp. 122–7.

64 Isaiah 65: 12, 17. (NEB)

Chapter 9: Jewish Apocalypses (I)

1 On the history of the Jews in the relevant period: E. Schürer, *The History of the Jewish People in the Age of Jesus Christ (175 BC–AD 135)*, trans. from the 3rd/4th German edn. (1901–9), fully revised and brought up to date by G. Vermes and F. Millar, 3 vols., Edinburgh, 1973–87; and more briefly: D.S. Russell, *The Jews from Alexander to Herod*, London, 1967; H. Jagersma, *A History of Israel from Alexander the Great to Bar Kochba*, London, 1985. On Hellenism and its consequences amongst Palestinian Jews: V. Tcherikover, *Hellenistic Civilization and the Jews*, Philadelphia and Jerusalem, 1959; M. Hengel, *Judaism and Hellenism: Studies in their Encounter in Palestine during the Early Hellenistic Period*, trans. from the 2nd German edn., 2 vols., London and Philadelphia, 1974 (vol. 2 consisting of critical apparatus); F. Millar, 'The background of the Maccabaean revolution: reflections on Martin Hengel's *Judaism and Hellenism*', in JJS 29 (1978), pp. 1–21; A. Momigliano, *Alien Wisdom: the Limits of Hellenisation*, Cambridge, 1975 and New York, 1976. For a briefer account: Schürer, *op. cit.*, vol. 1, pp. 125 sq.

2 Works on Jewish apocalyptic, or Jewish and early Christian apocalyptic in general, in order of publication: H.H. Rowley, *The Relevance of Apocalyptic*, 1944 (3rd rev. edn. 1964); J. Bloch, *On the Apocalyptic in Judaism*, Philadelphia, 1952; D.S. Russell, *The Method and Message of Jewish Apocalyptic, 200 BC–AD 100*, London, 1964; J.D. Schreiner, *Alttestamentlich-jüdische Apokalyptik: Eine Einführung*, Munich, 1969; W. Schmithals, *The Apocalyptic Movement. Introduction and Interpretation,*

Nashville, 1975 (trans. from the German, 1973); M.E. Stone, *Scriptures, Sects and Visions*, Philadelphia, 1980; G.W.E. Nickelsburg, *Jewish Literature between the Bible and the Mishnah*, London, 1981; C. Rowland, *The Open Heaven. A Study in Apocalyptic in Judaism and early Christianity*, London, 1982; J.J. Collins, *The Apocalyptic Imagination: An Introduction to the Jewish Matrix of Christianity*, New York, 1984.

Among the vast number of articles the following are particularly relevant: P. Vielhauer, 'Apokalypsen und Verwandtes', being the introduction to E. Hennecke and W. Schneemelcher, *Neutestamentliche Apokryphen*, 2, Tübingen, 1964, pp. 408–27 (also in 1963 ET of the same work); W.R. Murdock, 'History and revelation in Jewish apocalypticism', in *Interpretation. A Journal of Bible and Theology*, Union Theological Seminary, Virginia, 21 (1967), pp. 167–87; two articles in R.W. Funk (ed.), *Apocalypticism* (*Journal for Theology and Church*, vol. 6), New York, 1969: H. Betz, 'On the problem of the religio-historical understanding of apocalyptic', at pp. 134–56, and F.M. Cross, 'New directions in the study of apocalypticism', at pp. 157–65; P.D. Hanson, 'Jewish apocalyptic against its Near Eastern environment', in *Revue biblique*, Paris, 78 (1971), pp. 31–58; *id.*, 'Apocalypticism' and 'Apocalypse, genre', in *Interpreter's Dictionary of the Bible: Supplementary Volume*, Nashville, Tennessee, 1976, pp. 27–34; *id.*, 'An overview of early Jewish and Christian apocalypticism' (appendix to the 2nd edn. of *The Dawn of Apocalyptic*, Philadelphia, 1979); Hans-Peter Müller, 'Mantische Weisheit und Apokalyptik', in VTS 22 (1972) (Uppsala Congress 1971 volume), pp. 268–93; two essays in J. Maier and J. Schreiner (eds.), *Literatur und Religion des Frühjudentums*, Gütersloh, 1973: Karlheinz Müller, 'Die Ansätze der Apokalyptik', at pp. 31–42, and J. Schreiner, 'Die apokalyptische Bewegung', at pp. 214–53; the following articles by J.J. Collins: 'Apocalyptic eschatology as the transcendence of death', in CBQ 196 (1974), pp. 5–22; 'The symbolism of transcendence in Jewish apocalyptic', in *Biblical Research*, Chicago, 19 (1974), pp. 5–22; 'The court-tales in Daniel and the development of apocalyptic', in JBL 94, (1975) pp. 21–234; 'Jewish apocalyptic against its Hellenistic Near Eastern environment', in *Bulletin of the American School of Oriental Research*, No. 220, December 1975, pp. 27–36; 'Cosmos and salvation. Jewish wisdom and apocalyptic in the Hellenistic age', in HR 17 (1977) pp. 121–42; 'The Jewish apocalypses', in Collins (ed.) *Apocalypse: The Morphology of a Genre* (*Semeia*, 14), Missoula, 1979, pp. 21–60; two articles in F.M. Cross *et al.* (eds.), *Magnalia Dei: the Mighty Acts of God. Essays . . . in Memory of G.E. Wright*, Garden City, New York, 1976: P.D. Hanson, 'Prolegomena to the study of Jewish apocalyptic', at pp. 389–413, and M.E. Stone, 'Revealed things in apocalyptic literature', at pp. 414–52.

The contributions in HELLHOLM help to place Jewish apocalyptic in a wider context, historical and geographical; those by J. Carmignac, J.C.H. Lebram, M. Philonenko, K. Koch, E.P. Sanders and H. Stegemann are moreover particularly relevant to the present chapter. Other relevant articles will be found in the following: L. Monloubou (ed.), *Apocalypse et théologie de l'espérance*, Paris, 1977; M. Philonenko and M. Simon (eds.), *Études d'histoire des religions*, vol. 3: *L'Apocalyptique*, Paris, 1977.

The progress of scholarship in this field is surveyed up to the late 1940s in Johann M. Schmidt, *Die jüdische Apokalyptik. Die Geschichte ihrer Erforschung von den Anfängen bis zu den Textfunden von Qumran*, Neukirchen-Vluyn, 1969; up to the 1960s in Klaus Koch, *Ratlos vor der Apokalyptik*, Gütersloh, 1970 (ET *The Rediscovery of Apocalyptic*, London, 1972); and up to the late 1970s in M. Delcor, 'Bilan des études sur l'apocalyptique', in Monloubou, *op. cit.*, pp. 27–42; in J. Barr, 'Jewish apocalyptic in recent scholarly study', in *Bulletin of the John Rylands Library*, Manchester, 58 (1976), pp. 9–35; in R.J. Bauckham, 'The rise of apocalyptic', in *Themelios*, London, n.s. 3, no. 2 (1978), pp. 10–23; and in M.A. Knibb, 'Prophecy and the emergence of the Jewish apocalypses', in R. Coggins *et al.* (eds.), *Israel's Prophetic Tradition: Essays in Honour of Peter R. Ackroyd*, Cambridge, 1982, pp. 155–80, which includes a comprehensive bibliography. For further bibliographical references see G. Delling (ed.), *Bibliographie zur jüdisch-hellenistischen und intertestamentarischen Literatur 1900–1965*, Berlin, 1969 (2nd edn. 1975), and J.H. Charlesworth, *The Pseudepigrapha and Modern Research*, Missoula, 1976, pp. 66–8. More general surveys of the development of Judaism in the relevant period, but which give considerable attention to apocalyptic, are W. Bousset, *Die Religion des Judentums im späthellenistischen Zeitalter*, 3rd edn., revised by H. Gressmann, Tübingen, 1926; P. Grelot, *L'espérance juive à l'heure de Jésus*, Paris, 1978; D.E. Gowan, *Bridge between the Testaments: A Reappraisal of Judaism from the Exile to the Birth of Christianity*, 2nd edn., Pittsburgh, 1980; and vol. 2 of Schürer/Vermes/Millar, esp. pp. 448 sq. Though a notable work in its day, P. Volz, *Die Eschatologie der jüdischen Gemeinde im neutestamentlichen Zeitalter*, Tübingen, 1934, which is a second edition of a work originally published in 1903, is inevitably out of date in its approach as well as in its factual statements.

3 The way ancient Jews regarded time, tradition, personality and inspiration seems to have had some bearing on the matter; *cf.* Russell, *op. cit.*, pp. 158–73.

4 Daniel 10: 4–14. On angels and their functions see the article 'Angels and angelology' in the *Encyclopaedia Judaica*, 2, Jerusalem, 1971, cols. 956–77. H.B. Kuhn, 'The angelology of the non-canonical Jewish apocalypses', in JBL 67 (1948), though partly invalidated by the subsequent redating of much apocalyptic, is still useful.

5 *Cf.* H.P. Müller *op. cit.*; *id.*, 'Magisch-mantische Weisheit und die Gestalt Daniels', in UF 1 (1969), pp. 79–94; Bauckham, *op. cit.*, pp. 13–17; Collins, 'The court-tales in Daniel'. The most recent treatment is also the most exhaustive: H.S. Kvanig, *Roots of Apocalyptic. The Mesopotamian Background of the Enoch Figure and of the Son of Man*, Neukirchen-Vluyn, 1988.

6 It may be that the apocalyptists also drew on a native Israelite tradition of wisdom associated with the royal cult, and transmitted by channels of which we know nothing; *cf.* M. Barker, *The Older Testament. The survival of themes from the ancient royal cult in sectarian Judaism and early Christianity*, London, 1987.

7 For the *Demotic Chronicle*: C.C. McCown, 'Hebrew and Egyptian apocalyptic literature', in HTR 18 (1925), pp. 357–411, with translation at p. 389.

For the *Oracle of the Potter*: L. Koenen, 'The prophecies of a potter: a prophecy of world-renewal becomes an apocalypse', in D.H. Samuel (ed.), *Proceedings of the Twelfth International Congress of Papyrology*, Toronto, 1970, pp. 249–54. For the *Oracle of Hystaspes*: H. Windisch, *Die Orakel des Hystaspes*, Amsterdam, 1929; and *cf.* F. Cumont, 'La fin du monde selon les mages occidntaux', in RHR 103 (1931), pp. 29–96, esp. pp. 64 sq. See also Hengel, *op. cit.*, vol. 1, pp. 184–6, and bibliographical references in vol. 2, pp. 124–5.

8 Relatively recent studies of and commentaries on Daniel are those of E.W. Heaton (London, 1956); N.W. Porteous (London, 1965); M. Delcor (Paris, 1971); A. Lacocque, Neuchâtel and Paris, 1976 (ET Atlanta, 1979); R. Hammer (Cambridge, 1976, in the series *The Cambridge Bible Commentary*); L.F. Hartman and A.A. Di Lella (Garden City, New York, 1978, as a volume in the Anchor Bible); J. Lebram, 'Daniel/Danielbuch und Zusätze', in S. Schwertner (ed.), *Theologische Realenzyklopädie* 8, Berlin and New York, 1981, pp. 325–49. K. Koch, T. Niewisch, and J. Tubach, *Das Buch Daniel*, Darmstadt, 1980, surveys the state of knowledge at that date.

On the eschatology of Daniel in particular: J.J. Collins, *The Apocalyptic Vision of the Book of Daniel*, Missoula, 1977; P. Grelot, 'Histoire et eschatologie dans le livre de Daniel', in Monloubou, *op. cit.*, pp. 63–109 (see note 2 above); P.R. Davies, 'Eschatology in the Book of Daniel', in JSOT 17 (1980), pp. 33–53.

9 Daniel 2: 44–5 and 2: 28.

10 On the relationship between Daniel 2 and other treatments of the theme: Eduard Meyer, *Ursprung und Anfänge des Christentums*, vol. 2, Stuttgart and Berlin, 1921, pp. 189–91; H.H. Rowley, *Darius the Mede and the Four World Empires in the Book of Daniel*, Cardiff, 1935; J.W. Swain, 'The theory of the four monarchies: opposition history under the Roman empire', in *Classical Philology*, Chicago, 35 (1940), pp. 1–21, esp. pp. 9–11; D. Flusser, 'The four empires in the Fourth Sibyl and in the Book of Daniel', in *Israel Oriental Studies*, vol. 2, 1972, pp. 148–75; J.J. Collins, 'The place of the Fourth Sibyl in the development of Jewish Sibyllina', in JJS 25 (1974), pp. 365–80; *id.*, *Apocalyptic Vision*, pp. 36–46; G.F. Hasel, 'The four world empires of Daniel 2 against the Near Eastern environment', in JSOT 12 (1979), pp. 17–30. As Hasel points out, the relevance of the Babylonian text known as the *Dynastic Prophecy* is, to say the least, doubtful. On the other hand there is a striking resemblance between Nebuchadnezzar's dream and the dream attributed to Zoroaster in two Pahlavi commentaries on a lost Avestan text, the *Vahman Yasht*. In Zoroaster's dream too each of four periods (though not empires) is symbolised by a metal, and the fourth, 'iron-mixed', is by far the worst. Moreover this fourth period is to end just one thousand years after Zoroaster, which means, with the appearance of the first *saoshyant*. For the Pahlavi commentaries see B.T. Anklesaria, *Zand-ī Vohūman Yasn*, Bombay, 1957, chapters 1, 3 and 4. An older translation is to be found in *The Sacred Books of the East*, vol. 5, Oxford, 1880, pp. 191–3, and vol. 37, Oxford, 1891, pp. 18 sq.

11 Daniel 7: 7–8.

12 Psalm 96: 12–13; Zechariah 14: 5; Joel 3: 12.

13 *Cf.* Collins, *Apocalyptic Vision*, pp. 99–104; G.R. Beasley-Murray, 'The interpretation of Daniel 7', in CBQ 45 (1983), pp. 44–58.

14 *Cf.* Russell, *op. cit.*, pp. 244–9; G.B. Caird, *Principalities and Powers*, Oxford, 1956, pp. 4–6.

15 Daniel 10: 13, 21; 11: 1.

16 Daniel 11: 45–12: 1.

17 Daniel 8: 10–11; and *cf.* Job 38: 7. See also Delcor, *op. cit.*, p. 173; J.J. Collins, 'The Son of Man and the Saints of the Most High in the Book of Daniel', in JBL 93 (1974), Part 1, pp. 50–66.

18 *Cf.* A.S. Palmer, 'The fall of Lucifer', in *Hibbert Journal*, London, 11(1913), pp. 766–86, esp. pp.

772–3; Bousset/Gressmann, *op. cit.*, pp. 322–3.

19 *Cf.* O. Morkhølm, *Studies in the Coinage of Antiochus IV of Syria*, Copenhagen, 1963, pp. 57 sq.; A. Hultgård, *L'eschatologie des Testaments des Douze Patriarches*, 1, Uppsala, 1977, pp. 330–31, and plate facing p. 336; J.G. Bunge, '"Antiochus-Helios". Methoden und Ergebnisse der Reichspolitik Antiochus' IV Epiphanies von Syrien im Spiegel seiner Münzen', in *Historia, Zeitschrift für alte Geschichte* 24, Wiesbaden, 1975, pp. 164–88.

20 On the Son of Man in Daniel: A. Caquot, in *Semitica*, Paris, 17 (1967), pp. 37–71, and M. Casey, *The Son of Man*, London, 1979 (at pp. 30 sq.), provide surveys of the various interpretations offered up to those dates. For the Son of Man as a human being see e.g. H. Schmid, 'Daniel, der Menschensohn', in *Judaica*, Zurich, 27 (1971), pp. 192–220. Hartman and Di Lella *op. cit.* (see note 8 above) pp. 97 sq., and Casey, *op. cit.*, pp. 25 sq. interpret the Son of Man as a symbol for the righteous Jews. Lacocque, *op. cit.*, and Collins, in *The Apocalyptic Vision in the Book of Daniel*, in *The Apocalyptic Imagination*, and already in 'The Son of Man and the Saints of the Most High in the Book of Daniel', in JBL 93, (1974) identify him with Michael. Beasley-Murray, *op. cit.* (see note 13), pp. 55 sq., identifies him with the Messiah.

21 Daniel 7: 14.

22 Some scholars have identified the 'holy ones' as angels: M. Noth, 'The Holy Ones of the Most High', in *The Laws of the Pentateuch and other Essays*, Philadelphia, 1967, 215–28 (the German essay was orginally published in 1955); L. Dequeker, in *Ephemerides Theologicae Lovanienses*, Leuven, 36 (1960), pp. 353–92; *id.*, 'The "Saints of the Most High" in Qumran and Daniel', in *Oudtestamentische Studien*, Leiden, 18 (1973), pp. 108–87; J. Coppens, 'La vision danielique du Fils d'Homme', in VT 19 (1969), pp. 171–82; *id.*, 'Le chapitre VII de Daniel. Lecture et commentaire', in *Ephemerides Theologicae* 54 (1978), pp. 301–22; Collins, see note 19 above.

Grounds for preferring the interpretation offered in this chapter — that the 'holy ones' are righteous Jews — are to be found in: C.H.W. Brekelmans in P.A.H. de Boer (ed.), *Oudtestamentische Studien* 14, (1965), pp. 305–29; A. Caquot (1967), see note 19 above; R. Hanhart in VTS 16 (1967), pp. 90–101; A. Lenglet in *Biblica* 53 (1972), pp. 169–90; G.F. Hasel in *Biblica* 56 (1975), pp. 173–92; V.S. Poythress in VT 26 (1976), pp. 208–13. Hartman and Di Lella, Lacocque, Casey (see notes 8 and 20) agree. Koch *et al.*, *Das Buch Daniel*, p. 239, points out that the Masoretic rendering should be translated as 'the holy ones of the highest ones'. The implication would be that world dominion is to be bestowed on the (righteous) Jews in virtue of their close connection with the angels, who comprise the highest category of the holy ones.

23 Daniel 5: 18.

24 Daniel 7: 27, 2: 44.

25 Daniel 12: 10.

26 On the significance of this prophecy see G.W.E. Nickelsburg, *Resurrection, Immortality, and Eternal Life in Intertestamental Judaism*, Cambridge, Mass., and London, 1977, pp. 18–27. It now seems unlikely that Isaiah 26: 19 really points forward to the passage in Daniel; *cf.* D.G. Johnson, *From Chaos to Restoration. An Integrative Reading of Isaiah 24–27*, Sheffield, 1988, pp. 80–81.

27 2 Maccabees 14: 45–6; and *cf.* 7: 11. (NEB)

Chapter 10: Jewish Apocalypses (II)

1 Two reliable translations are now available: M.A. Knibb, *The Ethiopic*

Book of Enoch: a new edition in the light of the Aramaic Dead Sea fragments, vol.2, Oxford, 1978; and M. Black, (with J. VanderKam and O. Neugebauer) *The Book of Enoch or 1 Enoch: a new English edition with commentary and notes*, Leiden, 1985. These have replaced what was for more than half a century the standard translation: the second, revised edition of R.H. Charles, *The Book of Enoch*, Oxford, 1912. Quotations in the present chapter are taken from Knibb.

Relatively recent studies of *1 Enoch* or of aspects or parts of it (except for the *Similitudes*): P. Grelot, 'La légende d'Hénoch dans les apocryphes et dans la Bible: origine et signification', in *Recherches de Science religieuse*, Paris, 46 (1958), pp. 5–26, 181–210; *id.*, 'L'eschatologie des Esséniens et le livre d'Hénoch', in RQ 1 (1958), 113–31; *id.*, 'Hénoch et ses écritures', in *Revue biblique*, 82 (1975), pp. 481–500; J.T. Milik, 'Problèmes de la littérature hénochique à la lumière des fragments araméens de Qumran', in HTR 64 (1971), pp. 333–78; *id.*, *The Books of Enoch: Aramaic Fragments of Qumran, Cave 4*, Oxford, 1976, Introduction; J.C. Greenfield and M.E. Stone, 'The Books of Enoch and the traditions of Enoch', in *Numen*, Leiden, 6 (1979), pp. 89–103 (includes critique of Milik's datings); M. Black, 'The fragments of the Aramaic Enoch from Qumran', in W.C. van Unnik (ed.), *La littérature juive entre Tenach et Mischna, quelques problèmes (Recherches bibliques 9)*, 1974, pp. 15–28; *id.*, 'The New Creation in 1 Enoch', in R.W.A. McKinney (ed.), *Creation, Christ and Culture*, Edinburgh, 1976, pp. 13–21; M.E. Stone, 'The Book of Enoch and Judaism in the third century BCE', in CBQ 40, (1978), pp. 479–92; *id.*, 'Enoch and apocalyptic origins', (chapter 5 of his *Scriptures, Sects and Visions*, Philadelphia, 1980); L. Hartman, *Looking for a Meaning: A Study of 1 Enoch 1–5*, Gleerup, 1979; J.H. Charlesworth, 'The SNTS Pseudepigrapha Seminars at Tübingen and Paris on the Books of Enoch', in NTS 25 (1979), pp. 315–23; D. Dimant, 'The biography of Enoch and the Books of Enoch', in VT 33 (1983), pp. 14–29; O. Neugebauer, *The Astronomical Chapters of the Ethiopic Book of Enoch (72–82)*, Copenhagen, 1981; J.J. Collins, 'The apocalyptic technique: setting and function of the Book of Watchers', in CBQ 44 (1982); J.C. VanderKam, 'The theophany of Enoch 1.3b–7.9', in VT 23 (1979), pp. 129–50; *id.*, *Enoch and the Growth of an Apocalyptic Tradition*, Washington, D.C., 1984; S. Uhlig, *Das äthiopische Henochbuch*, Gütersloh, 1984; M. Barker, *The Older Testament*, 1987, see note 6 to Chapter 9; the following articles by G.W.E. Nickelsburg: 'The apocalyptic message of 1 Enoch 92–105', in CBQ 39 (1977), pp. 309–28; 'Apocalyptic and myth in Enoch 6–11', in JBL 96 (1977), pp. 383–405; 'Enoch, Levi and Peter: recipients of revelation in Upper Galilee', *ibid.*, 100, (1981), pp. 575–600; 'The Epistle of Enoch and the Qumran literature', in JJS 33 (1982), pp. 333–49; the following papers in P.J. Achtemeier (ed.), *Society of Biblical Literature 1978 Seminar Papers*, 1, Chico, Cal., 1978: J.J. Collins, 'Methodological issues in the study of 1 Enoch'; G.W.E. Nickelsburg, 'Reflections upon reflections: a response to John Collins' "Methodological issues . . ." '; D. Dimant, '1 Enoch 6–11: a methodological perspective'. B.Z. Wacholder, *Eupolemus: a study of Judaeo-Greek Literature*, Cincinnati, 1974, pp. 71 sq. considers Enoch as a model of the 'wise man'.

2 Genesis 5: 21–4.

3 *Jubilees* 4: 19, 23.

4 Reliable translations of the *Book of Jubilees* are those by R.H.

Charles, London, 1902, and by O.S. Wintermute in J.H. Charlesworth (ed.), *The Old Testament Pseudepigrapha*, 2, London, 1985, pp. 52–142, with introduction at pp. 32–50. Quotations in the present chapter are taken from the former. Useful studies: M. Testuz, *Les idées religieuses du Livre des Jubilées*, Geneva and Paris, 1960; G.L. Davenport, *The Eschatology of the Book of Jubilees*, Leiden, 1971; J.C. VanderKam, *Textual and Historical Studies in the Book of Jubilees*, Missoula, 1977.

5 Damascus Document 16: 3–4.

6 For the following *cf.* M. Limbeck, *Die Ordnung des Heils. Untersuchungen zum Gesetzesverständnis des Frühjudentums*, Düsseldorf, 1971, pp. 64–82; U. Luck, 'Das Weltverständnis in der jüdischen Apokalyptik', in *Zeitschrift für Theologie und Kirche*, Tübingen, 73 (1976), pp. 283–305.

7 *Jubilees* 2: 2.

8 *1 Enoch* 82: 8.

9 *Ibid.* 18: 2; *cf.* 34: 2–36, 1; 76:1–7.

10 *Ibid.* 2: 1–5; 4; *cf.* 69: 15–33.

11 *Cf.* Ch. Münchow, *Ethik und Eschatologie, Ein Beitrag zum Verständnis der frühjudischen Apokalyptik mit einem Ausblick auf das Neue Testament*, Göttingen, 1981, pp. 16–64; M.-Th. Wacker, *Weltordnung und Gericht: Studien zu 1 Henoch 22*, Würzburg, 1982, esp. pp. 257, 298–305, 314–15.

12 *Jubilees* 5: 10, 13.

13 *Cf.* C.A. Newsom, 'The development of 1 Enoch 6–19: cosmology and judgment', in CBQ 42 (1980), pp. 310–29, esp. pp. 322 sq.

14 *Jubilees* 15: 26–7.

15 On the solar calendar: A. Jaubert, 'Le calendrier des Jubilées et de la secte de Qumran: ses origines bibliques', in VT 3 (1953), pp. 250–64; *id.*, 'Le calendrier des Jubilées et les jours liturgiques de la semaine', *ibid.*, 7 (1957), pp. 35–61; J. Morgenstern, 'The Calendar of the Book of Jubilees', *ibid.*, 5 (1955), pp. 34–76; J.C. VanderKam, 'The origin, character, and early history of the 364-day calendar: a reassessment of Jaubert's hypotheses', in CBQ 41 (1979), pp. 390–411; P.R. Davies, 'Calendrical change and Qumran origins. An assessment of VanderKam's theory', in CBQ 45 (1983), pp. 80–9; R.T. Beckwith 'The earliest Enochic literature and its calendar', in RQ 10 (1981), pp. 365–403.

16 *1 Enoch* 72: 35–7.

17 *Jubilees* 2: 9.

18 *Jubilees* 6: 33.

19 *Cf.* P.L. Day, *An Adversary in Heaven: Satan in the Hebrew Bible*, Atlanta, 1988.

20 Exodus 4: 24–5.

21 *Jubilees* 48: 3.

22 Recent works dealing with early versions of the Devil, and their relationship to the chaos-monsters of still earlier times: J.B. Russell, *The Devil: Perceptions of Evil from Antiquity to Primitive Christianity*, Ithaca, N.Y. and London, 1977; B. Teyssèdre, *Naissance du Diable. De Babylone aux grottes de la mer Morte*, Paris, 1985; N. Forsyth, *The Old Enemy: Satan and the Combat Myth*, Princeton, 1987.

23 On the earlier history of the myth of the Watchers, and related myths: B.J. Bamberger, *Fallen Angels*, Philadelphia, 1952, esp. pp. 15–59; A. Lods, 'La chute des anges', in RHPR 7 (1927), pp. 295–315. For a variety of interpretations: P.D. Hanson, 'Rebellion in Heaven, Azazel, and the euhemeristic heroes in 1 Enoch 6–11', in JBL 96 (1977) pp. 195–233; G.W.E. Nickelsburg, 'Apocalyptic and Myth in 1 Enoch 6–11', *ibid.*, pp. 383–405; D. Suter, 'Fallen angel, fallen priest: the problem of family purity in 1 Enoch 6–16', in HUCA 50 (1979), pp. 115–35; Barker, *The Older Testament*, esp. pp. 21 sq., 94; Forsyth, *op. cit.*, pp. 160 sq.

24 *1 Enoch* 8: 2.

25 *Cf. 1 Enoch* 15: 10–12.

26 *Jubilees* 10: 1–9.

27 *Ibid.* 11: 2, 3 and 5; *cf.* 10: 8–12.
28 *Ibid.* 10: 12.
29 *Cf. Jubilees* chapter 23.
30 *Ibid.* 12: 20.
31 *Ibid.* 19: 28.
32 *Ibid.* 23: 25.
33 *Ibid.* 23: 23.
34 *Cf. ibid.* 22: 22.
35 *1 Enoch* 11 sq.
36 *Jubilees* 50: 5.
37 *Jubilees* 23: 27–8. 'Nor one who is full of days' is an emendation by VanderKam, *op. cit.*, p. 269, on the basis of Ethiopic manuscripts.
38 *1 Enoch* 24–5; 58.
39 *1 Enoch* 90: 38.
40 On the Scrolls and the Qumran community: G. Vermes, *The Dead Sea Scrolls: Qumran in Perspective*, Cleveland and London, 1978, which includes a comprehensive bibliography to that date. On the world-view of the Community see also: H. Ringgren, *The Faith of Qumran: Theology of the Dead Sea Scrolls*, Philadelphia, 1963; P. von der Osten-Sacken, *Gott und Belial: Traditionsgeschichtliche Untersuchungen zum Dualismus in den Texten aus Qumran*, Göttingen, 1969; E.H. Merrill, *Qumran and Predestination*, Leiden, 1975.

On eschatology in particular: Y. Yadin, *The Scroll of the War of the Sons of Light against the Sons of Darkness*, Oxford, 1962, esp. pp. 229–42, on the eschatological role of angels; H.W. Kuhn, *Enderwartung und gegenwärtiges Heil: Untersuchungen zu den Gemeindeliedern von Qumran*, Göttingen, 1966; P. Grelot, 'L'eschatologie des Esséniens et le livre d'Hénoch', in RQ 1 (1958), pp. 112–31; J. Licht, 'An analysis of the Treatise on the Two Spirits', in C. Roth and Y. Yadin, *Aspects of the Dead Sea Scrolls*, Jerusalem, 1958, pp. 88–100; *id.*, 'Time and eschatology in apocalyptic literature and Qumran', in JJS 16 (1967), pp. 117–82; J. Pryke, 'Eschatology in the Dead Sea Scrolls', in M. Black (ed.), *The Scrolls and Christianity*, London, 1969, pp. 45–57; J. Carmignac, 'La future intervention de Dieu', in M. Delcor (ed.), *Qumran. Sa piété, sa théologie et son milieu*, Paris and Leuven, 1978, pp. 119–29; A. Caquot, 'Le Messianisme qumranien', *ibid.*, pp. 231–47; J.J. Collins, 'Patterns of eschatology at Qumran', in B. Halpern and J.D. Levenson, *Traditions in Transformation: Turning Points in Biblical Faith*, Winona Lake, Indiana, 1981, pp. 351–75. On the calendar in particular: E. Ettisch, 'Der grosse Sonnenzyklus und der Qumrankalender', in *Theologische Literaturzeitung* 88 (1963), cols. 185–94; M.D. Herr, 'The Calendar', in *Compendia Rerum Judaicarum ad Novum Testamentum*, 1, pt. 2, Assen, 1976, pp. 834 sq.

Translations of the Scrolls include: T.H. Gaster, *The Dead Sea Scriptures in English Translation*, Garden City, New York, 2nd edn., 1964; A. Dupont-Sommer, *The Essene Writings from Qumran*, Oxford, 1961; G. Vermes, *The Dead Sea Scrolls in English*, 2nd edn., Harmondsworth, 1975, and 3rd edn., Sheffield, 1987. All quotations in the present chapter are from Vermes (1975), and in the following notes the page-numbers refer to that work. To facilitate the use of other translations references to the Scrolls themselves are also given, in brackets, with the customary abbreviations: 1 Q for Qumran Cave 1, S for the Community Rule, H for the Hymns, M for the War Rule, Melch for the Melkizedek Document, CD for Cairo Damascus Rule. Here too the very full references in Vermes (1975) are adopted.

After many years' delay a considerable amount of additional material from the Scrolls has recently been made available. It has been published, with commentary, in R. Eisenman and M. Wise, *The Dead Sea Scrolls Uncovered*, Shaftesbury, Dorset, and Rockport,

Mass., 1992. The implications are currently being assessed. However, the ideology that had emerged from the Scrolls previously published still looks much the same — except that it now seems certain, instead of merely probable, that a bodily resurrection of the righteous was expected.

41 pp. 93, 158 (1QS 11: 7–9).

42 pp. 92–3 (1QS 11: 6–8).

43 p. 72 (1Qs 1: 13–15).

44 p. 188 (1QH 12: 5).

45 pp. 75–6 (1QS 3: 13–4: 1).

46 Quoted by Vermes, *The Dead Sea Scrolls: Qumran in Perspective*, pp. 155–6.

47 pp. 147–8 (1QM 19: 2–8).

48 p. 146 (1QM 18: 1–3).

49 p. 267 (11 Q Melch 2: 9, 13). *Cf.* P.J. Kobelski, *Melchizedek and Melkiresa*, Washington, D.C., 1981, pp. 6–57; H.G. May, 'Cosmological reference in the Qumran doctrine of the Two Spirits and in Old Testament imagery', in JBL 72 (1963), pp. 1–14.

50 p. 103 (CD 6: 11).

51 p. 78 (1QS 4: 25).

52 p. 77 (1QS 4: 12–13).

53 p. 76 (1QS 4: 7–8).

54 p. 172 (1QH 6: 34–5). But see Vermes, *The Dead Sea Scrolls: Qumran in Perspective*, p. 187.

55 *Cf.* Vermes, *The Dead Sea Scrolls in English*, p. 158 (1QH 3: 20–22).

56 On Zurvanism see below, p. 221.

Chapter 11: The Jesus Sect

1 The literature on Christian origins is vast. For a valuable bibliography of twentieth-century works down to the mid-1980s see C. Rowland, *Christian Origins. An Account of the Setting and Character of the Most Important Messianic Sect of Judaism*, London 1985. Other wide-ranging works on the subject to which the present account in indebted include H.C. Kee, *Christian Origins in Sociological Perspective*, London, 1980; A.E. Harvey, *Jesus and the Constraints of History*, London, 1982; E.P. Sanders, *Jesus and Judaism*, London, 1983. Of the innumerable works on background, life and teaching of Jesus himself, two by G. Vermes, *Jesus the Jew, a Historian's Reading of the Gospels*, London, 1973, *The Religion of Jesus the Jew*, London, 1993, proved particularly helpful. P. Fredriksen, *From Jesus to Christ*, New Haven and London, 1988, is enlightening on the changing interpretations of Jesus in the gospels and the Pauline writings.

2 On the wandering charismatics: Kee, *op. cit.*, esp. chapter 3; G. Theissen, *The First Followers of Jesus: A Sociological Analysis of the Earliest Christianity*, London, 1978.

3 The centrality of the kingdom of God in the thought and teaching of Jesus was not always appreciated. The scholar who first drew attention to it was Johannes Weiss, *Die Predigt vom Reiche Gottes*, 1892 (first edition, 67 pp.), and 1900 (revised edition, 214 pp.); ET *The Proclamation of the Kingdom of God*, London and Philadelphia, 1971. Albert Schweitzer produced an eloquent but methodologically faulty popularisation and elaboration of Weiss's discovery in *Von Reimarus zu Wrede*, Tübingen, 1906; the second and later editions were entitled *Geschichte der Leben-Jesu-Forschung*; ET *The Quest for the Historical Jesus*, London, 1910, New York, 1922; many subsequent editions. For a penetrating critique of Schweitzer: T.F. Glasson, 'Schweitzer's influence: blessing or bane?' in *Journal of Theological Studies*, Oxford, 28 (1977), 289–302. Weiss is sounder than Schweitzer, and would be even sounder if he had used the term 'eschatological' instead of 'apocalyptic'.

4 e.g., in addition to the works by Rowland, Sanders, and Vermes specified in note 1, W.G. Kümmel, *Promise and Fulfilment*, ET from 3rd German edn., London, 1957; J.

Jeremias, *New Testament Theology*, 1, London, 1971, pp. 73 sq.; R.H. Hiers, *The Kingdom of God in the Synoptic Tradition*, Gainesville, Florida, 1970; *id.*, *The Historical Jesus and the Kingdom of God*, Gainesville, 1973; B.F. Meyer, *The Aims of Jesus, London*, 1979. For surveys of other interpretations: G. Lundström, *The Kingdom of God in the Teaching of Jesus. A Study of Interpretation from the Last Decades of the Nineteenth Century to the Present Day* (ET from the Swedish), Edinburgh, 1963; N. Perrin, *The Kingdom of God in the Teaching of Jesus*, Philadelphia and London, 1963. For a useful anthology of interpretations: B. Chilton (ed.), *The Kingdom of God*, Philadelphia and London, 1984; to which should be added: G.R. Beasley-Murray, *Jesus and the Kingdom of God*, Grand Rapids, and Exeter, England (with exhaustive bibliography).

5 See above, pp. 182–3, 190. [308 in MS]

6 Isaiah 11: 5–9; *cf.* Jeremias, *op. cit.*, pp. 68 sq.

7 *Cf.* B. Noack, *Satanas und Sotería: Untersuchungen zur neutestamentlichen Dämonologie,* Copenhagen, 1948; J.M. Robinson, *The Problem of History in Mark*, London, 1957, pp. 43–51; Hiers, *Kingdom of God*, esp. pp. 30–39; *id.*, *Historical Jesus*, pp. 59–64; Jeremias, *op. cit.*, pp. 94–5; J.B. Russell, *The Devil. Perceptions of Evil from Antiquity to Primitive Christianity*, Ithaca and London, 1977, pp. 227–39; R. Yates, 'Jesus and the Demonic in the Synoptic Gospels', in *Irish Theological Quarterly*, 44, Maynooth College, Co. Kildare, 1977, pp. 39–57; Vermes, *Jesus the Jew*, pp. 61 sq.; *id.*, *Gospel of Jesus*, p. 9; H.C. Kee, *Miracle in the Early Christian World. A Study in Sociohistorical Method*, New Haven and London, 1983, pp. 146, chapter 5; N. Forsyth, *The Old Enemy. Satan and the Combat Myth*, Princeton, 1987, pp. 285–7; and see note 5 above. For later developments: H.A. Kelly, *The Devil at Baptism*, Ithaca and London, 1985.

8 Mark 1: 24.

9 *Cf.* Luke 11: 20, Matthew 12: 28.

10 *Cf.* Mark 3: 27.

11 *Cf.* on the synonyms: Vermes, *Jesus the Jew*, p. 69.

12 *Cf.* Luke 10: 17–20; Meyer, *Aims of Jesus*, p. 156.

13 *Cf.* Mark 13: 7–10, 24–5.

14 *Cf.* Hiers, *Historical Jesus*, pp. 25–6.

15 Isaiah 35: 5–6.

16 Matthew 15: 31.

17 Isaiah 25: 6.

18 Mark 14: 25.

19 *Cf.* Mark 11: 12–14; and Hiers, 'Not the Season for Figs', in JBL 87 (1968), pp. 394–400; *id.*, *Historical Jesus*, pp. 83–5; and for a critique of this interpretation see W.R. Telford, *The Barren Temple and the Withered Tree*, Sheffield, 1980, pp. 206–208.

20 For Papias: U.H.J. Körtner, *Papias von Hieropolis*, Göttingen, 1983.

21 This fragment is preserved in Irenaeus, *Adversus Haereses*, Book 5, chapter 33, para 3. Translation by the author.

22 *2 Baruch* 29: 5–8.

23 *Cf.* Irenaeus, *op. cit.*, Book 5, chapters 32–34.

24 *Cf.* Matthew 11: 11; Luke 7: 28.

25 Mark 12: 25; Matthew 13: 43.

26 Augustine, *City of God*, book XX, chapters 14, 16, trans. John Healey, London and New York, 1945 etc. (Everyman's Library). *Cf.* Thomas E. Clarke, 'St Augustine and cosmic redemption', in *Journal of Theological Studies*, Baltimore, 19 (1958), pp. 133–64; *id.*, *The Eschatological Transformation of the Material World according to St Augustine*, Woodstock, Maryland, 1956.

27 Luke 7: 22.

28 Matthew 19: 30.

29 Luke 6: 20–21. (RSV)

30 Matthew 25: 35.

31 Mark 10: 21. (RSV)

32 Luke 14: 13–14. (RSV)

33 *Cf.* Matthew 15: 24; 10: 6.

34 Mark 7: 27–9.
35 Luke 16: 17; *cf.* Matthew 5: 18.
36 *1 Enoch* 89–90 ('Animal Apocalypse'); 91: 30 ('Apocalypse of Weeks'); *Jubilees* 1: 15–17.
37 *Cf.* Sanders, *op. cit.*, 87, 106.
38 Luke 22: 28–9; *cf.* Matthew 19: 28.
39 Matthew 18: 1.
40 Matthew 20: 21.
41 *Cf.* Harvey, *op. cit.*, p. 141.
42 Luke 4: 18–19; *cf.* Isaiah 6: 1–2.
43 R. Bornkamm, *Theology of the New Testament*, 1, London, 1952, p. 180.
44 1 Corinthians 15: 4–8, 11–14.
45 Acts 1: 6.
46 See note 1 to Chapter 10 for translations of *1 Enoch.* On other figures similar to the Enoch of the *Similitudes*: J. Theisohn, *Der auserwählte Richter*, Göttingen, 1975.
47 *Cf.* G.R. Beasley-Murray, *op. cit.* (under note 4), pp. 63–8 (Excursus: The Date of the Similitudes of Enoch).
48 *1 Enoch* 46: 1; 45: 3; and *cf.* 51: 3.
49 *ibid.*, 46: 4–7.
50 *ibid.*, 38: 1; 46: 6; 62: 3–12; 54: 1–2.
51 *ibid.*, 69: 27–9.
52 *ibid.*, 50: 1–2.
53 *ibid.*, 51: 5.
54 *ibid.*, 45: 4–5; 62: 14.
55 *ibid.*, 58: 3; 51: 4; 62: 16.
56 *ibid.*, 71: 14–17.
57 *Cf.* B. Lindars, *Jesus Son of Man*, London, 1983, esp. p. 14.
58 Luke 24: 26.
59 Philippians 2: 9–10.
60 Acts 17: 31.
61 1 Corinthians 7: 29; Romans 13: 12; 1 Peter 4: 7.
62 Mark 9: 1.
63 1 Thessalonians 4: 13–18. *Cf.* G. Kegel, *Auferstehung Jesu — Auferstehung der Toten*, Gütersloh, 1970.
64 On the self-awareness of the primitive Church: R. Bultmann, *Theology of the New Testament*, London, 1, pp. 33–62.
65 Luke 12: 32.
66 *Didache* 10: 5 sq., trans. Kirsopp Lake, in *The Apostolic Fathers*, vol. I, 1. London, 1912 (Loeb Classical Library).
67 *Cf.* Acts 11: 28; 21: 9–11.
68 1 Thessalonians 5: 2, 6.
69 Matthew 3: 12.
70 Matthew 10: 32–3.
71 Matthew 25: 31–4, 41.
72 Matthew 13: 41–3.
73 2 Thessalonians 1: 6–10.

Chapter 12: The Book of Revelation

1 Valuable works on Revelation include: R.H. Charles, *A Critical and Exegetical Commentary on the Revelation of St John*, London and New York, 1920; G.B. Caird, *A Commentary on the Revelation of St John the Divine*, London and New York, 1966; W. Harrington, *Understanding the Apocalypse*, Washington, 1969; P.S. Minear, *I Saw a New Earth*, 1968; A. Yarbro Collins, *Crisis and Catharsis. The Power of the Apocalypse*, Philadelphia, 1984; L.L. Thompson, *The Book of Revelation: Apocalypse and Empire*, New York and Oxford, 1990.
2 Revelation 1: 10–20. Unless otherwise stated, all the following biblical references are to the Book of Revelation.
3 3: 4–5.
4 3: 10.
5 2: 26–7.
6 That Revelation owes much to the Near Eastern combat myth was argued already in H. Gunkel, *Schöpfung und Chaos in Urzeit und Endzeit*, Göttingen, 1885, at a time when the only known version of the myth was *Enuma elish.* For a more up-to-date presentation of the argument see R. Halver, *Der Mythos im letzten Buch der Bibel*, Hamburg-Bergstadt, 1964.
7 12:12; 12: 17.
8 13: 7.
9 *Cf.* Thompson, *op. cit.*, pp. 16, 104.

10 *Ibid.*, esp. pp. 95, 132, 171–81.
11 19: 16.
12 19: 17.
13 18: 2.
14 18: 20.
15 14: 9.
16 16: 2–10; 14: 11.
17 20: 3.
18 *Cf.* Ezekiel 38: 1–39.
19 *Cf.* A. Wikenhauser, *Die Offenbarung des Johannes*, 3rd edn., Regensburg, 1959 (*Regensburger Neues Testament* 9); W.W. Reader, *Die Stadt Gottes in der Johannesapokalypse*, Göttingen, 1971, pp. 240–1.
20 21: 7.
21 21: 1–5.
22 22: 2.
23 22: 12, 20.

Chapter 13: Jews, Zoroastrians and Christians

1 The hypothesis is not generally familiar, and I myself came only very gradually to accept it as correct. On the other hand it is not a new notion. Amongst scholars it has been mooted at various times, albeit at very uneven levels of scholarship, since the appearance of *Zend-Avesta. Ouvrage de Zoroastre, contenant les idées théologiques, physiques et morales de ce législateur*, Paris, 1771, by that extraordinary traveller and linguist Abraham-Hyacinthe Anquetil-Duperron; for a brief account see J. Duchesne-Guillemin, *The Western Response to Zoroaster*, Oxford, 1958, chapter 6. The development of the discussion can be pursued through J.G. v. Herder, *Erläuterungen zum Neuen Testament aus einer neueröffneten morgenländischen Quelle*, 1775 (*Sämtliche Werke zur Religion und Theologie*, ed. J.G. Mueller, vol. 9, Stuttgart and Tübingen, 1829); J.S. Semler, appendix to an anonymous *Versuch einer biblischen Dämonologie*, 1776; Constantin-François Chasseboeuf, Comte de Volney, *Les Ruines, ou Méditation sur les révolutions des empires*, Paris, 1791, chapter 21; J.A.L. Richter, *Das Christentum und die ältesten Religionen des Orients*, 1819; W. Vatke, *Die Religion des Alten Testaments*, Berlin, 1835, pp. 542–51; D.G.C. von Cölln, *Biblische Theologie*, Leipzig, 1836, pp. 346–52; E. Stave, *Über den Einfluss des Parsismus auf das Judentum*, Haarlem, 1898, esp. part 3, pp. 117–280; Lawrence H. Mills, *Zarathustra, Philo, the Achaemenids and Israel*, Leipzig, 1904, esp. part 2, pp. 210–460; E. Meyer, *Ursprung und Anfänge des Christentums*, vol. 2, 1921; D.W. Bousset, *Die Religion des Judentums im späthellenistischen Zeitalter*, 3rd edn., ed. H. Gressmann, Tübingen, 1926, pp. 469–524; A. von Gall, *Basileia tou Theou. Eine religionsgeschichtliche Studie zur vorkirchlichen Eschatologie*, Heidelberg, 1926; R. Otto, *The Kingdom of God and the Son of Man*, trans. from the revised German edn., London, 1938; Ch. Autran, *Mithra, Zoroastre et la préhistoire aryenne du christianisme*, Paris, 1935, part 2, pp. 143–269; G. Widengren, 'Quelques rapports entre Juifs et Iraniens à l'époque des Parthes', in VTS 4 (1957), pp. 197–241; *id.*, *Iranische-semitische Kulturbegegnung in parthischer Zeit*, Cologne and Opladen, 1960; *id.*, 'Iran and Israel in Parthian times with special reference to the Ethiopic Book of Enoch', in *Temenos* 2, Helsinki, 1966, pp. 139–77; S.K. Eddy, *The King is Dead. Studies in the Near Eastern Resistance to Hellenism*, Lincoln, Nebraska, 1961; Morton Smith, 'II Isaiah and the Persians', in JAOS 83 (1963), pp. 415–21; D. Winston, 'The Iranian component in the Bible, Apocrypha and Qumran: a review of the evidence', in *HR* 5 no. 2 (1966), pp. 183–216; J.R. Hinnells, 'Zoroastrian saviour imagery and its influence on the New Testament', in *Numen* 16 (1969), pp. 161–84; *id.*, 'Iranian influence upon the New Testa-

ment', in *Commémoration Cyrus*, 2, *Acta Iranica* 2 (1974), 271–84; *id.*, 'Zoroastrian influence on the Judaeo-Christian tradition', in *Journal of the K.R Cama Oriental Institute* 65, Bombay, 1976, pp. 1–23; A. Hultgård, 'Das Judentum in der hellenistisch-römischen Zeit und die iranische Religion — ein religionsgeschichtliches Problem', in *Aufstieg und Niedergang der römischen Welt*, ed. H. Temporini and W. Haase, Berlin and New York, 2, 1979, pp. 512–90, with bibliography p. 583 sq.; S. Shaked, 'Iranian influence on Judaism: first century BCE to second century CE', in *Cambridge History of Judaism*, 1, Cambridge, 1984, pp. 308–25; M. Boyce, 'Persian religion in the Achaemenid age', *ibid.*, pp. 308–25; id., *A History of Zoroastrianism*, 3, Leiden etc., 1991, chapter 11. E. Böklen, *Die Verwandtschaft der jüdisch-christlichen und der persichen Eschatologie*, Göttingen, 1902, stressed the many similarities between the two eschatologies but, owing to the uncertainty, at that time, of the dating of the *Avesta*, left the question of influence open.

Zoroastrian influence has been denied in e.g. N. Söderblom, *La Vie future d'après le Mazdéisme*, 1901; J.H. Moulton, *Early Zoroastrianism*, 1913, chapter 11; I. Scheftelowitz, *Die Altpersiche Religion und das Judentum*, 1920; Cardinal Franz König, *Zarathustras Jenseitsvorstellungen und das Alte Testament*, Vienna, 1964, esp. pp. 243–9. Of these, however, Söderblom gives a misleading account of Zoroastrian beliefs, and König limits himself to a period in Israelite belief so early as to be irrelevant.

2 *Cf.* Th. H. Gaster, art. 'Satan' in *The Interpreter's Dictionary of the Bible*, New York and Nashville, 1962, vol. 4, esp. p. 226.

3 See above, pp. 102–3.

4 On the *Vahman Yasht* and its influence on Daniel see Boyce, *History*, vol. 3, pp. 385–6, with n 106.

5 For a fuller account of Zoroastrian-Jewish contacts: Boyce, *History*, 3, chapter 11, esp. pp. 410 sq.

6 On the *Oracles of Hystaspes: cf.* Windisch, *Die Orakel des Hystaspes (Verhandelingen der Koninklijke Akademie van Wetenschappen te Amsterdam*, 28, 3 (1929)). See also Boyce, *History*, 3, pp. 376 sq., with bibliography at n 59.

7 Jewish-Parthian relations are considered in the works of Widengren and Hinnells listed under note 1 above.

8 *Cf.* K.G. Kuhn, 'Die Sektenschrift und die iranische Religion', in *Zeitschrift für Theologie und Kirche* 49 (1952), pp. 296–316; H. Wildenberger, 'Der Dualismus in den Qumranschriften', in *Asiatische Studien* 8, Bern, 1954, pp. 163–77; J. Duchesne-Guillemin, 'Le Zervanisme et les manuscrits de la mer Morte', in IIJ 1 (1957). For a different but compatible approach: S. Shaked, 'Qumran and Iran: further considerations', in *Israel Oriental Studies* 2, Tel Aviv, 1972, pp. 433–44.

9 It is unfortunate that certain scholars belonging to, or influenced by, the German 'history of religion' school have tried to derive the transcendent Messiah of Christianity from a hypothetical Gnostic heavenly redeemer, who in turn was supposed to derive from the primal man of Zoroastrianism, Gayomart. That argument has been shown to be erroneous: see K. Colpe, *Die religionsgeschichtliche Schule: Darstellung und Kritik ihres Bildes vom gnostischen Erlösermythus*, Göttingen, 1961. It should not distract attention from the very real similarity between the Saoshyant and the Christ of the Book of Revelation.

10 *Cf.* Hinnells, 'Iranian influence upon the New Testament', pp. 279–80.

Afterword

1 In his exhaustive study, *When Time Shall Be No More. Prophecy Belief in Modern American Culture*, Cambridge, Mass., and London, 1992, Paul Boyer concludes (p. 15) that apocalyptic and millenarian expectations "*pervaded* U.S. thought and culture as the twentieth century drew to its close." The argument about the quasi-millenarian elements in Marxist-Leninist ideology is developed in Cohn, *The Pursuit of the Millennium*, London and New York, 1957, esp. the Preface and the Conclusion, and more fully in the Conclusion to the second edition (1962). By the time the third edition appeared in 1970, the notion had become so familiar that it seemed appropriate to reduce the argument to a brief reference. In the fourth edition (1993) the relevant part of the 1962 Conclusion is reinstated, as by now it has acquired a certain historical interest.

Index